BLAME
AND
PUNISHMENT

ESSAYS IN THE CRIMINAL LAW

For June

BLAME AND PUNISHMENT

ESSAYS IN THE CRIMINAL LAW

SANFORD H. KADISH

MACMILLAN PUBLISHING COMPANY

NEW YORK

Collier Macmillan Publishers

LONDON

ℒℂ

Macmillan Publishing Company
866 Third Avenue, New York, N.Y. 10022

Collier Macmillan Canada, Inc.

Library of Congress Catalog Card Number: 87–5610

Printed in the United States of America

1   2   3   4   5   6   7   8   9   10

Library of Congress Cataloging-in-Publication Data

Kadish, Sanford H.
  Blame and punishment.

  Includes index.
  1. Criminal law—United States.   2. Criminal liability—United States.   3.
  Punishment—United States.   I. Title.
  KF9219.K33   1987   345.73   87-5610
  ISBN 0-02-916691-8   347.305

We are grateful to the journals that originally published the essays in this book, as listed
on p. x of the Introduction, for their permission to reprint the articles here.

2-12-88

CONTENTS

INTRODUCTION

The essays in this volume grew out of many years of study and teaching of the substantive criminal law. They were written over a period of more than two decades with no thought that they would compose a book. Taken together, therefore, they do not constitute either an integrated argument or a comprehensive account of the law. On the other hand, they possess a unity as my own efforts to deal with aspects of what I saw (and still see) as the salient problems of the substantive criminal law over this period—the overuse of the criminal law, the conditions morally required for finding individuals punishable for harms, the need for comprehensive law reform and the use and abuse of discretion.

The essay constituting Chapter One, in the form of an imagined (but yet non-fictional) conversation with a dissatisfied law student, attempts to identify the range of the fundamental problems of the criminal law and to argue their larger significance.

Chapter Two contains three studies of the besetting problem of overuse of the criminal law. The first two, Essays 2 and 3, develop the damaging consequences of the use of the criminal sanction and argue for decriminalization of a wide range of conduct. The third, Essay 4, considers the merits of the case for extending the use of the criminal sanction to enforce economic regulations.

The next three chapters are devoted to studies of the most vital feature of a body of substantive criminal law—its specification of the conditions justifying the imposition of blame and punishment upon an individual.

Chapter Three deals with the law of excuse, a group of defenses that define the conditions under which persons are relieved of liability for criminal harms they have committed because of something special to themselves or to their situation that makes it unjust to blame them. The first essay, Essay 5, explores the proposal to eliminate the requirement of blameworthiness from the criminal law. The second, Essay 6, surveys the legal excuses allowed by the criminal law, develops their rationale, and assesses the extent to which they track the moral requirements for assigning blame.

Chapter Four is about justification, a concept that refers, by contrast, to the circumstances in which persons may not be subjected to criminal liability because their action, considered all in all, was the right thing to do. The essay it contains, Essay 7, develops an analysis and an interpretation of the factors determining when the life of another may justifiably be taken or risked under the law.

The question of when a person may be blamed for a consequence of his action is the subject of Essay 8 in Chapter Five, which is devoted to the law of complicity, the law determining when a person is accountable for the criminal action of another. In this study, complicity is contrasted with the law of causation (which determines when a person is accountable for a happening that follows his action), and an effort is made to identify the principles underlying the legal doctrine which gives it coherence.

Chapter Six introduces the subject of reform of the criminal law through a historical study (Essay 9) of efforts to codify the law in common law jurisdictions.

Essay 10, constituting the last chapter, Chapter Seven, addresses the subversion of the substantive criminal law threatened by the exercise of substantially uncontrolled discretion by police and sentencing judges.

Following the usual practice with collections of this kind I have left these studies as they were when first published, except for some minor deletions and stylistic changes, as well as two updating postscripts.

The essays in this book were originally published as the following articles: Why Substantive Criminal Law—A Dialogue, 29 *Cleveland-Marshall Law Review* 1 (1980); The Crisis of Overcriminalization, 374 *The Annals of the American Academy of Political and Social Science*, 157 (1967); More on Overcriminalization, 15 *U.C.L.A. Law Review* 719 (1972); Some Observations on the Use of Criminal Sanctions in Enforcing Economic Regulations, 30 *University of Chicago Law Review* 423 (1963); The Decline of Innocence, 26 *Cambridge Law Journal* 273 (1968); Respect for Life and Regard for Rights in the Criminal Law, 64 *California Law Review* 871 (1976); Complicity, Cause and Blame, 73 *California Law Review* 323 (1985); Codifiers of the Criminal Law, 78 *Columbia Law Review* 1098 (1978); Legal Norm and Discretion in the Police and Sentencing Process, 75 *Harvard Law Review* 904 (1962). The essay, Excusing Crime, is also being published in Volume 75, No. 1 of the *California Law Review*, 1987. I am thankful to each of these journals for consenting to the republication of the articles in this book.

Sanford H. Kadish
Berkeley, January 1987

CHAPTER ONE

THE SIGNIFICANCE OF THE CRIMINAL LAW

1
WHY SUBSTANTIVE CRIMINAL LAW— A DIALOGUE

In this dialogue I have tried to address criticisms of the substantive criminal law, as a course and as a subject matter, made by a number of my students over several decades of teaching the subject. In a way it is rather personal since it consists of the criticisms of my students and my apologia for what I have tried to do. That, however, would hardly be worth doing unless it is the case, as I believe it is, that these criticisms are widespread and that my responses speak to what is generally done in criminal law courses in this country.

The subject of this piece suggested its dialogue form, for as I thought about it, my head was filled with echoes of fragments of conversations I have had with many students—or Walter Mitty-like, imagined I should like to have had.

Student. I just returned from a clinical stint with the Public Defender and I have a lot of questions about the substantive criminal law in general and its teaching in particular.

Professor. Shall we start with the law itself or with its teaching and place in the curriculum?

S. I find it hard to sort out my questions in those categories, they overlap so much. Let me start with what struck me at the Public Defender's office. No one worried much about the substantive criminal law. In fact, there was not much law involved, period. There was mainly wheeling and dealing, but I'll get to that later. Anyway, I did memos about search and seizure, stop and frisk, police interrogation, and the like, but I never had to write on the rules of criminal law. There was no reason to. The guy was charged with making a drug sale, or with going after someone with an iron pipe or a knife, or with mugging an old man, or grabbing a woman's purse and running off with it. The substantive law was no problem. There was nothing to argue about. What we spent our time on was the facts, the evidence, and the proof. The most important question was whether we could exclude some damaging evidence because of police misconduct. I figured that maybe my experience was unusual, so I asked around. Turns out it was not unusual at all. The old pros said that that was the way it always went. So why did

I spend most of my first course in criminal law studying areas criminal lawyers do not use much and comparatively little time with the subjects they use day in and day out?

P. I take it your complaint is that the subject taught is impractical.

S. Right, and a waste of time too.

P. I don't see it that way at all. First, you have to admit that before you graduate, you will have had an opportunity to take courses in the areas of law you regard as practical—specifically the specialized courses in criminal procedure and evidence. Even if our objective was to train you to be a defender or prosecutor, it doesn't follow that we should do it all in one course, in the first year.

S. No of course not, but you'd at least want to make a start, and I don't see how the course in criminal law does that.

P. Sure you do, if the defender or the prosecutor were not familiar with the elements of crimes, including the often tricky mens rea issues, as well as what conduct is prohibited, and the many possible defenses, they couldn't function. The daily grist of the urban criminal courts doesn't regularly pose many major substantive legal problems, but well trained lawyers can often find them. The major advances in substantive criminal law, apart from statutes, come from cases in which defendants are represented by broadly educated lawyers with rich sophistication in the subtlety and complexity of the criminal law. Take the innovative use of duress or necessity as a defense to charges of prison escape, or the effort to enlarge the defense of insanity to include incapacity produced by severe social disadvantage, or the attempt to assimilate drug or alcohol addiction to the defense of the involuntary act. Even beyond that, there's more to the practice of criminal law than the routine grist of the urban courts. Consider, for example, the complex problems for defense and prosecution alike in the growing use of the law of conspiracy to deal with racketeering and other forms of organized crime; or in the defense of mistake of law to charges of lawbreaking by governmental officials; or of increasing efforts to enforce criminal sanctions against corporations. No indeed, even for students who plan to make criminal law practice their area, I can't agree that the substantive criminal law course is plainly impractical.

S. Well sure, you can give examples like that, but the course isn't devoted just to those things. Most of it, or at least a great deal of it, deals with matters you'd have a hard time justifying as practical.

P. If you mean to say that a good part of what you study is not directly useful in a lot of the criminal practice, I have to agree. But as you must have noticed from your other courses, it isn't our purpose merely to offer you immediate practical training in the handling of routine cases. That would be a great waste and would make it doubtful whether we could justify being part of a university. For example, the property law course is not directed toward forming property law practitioners, nor is the torts class designed to equip you to be negligence lawyers. Sure, we are in business to educate lawyers, but that means a great deal more than giving you the knowledge and skills to practice in particular areas. We're laying the foundation for your legal education, to be further developed later in law school and beyond. Look at it this way: would requiring criminal law make sense if we thought we were just training criminal practitioners in that course? Surely not. Our students will be public interest lawyers, corporate lawyers, tort lawyers, and tax lawyers; many will also be judges and legislators. Some students will even be law professors. Even those who become criminal lawyers won't be just defenders and prosecutors; they'll constitute a group of specialists with great knowledge of and a great stake in a vitally significant institution whose workings make a tremendous difference to the lives of countless people and the welfare of our society. Does it make sense to fashion a required course in criminal law for all these people narrowly directed to training for criminal practice? We have other objectives in mind beside training people to operate the machinery of urban criminal courts.

    S. Could you spell out those objectives a bit more clearly?

    P. Sure. The first of those objectives is to contribute to your general legal education, quite apart from the criminal law. The concepts of criminal law are splendid vehicles for rigorous legal analysis, for generalizing, distinguishing, and searching for contradiction and consistency—legal and factual impossibility, preparation and attempt, mens rea, intention, voluntary act, and causation. The subject provides an opportunity to work with statutory materials not too complex for a beginner. It allows for the comparison of adjudication and legislation as two means of changing and developing the law. It confronts the student with how the law can approach resolution of issues where deeply held values are so in conflict that there is peril and loss whichever move one makes. And one of its central issues is exploring the ramifications of a person's moral fault and responsibility for what happens, and for what others do as a consequence of one's own actions—a pervasive issue in all private law.

    There is a lot more to be said on this, but I don't want this discussion to sound too much like a curriculum committee meeting. Let me advance another objective of much larger import derived from the significance of substantive criminal law to the community and to individuals.

    I cannot do better in making this point than to quote from an eloquent statement by Professor Herbert Wechsler, used as an epigraph to a criminal law casebook you may be familiar with.

> Whatever views one holds about the penal law, no one will question its importance in society. This is the law on which men place their ultimate reliance for protection against all the deepest injuries that human conduct can inflict on individuals and institutions. By the same token penal law governs the strongest force that we permit official agencies to bring to bear on individuals. Its promise as an instrument of safety is matched only by its power to destroy. If penal law is weak or ineffective, basic human interests are in jeopardy. If it is harsh or arbitrary in its impact, it works a gross injustice on those caught within its toils. The law that carries such responsibilities should surely be as rational and just as law can be. Nowhere in the entire legal field is more at stake for the community or for the individual.[1]

In the light of this, it seems essential that law schools try to educate their students broadly and deeply in the criminal law, for it is our future lawyers who will have the most to say about how the system works and how just, rational, and effective it will be.

   S. Now, I don't disagree with that at all. I just cannot see how it follows that we should devote the major part of the first year course to the substantive criminal law rather than to the great issues of criminal law today—urban crime and its relation to ghetto life; race and crime; the injustices in our society that produce crime; the degradation of our prisons and jails; corruption in government; the arrogance and brutality of police; . . .

   P. Wait, wait. I get your point. I'm not denying these issues are matters of great importance. Still and all, this is a law school and it is a first year law course we are talking about. If we take the subject to be the phenomenon of crime and societal responses to it in America today, there is very little that could not justifiably be included. If we were to address these matters seriously and not as an exercise in ideological polemics, it would be necessary to assess historical and cultural issues, problems of sociology, economics, and social psychology. The inquiries would require careful empirical work as well as thorough examination of theoretical and methodological considerations. That is a tall order for a class of harried beginning law students struggling with three or four other courses. I agree that the criminal law, like all law, is a product of social organization with deep roots in human and social behavior. To some degree it is possible to call attention to some of the ways this is so. But to do more in a basic criminal law course, as opposed to advanced seminars in manageable pieces of the puzzle, would tend to sacrifice the study of law as a distinctive institution. Of course we should deal with the criminal law critically and deeply, but I don't think we err in making law the central focus.

   S. But how does that make the case for substantive criminal law? On that view, the centerpiece of the course should be the administration of justice in this country—the law governing police practices and their enforcement through the exclusionary rule, the developing law with respect to prisoners' rights, and so on. This is law, not the whole realm of human and social behavior, but it's the law that really connects with the life of individuals and the quality of our society. And it just so happens it is practical as well, which even you would not count as a disadvantage, I should think.

P. No, of course not. I don't underestimate the significance of these matters. We do teach them, as I said, sometimes as part of first year criminal law, often as advanced courses in criminal procedure and specialized seminars. The issue between us is not the importance of the administration of the law, but the importance of the substantive law. We have to consider why the substantive criminal law is also justified on the criteria we are talking about now, that is, why it also connects, as you say, with matters of great social concern.

S. All right, why?

P. The substantive criminal law connects with matters of great social concern because upon it all of our criminal and penal institutions rest. You regard the administration of justice as important. It is. But what is being administered? Surely not justice as an abstract goal—you, I gather, would be the last to say that. What is it then, if not the substantive criminal law? There can be no authorized police inquiry, arrest, prosecution, conviction, or sentence that is not based on the rules and doctrines of the substantive criminal law. This is the law that finally legitimates or fails to legitimate what is done by the agencies of criminal justice. It does so in two basic ways. First, it defines who is accountable, on pain of punishment, for what actions in what circumstances. Second, it defines by implication—a very consequential implication—all the other actions and circumstances in which people are *not* subject to the sanctions of the law. These two functions are crucial for the security of the people and the stability of society. What would you have without the substantive law? Only the unrestrained exercise of force by public officials upon anyone and for such purposes as they happen to decide upon. At best, officials would take it upon themselves to do the right thing, as *they* might view it.

S. But that's precisely what does happen in practice. That's why I wonder how much difference it makes what the doctrines and definitions of the criminal law happen to be. The discretionary judgments of officials pretty well undercut the role of the substantive criminal law you are speaking about. Police detain and arrest not just by the book, but by their own notions of how law enforcement can best be advanced. Prosecutors exercise broad freedom on whether and what to charge. Defendants get convicted of crimes through free-wheeling bargaining between prosecutor and defense counsel, rather than through an objective as-

sessment of the distinctions made by the criminal law. Even when cases
go to trial, I can't believe juries are much affected by the elaborate and
confusing instructions they get on the doctrines of the criminal law. Even
lawyers and judges have a tough time with them. In the end, juries
convict or acquit on how it all strikes them. And in sentencing, judges
have such a wide choice once the defendant is convicted of some crime
that it often doesn't make a great deal of difference of what crime the
person is convicted.

P. There's much in what you say. But I must say, with respect, you
mistake what it all goes to prove. First, in decrying excessive discretion as you do, your premise has to be that the rules of law *should* control discretion, but do not. That concedes the importance of substantive
law in any proper criminal law system. Your arguments make a case
for studying how and where the rules become eclipsed by uncontrolled
discretion and what can be done about it. They don't make a case for
not studying critically the criteria governing determinations of guilt
and punishment, which, after all, are just what the substantive law
consists of.

Beyond that, however, you make too much of the fact that rules of
law don't always operate in practice the way they are designed to operate.
From this, it doesn't follow that the rules do not matter at all. Take the
free-wheeling bargaining you refer to. Surely the substantive rules of
law do operate here—not in an adjudicatory context to be sure, but in
a settlement context in which judgments of the applicable rules and the
proveable facts set the framework for the negotiation. True, the substantive law does matter less because of the discretionary elements in
the system you point to, and any sensible examination of the rules of
law would extend to how far they are blunted in practice. But do they
matter so much less that they lose the significance I attribute to them?
I don't think so.

Look at it this way. Taking the criminal law as a body of specifications
of who may be prosecuted and convicted for what crimes in what circumstance and subject to what punishment, you can ask two questions
about their effect in practice. First, do they serve in practice to prevent
the imposition of criminal sanctions for conduct not made criminal?
Second, do they control the actions of officials within the ambit of what
is proscribed?

Consider the first question. If it were the case that in practice the
specifications of the criminal law were disregarded in the sense that
people were systematically prosecuted, convicted, and sentenced beyond
what they authorized, your point would be strong. But this is not the
case, and I don't think that you are saying it is. Persons can't be prosecuted and convicted of what is not made criminal, and they can't be
punished beyond what the law allows. The courts function in practice,

not just in theory, to prevent excesses of these sorts. Juries, for example, may as you say, have trouble with the legal instructions because they don't understand them or because they just don't like them, but no verdict of guilty can stand unless the court concludes a reasonable jury could find it on the law beyond a reasonable doubt. So, even if we look at the rules of the criminal law as marking the outer perimeter of criminality and punishability, and put aside the distinctions it makes within those perimeters, the criminal law has the telling import I attribute to it. Its existence serves to protect the individual against punishment by the state, not just on the books, but in practice. This is the distinctive function of the whole criminal code—its definitions of criminal actions, culpable states of mind, doctrines of liability, as well as its doctrines of excuse and justification.

Consider the positions commonly taken by law students—that the law of rape should be enlarged; that the rules of corporate criminality should be changed to facilitate convictions of corporate wrong-doing; that environmental spoilation should be made criminal; that the criminal law should be extended over economic offenses; that such defenses as mistake of law and official authorization should be narrowed to avoid the escape of governmental officials who direct criminal activities; that the possession of firearms should be made criminal; that the lawful use of deadly force in law enforcement should be narrowed. Surely you agree that these proposals can make a real difference, and that those urging them are not wasting everyone's time with things that do not matter.

The same is equally true of areas where the law arguably goes too far in defining conduct as criminal. Need I remind you of the debate over decriminalizing such conduct as the use of marijuana and other drugs, deviant sexual behavior, or prostitution? I do not think you would regard these issues as inconsequential because of the large elements of discretion in the system.

Let me go back to pick up the second question I raised about the effect of the substantive criminal law in practice—the extent to which the distinctions among kinds of criminality and degrees of punishment actually determine the behavior of law enforcing agencies. Here your point is the strongest. As you say, the vast amount of discretion by prosecutors and the prevalence of plea bargaining distort the legislative patterns. The precise crime or crimes committed by the defendant, as measured by the criminal law on the books, may be very different from the crime the defendant is convicted of as a result of prosecutorial discretion, plea bargaining and jury compromising. Moreover, the defendant may be sentenced far less severely than the law allows. I want to stress, however, that the difference lies in the defendant being convicted and punished for *less* than the law authorizes, not more. The prosecutor, for example, cannot bargain credibly for *more* than the law authorizes, not at least if the defendant is properly represented.

Now, I have to concede that discretionary judgments sometimes distort the legal distinctions over shades of criminality found in the substantive law. An example of this is Professor Zimring's study of those convicted of varying classes of culpable homicide in Pennsylvania.[2] The study showed that the discretionary elements in the system produced a pattern of conviction and punishment strikingly at odds with the grading of culpable homicide mandated by the homicide statute and its judicial interpretations. But what follows from this fact is that a rounded treatment of substantive rules and doctrines of the criminal law should include treatment of those features of the working system that tend to frustrate or distort the system's design. One would want to look at those features critically. To what extent are they dispensable irrationalities, adhered to because of economy or sheer expedience or inertia, as is often said of plea bargaining? To what extent do they represent a judgment that equity and discretion are indispensable to a just criminal law, as is often said of juries? In either event, what should be done differently in formulating criminal doctrines to account for these discretionary features?

You see, I concede the force of part of what you say, but I cannot concede that the existence of these discretionary features renders unreal and unworthy of critical study the law's distinctions in shades of guilt or punishment. While strict rule-of-law determinations don't always work in practice—because of imperfections in administration or because they can't altogether do so without displacing a desired flexibility—it doesn't follow that formulating rules is a waste of time. Of course rules influence prosecutors and jurors in varying degrees. We want to know how and why their influence varies to enable us to improve the law's effectiveness. This is a vital question of means. But we also have to refine and articulate those differential judgments of fault and punishability that make for a more just criminal law. Only by so doing can we discover how we want judgments to be made, that is, the criteria we want to govern in place of the discretion exercised by criminal justice agencies. This is a question of ends.

S. Yes, but even accepting all that, are these restraints what the criminal law is mainly about, or is it rather the exercise of coercive power by the state to make people conform? We talk about what people may be punished for and for how much and in what circumstances. Underlying all this talk is the premise that punishing people is an acceptable and justifiable thing for our society to do. I don't accept that premise.

P. Why do you have to? You aren't the first person to doubt that punishment actually deters others from crime, that we can justly use offenders for this purpose, that retribution is a defensible basis for punishment, or to prefer rehabilitative approaches to punishment. Of course these matters are not to be taken for granted. They should be high on the agenda of any course in criminal law.

S. No, that's not what bothers me. I'm not one who believes there is no evil in the world or that evil-doers should not be punished. On the contrary. My point is that the principal evil in our society is done by those who control the criminal law—including those who write it and those who enforce it. The well-to-do and the powerful are the chief beneficiaries of the criminal law. The poor, the powerless, the outsider, racial and ethnic minorities—these are its chief victims. The criminal law is an instrument whereby those in power preserve society as it is, with all its injustices. When we study it as you would have us do, raising the questions you would have us raise, you are asking us to act and think as if it were otherwise. I regard that as an immoral enterprise and I resent being drawn into it.

P. Will you forgive me if I say you are overreacting? Do you really think that no punishment of anyone can be morally justified in America today—not rapists, or child molesters, or the Watergate perpetrators, or law-breaking corporations and those who run them, or polluters, or corrupt politicians? Come on, your gripe is that we don't punish enough, and that that itself is an injustice. Isn't that so? You don't have such persons in mind when you make your point about the injustice of punishment. But don't you have to?

And how about those others you do have in mind? Would our society be better if people who kill or assault others, or steal their possessions, or rob them, or invade their homes, or purvey dangerous addictive drugs, if these people were not punished? Do not think for a minute it is just the privileged white middle class which is victimized by these crimes. Speak to families trying to make it in the ghettos of our cities. You will learn otherwise.

I know you have sympathy with the great mass of offenders who populate our awful jails and prisons. You see who they are and where they come from and you lay the responsibility at the door of society. You blame poverty, unemployment, racial prejudice and discrimination. These social injustices are real, but after all, it was not the criminal law which produced them.

S. No, but our criminal laws help to maintain them.

P. I am sorry, I just do not understand that. How does society perpetrate poverty, prejudice, and oppression by prosecuting and punishing people who assault and rob other people?

S. I'll tell you how—by totally distracting people from where the real problem lies; by turning their attention from the root causes of these crimes in social injustice to the overt symptoms of these evils. It's all so easy. Criminals are evil, hateful individuals, so all you need is a dose of law and order to set things right. Arrest them, convict them, and lock them away in vile and degrading jails and prisons, and if crime continues do the same for more of them for longer terms.

P. Well, I hope I don't have to defend a simplistic law-and-order mentality in order to defend the institution of criminal law. I think it is true that public opinion and the legislatures that reflect it do tend to react that way. One hopes that our graduates will have a more sophisticated view. All the same, it strikes me as equally simplistic to dwell exclusively on social injustice as the cause of crime. First, while no one doubts the connections between crime and poverty, discrimination and other social injustices, it's not at all clear how close these connections are. No one has succeeded in establishing the etiology of crime in any single factor. Second, whatever the causes, crime is a source of profound fear, insecurity, and injury to people in this country. They may legitimately demand protection against it, through our laws, while the process of finding and dealing with its causes goes on.

But all this was by way of saying why I thought your moral distaste for the criminal law was misplaced. I would like now to make a more daring claim. I suggest to you that it is precisely for those who are most sensitive to issues of moral rights that the substantive criminal law should have the greatest appeal. May I ask you this: feeling as you do, how is it that you don't have similar distaste for criminal procedure?

S. I'm not sure. Partly because it strikes me as practical—something I am going to be using whenever I have a criminal matter. But maybe there's more to it. Perhaps, it's the way in which criminal procedure is taught nowadays. It is mainly about constitutional prohibitions on the law enforcement process, and these prohibitions involve basic rights of individuals against the government—search and seizure, interrogation, right to counsel, self-incrimination. In a way, it's a course in civil liberties.

P. All right, I want to claim the same for the substantive criminal law course. It too is a course in civil liberties. Underlying the great bulk of the doctrines of the criminal law is the conception of personal responsibility. This is no artificial construct of the criminal law. It is deeply rooted in our moral sense of fitness that punishment entails blame and that, therefore, punishment may not justly be imposed where the person is not blameworthy. The whole so-called general part of the criminal law, as well as the mens rea definitions in the special part, are devoted to articulating the minimum conditions for the attribution of blame and the various features of conduct that warrant differential judgments of blameworthiness.

One finds instances where punishment seems to be imposed in the absence of blame—strict liability for example, or more arguably, liability for negligence. One also finds instances where people are punished for what they are not to blame, rather than for what they are to blame—

felony murder, for example. But note the arguments offered to support these instances. They are either that, contrary to common belief, blame is appropriate, or that these are exceptional situations in which the exigencies of law enforcement outweigh the injustice of punishing the individual. The moral claim of the individual that he may not be subjected to punishment where he cannot be said to be blameworthy, as judged by our fundamental conceptions of morality and corrective justice, is a central issue to be faced in every case even when it is found not to be controlling.

If you conceive the doctrines of criminal law as I'm suggesting, you'll find the issue of moral accountability everywhere. Indeed, nowhere are its conditions more systematically examined and refined than in the substantive criminal law. When and why does it affect liability that the defendant misunderstood the situation? When a harm ensues that would not have happened had the defendant not acted as he did, is the defendant to be held for that result? Certainly not always, but whatever the formulas—proximate cause, concurrent cause, etc.—the governing question is whether our moral ideas of causation permit the defendant to be held accountable for the result. Consider the doctrines of accomplice liability. It's no accident that the doctrines mainly track our moral judgments of when one person may be held accountable for the actions of others, and only when they do not, do they become problematical.

Then there's the law of excuses, which plainly has its roots in conceptions of moral accountability. When and why do we afford a defense where the defendant acted under the threats of another; or when he acted under the influence of alcohol; or when he acted in a haze after a blow? Again the notion of the injustice of blame when the person could not have done otherwise is central to any resolution of these issues. Consider also the defense of legal insanity. Why do we have such a defense except for our feeling that it would be morally intolerable to punish persons who are not responsible? This is the ultimate ground for the resistance to proposals to abolish the defense. The long-standing controversy over the legal test of insanity centers on means, not ends—how best to identify for the jury those features of a person's mental abnormality that are relevant to an assessment of his moral responsibility.

S. Are you really saying that the doctrines of the criminal law mirror our moral judgments about the justice of punishing particular individuals?

P. I regret the hint of skepticism in your observation, but the answer is yes, in part. But only in part. The criminal law is not a moral code. It is a code of law, which has to be administered practically to accomplish its purpose. In most any criminal law—certainly in our own—compromises are made in the name of effectiveness and administration. I already pointed out an instance of this, strict criminal liability, but surely there are many others. Indeed, I would think that very few provisions of the law are precisely what would be indicated by moral considerations of personal responsibility. Take, for example, the whole resort to what is called an objective standard, as it operates in defining culpable negligence, or as it operates in the various excuses to criminal conduct. A strictly moral approach would condition blame on what could be expected of the particular individual, not on what could be expected of a reasonable person. As Holmes observed, if moral ground were to control punishment "the first thing to be considered would be those limitations in the capacity for choosing rightly which arise from abnormal instincts, want of education, lack of intelligence, and all the other defects which are most marked in the criminal classes."[3] If one imposed liability for unintended or unforeseen consequences, one would want to know whether the defendant exercised that care of which he was capable; in defining the defense of duress one would ask whether the defendant exercised the self-control of which *he* was capable, rather than that of a person of reasonable firmness.

But you see the problem. How do we determine what the defendant was capable of? When you are discussing moral issues abstractly, you do not face this dilemma. You can simply conclude that if the person could have taken care and did not, then he is morally censorable, but not otherwise. However, the criminal law does not allow this. The court and jury must decide, not conditionally but absolutely, whether the defendant is guilty. What do you do when you lack the means to make reliable judgments of facts on which moral blame rests? One possibility—and it is commonly what our criminal law does—is to make compromises and approximations. You ask the jury to decide not if the *defendant* exercised the care or the power of resistance he was capable of (how could they reliably know?), but whether he exercised the care or power of resistance a *reasonable person* would be capable of. That way you have a test a jury can administer. Administrability, I might add, is no minor consideration in dealing with possible defenses that rest altogether on the personality and character of the defendant. For without an objective element, there are no ascertainable limits to these defenses and the deterrent threat of punishment could be seriously weakened.

A rather nice example is the defense of legal insanity. Periodically there are serious proposals to abolish the defense. Sometimes abolition is proposed by those who see it as a loophole in the law through which the guilty escape punishment. At other times it is proposed by those who see it as a cruel hoax whereby some offenders are subjected to a worse and longer confinement in so-called hospitals than they would be in a prison. These are not captious arguments. What accounts for the lineage and durability of the insanity defense is a very fundamental moral conception of the wrongness of imposing the stigma of punishment on those who cannot fairly be blamed.

At the same time the defense has never been defined altogether as its rationale would require. Is it not possible that a person, to use the terms of the most widely accepted test, may lack knowledge of the wrongfulness of his act or be unable to conform his conduct to the requirements of the law, *even though* he has no medically identifiable mental disease or defect? Why insist, then, on such a disease as a necessary condition of the defense? The explanation lies in the weight accorded expediency in the administration of the criminal justice system. Without tying the defense to mental disease, the defense is limitless and unascertainable— we have no means of distinguishing those who would not from those who could not. The requirement of mental disease does not assure our ability to make the distinction, but it serves at least to confine the exception to punishability to a narrow band of offenders and provides some basis for managing an otherwise unworkable distinction.

S. So you end up giving me more evidence of how the criminal law pursues its goals through invasion of the moral rights of individuals. That is what I keep trying to tell you about your favorite subject. It's the nature of the beast and maybe it's necessary in some sense, but I have no heart for it.

P. Well, I am saying that utilitarian considerations sometimes prevail over justice to the individual, but I don't think that justifies your feelings about the criminal law. Let me briefly state three reasons why. First, it is not the case that law enforcement exigencies systematically prevail over justice to the individuals. If that were the case, we would have a very different criminal law than we have today, without mens rea, excuses, or any concessions to the plight of the individual. Second, the value of personal justice is always present as an extremely powerful reason to shape the law in one way. It's always a central issue to be dealt with in study and criticism of the criminal law, or in confronting substantive issues in litigation by prosecutor and defense counsel. Sometimes it prevails, sometimes it is compromised, occasionally it is given no force. The criminal doctrine that emerges is in most cases at least influenced by recognition of this value of personal justice. Third, it is not always wrong to give weight to considerations of more effective law enforcement. Certainly the majority of my students would agree when the conduct that's made criminal is of particular concern to them. I hear few complaints from students about imposing strict liability on persons or corporations who package unfit or mislabeled drugs or foods, or who commit pollution by their industrial processes; and I hear strong arguments from many students for eliminating any requirement that a particular defendant be aware of the woman's resistance when prosecuted for raping her or even trying to do so. I don't say these positions are necessarily wrong. The protection of the consumer, the environment, and of women from these harms is a legitimate, even urgent, good. Sometimes the urgency is great enough to make a case for compromising our commitment to justice to the individual. As Justice Holmes observed, with characteristic bluntness, what "accounts for the law's indifference to a man's particular temperament, faculties, and so forth" is that "public policy sacrifices the individual to the general good."[4] This is a problem not unique to criminal law. It is encountered in every field of law. The hard questions are why and how and when and how much—questions of great importance for any legal system and worthy of all the attention we can give them.

S. I don't know—can I be completely candid?

P. How can I say no?

S. You do tend to get lyrical while talking about your subject, but in the end what does it come to? You speak of concern for justice as a justification for concern with the substantive criminal law, but how much does it touch what really matters? The world is rife with immense social wrongs—poverty, discrimination, inequalities, degrading jails and prisons. What we need are blueprints for massive reform and you give us exquisite line drawings.

P. We seem to be back where we were a while ago. All I can say is that the shape of the substantive criminal law has a bearing on the moral conditions of any society. It's not everything. A just and sound criminal law will not eliminate the evils you speak of, but an unjust and ill-considered one will surely add to those evils. Consider a world as it is now, with all the injustices that rankle you, but with a criminal law that has abandoned personal responsibility as a touchstone. Only harm or the threat of harm need be shown to trigger the state's authority to punish. Once that were shown there would be no escape unless a judge or an official so chose. There would be very little to argue because there would be very little law. It would be all the same whether the person meant the harm, or was negligent, or was himself blameless. There would be no excuse or justification which legally checked the power of officials. I leave the rest to your imagination. Whenever you are inclined to think of the criminal law as small potatoes—as "exquisite line drawings," in your phrase—think of what our society would be like with a criminal law shorn of its commitment to the concept of moral responsibility.

S. I'm beginning to see why we look at things so differently. You see the doctrines of criminal law as serving the traditional libertarian values of individual responsibility and you seem to think those values are the most important in the world. I just can't get as fired up about them as you do. For me the greatest threat to our democratic society comes from the gross inequality in the distribution of resources and the degradation and deprivation of the poor and the minorities who are denied their rights. Therefore, when I look at the criminal law, I'm less impressed with its finely drawn principles of blame and responsibility than with the people who are victimized by it—the poor and the minorities whose neglect represents the greatest injustice in our society.

P. That's a fair statement, though I'm not inclined to think it leaves our positions as irreconcilable as you imply. There are situations in which the values of liberty and equality conflict, but I don't think this is one of them. Corrective justice and distributive justice are both central features of our morality. We don't deny the one in praising the other. As for the great majority of defendants and prisoners being the poor and minorities, I don't deny this either, and I share your feelings. However, as I tried to say before, the cause of this is not in any meaningful sense the substantive criminal law, but social conditions quite remote from it. It behooves you from your perspective as well as me from mine to respect the importance of a just and rational body of substantive criminal law.

S. We should end on a note of harmony and that is as close to it as we are likely to get. Thanks, Professor.

THE REACH OF THE CRIMINAL LAW

2
THE CRISIS OF
OVERCRIMINALIZATION

Since World War II there have been striking achievements in reform of the substantive criminal law. Largely under the impetus of the American Law Institute's Model Penal Code, a number of states have completed revisions of their criminal codes, and still more are in the process. The importance of this reform for criminal justice cannot be overstated.

But there is a significant feature of substantive law revision that these reforms have succeeded in reaching only in part. By and large, these efforts have dealt with offenses entailing substantial harm to persons, property, and the state, against which the criminal law is generally accepted as the last and necessary resort. But American criminal law typically has extended the criminal sanction well beyond these fundamental offenses to include very different kinds of behavior, kinds which threaten far less serious harms, or else highly intangible ones about which there is no genuine consensus, or even no harms at all. The existence of these crimes and attempts at their eradication raise problems of inestimable importance for the criminal law. Indeed, it is fair to say that until these problems of overcriminalization are systematically examined and effectively dealt with, some of the most besetting problems of criminal-law administration are bound to continue.

The subjects raising the central issue of overcriminalization cut a wide swath through the laws of most jurisdictions. In the process of revising the California criminal law, we encountered a mass of crimes outside the Penal Code, matching the Penal Code itself in volume, and authorizing criminal convictions for such offenses as failure by a school principal to use required textbooks,[1] failure of a teacher to carry first-aid kits on field trips,[2] gambling on the result of an election,[3] giving private commercial performances by a state-supported band,[4] and allowing waste of an artesian well by the landowner.[5] Then there are the criminal laws, enforced by state police forces, which have been the primary means used to deal with the death and injury toll of the automobile. Indications are that this response may ultimately do more harm than good by blocking off politically harder, but more likely, remedial alternatives.[6] Problematic also has been the use of criminal sanctions to enforce economic regulatory measures, a matter which I have dealt with elsewhere.[7] And there are other instances as well. In this piece I want to comment on the problems of overcriminalization in just three kinds of situations, in each of which the costs paid primarily affect the day-to-day business of law enforcement. These are the situations in which the criminal law is used: (1) to declare or enforce public standards of private morality, (2) as a means of providing social services in default of other public agencies, and (3) as a disingenuous means of permitting police to do indirectly what the law forbids them to do directly.

ENFORCEMENT OF MORALS

The use of the criminal law to prohibit moral deviancy among consenting adults has been a recurring subject of jurisprudential debate. Stephens in the last century[8] and Lord Devlin in this century have urged the legitimacy of criminal intervention on the ground that "society cannot ignore the morality of the individual any more than it can his loyalty; it flourishes on both and without either it dies."[9] The contrary view, vigorously espoused by John Stuart Mill in the nineteenth century,[10] and by H. L. A. Hart[11] and many others in recent years, is, in the words of the Wolfenden Report:

> Unless a deliberate attempt is to be made by society, acting through the agency of the law, to equate the sphere of crime with that of sin, there must remain a realm of private morality and immorality which is, in brief and crude terms, not the law's business.[12]

It is not my purpose here to mediate or resolve that dispute. My objective is to call attention to matters of the hardest concreteness and practicality, which should be of as much concern in reaching final judgment to a Devlin as to the staunchest libertarian; namely, the adverse consequences to effective law enforcement of attempting to achieve conformity with private moral standards through use of the criminal law.

SEX OFFENSES

The classic instance of the use of the criminal law purely to enforce a moral code is the laws prohibiting extra-marital and abnormal sexual intercourse between a man and a woman. Whether or not Kinsey's judgment is accurate that 95 percent of the population are made potential criminals by these laws,[13] no one doubts that their standard of sexual conduct is not adhered to by vast numbers in the community, including the otherwise most respectable (and, most especially, the police themselves);[14] nor is it disputed that there is no effort to enforce these laws. The traditional function of the criminal law, therefore—to curtail socially threatening behavior through the threat of punishment and the incapacitation and rehabilitation of offenders—is quite beside the point.

Thurman Arnold surely had it right when he observed that these laws "are unenforced because we want to continue our conduct, and unrepealed because we want to preserve our morals."[15]

But law enforcement pays a price for using the criminal law in this way. First, the moral message communicated by the law is contradicted by the total absence of enforcement; for while the public sees the conduct condemned in words, it also sees in the dramatic absence of prosecutions that it is not condemned in deed. Moral adjurations vulnerable to a charge of hypocrisy are self-defeating no less in law than elsewhere. Second, the spectacle of nullification of the legislature's solemn commands is an unhealthy influence on law enforcement generally. It tends to breed a cynicism and an indifference to the criminal-law processes which augment tendencies toward disrespect for those who make and enforce the law, a disrespect which is already widely in evidence. In addition: "Dead letter laws, far from promoting a sense of security, which is the main function of the penal law, actually impair that security by holding the threat of prosecution over the heads of people whom we have no intention to punish."[16]

Finally, these laws invite discriminatory enforcement against persons selected for prosecution on grounds unrelated to the evil against which these laws are purportedly addressed, whether those grounds be "the prodding of some reform group, a newspaper-generated hysteria over some local sex crime, a vice drive which is put on by the local authorities to distract attention from defects in their administration of the city government."[17]

The criminalization of consensual adult homosexuality represents another attempt to legislate private morality. It raises somewhat different problems from heterosexual offenses, in that there are some attempts at enforcement. The central questions are whether the criminal law is an effective way of discouraging this conduct and how wasteful or costly it is.

Despite the fact that homosexual practices are condemned as criminal in virtually all states, usually as a felony with substantial punishment, and despite sporadic efforts at enforcement in certain situations, there is little evidence that the criminal law has discouraged the practice to any substantial degree. The Kinsey Report as well as other studies suggest a wide incidence of homosexuality throughout the country. One major reason for the ineffectiveness of these laws is that the private and consensual nature of the conduct precludes the attainment of any substantial deterrent efficacy through law enforcement. There are no complainants, and only the indiscreet have reasons for fear. Another reason is the irrelevance of the threat of punishment. Homosexuality involves not so much a choice to act wickedly as the seeking of normal sexual fulfillment in abnormal ways (though not abnormal to the individual) preferred by the individual for reasons deeply rooted in his development as a personality. Moreover, in view of the character of prison environments, putting the homosexual defendant into the prison system is, as observed recently by a United States District Court Judge, "a little like throwing Bre'r Rabbit into the briarpatch."[18]

On the other hand, the use of the criminal law has been attended by grave consequences. A commonly noted consequence is the enhanced opportunities created for extortionary threats of exposure and prosecution. Certainly, incidents of this kind have been reported often enough to raise genuine concern.[19] But, of more significance for the administration of justice, enforcement efforts by police have created problems both for them and for the community. Opportunities for enforcement are limited by the private and consensual character of the behavior. Only a small and insignificant manifestation of homosexuality is amenable to enforcement. This is that which takes place, either in the solicitation or the act, in public places. Even in these circumstances, it is not usual for persons to act openly. To obtain evidence, police are obliged to resort to behavior that tends to degrade and demean both themselves personally and law enforcement as an institution.[20] However, one may deplore homosexual conduct, no one can lightly accept a criminal law that requires for its enforcement that officers of the law sit concealed in ceilings, their eyes fixed to "peepholes," searching for criminal sexuality in the lavatories below;[21] or that they loiter suggestively around public toilets or in corridors hopefully awaiting a sexual advance.[22] Such conduct corrupts both citizenry and police and reduces the moral authority of the criminal law, especially among those portions of the citizenry—the poor and subcultural—who are particularly liable to be treated in an arbitrary fashion. The complaint of the critical that the police have more important things to do with their time is amply attested by the several volumes of the National Crime Commission's reports.

The offense of prostitution creates similar problems. Although there are social harms beyond private immorality in commercialized sex—spread of venereal disease, exploitation of the young, and the affront of public solicitation, for example—the blunt use of the criminal prohibition has proven ineffective and costly. Prostitution has perdured in all civilizations; indeed, few institutions have proven as hardy. The inevitable conditions of social life unfailingly produce the supply to meet the ever-present demand. As the Wolfenden Report observed: "There are limits to the degree of discouragement which the criminal law can properly exercise towards a woman who has deliberately decided to live her life in this way, or a man who has deliberately chosen to use her services."[23] The more so, one may add, in a country where it has been estimated that over two-thirds of white males alone will have experience with prostitutes during their lives.[24] The costs, on the other hand, of making the effort are similar to those entailed in enforcing the homo-sexual laws—diversion of police resources; encouragement of use of illegal means of police control (which, in the case of prostitution, take the form of knowingly unlawful harassment arrests to remove suspected prostitutes from the streets[25] and various entrapment devices, usually the only means of obtaining convictions)[26]; degradation of the image of law enforcement; discriminatory enforcement against the poor; and of-ficial corruption.

To the extent that spread of venereal disease, corruption of the young, and public affront are the objects of prostitution controls, it would require little ingenuity to devise modes of social control short of the blanket criminalization of prostitution which would at the same time prove more effective and less costly for law enforcement. Apparently, the driving force behind prostitution laws is principally the conviction that prostitution is immoral. Only the judgment that the use of the criminal law for verbal vindication of our morals is more important than its use to protect life and property can support the preservation of these laws as they are.

ABORTION

The criminal prohibition of abortions is occasionally defended on the ground that it is necessary to protect the mother against the adverse physical and psychological effects of such operations. There seems little doubt, however, that these laws serve to augment rather than to reduce the danger. The criminal penalty has given rise to a black market of illegal abortionists who stand ready to run the risk of imprisonment in order to earn the high fees produced by the law's discouragement of legitimate physicians. As a consequence, abortions are performed in kitchens and private rooms instead of in properly equipped hospitals, and often by unqualified amateurs rather than by licensed physicians. A relatively simple and nondangerous operation on patients strongly desirous of avoiding parenthood is therefore converted into a surrep-titious, degrading, and traumatic experience in which the risk to the mental and physical well-being of the woman is many times increased. Indeed, the evidence is irresistible that thousands of lives are needlessly lost yearly at the hands of illegal abortionists.[27]

It is plain, therefore, that the primary force behind retention of the abortion laws is belief that it is immoral. One of the serious moral ob-jections is based on the view that the unborn fetus, even in its early stages of development, has an independent claim to life equivalent to that of a developed human being. Even those holding this judgment, however, can scarcely ignore the hard fact that abortion laws do not work to stop abortion, except for those too poor and ignorant to avail themselves of blackmarket alternatives, and that the consequence of their retention is probably to sacrifice more lives of mothers than the total number of fetuses saved by the abortion laws.

While there are no reliable figures on the number of illegal abortions, estimates have ranged from a hundred thousand to a million and a half yearly.[28] Among the factors responsible for this widespread nullification, two appear to predominate. The first is that there is no general consensus on the legitimacy of the moral claim on behalf of the fetus. While it is vigorously asserted by some portions of the community, it is as vigorously denied by others of equal honesty and respectability. In democratic societies, fortunately, the coercive sanctions of the criminal law prove unacceptable and unworkable as a means of settling clashes of sharply divided moralities. Second, the demand for abortions, by both married and unmarried women, is urgent and widespread, arising out of natural and understandable motives manifesting no threat to other persons or property. As with most morals offenses, therefore, sympathy for the offender combines with an unsettled moral climate to preclude any real possibility of enforcement.

GAMBLING AND NARCOTICS

Laws against gambling and narcotics present serious problems for law enforcement. Despite arrests, prosecutions and convictions, and increasingly severe penalities, the conduct seems only to flourish. The irrepressible demand for gambling and drugs, like the demand for alcohol during Prohibition days, survives the condemnation of the criminal law. Whether or not the criminal restriction operates paradoxically, as some have thought, to make the conduct more attractive, it is clear that the prohibitions have not substantially eliminated the demand.

Nor have the laws and enforcement efforts suppressed sources of supply. No one with an urge to gamble in any fair-sized city of this country has far to go to place an illegal bet. And in the case of narcotics, illicit suppliers enter the market to seek the profits made available by the persistence of the demand and the criminal law's reduction of legitimate sources of supply, while "pusher"-addicts distribute narcotics as a means of fulfilling their own needs. Risk of conviction, even of long terms of imprisonment, appears to have little effect. Partly, this is because the immediate and compelling need of the "pusher"-addict for narcotics precludes any real attention to the distant prospect of conviction and imprisonment. For large-scale suppliers, who may not be addicts, the very process of criminalization and punishment serves to raise the stakes—while the risk becomes greater, so do the prospects of reward.[29] In addition, experience has demonstrated that convictions are difficult to obtain against large, nonaddict, organized dealers.

Our indiscriminate policy of using the criminal law against selling what people insist on buying has spawned large-scale, organized systems, often of national scope, comprising an integration of the stages of production and distribution of the illicit product on a continuous and thoroughly business-like basis. Not only are these organizations especially difficult for law enforcement to deal with; they have the unpleasant quality of producing other crimes as well because, after the fashion of legitimate business, they tend to extend and diversify their operations. After repeal of Prohibition, racketeering organizations moved into the illegal drug market. Organizations which purvey drugs and supply gambling find it profitable to move into loan-sharking and labor racketeering. To enhance their effectiveness, these organized systems engage in satellite forms of crime, of which bribery and corruption of local government are the most far-reaching in their consequences.[30] Hence the irony that, in some measure, crime is encouraged and successful modes of criminality are produced by the criminal law itself.

Another significant cost of our policy is that the intractable difficulties of enforcement, produced by the consensual character of the illegal conduct and the typically organized methods of operation, have driven enforcement agencies to excesses in pursuit of evidence. These are not only undesirable in themselves, but have evoked a counterreaction in the courts in the form of restrictions upon the use of evidence designed to discourage these police practices. One need look no farther than the decisions of the United States Supreme Court. The two leading decisions on entrapment were produced by overreaching undercover agents in gambling[31] and narcotics prosecutions,[32] respectively. Decisions involving the admissibility of evidence arising out of illegal arrests have, for the most part, been rendered in gambling, alcohol, and narcotics prosecutions.[33] Legal restraints upon unlawful search and seizure have largely grown out of litigation over the last five decades concerning a variety of forms of physical intrusion by police in the course of obtaining evidence of violations of these same laws.[34] The same is true with respect to the developing law of wire-tapping, bugging, and other forms of electronic interception.[35] Indeed, no single phenomenon is more responsible for the whole pattern of judicial restraints upon methods of law enforcement than the unfortunate experience with enforcing these laws against vice.

There is, finally, a cost of inestimable importance, one which tends to be a product of virtually all the misuses of the criminal law discussed in this paper. That is the substantial diversion of police, prosecutorial, and judicial time, personnel, and resources. At a time when the volume of crime is steadily increasing, the burden on law-enforcement agencies is becoming more and more onerous, and massive efforts are being considered to deal more effectively with threats to the public of dangerous and threatening conduct, releasing enforcement resources from the obligation to enforce the vice laws must be taken seriously. Indeed, in view of the minimal effectiveness of enforcement measures in dealing with vice crimes and the tangible costs and disadvantages of that effort, the case for this rediversion of resources to more profitable purposes becomes commanding. It seems fair to say that in few areas of the criminal law have we paid so much for so little.

One might, even so, quite reasonably take the position that gambling and narcotics are formidable social evils and that it would be dogmatic to insist that the criminal law should in no circumstances be used as one way, among others, of dealing with them. The exploitation of the weakness of vulnerable people, in the case of gambling, often results in economic loss and personal dislocations of substantial proportions. And the major physical and emotional hardships imposed by narcotics addiction raise even more serious evils. Still, such a view would scarcely excuse perpetuating the pattern of indiscriminate criminalization. There are obvious ways at least to mitigate the problems described; for example, by narrowing the scope of criminality. In the case of gambling, there is an overwhelming case for abandoning the traditional approach of sweeping all forms of gambling within the scope of the prohibition, while relying on the discretion of police and prosecutor to exempt private gambling and charitable and religious fund-raising enterprises.[36] At least, the evil of delegating discretion in such magnitude as to abandon law can be remedied by a more careful legislative definition of precisely the form of gambling conduct which the legislature means to bring within the criminal sanction. In the case of narcotics, our legislatures have tended indiscriminately to treat all narcotics as creative of the same dangers despite the strong evidence that some drugs, particularly marijuana, present evils of such limited character that elimination of the criminal prohibition is plainly indicated.[37] In short, there is much of value that could be done even if the whole dose of repeal were too much to swallow.

PROVISION OF SOCIAL SERVICES

In a number of instances, which, taken together, consume a significant portion of law enforcement resources, the criminal law is used neither to protect against serious misbehavior through the medium of crime and punishment nor to confirm standards of private morality, but rather to provide social services to needy segments of the community. The drunk, the deserted mother, and the creditor have been the chief beneficiaries. In each instance, the gains have been dubious in view of the toll exacted on effective law enforcement.

THE DRUNK

Using the criminal law to protect against offensive public behavior, whether by drunken or by sober persons, is not the issue here. The trouble arises out of the use of laws against public drunkenness to deal with the inert, stuporous drunk in the public streets and alleyways, who constitutes a danger to himself and an ugly inconvenience to others. Staggering numbers of these drunks are fed daily into the criminal machinery. Indeed, more arrests are made for this offense than for any other—35 to 40 percent of all reported arrests. Not only does the use of the criminal law, therefore, divert substantial law enforcement resources away from genuinely threatening conduct, but the whole criminal justice system is denigrated by the need to process massive numbers of pathetic and impoverished people through clumsy and inappropriate procedures. Hearings and trials degenerate into a mockery of the forms of due process, with mass appearances, guilt assumed, and defendants unrepresented. Even if the social and personal problems of drunkenness were, in some measure, helped by this effort, these costs would make the investment doubtful. In fact, apart from a very temporary cleaning of the streets by the police, the effort is notoriously unsuccessful. Poverty, rootlessness, and personal inadequacy, which are at the bottom of alcoholism, are scarcely deterrable by the threat of criminal conviction. And rehabilitation in the human warehouses of our city jails is unthinkable.

THE CREDITOR AND THE DESERTED MOTHER

The bad-check laws and the family-nonsupport laws are two other instances in which the criminal law is used in practice to provide social services; in these cases, to assist a merchant in obtaining payment and to assist needy families in obtaining support from a deserting spouse. The issue for legislative choice is straightforward: Is it ultimately worthwhile to employ the resources of police, prosecutors, and the criminal process generally in order to supplement civil remedies, even though such use entails a diversion of law enforcement energies from more threatening criminal conduct?

Checks, of course, can be instruments of serious fraud for which it is proper to employ the sanctions of the criminal law. However, the typical bad-check laws provide for serious punishment as well for the person who draws a check on his account knowing that at the time it has insufficient funds to cover the check. Usually, the intent to defraud is presumed in these cases. Merchants, of course, are aware of the risk of accepting payment in checks, but expectedly prefer not to discourage sales. The effect of the insufficient-fund bad-check laws, therefore, is to enable them to make use of the resources of the criminal law to reduce what, in a sense, are voluntarily assumed business risks. When complaints are filed, the police, or sometimes the prosecutor, investigate to determine if there was a genuine intent to defraud or if the accused is a habitual bad-check writer. If not, the usual practice is to discourage prosecution and instead to assume the role of free collection agencies for the merchants.[38]

The cost to law enforcement is, again, the diversion of resources from genuine threatening criminality. It is not clear that it is anything but habit that keeps states from narrowing their bad-check laws to exclude the occasional bad-check writer where there is no proof of intent to defraud. This would make it more difficult for merchants to obtain payment, but it is hard to see why it would not be preferable to conserve precious law enforcement resources at the far lesser cost of requiring the merchant to choose between being more conservative in accepting checks and assuming the risk as a business loss.

Nonsupport complaints by wives against deserting husbands are handled similarly. The objective of law enforcement personnel—the probation officer, a deputy in the prosecutor's office, a welfare agency—is not to invoke the criminal process to punish or rehabilitate a wrongdoer but to obtain needed support for the family.[39] Instead, jailing the father is the least likely means of obtaining it. As in the bad-check cases, the chief effect on law enforcement officers is that this duty amounts to still another diversion from their main business. Unlike the bad-check cases, however, here the criminal process is being used to provide a service which, indisputably, the state has an obligation to provide. It is apparent from the economic status of those usually involved that the service amounts to the equivalent of legal aid for needy families. Still, although the service is a useful one, it makes little sense to provide it through the already overburdened criminal processes. Although the obligation is performed by police and prosecutors with some success, it is done reluctantly and usually less effectively than by a civil agency especially designed to handle the service. In addition, it is performed at a sacrifice to those primary functions of protecting the public against dangerous and threatening conduct which only the criminal law can perform.

AVOIDING RESTRAINTS ON LAW ENFORCEMENT

Another costly misuse of the substantive criminal law is exemplified in the disorderly conduct and vagrancy laws. These laws are not crimes which define serious misconduct that the law seeks to prevent through conviction and punishment. Instead, they function as delegations of discretion to the police to act in ways which formally we decline to extend to them because it would be inconsistent with certain fundamental principles with respect to the administration of criminal justice. The disorderly conduct laws constitute, in effect, a grant of authority to the police to intervene in a great range of minor conduct, difficult or impossible legally to specify in advance, in which the police find it desirable to act. The vagrancy laws similarly delegate an authority to hold a suspect, whom police could not hold under the law of arrest, for purposes of investigation and interrogation.

Disorderly conduct statutes vary widely. They usually proscribe such conduct as riot, breach of the peace, unlawful assembly, disturbing the peace, and similar conduct in terms so general and imprecise as to offer the police a broad freedom to decide what conduct to treat as criminal. A New York Court of Appeals judge observed of that state's disorderly conduct statute: "It is obviously one of those dragnet laws designed to cover newly invented crimes, or existing crimes that cannot be readily classified or defined."[40] In examining disorderly conduct convictions, the Model Penal Code found that the statutes have been used to proscribe obscenity in a sermon, swearing in a public park, illicit sexual activity, picketing the home of a nonstriking employee, picketing the United Nations, obstructing law enforcement, shouting by a preacher whose "Amen" and "Glory Hallelujah" could be heard six blocks away, and talking back and otherwise using loud and offensive language to a policeman.[41] But the reported decisions give only a remote hint of the use of these laws since convictions are appealed only in a minute percentage of the cases.[42] In fact, arrests for disorderly conduct exceed those of arrests for any other crime except drunkenness—in 1965, a half-million arrests out of a total of five million were made for disorderly conduct.[43]

Vagrancy-type laws define criminality in terms of a person's status or a set of circumstances. Often, no disorderly conduct need be committed at all. The usual components of the offense include living in idleness without employment and having no visible means of support; roaming, wandering, or loitering; begging; being a common prostitute, drunkard, or gambler; and sleeping outdoors or in a residential building without permission. Beginning in feudal days, when these laws had their beginning, they have been pressed into a great variety of services. Today, they are widely and regularly used by police as a basis for arresting, searching, questioning, or detaining persons (who otherwise could not legally be subjected to such interventions) because of suspicion that they have committed or may commit a crime or for other police purposes, including cleaning the streets of undesirables, harassing persons believed to be engaged in crime, and investigating uncleared offenses. The story has been told in a number of descriptive studies in recent years.[44]

Both the disorderly-conduct and vagrancy laws, therefore, constitute a powerful weapon in the hands of police in the day-to-day policing
of urban communities. Since "penalties involved are generally minor,
and defendants are usually from the lowest economic and social levels,"[45]
they have proved largely immune from the restraints of appellate sur-
veillance and public criticism. A weighing of the long-term costs of use
of these laws against their immediate benefit to law enforcement suggests
the wisdom of either scrapping them or at least substantially narrowing
their scope.

The chief vice of these laws is that they constitute wholesale abandonment of the basic principle of legality upon which law enforcement
in a democratic community must rest—close control over the exercise
of the delegated authority to employ official force through the medium
of carefully defined laws and judicial and administrative accountability.
If I may, in the circumstances, take the liberty of quoting the language
of Chapter VIII:

> The practical costs of this departure from principle are significant. One
> of its consequences is to communicate to the people who tend to be the
> object of these laws the idea that law enforcement is not a regularized,
> authoritative procedure, but largely a matter of arbitrary behavior by
> the authorities. The application of these laws often tends to discriminate
> against the poor and subcultural groups in the population. It is unjust
> to structure law enforcement in such a way that poverty itself becomes
> a crime. And it is costly for society when the law arouses the feelings
> associated with these laws in the ghetto—a sense of persecution and
> helplessness before official power and hostility to police and other au-
> thority that may tend to generate the very conditions of criminality
> society is seeking to extirpate.[46]

I would only add that police conduct undertaken under color of these
laws produces the typical resentment associated with what is perceived
as double-dealing. There is, after all, what can reasonably be taken for
hypocrisy in formally adhering to the constitutional, statutory, and judicial restrictions upon the power of the police to arrest, search, and
otherwise intervene in the affairs of citizens on the streets, while actually
authorizing disregard of those limitations, principally against the poor
and disadvantaged, through the subterfuge of disorderly conduct and
vagrancy laws.

The proper legislative task is to identify precisely the powers which
we want the police to have and to provide by law that they shall have
these powers in the circumstances defined. Amending the law of attempt
to make criminality commence earlier in the stages of preparation than
now generally is the case would help to some degree. More substantial
moves in this direction are exemplified in the attempts to authorize
stopping and questioning short of arrest such as those of the New York

"Stop and Frisk" law and the proposals of the American Law Institute's Model Pre-Arraignment Code. Unfortunately, however, the future is not bright. Increasingly, in recent years, the Supreme Court has been imposing constitutional restraints upon powers which the police and most legislatures strongly believe the police should have. If anything, therefore, the temptation to invent subterfuge devices has increased. This is another of the unfortunate consequences of the tension between the police and the courts. But until law enforcement comes to yield less grudgingly to the law's restraints in the process of imposing its restraints upon others, the problem will long be with us.

CONCLUDING REMARKS

The plain sense that the criminal law is a highly specialized tool of social control, useful for certain purposes but not for others; that when improperly used it is capable of producing more evil than good; that the decision to criminalize any particular behavior must follow only after an assessment and balancing of gains and losses—this obvious injunction of rationality has been noted widely for over 250 years, from Jeremy Bentham[47] to the National Crime Commission,[48] and by the moralistic philosophers[49] as well as the utilitarian ones.[50] And those whose daily business is the administration of the criminal law have, on occasion, exhibited acute awareness of the folly of departing from it.[51] The need for restraint seems to be recognized by those who deal with the criminal laws, but not by those who make them or by the general public, which lives under them. One hopes that attempts to set out the facts and to particularize the perils of overcriminalization may ultimately affect the decisions of the legislatures. But past experience gives little cause for optimism.

Perhaps part of the explanation of the lack of success is the inherent limitation of any rational appeal against a course of conduct which is moved by powerful irrational drives. Explaining to legislatures why it does more harm than good to criminalize drunkenness or homosexuality, for example, has as little effect (and for the same reasons) as explaining to alcoholics or homosexuals that their behavior does them more harm than good. It may be that the best hope for the future lies in efforts to understand more subtly and comprehensively than we do now the dynamics of the legislative (and, it must be added, popular) drive to criminalize. The sociologists, the social psychologists, the political scientists, the survey research people, and, no doubt, others will have to be conscripted for any effort of this kind. A number of studies have already revealed illuminating insights into the process of conversion of popular indignation into legislative designation of deviancy,[52] the nature of the competitive struggles among rival moralities, and the use of the criminal law to solidify and manifest victory.[53] We also have a degree of understanding of the effect of representative political processes on the choice of sanctions and the dynamics of law enforcement by the police.[54] Perhaps by further substantial research along these lines—research that would put the process of overcriminalization by popularly elected legislators itself under the microscope—we will understand better the societal forces which have unfailingly produced it. Understanding, of course, is not control, and control may prove as hopeless with it as without it. But scientific progress over the past one hundred years has dramatized the control over the physical environment which comes from knowledge of its forces. It may prove possible to exert in like manner at least some measure of control over the social environment. It is an alternative worth pursuing.

POSTSCRIPT

Contrary to my pessimistic predictions in 1967 the law did change in the intervening decade and a half. Laws against fornication, adultery, and deviant sex practices within marriage have been repealed in perhaps half the states. Some states have now even legalized consensual sodomy, though most have not. See AMERICAN LAW INSTITUTE, MODEL PENAL CODE AND COMMENTARIES, Part II, pp. 364, 372, 439 (1980).

In addition, several decisions of the United States Supreme Court have had an important impact on the issue of criminalization:

(i) In *Roe v. Wade,* 410 U.S. 113 (1973), the Supreme Court invalidated laws prohibiting abortion as invasive of a right to privacy protected by the due process clause. Though the Court permitted some restraints on abortion in later stages of pregnancy, the effect of the decision was substantially to end enforcement of the laws against abortion. Subsequent developments in the climate of public opinion and expected changes in the composition of the Court raise some doubt as to the longevity of this decision.

(ii) It was thought in some quarters that the theory of *Roe v. Wade* would lead the Court likewise to invalidate sodomy laws as applied to consenting adults. The Supreme Court held otherwise in *Bowers v. Hardwick,* 106 Sup.Ct. 2841 (1986).

(iii) In its decision in *Papachristou v. City of Jacksonville,* 405 U.S. 156 (1972), the Court imposed severe constitutional restrictions on the enforcement of disorderly conduct and vagrancy laws, which served to make these laws less of a problem than they were before.

(iv) Finally, by a closely divided vote, the Court in *Powell v. Texas*, 392 U.S. 514 (1968), turned aside an effort to have the enforcement of public intoxication laws against alcoholics declared unconstitutional. Efforts in other courts to establish a constitutional bar to the enforcement of narcotic laws against addicts have also been largely unsuccessful. See, *e.g.*, *United States v. Moore*, 486 F.2d 1139 (D.C. Cir. 1973); *People v. Davis*, 33 N.Y.2d 221, 306 N.E.2d 787 (1973).

3
MORE ON
OVERCRIMINALIZATION

I am grateful to the editors of the Law Review for inviting me to comment on Mr. Junker's article.* It gives me a chance to clarify some of the points I have elsewhere tried to make which, judging from Mr. Junker's article, appear to need it.

Mr. Junker apparently agrees with the conclusion of those he criticizes, myself and several others, that the criminal law has made excessive use of the criminal sanction in the respects we describe. What he quarrels with is the arguments we make to support that conclusion. Fair enough. I am not inclined to regard it as treason in an ally to attack the good hearted for being weak minded, least of all among those who presume to scholarship. Indeed, as T. S. Eliot has Thomas Becket reflect, "The last temptation is the greatest treason; To do the right deed for the wrong reason." So if there's treason around it is we who are charged with it.

Then what is Mr. Junker's argument? Let me deal first with what he offers as his "general conclusion." It is that "the proferred arguments are parasites in search of a host"; that we have failed to develop principles to support the proposition that private behavior should not be prohibited by the criminal law; that such principles are essential to the argument, for without them it can always be retorted that despite the great practical costs of enforcing such laws, which we argue at length, the price should be paid anyway.

Now I am not one to make little of the search for the high ground of principle. The moral and philosophical questions on what is and what is not the law's business—debated elegantly by Mill and Stephan in the last century and as well by Hart and Devlin more recently—are of great significance on many counts. But is it really necessary to get the answers to those questions to make *a case* for decriminalizing abortion, homosexuality, prostitution, marijuana use, and the rest? Surely not. Speaking for myself at least (I have no charter to speak for my brethren under attack), the argument that Mr. Junker attacks was quite straightforward in structure. It was as follows: You apparently want to keep certain

* Junker, *Criminalization and Crimogenisis*, 19 U.C.L.A. LAW REV. 694 (1972).

conduct criminal just because it's immoral (homosexuality, abortion, prostitution), or because it enables police and prosecutors to provide some service or other (check laws, family support laws), or because it gives police authority over suspected criminals they otherwise would not have (vagrancy, disorderly conduct). But have you considered how the inevitable process of actual enforcement of such laws (a) so poorly serves the objectives you have in mind, and (b) in any event produces a variety of substantial costs, including adverse consequences for the effective enforcement of the criminal law generally? These practical considerations are so great that they should persuade you to decriminalize the law in these areas.[1]

It eludes me why this line of argument is fatally flawed by failing to demonstrate a general principle in terms of which conduct should not be made criminal. Of course, the argument rests on a major premise. But that premise is not at all a covert conclusion as to the limits of the legitimate use of the criminal sanction. It is simply that if something costs too much for what you get, you'd be foolish to buy it. Concededly, I don't generalize a principle for determining how much of which costs are too much for which benefits. Frankly, I wouldn't know how to go about it. The argument asserts the conclusion that the specified costs are too much for the specified gains and invites agreement in the hope that presenting a bill of particulars of the nature and magnitude of the costs may help to achieve it.

Consider an example. At the end of my discussion of sex offenses, I observed: "Only the judgment that the use of the criminal law for verbal vindication of our morals is more important than its use to protect life and property can support the preservation of these laws as they are."[2] Mr. Junker criticizes this statement because it fails to demonstrate a set of principles in terms of which it is improper to use the criminal law for verbal vindication of our morals, arguing that in the absence of such principles I haven't made a case for repeal. Of course not—not, that is, if one wants to insist that verbal vindication *is* more important than more effective enforcement of laws protecting life and property. That's exactly what the statement asserts. The argument was plainly not that one is not *entitled* to use the criminal law for verbal and symbolic purposes, only that it was *foolish* to do so if you give protection of life and property a higher priority.

This same misconstrual of the argument leads Mr. Junker to another of his critical themes—*i.e.*, if we meant what we said we'd be advocating repeal of a lot more of the criminal law than we do. Illegal police practices occur as often in connection with weapons offenses as with narcotics offenses. How, then, can Morris and Hawkins urge repeal of the latter and extension of the former? If absence of complainants produces underenforcement which invites discriminatory enforcement, then why not repeal bribery and weapons offenses as well as sex and drug offenses? If the costs we describe inhere in enforcing drug laws against adults, they inhere in juvenile enforcement as well—but we don't urge repeal of the latter. Hence we don't mean what we say. And our real reasons for urging repeal of those laws we don't discuss or defend.

This is a further manifestation of Mr. Junker's winning but misplaced figure of the parasite in search of a host. Again he has the argument wrong. The argument is not that any of these adverse consequences affords a sufficient reason for abandoning every criminal law whose use produces it. It is simply that in any use of the criminal law a particular adverse consequence may be so severe and so combined with other kinds of adverse consequences (e.g., not only discriminatory enforcement, but police corruption, police illegality, loss of respect for law) that, considering the relative importance of the purposes of that law and the extent to which they are achieved, a prudential judgment would be to abandon it.

Now this kind of case can be made more strongly for certain kinds of laws than for others. "Morals offenses" tend to come off particularly badly with this sort of cost accounting. But that doesn't mean that any law whose criminal enforcement produces any of these adverse consequences, to be consistent, must also fall. Take gun control, for example. Its enforcement may well exact some costs of the kind we called attention to in urging repeal of private morals offenses: a significant minority of law abiding citizens are firmly attached to their right to buy and possess guns free of control; the mere illegal possession of guns produces no complaining victim; enforcement requires searches of the person which can lead to abuse; discriminatory enforcement is likely against groups the police fear or dislike. These plausible apprehensions are enough to justify some second thoughts about gun control laws. But they don't themselves make the case against these laws. What has to be weighed is the objective of gun control laws (the saving of human lives) and the chances that gun control laws would operate to achieve that goal. So long as a strong case can be made in light of these kinds of considerations (and I believe it can and has been made[3]), Mr. Junker's decriminalizers should be able to favor such laws without being accused of playing an intellectual shell game.

There is a big problem in this cost-benefit approach to deciding what to make criminal. The problem is that it is easier to state what the costs and benefits may be than to measure their quantity with any degree of accuracy or to assess them with reliability and objectivity. My colleague, Phillip Johnson, called attention to this when he observed: "In the end the comparison of costs and benefits is just a useful way of thinking about the problem. When it begins to seem to lead to definite answers, one begins to suspect that the proponent's personal moral philosophy is quantifying the uncertainties."[4] I agree with that. It's Mr. Junker's best point. I think he threw it away going after bigger fish that weren't there.

4

THE USE OF CRIMINAL SANCTIONS IN ENFORCING ECONOMIC REGULATIONS

Those who have had occasion to look for answers to the problems of the use of sanctions, taken to include the whole range of official modes of securing compliance with norms of conduct, have commonly agreed for some time now that there are few to be found.[1] In view of the antiquity of the legal experience, which for the most part has always entailed the use of sanctions of one kind or another, this is a remarkable verdict. Indeed, works written at the turn of the eighteenth century by Jeremy Bentham[2] are still the basic works in the area, a sobering observation which could scarcely be made of more than a handful of subjects of inquiry. In this state of affairs it is not very surprising that we are largely ignorant of the impact of the penal sanction, which is only one aspect of the larger problem of sanctions; and it is still less surprising that we know little about the use of the penal sanction in an area of relatively recent development, economic regulatory legislation. These are only sectors of a much larger unexplored terrain.

Moreover, unnecessary confusion has become an ally of ignorance in impeding understanding of these areas. Because strong ideological differences separate the proponents and opponents of economic regulation, judgments about the effect of penal sanctions in achieving compliance tend to turn upon judgments about the merits of the substantive regulation. Liberally oriented social scientists, otherwise critical of the case made for the deterrent and vindicatory uses of punishment of ordinary offenders, may be found supporting stern penal enforcement against economic violators.[3] At the same time conservative groups, rarely foes of rigorous punishment for ordinary offenders, appear less sanguine for the criminal prosecution when punishment of business offenders is debated.[4]

This statement of the undeveloped state of the art is by no means designed as an introduction to an ambitious effort to close the ancient gap in understanding. Quite the contrary, it is meant rather to excuse the modest ambit of these observations. What I would like to accomplish is to outline the special characteristics of economic regulatory legislation relevant to the use of the criminal sanction; to indicate what implications they have for effective use of the criminal law; and to suggest relevant concerns in the use of this sanction beyond the goal of enforcing the specific regulatory norm.

I

The kind of economic regulations whose enforcement through the criminal sanction is the subject of this inquiry may be briefly stated: those which impose restrictions upon the conduct of business as part of a considered economic policy. This includes such laws as price control and rationing laws, antitrust laws and other legislation designed to protect or promote competition or prevent unfair competition, export controls, small loan laws, securities regulations, and, perhaps, some tax laws. Put to one side, therefore, are regulations directly affecting business conduct which are founded on interests other than economic ones; for example, laws regulating the conduct of business in the interest of public safety and general physical welfare. Also to one side are laws indirectly affecting business conduct by their general applicability; for example, embezzlement, varieties of fraud and related white-collar offenses.

The class of regulations so defined possesses several characteristics that have a direct bearing upon the uses and limits of the criminal sanction as a means of achieving compliance. The first is the very feature suggested as the identifying characteristic of such legislation; that is, the nature of the interest protected. Certainly the use of criminal sanctions to protect interests of an economic character is not a contemporary departure. The extension of the classic larceny offense by courts and legislatures to embrace fraud, embezzlement and similar varieties of misappropriation that threatened newly developing ways of transacting business is a well documented chapter in the history of the criminal law.[5] Indeed the process continues today.[6] But there is an important difference between the traditional and expanded property offenses and the newer economic regulatory offenses—a difference reflecting the shift from an economic order that rested on maximum freedom for the private entrepreneur to one committed to restraints upon that freedom. The traditional property offenses protect private property interests against the acquisitive behavior of others in the furtherance of free private decision.[7] The newer offenses, on the other hand, seek to protect the economic order of the community against harmful use by the individual of his property interest. The central purpose, therefore, is to control private choice, rather than to free it. But the control imposed (and this too has significance) is not total, as it would be in a socialistic system. Private economic self-determination has not been abandoned in favor of a wholly state regulated economy. Indeed, the ideal of free enterprise is maintained, the imposed regulations being regarded as necessary to prevent that ideal from consuming itself.[8] Whether the criminal sanction may safely and effectively be used in the service of implementing the large-scale economic policies underlying regulatory legislation of this kind raises fundamental questions.

A second relevant feature of these laws concerns the nature of the conduct restrained. Since it is not criminal under traditional categories of crime and, apart from the regulatory proscription, closely resembles acceptable aggressive business behavior, the stigma of moral reprehensibility does not naturally associate itself with the regulated conduct.[9] Moreover, the conduct is engaged in by persons of relatively high social and economic status; since it is motivated by economic considerations, it is calculated and deliberate rather than reactive; it is usually part of a pattern of business conduct rather than episodic in character; and it often involves group action through the corporate form.

The third noteworthy attribute of this legislation is the role provided for the criminal sanction in the total scheme of enforcement. Typically the criminal penalty is only one of a variety of authorized sanctions which may include monetary settlements, private actions (compensatory or penal), injuctions, inspections, licensing, required reporting or others. Its role, therefore, is largely ancillary and takes either or both of two forms. On the one hand, the criminal penalty may serve as a means to insure the functioning of other sanctions, as, for example, penalties for operating without a license, or without prior registration or reporting. On the other hand, the criminal sanction may serve as a separate and supplementary mode of enforcement by directly prohibiting the conduct sought to be prevented, as in the Sherman Act. Furthermore, implicit in the legislative scheme is the conception of the criminal sanction as a last resort to be used selectively and discriminatingly when other sanctions fail. The array of alternative non-penal sanctions appears unmistakably to carry this message. That this is assumed by enforcement authorities is apparent from the relative infrequency of the use of the criminal as compared to other sanctions,[10] and in the occasional appearance of published criteria of enforcement policy.[11] And in some legislation, of course, the message of selective enforcement is explicit in the law.[12] Finally, the responsibility for investigation, detection and initiating prosecution is often vested in a specialized agency or other body rather than left with the usual institutions for policing and prosecuting criminal violations. Moreover, these bodies, such as the Office of Price Administration during the war, or the Securities and Exchange Commission, commonly are not specialized organs of criminal enforcement, but are the agencies broadly charged with administering the legislative scheme.

This statement of the relevant features of the laws under inquiry, in terms of the interest protected, the behavior regulated and the contemplated role of the criminal penalty, is not meant to suggest that these laws are ultimately unique in the problems they raise for criminal enforcement. Apart from the nature of the interest protected, most, if not all, of these characteristics may be found in other areas of the criminal law: upper-class criminality in white-collar crime generally; selectivity in enforcement in the whole range of the criminal law, to a greater or lesser degree; deliberate, patterned conduct for gain engaged in by organizations in many other classes of offenses. And even though the nature of the interest protected is by definition unique, many of the problems it poses, such as making criminal morally neutral behavior, are common to other areas as well. All that is suggested is that if one asks, "What problems are raised for the effective use of the criminal sanction as a mode of achieving compliance in this area?" the beginnings of an answer are to be found in this congeries of characteristics. It remains now to suggest what bearing they have.

II

I propose to deal with the relevance of these characteristics in terms of three major problems: the problem of defining the proscribed conduct, the problem of corporate criminality, and the problem of moral neutrality.

A. THE PROBLEM OF DEFINING THE PROSCRIBED CONDUCT

The fact that the protected interest is the preferred functioning of the economic system, and entails only partial restriction upon the operation of American business, bears directly upon the task of defining the proscribed behavior with sufficient specificity to meet the requirement of fair notice generally applicable to criminal legislation. Where the criminal sanction is used to police other enforcement devices, as for example, when it becomes criminal to market a security issue without registration or to do business without a license, the standard is met without difficulty. But the requirement of specificity is notably difficult of fulfillment where the crime itself purports to define the substantive economic behavior sought to be avoided. A notable example is the Sherman Act's prohibition of "restraint of trade or commerce" and "illegal monopolization."[13] Only to a small degree, if at all, is the difficulty remediable by better draftsmanship. As Thurman Arnold observed, "antitrust policy touches fields and boundaries which recede as you approach them and disappear each time you try to stake them out."[14] The reason for this arises from several sources. First, the economic policy is itself unclear, constituting largely a vague aspiration for a proper balance among competing economic goals.[15] Second, illegality must turn on judgments that are essentially evaluative in character, rather than upon purely factual determinations. Third, the inevitable development of novel circumstances and arrangements in the dynamic areas under regulation would soon make precise formulations obsolete, even to the limited extent they proved feasible.[16]

A key question is whether what would be an intolerable vagueness in conventional crime is less objectionable here in view of the preventive character of these laws. But deferring this question for the moment, are there alternatives for meeting the difficulty short of eschewing criminal sanctions where the conduct cannot be defined with acceptable specificity?

The requirement in an otherwise unconstitutionally vague definition of criminal conduct that the defendant must be shown to have acted willfully or knowingly has sometimes been held to remedy the defect of definition. Thus the Supreme Court found no unfairness in convicting a motor company for failing to reroute their explosive-laden truck "as far as practical, and where feasible" to avoid congested areas, where it was necessary to prove that this was done "knowingly";[17] or in convicting a taxpayer for attempting to evade taxes by making "unreasonable" deductions for commissions paid to stockholders as compensation for service, where the action was taken "willfully."[18] A requirement that the defendant have intentionally committed the act with a full and correct understanding of the factual circumstances is of no help to a defendant faced with an unclear definition of the conduct forbidden. On the other hand, however vague the line between what is permissible and what is criminal, where the actor is aware that his conduct falls squarely within the forbidden zone he is in no position to complain.[19] "A mind intent upon willful evasion is inconsistent with surprised innocence."[20] Apparently, therefore, it is scienter in this sense, that is, knowledge by the actor that he is violating the law, which is held in these cases to eliminate the vagueness problem. Yet this premise probably affords defenses to a larger group than intended, since a defendant who knew nothing of the existence of the law would be in as good a position as one who did not know that his action came within its terms.[21] If the prosecution must prove that the defendant knew his conduct fell within the terms of the law, it could hardly do so without proof as well that he knew of its existence. A legislature, however, could presumably resolve the semantic impasse by making it a defense that the defendant did not know his acts fell within its terms, or perhaps, more narrowly, that he could not reasonably know it, though not a defense simply that he did not know of the law's existence.[22]

Another approach to mitigating the difficulties of a vague formulation is through administrative choice of cases to prosecute. If the enforcement agency initiates criminal prosecution solely where the meaning of the statute has become acceptably clear through judicial interpretation, the unfairness of the original unclarity may be thought adequately reduced. An example is the announced policy of the Department of Justice to institute criminal prosecutions for Sherman Act violations only where there is a per se violation, such as price fixing, a violation accompanied by a specific intent to restrain competition or monopolize, the use of predatory practices, or where the defendant has before been convicted of a Sherman Act violation.[23] This approach, unlike the legislative requirement of scienter, is of no avail where the vagueness of the statutory formulation renders the law constitutionally unenforceable. It is also dependent upon the existence of means other than criminal prosecutions to develop clarifying interpretation. In the Sherman Act this is provided through the civil suit as a parallel means of enforcing the identical standard of conduct. This, in turn, however, may be a mixed blessing. One of the purposes of looseness and generality in the formulation of the standard is to create a flexibility that will allow judicial interpretation to keep pace with the changes in the character of the area under regulation. Courts may prove understandably reluctant to sustain expansive, although desirable, interpretations where the consequence will be to subject defendants to criminal as well as civil sanctions.

There are several alternatives to civil litigation as a means of producing clarifying interpretation. The most obvious is to delegate to the responsible administrative agency the authority to issue so-called legislative regulations in implementation of the statutory scheme.[24] Providing criminal penalties for violations of these regulations[25] then eliminates the vagueness problem to the extent of the clarity of the regulation.[26] There is still, to be sure, a requirement of some specificity in the legislative standard from which the agency derives its authority. But this raises the different, though related, issue of delegation of powers, where requirements of specificity are considerably less than those applicable to criminal statutes.[27] The declaratory order, in which the agency renders an advisory judgment on the legality of a contemplated course of action, is another possibility. This has utility both in providing further clarification of the applicability of regulations and in rendering interpretive guidance of the law when it, rather than a regulation, is the direct source of the prohibition. Section 5 of the Administrative Procedure Act[28] provides a precedent for such an order, although the use authorized therein is considerably more limited than it might be.[29]

Still another alternative is flatly to prohibit certain kinds of activity, except where an administrative agency, interpreting and applying general legislative standards, expressly allows it, as by issuing a license. The criminal penalty may then be imposed for the clearly defined offense of engaging in the activity without authorization.[30] This, of course, is to use the criminal sanction, as previously suggested, as a means of enforcing another, non-criminal sanction. It is readily usable in such narrow areas as marketing securities, or engaging in other particular types of business. It is impractical where the thrust of the prohibition goes to ways of conducting any and all kinds of business, as in the Sherman Act.

B. THE PROBLEM OF CORPORATE CRIMINALITY

Conduct reached by economic regulatory legislation is typically group conduct often engaged in through the corporate form. This raises the formidable issue of corporate criminality. From the legislative viewpoint, the principal questions are twofold. First, what difficulties beset enforcement agencies in affixing criminal liability upon responsible actors where the principal violator is the corporation? Second, in any event, what are the possibilities of effective enforcement through the imposition of criminal penalties upon the corporation itself?

Fixing criminal liability upon the immediate actors within a corporate structure generally poses no special problem.[31] But the immediate actors may be lower echelon officials or employees who are the tools rather than the responsible originators of the violative conduct. Where the corporation is managed by its owners, the task of identifying the policy formulators is not acute. But where the stock of the corporation is widely held, the organization complex and sprawling, and the responsibility spread over a maze of departments and divisions, then, as has recently been shown,[32] there may be conspicuous difficulties in pinpointing responsibility on the higher echelon policymaking officials. The source of the difficulty is the conventional requirement that to hold one person criminally liable for the acts of another he must have participated in the acts of the other in some meaningful way, as by directing or encouraging them, aiding in their commission,[33] or permitting them to be done by subordinates whom he has power to control.[34] The difficulty is exemplified in the now famous antitrust prosecution of the electrical equipment manufacturers. Here the high policy makers of General Electric and other companies involved escaped personal accountability for a criminal conspiracy of lesser officials that extended over several years to the profit of the corporations, despite the belief of the trial judge and most observers that these higher officials either knew of and condoned these activities or were willfully ignorant of them.[35]

It cannot be known to what extent this legal obstacle to convicting the policy initiators actually reduces the efficacy of the criminal sanction in achieving compliance. Certainly, it would prove more significant in those areas, like antitrust, where giant corporations are the principal targets of the law, than in areas where they are not. But other factors may be more influential in preventing widescale successful prosecution of individual corporate officials; under the antitrust laws, for example, there have been strikingly few convictions of corporate officials, even of officials of closely held corporations and the lesser officials of large, public corporations.[36]

At all events, one means of reducing the difficulty would be to alter by statute the basis of accountability of corporate directors, officers or agents. An amendment, for example, of the antitrust law was recently proposed which would have changed the present basis of accountability (that such persons "shall have authorized, ordered or done" the acts)[37] to make it suffice that the individual had knowledge or reason to know of the corporate violation and failed to exercise his authority to stop or prevent it.[38] This falls short of outright vicarious liability since accountability is made to turn on fault in not knowing and acting rather than on a relationship simpliciter. Essentially it makes a negligent omission the basis of accountability. Still a standard of accountability resting on precisely how much of the far-flung operations of a nation-wide corporation an official should reasonably be aware of approaches vicarious liability in its indeterminateness, since neither the common experience of the jury nor even specialized experience affords substantial guidance. In effect, it introduces an element of uncertainty concerning accountability into laws that often, like the Sherman Act, are already marked by uncertainty concerning the conduct forbidden.[39]

I defer to a later point the issue of whether such scruples are appropriate in business offenses.[40] To the extend they are, a possible alternative is the legislative formulation of rules and standards of accountability. Where state regulatory laws are involved this might be accomplished through amendment of the corporation laws to fix the lines of accountability in intra-corporate relationships compatibly with the needs of an effective system of regulation. The problem, however, arises principally with national regulatory laws sought to be applied to officials of large interstate corporations. Professor Watkins has long suggested a federal incorporation law to restore responsibility in such corporate structures by eliminating the diverse and confusing lines of accountability under state corporation laws.[41] If, as he suggests, the problem of fixing accountability is due neither to the complexity of business nor to willful attempts to baffle outsiders, but rather to "the absence of uniform standards and rules for delegation of authority in these huge corporations in which nobody appears to know who is responsible for what,"[42] there may be no just means for meeting the problem short of his proposal. On the other hand, the complexity of the task and the further inroad into an area of traditional local jurisdiction might not be regarded as worth the cost, since the legal standards of accountability may prove to be only one of several factors, and not necessarily the most crucial, as we will see, militating against enforcement through conviction of corporate officials.

Fixing criminal liability upon the corporation itself has posed fewer legal obstacles in the enforcement of regulatory legislation. The earlier conceptual difficulties of ascribing criminal intent to a fictitious entity have been largely removed by the developing law. And whatever doubt may exist is readily met by expressly providing for corporate liability in the regulatory statute.[43] But the problem of corporate accountability—that is, when the entity is liable for conduct of its agents at various levels of responsibility—is analogous to the problem of holding corporate officials accountable for the acts of lesser agents. It has been resolved more sweepingly in the case of the entity. For acts of its high managerial agents it is by definition accountable since a corporation cannot act by itself. For the acts of its lesser agents the tendency has been, at least in the regulatory offenses, to hold the corporation accountable for the acts of employees within the scope of their employment[44] or while acting as employees.[45] Whether the consequential imposition of vicarious responsibility upon the corporate entity, as well as upon shareholders, is justified raises the question of the deterrent efficacy of convicting and fining the corporate entity.

The case for corporate criminality rests presumably upon the inadequacy of the threat of personal conviction upon the individual actors. As said earlier, difficulties of proof under legal principles of accountability have interfered with effective prosecution of high corporate officials. And the commonly observed jury behavior of convicting the corporate defendant while acquitting the individual defendants, even where proof is apparently strong, further supports the case for the alternate sanction.[46] Moreover, "there are probably cases in which the economic pressures within the corporate body are sufficiently potent to tempt individuals to hazard personal liability for the sake of company gain, especially where the penalties threatened are moderate and where the offense does not involve behavior condemned as highly immoral by the individual's associates."[47] Yet the question remains of the effectiveness of corporate criminality as a supplementary deterrent.

The only two practically available modes of imposing criminal sanctions upon the corporate defendant are through the stigma of conviction and the exaction of a fine. The former, classified by Bentham as the "moral or popular" sanction, operates as he suggested through the adverse reactions to the conviction of persons in the community.[48] Whether there is any substantial moral opprobrium attached to violation of economic regulatory legislation (even where individuals are convicted) I defer until later. Assuming there is, can it be said to have any appreciable significance when directed to a corporate entity? There is no substantial empirical basis for answering this question.[49] It seems unlikely that whatever moral stigma may attach to a convicted corporation would be felt in any effectual way by the corporate individuals, especially in large corporations where responsibility is diffused.[50] On the other hand, the point has been made[51] (though denied as well)[52] that the corporate stigma may operate as a deterrent by impairing the reputation of the corporation in its business operations and hence adversely affecting its economic position. Until there is more to go on one can only guess at the validity of this observation, though there is reason to expect that the impact of the conviction would operate differentially, depending on the size of the corporation, the extent of competition and the dominance of its market position, the degree to which its conviction attracted public notice, and the like.

The exaction of a corporate fine serves in part to give color to the moral stigma of conviction. Insofar as this is its role, its value depends upon the existence and power of the stigma to deter. On the other hand, the use of the corporate fine apart from the stigma of conviction raises no issue peculiar to the criminal sanction, since civil fines afford identical deterrent possibilities. Whether it would prove effective to increase the economic hazard of misconduct by authorizing higher fines than those now commonly authorized[53] depends on such considerations as the general ability of the corporation to recoup its losses through its pricing policy[54] and the likelihood that courts would impose the higher fines.[55] An alternative recently proposed would substitute for the fine a governmental proceeding designed to compel the corporation to disgorge the profits attributable to its violation.[56] These alternatives raise substantial questions concerning sanctions, but not the criminal sanction, strictly speaking.

C. THE PROBLEM OF MORAL NEUTRALITY

Viewed in the large, the characteristic of the conduct typically proscribed by economic regulatory legislation most relevant for the purposes of criminal enforcement is that it is calculated and deliberative and directed to economic gain.[57] It would appear, therefore, to constitute a classic case for the operation of the deterrent strategy. Nonetheless, it is a widely shared view that the strategy has not worked out in fact, that the criminal sanction has not proved a major weapon for achieving compliance. Part of the explanation may be attributable to the difficulties of enforcement suggested above, such as the resistance to vaguely defined standards of criminality, the difficulty of fixing culpability upon high corporate officials, and the muffled and absorbable impact of corporate criminal sanctions. But it is likely that other factors play a more dominant role.

A common explanation of the failure of the criminal sanction is simply that the powerful business interests affected do not want these laws enforced and employ their power and position in American life to block vigorous enforcement. Influence is exercised over the legislatures to keep enforcement staffs impoverished and sanctions safely inefficacious. Enforcement officials, as prospective counsel for business interests, and judges as former counsel, identify with these interests and resist criminal enforcement. Moreover, news media, under the control of these same groups, work to create hostility to these laws and their vigorous enforcement and sympathy for the violators. In short, "those who are responsible for the system of criminal justice are afraid to antagonize businessmen. . . . The most powerful group in medieval society secured relative immunity from punishment by 'benefit of clergy,' and now our most powerful group secures relative immunity by 'benefit of business.'"[58]

It would be dogmatic to assert that influences of this kind do not exist, but it may be doubted that they play a dispositive role. Business surely constitutes a powerful interest group in American life; but the profusion of regulatory legislation over the ardent protests of important economic interests in the past thirty years is some evidence that is is not all-powerful. Opposing forces have been able to marshal considerable public sentiment against a variety of business practices. Moreover, it is perhaps an oversimplification to identify all business as united in monolithic opposition. There is less a single business interest than a substantial variety of business interests. What then, in addition to business propaganda and influence, has accounted for the failure of the criminal sanction? Or, if we must have a villain, how has it been that business, which has not always gotten its way, has been this successful in devitalizing the use of that sanction?

It is a plausible surmise that the explanation is implicated in another feature of the behavior regulated by these laws, namely, that it is not generally regarded as morally reprehensible in the common view, that, indeed, in some measure it is the laws themselves that appear bad, or at least painful necessities, and that the violators by and large turn out to be respectable people in the respectable pursuit of profit. It is not likely that these popular attitudes are wholly products of a public-relations campaign by the affected business community. The springs of the public sentiment reach into the national ethos, producing the values that the man of business himself holds, as well as the attitude of the public toward him and his activities. Typically the conduct prohibited by economic regulatory laws is not immediately distinguishable from modes of business behavior that are not only socially acceptable, but affirmatively desirable in an economy founded upon an ideology (not denied by the regulatory regime itself) of free enterprise and the profit motive. Distinctions there are, of course, between salutary entrepreneurial practices and those which threaten the values of the very regime of economic freedom. And it is possible to reason convincingly that the harms done to the economic order by violations of many of these regulatory laws are of a magnitude that dwarf in significance the lower-class property offenses.[59] But the point is that these perceptions require distinguishing and reasoning processes that are not the normal governors of the passion of moral disapproval, and are not dramatically obvious to a public long conditioned to responding approvingly to the production of profit through business shrewdness, especially in the absence of live and visible victims. Moreover, in some areas, notably the antitrust laws, it is far from clear that there is consensus even by the authors and enforcers of the regulation—the legislators, courts and administrators—on precisely what should be prohibited and what permitted, and the reasons therefor.[60] And as Professor Freund observed, "if a law declares a practice to be criminal, and cannot apply its policy with consistency, its moral effect is necessarily weakened."[61]

The consequences of the absence of sustained public moral resentment for the effective use of the criminal sanction may be briefly stated. The central distinguishing aspect of the criminal sanction appears to be the stigmatization of the morally culpable.[62] At least it tends so to be regarded in the community. Without moral culpability there is in a democratic community an explicable and justifiable reluctance to affix the stigma of blame.[63] This perhaps is the basic explanation, rather than the selfish machinations of business interests, for the reluctance of administrators and prosecutors to invoke the criminal sanction, the reluctance of jurors to find guilt and the reluctance of judges to impose strong penalties.[64] And beyond its effect on enforcement, the absence of moral opprobrium interferes in another more subtle way with achieving compliance. Fear of being caught and punished does not exhaust the deterrent mechanism of the criminal law. It is supplemented by the personal disinclination to act in violation of the law's commands, apart from immediate fear of being punished.[65] One would suppose that especially in the case of those who normally regard themselves as respectable, proper and law-abiding, the appeal to act in accordance with conscience is relatively great. But where the violation is not generally regarded as ethically reprehensible, either by the community at large or by the class of businessmen itself, the private appeal to conscience is at its minimum and being convicted and fined may have little more impact than a bad selling season.[66]

Are there modes of dealing with these consequences of making morally neutral behavior criminal? A commonly suggested remedy for inadequate enforcement is a compaign of strict enforcement aided by strengthened prosecution staffs, and perhaps more severe penalties.[67] But to the extent that the deficiency in enforcement is attributable to the moral inoffensiveness of the behavior, the major limitation of such a call to arms is that it is addressed to the symptom rather than the cause. How will legislatures be convinced to expend substantial sums for criminal enforcement, or prosecutors to go for the jugular, or courts or juries to cooperate in the face of a fundamental lack of sympathy for the criminal penalty in this area? Enlarged resources for prosecution may well afford staff enthusiasts an opportunity for more vigorous enforcement, but one may doubt that it can achieve more than a minor flurry of enforcement.[68]

An attack on the cause, insofar as moral neutrality is the cause, would presumably require a two-pronged program: one directed at the obstacle of popular nullification; the other at inculcating the sentiment of moral disapproval in the community.[69] Each, of course, would inevitably have an effect upon the other. The former might proceed, not simply by allocating greater enforcement resources, but by arrangements that would reduce the traditional discretionary authority of the various bodies involved in criminal law enforcement. For example, the decision to prosecute might be exclusively centered in the agency responsible for the whole regulatory program; conservative legal interpretation might be dealt with by authorizing agency interpretative regulations which are made relevant in criminal prosecutions[70]; the temporizing of juries might be avoided by eliminating, where possible, jury trials; the judge's sentencing discretion might be curtailed by mandatory minimum penalties.[71] There is, of course, the substantial task of persuading legislatures to abjure the traditional mediating institutions of the criminal law in an area where, the moral factor being largely absent, they might be thought to have their historic and most useful function to perform. But if enacted, one might reasonably suppose that such legal arrangements could result in a somewhat more frequent and rigorous use of the criminal sanction and a heightening of the deterrent effect of the law.

The other prong of the program, the cultivation of the sentiment of moral disapproval, is perhaps closer to the heart of the matter. To some extent the more frequent enforcement and the more stringent punishment of violators may tend to serve this objective as well as its more direct in terrorem purposes, especially where cases are selected for enforcement with this end in view.[72] Whether a governmentally mounted campaign should be employed as well to give widespread publicity to successful convictions and to shape the public conscience in other ways may be questioned from various viewpoints, but it surely would be consistent with the basic strategy of using criminal sanctions in these areas.

How effective a campaign of selected prosecutions and attendant publicity would prove in creating a changed moral climate is problematical. Certainly one cannot confidently deny that the spectacle of frequent conviction and severe punishment may play a role in molding the community's attitudes toward the conduct in question. Experience offers uncertain guidance. Tax evasion has a history that provides some support. We have come a considerable distance, though not all the way,[73] from the day when an English judge could observe from the bench, "there is not behind taxing laws, as there is behind laws against crime, an independent moral obligation."[74] The change was accompanied in this country by a gradual tightening of the criminal sanction. In 1924 tax evasion was upgraded from a misdemeanor to a felony and maximum imprisonment raised from one to five years[75]; reforms in 1952 converted the criminal prosecution from a tax recovery device and weapon against the professional racketeer to a means of general deterrence of tax evasion by widespread and selected enforcement against all levels of violators.[76] While the tax evasion prosecution is still something of a special case, the record of successful prosecution has become genuinely impressive and the tax evasion conviction a sanction of some consequence.[77] Experience such as this, however, gives little more than support for the plainly plausible assumption that criminal enforcement may play some part. One cannot be sure of the extent to which other factors, not necessarily present in areas other than tax, created the conditions for optimum use of the criminal sanction as a moralizing weapon, or indeed, of the extent to which other influences rather than, or in addition to, the criminal sanction, produced the changed climate. The caution is further indicated (though, of course, not demonstrated) by less successful experiences in attempting to deal through the criminal law with behavior that did not attract any substantial degree of reprobatory unanimity, such as prohibition or gambling. At all events, Mannheim's caveat is a useful one: "It is only in a Soviet state and through a legal system on the lines of the Soviet penal code, which deliberately uses the political weapon of criminal prosecution to shape the economic system according to its ideology, that old traditions of such strength can be comparatively quickly destroyed."[78]

III

I have reserved for last those issues and concerns that arise out of goals other than the effectiveness of the criminal sanction in achieving compliance. Those which most prominently compete for consideration are: first, the sentiment of fundamental fairness—justice, in a word; and second, the retention of the vitality of the criminal law in its traditional sphere of application. They come into play in connection with

two aspects of the use of the criminal law to enforce economic regulatory laws; namely, the loosening of minimum requirements for
culpability in the cause of enforcement efficiency, and the criminalizing
and punishing of behavior that does not generally attract the sentiment
of moral reprobation.

A. REQUIREMENTS OF CULPABILITY

At several points attention has been called to the obstacles to effective
prosecution created by certain conventional requirements of the criminal
law; for example, the requirement of specificity in defining the prohibited conduct and the requirement of minimum conditions of accountability in holding persons responsible for the acts of others. Whatever
basis these requirements have in the area of traditional crime, may they
properly be diluted or dispensed with in the area of economic regulatory
crime? The issue is fundamentally the same as that posed by the use of
strict criminal liability, though, interestingly enough, this appears to have
been much less commonly employed in economic regulation than in
those controls on business directed to public health and safety.

The case for the irrelevance of these traditional requirements is
reflected in the observation of a trust-buster of an earlier generation:
"The rights of the accused which are of the utmost importance where
liberty of an individual is in jeopardy, are irrelevant symbols when the
real issue is the arrangement under which corporations in industry compete."[79] In essence the concept is that the purpose behind the criminal
sanction in this area is not penalization, but regulation. Unlike the area
of conventional crime against person and property where criminalization
serves to reassure the community, to express condemnation and to set
in motion a corrective or restraining regime, as well as to deter proscribed
behavior, here the concern is solely with this last factor. "[T]he problem
of responsibility is not the general social phenomenon of moral delinquency and guilt, but the practical problem of dealing with physical
conditions and social or economic practices that are to be controlled."[80]

A countervailing consideration commonly adduced in discussions
of strict liability is equally applicable where culpability requirements are
otherwise withdrawn by statutes that do not adequately announce what
is prohibited or that impose varieties of vicarious responsibility. Absent
these requirements, it cannot be said, except in a strictly formal sense,
that the actor made a choice to commit the acts prohibited. Hence, it is
said that the law has no deterrent function to perform, offering no lesson
to the actor or to other persons, beyond the Pickwickian instruction that
even if he does the best he can, or anyone could, to comply with the law
he may nonetheless be punished.[81] Yet the argument does not quite
persuade. For it may as plausibly be argued that the consequence of

dispensing with the requirement of proof of culpability eases the task of the enforcing authorities, rendering successful prosecution more likely and, through discouraging insistence on trial and simplifying the issues when trials are held, enhances the efficiency of prosecution. In a word, certainty of conviction is increased. This may readily exert an added deterrent force upon the actor faced with a choice, since the chances of escaping punishment for a culpable choice, intentional or negligent, are decreased.[82] And even where there is no immediate choice, the effect could sometimes be to influence persons to arrange their affairs to reduce to a minimum the possibilities of accidental violation; in short, to exercise extraordinary care. Further, the persistent use of such laws by legislatures and their strong support by persons charged with their enforcement makes it dogmatic to insist they cannot deter in these ways.

Closer, perhaps, to the core of the opposition to dispensing with culpability is the principle that it is morally improper and ultimately unsound and self-defeating to employ penal sanctions with respect to conduct that does not warrant the moral condemnation that is implicit, or that should be implicit, in the concept of a crime.[83] The issue is whether these considerations are adequately dealt with by the contention that laws dispensing with culpability are directed to regulation rather than penalization.

The contention plainly proves too much. If the sole concern is a non-reprobative deterrent threat, then it follows that the sanction should be drastic and certain enough to overcome the motive of economic gain, and not necessarily that the sanction should be criminal. Civil fines, punitive damages, injuctions, profit divestiture programs or other varieties of non-criminal sanctions would thus appear to offer equivalent possibilities of enforcing the regulatory scheme. Indeed, these alternatives might enhance the possibilities, since proof and evidentiary requirements are more onerous in criminal prosecutions than in civil suits. The conclusion appears difficult to resist that insistence on the criminal penalty is attributable to a desire to make use of the unique deterrent mode of the criminal sanction, the stigma of moral blame that it carries. If so, the argument of regulation rather than penalization turns out in the end to be only a temporary diversion that does not escape the need to confront the basic issue: the justice and wisdom of imposing a stigma of moral blame in the absence of blameworthiness in the actor.

So far as the issue of justice is concerned, once having put the moral question the footing becomes unsteady. Is the moral difficulty inconsequential, requiring simply the side-stepping of an otherwise useful symbol that happens to stand in the way of attaining immediately desirable goals?[84] Does it yield to a pragmatic evaluation in terms of an estimate of the soundness of departing from principle to some degree in particular cases in order to attain goals of greater consequence?[85]

Does it present an insuperable objection entailing commitment to values of such profundity that compromise is unthinkable?[86] For present purposes it is perhaps enough to put the questions, though three points may be suggested. First, the starkness of the moral issue is to some degree assuaged by regarding laws dispensing with culpability as empowering enforcement officials to use their discretion to select for prosecution those who have in their judgment acted culpably. Plainly, however, the issue is not escaped since it remains to justify dispensing with the safeguards of trial on this single and crucial issue.[87] Second, the recognition of the moral impasse does not necessarily require agreement that the criminal law *should* use its weapons for the purpose of fixing moral obloquy upon transgressors. It is sufficient that it is broadly characteristic of the way criminal conviction operates in our society. Third, and in consequence, the moral difficulty exists only so long as and to the extent that criminal conviction retains its aura of moral condemnation. The impasse lessens to the extent that the element of blame and punishment is replaced by a conception of the criminal process as a means of social improvement through a program of morally neutral rehabilitation and regulation.[88] (Though such a development has important implications which I mean to return to shortly.)

Concerning the issue of ultimate wisdom, the point frequently made respecting strict liability is equally applicable to the dilution of these aspects of culpability typically at issue in economic regulatory legislation. The dilution is not readily confined within the narrow area for which it was designed, but tends to overflow into the main body of conventional crimes. The distinction between offenses that regulate and those that penalize in the traditional sense proves inadequate to divide the waters. For example, traditional concepts of liability in the main body of criminal law tend to receive a new and diluted form when construed as part of a regulatory statute.[89] Moreover, the habituation of courts and legislatures to crimes dispensing with culpability in the regulatory area may readily dull legislative and judicial sensitivity to the departures from minimum culpability requirements already fixed in the main body of the criminal law.[90] This expansion of criminality without culpability in statutory offenses and convictions, and its spread and solidification in the general criminal law heightens the moral difficulty. As the area expands and deepens it becomes necessary at some point to face the issue as entailing a judgment on the abandonment of principle rather than one on the wisdom of utilitarian compromise for a larger good. Moreover, the risks entailed in depreciating the impact of condemnation in a criminal conviction become greater to the extent that conviction without culpability becomes more common and pervasive. To the extent that the crucial distinguishing factor of the criminal sanction is "the judgment of community condemnation which accompanies and justifies its imposition,"[91] and to the extent that this characteristic contributes substantially to its effectiveness in influencing compliance with proscribed norms, the proliferation of convictions without grounds for condemnation tends in the long run to impair the identity of the criminal sanction and its ultimate effectiveness as a preventive sanction, both in the area of economic crimes and in the areas of its traditional application.[92]

B. THE CRIMINALIZATION OF MORALLY NEUTRAL CONDUCT

But let it be assumed that the traditional grounds of culpability have been adhered to so that the defendant can fairly be held accountable for a choice to violate the economic prohibition. May there be costs, even so, in terms of principle and other goals, in employing the criminal sanction where the violative behavior does not attract in the community the moral disapprobation associated with a criminal conviction? How different and how similar are the considerations involved in dispensing with culpability? The question is the obverse of an aspect of the relation between criminal law and morals which has been much considered—the use of the criminal law to prohibit and condemn behavior that is widely (either actually or formally) viewed as morally reprehensible, where secular interest, in the sense of concerns beyond the immorality of individuals, do not exist.[93] Here the issue is the use of the criminal sanction to prohibit and condemn behavior that threatens secular interests, but that is not regarded as fundamentally and inherently wrong.

The central consequence of diluting or eliminating requirements of culpability is, as suggested, the criminalization and punishment of persons who cannot be said to warrant the condemnation thereby imported. It is this consequence that gives rise to the hard question of principle and practical consequences. In a sense a similar consequence follows from punishing conduct that is not itself blameworthy, even when culpably engaged in: persons are stigmatized with conviction for conduct not regarded as deserving the moral stigma. The problem of principle, however, is of considerably smaller dimension, since the choice to act in defiance of the criminal prohibition may be regarded as in some measure furnishing an independently adequate ground for condemnation. (Yet it is necessary to add that the ground exists only in cases where the culpability requirements are extended to include knowledge or culpable disregard of the existence of the prohibition, an extension only occasionally made in regulatory legislation.[94])

The danger of debilitating the moral impact of the criminal conviction and hence decreasing the overall effectiveness of the criminal law cannot as readily be put aside. As Professor Henry Hart has noted, "the criminal law always loses face if things are declared to be crimes which people believe they ought to be free to do, even wilfully."[95] It may be mitigated to a degree by maintaining a proper proportion in the punishment authorized for various offenses in accordance with the moral culpability of the behavior. The limitations of such a strategy are, first, that there is always a strong pressure to raise authorized penalties when violations become widespread or conspicuous, and second, that there is an irreducible minimum in the moral condemnation comported by conviction of crime. Such considerations have led one observer to "decry the trend toward an increasingly undiscriminating employment of this branch of the law, and to repudiate the suggestion that criminal law should be applied more extensively in the areas of ordinary economic relationships."[96]

It may of course be answered that the conviction of violators of laws of this character serves as a means of moral instruction to the community; in short, that the onus of conviction is transferred to the behavior prohibited. That there will be a transference would appear quite likely. But that it should necessarily or generally be expected to involve imparting moral onus to the behavior rather than moral indifference to the conviction is considerably less so. The more widely the criminal conviction is used for this purpose, and the less clear the immorality of the behavior so sanctioned, the more likely would it appear that the criminal conviction will not only fail to attain the immediate purpose of its use but will degenerate in effectiveness for other purposes as well.

There is another cost not paralleled in the dilution of culpability requirements. The behavior under discussion involves restraints upon the free operation of business without at the same time denying commitment to a free enterprise system. The demarcation of the line between the legitimate, indeed the affirmatively desirable, and the illegitimate in business conduct is continually in flux and subject to wide controversy in the community. To say there is no complete consensus on what business decisions should be regulated and what left free of regulation is to say what is minimally true. It would not follow from this that a legislature should abstain from enacting such controls as command a majority. But the appropriateness of the criminal sanction as a means of enforcing the imposed control is another matter. I have already suggested that the criminal remedy in this situation tends to be ineffective and destructive of its overall utility as a sanctioning device. Here the point is different. To the extent it is effective in generating strong moral commitments to the regulatory regime it supports it has the dangerous potential of introducing a rigidification of values too soon, of cutting off the debate, or at least restricting the ease of movement to new positions and a new consensus.[97] This seems to me the wisdom of Professor Allen's caveat that "the function of the criminal law in these areas is not to anticipate but to reflect and implement the consensus already achieved in the community."[98]

A word in conclusion on lines of legislative action. The widescale abandonment of the criminal sanction in those areas where its cost is excessive is as unlikely as it is desirable. Legislative habit and the simple logic of here and now expediency have a compulsion not to be denied by contemplation of long range consequences in areas removed from the immediate target of legislative concern. A more acceptable and hence more fruitful course is the development of means of reducing the costs of the use of the criminal sanction in economic regulations, which do not demand that it be abandoned altogether. If such means exist one would expect they would be found in ways of dealing with the central fact principally responsible for the predicament, the irreducible core of condemnation in a criminal conviction. One possible approach is to institutionalize a system of gradation of convictions, just as systems of grading punishment have long been a part of the law. There is no adequate basis for accomplishing this under present law. The distinction between offenses *mala prohibita* and *mala in se* carries something of the flavor, but it is an informal rather than an institutionalized distinction and lacks any clear meaning.[99] The felony-misdemeanor distinction has an established statutory basis. However, the categories have largely lost significance in distinguishing degrees of blameworthiness, some misdemeanors embracing crimes of serious moral import, and some felonies embracing relatively minor transgressions. Moreover, there is need for a category of offense carrying considerably less weight than a misdemeanor. The petty offense category which appears in many statutes is essentially a petty misdemeanor, retaining its label as a crime and being punishable with imprisonment.[100] In those cases in which the label has been removed, the substance (that is, provision for imprisonment) has not.[101]

The Model Penal Code has attempted to meet the inadequacies of existing law by adding to its three categories of crime (felonies, misdemeanors and petty misdemeanors) a separate noncriminal category designated a "violation"[102] which is punishable only by a sentence of fine (under 500 dollars or any higher amount equal to double the pecuniary gain made by the offender)[103] or civil penalty,[104] and which does not "give rise to any disability or legal disadvantage based on conviction of a criminal offense."[105] The design of this proposal "reflects the purpose of the Code to employ penal sanctions only with respect to conduct warranting the moral condemnation implicit in the concept of a crime."[106] Since strict liability even for crimes properly so regarded presents the same problem, the same solution is applied by treating crimes committed without culpability as "violations."[107]

While novel in American law, the German law has for some years adopted an approach quite similar to that proposed by the Model Penal Code.[108] Separate from a three level classification of crimes, properly so called (*Straftat*),[109] is another category of offense, the "regulatory violation" (*Ordnungswidrigkeit*).[110] These regulatory violations are not punishable by imprisonment. A fine is the sole available sanction, indeed a fine which bears a special designation (*Geldbusse*, literally "monetary repentance") as opposed to the penal fine (*Geldstrafe*, literally "monetary punishment").[111] These fines are not registered in the punishment registry[112] and are imposed at the first instance by the responsible administrative agency[113] subject to the right of the violator to object and to be tried in the courts.[114]

The feasibility of using the category of regulatory violation for sanctioning economic regulation is, of course, the principal issue. Here the German experience may offer some evidence for decision. Unfortunately there appear to be no empirical studies of the relative effectiveness of its use in Germany. But to judge from the statute books it is the typical non-civil sanction for economic misconduct. All antitrust violations,[115] for example, are regulatory violations, as are violations of other restrictions upon economic behavior such as certain behavior prohibited by the foreign trade law,[116] laws governing the operation of loan banks,[117] laws governing the closing of shops,[118] transportation rate laws,[119] and other laws. Particularly suggestive is the strategy used in connection with certain kinds of economic offenses as a means of individualizing the determination of whether a defendant's behavior is to be treated as a crime or a regulatory violation. For violations of certain price control laws, import restrictions and unlawful overcharging,[120] a legislative determination of the appropriate category of the offense is withheld in favor of a judicial determination in each case. The law requires an offense under these laws to be dealt with as a regulatory violation unless the nature either of the conduct or of the defendant warrants dealing with it as a crime. It is a crime when the conduct "by virtue of its scope or consequences is likely to prejudice the goals of the economic system, especially those of market or price regulations"; or when the defendant is a "repeated or professional violator or acts in culpable selfishness or otherwise irresponsibly, and by his conduct shows that he lacks respect for the public interest in the protection of the economic system, especially of the market or price regulations."[121] With all their vagueness these provisions suggest a need in any system that employs a noncriminal category of violation and uses it to deal with economic violations, for a flexible device whereby violations may, with changed public sentiment and in consideration of the extremity of the circumstances, be raised to the category of crime.

One can hardly say that this approach through a tertium quid is the clear answer to the problems of using criminal sanctions to enforce economic restrictions. There are many imponderables with respect to its effectiveness both as a preventive and as a means of reducing the costs of an indiscriminate use of the criminal sanction. On the side of preventive effectiveness, is the reprobative association of a genuine criminal conviction a needed weapon of enforcement? Would the semi-criminal category of offense convey enough of a sense of wrongness to perform its tasks? Can these laws be enforced efficiently enough without such associations? Is the loss of the power to imprison a substantial loss? Does what is left of the criminal process still provide efficiencies not available in the pure civil remedy? Will the regulatory offense prove politically acceptable to legislators and administrators as an alternative to outright criminalization? On the side of reducing costs, how much will it help that a new label has been created so long as the criminal process is used, or that imprisonment is not available as a sanction, when in fact it is rarely used anyway? And finally, is whatever is lost in effectiveness worth what is gained in other respects? One cannot be dogmatic in answering these questions. But one can, I think, insist that these are the kinds of questions which must be asked about this alternative as well as others if we are to escape the limited options inherited from different days in the use of the criminal sanction.

CHAPTER THREE

EXCUSE

5
THE DECLINE OF
INNOCENCE

The criminological positivists at the turn of the century started a good deal of creative thinking about the criminal law.[1] Some of their proposals have gained widespread acceptance in the criminal law as we know it today. Others made no headway at all. One particular proposal, and a very fundamental one indeed, began a controversy that has ebbed and flowed regularly since. That is the proposal to eliminate from the criminal law the whole apparatus of substantive principles, or at least some of them, such as the legal insanity defense, which owe their presence to the law's traditional concern for distinguishing the guilty and the innocent in terms of their blameworthiness. The essence of the proposal is that innocence in this sense, moral innocence, if you will, should not disqualify a person from the consequences of the penal law. Moral innocence should, it is urged, give way to social dangerousness as the basis for a criminal disposition.

In recent years there has been a resurgence of the controversy produced by serious proposals to eliminate the defense of legal insanity and, more radical still, to eliminate across the board the requirements of *mens rea* from the definition of criminal offenses and defenses. If I may raise my colors at the outset, I am frankly a friend to neither proposal. In this brief paper I would like to discuss the implications of these suggested reforms and to develop my reasons for believing that the case has not been made.

The term "*mens rea*" is rivaled only by the term "jurisdiction" for the varieties of senses in which it has been used and for the quantity of obfuscation it has created. A few introductory paragraphs on usage are inescapable if minds are to meet on the genuine issues.

The criminal law constitutes a description of harms which a society seeks to discourage with the threat of criminal punishment for those who commit those harms. At the same time the criminal law comprises an elaborate body of qualifications to these prohibitions and threats. It used to be common, and it still is not unknown, to express all of these qualifications to liability in terms of the requirement of *mens rea*. This is the thought behind the classic maxim, "*Actus non facit reum, nisi mens sit rea.*" Or in Blackstone's translation, "An unwarrantable act without a vicious will is no crime at all." The vicious will was the *mens rea*. Reduced to its essence it referred to the choice to do a blameworthy act. The requirement of *mens rea* was rationalized on the common sense view of justice that blame and punishment were inappropriate and unjust in the absence of that choice.

It is more helpful (and also more usual today) to speak more discriminatingly of the various classes of circumstances in which criminal liability is qualified by the requirement of blameworthiness. Putting aside the circumstances of justification and excuse (they are relevant but not central to the controversy), there are two principal categories of *mens rea* which should be distinguished.

The first category we can call *mens rea* in its special sense. In this special sense *mens rea* refers only to the mental state required by the definition of the offense to accompany the act that produces or threatens the harm. An attempt to commit a crime consists of an act which comes close to its commission done *with the purpose that the crime be committed*. Unlawful assembly is joining with a group in a public place *with intent to commit unlawful acts*. Larceny consists of the appropriation of another's property *knowing* it is not your own with *intent* to deprive the owner or possessor of it permanently. Receiving stolen goods is a crime when one receives those goods *knowing they are stolen*. Manslaughter is the killing of another by an act done with *awareness* of a substantial and unjustifiable risk of doing so.

That the absence of the *mens rea*, in this special sense of the required mental state, precludes liability in all of these cases is of course the merest tautology. This is the way these crimes are defined. But it is important to see that they are so defined because the special *mens rea* element is crucial to the description of the conduct we want to make criminal. And description is crucial in so far as it is regarded as important to exclude from the definition of criminality what we do not want to punish as criminal. To revert to the examples just given, it would not be regarded as appropriate to make criminal the taking of another's property where the taker believed honestly that he was taking his own property. Neither would it make sense to make a person guilty of receiving stolen goods where he neither knew nor had occasion to know that the goods were stolen. And surely we should see nothing criminal in joining a group in a public place, apart from the intent to commit unlawful acts.

The second category of *mens rea* qualifications to liability is that of legal responsibility, which includes the familiar defenses of legal insanity and infancy. These qualifications differ in several particulars from the *mens rea* qualifications of the first category. In requiring *mens rea* in the first, special, sense the law is saying that it does not hold a person where he has shown himself by his conduct, judged in terms of its totality, including his mental state, to be no different than the rest of us, or not different enough to justify the criminal sanction. In requiring *mens rea* in the sense of legal responsibility, the law absolves a person precisely because his deficiencies of temperament, personality, or maturity distinguish him so utterly from the rest of us to whom the law's threats are addressed that we do not expect him to comply.

Proposals to eliminate the defense of legal insanity entail the abolition of *mens rea* in this latter sense of legal responsibility. The elimination of *mens rea* in its special sense raises more radical challenges to the traditional criminal law. Let me start with legal insanity.

I

Devising an appropriate definition of legal insanity has been the subject of most of the argument concerning this defense. The modern starting point in England and the United States is the M'Naghten test formulated in 1843, which asks whether at the time of the act the accused was laboring under such a disease of the mind as not to know the nature and quality of the act he was doing, or that it was wrong.[2]

The justification for this formulation is that it does in fact exclude from liability a category of persons who by definition could not be deterred by the prospect of punishment, simply because they were incapable of choice, and whom, in consequence, it would be futile as well as unjust to punish. The definition of the exculpation, therefore, coincides with the rationale of the traditional requirement of *mens rea*. Nonetheless, the M'Naghten test has been vigorously and consistently criticized since its formulation. One can roughly identify four major themes of criticism, which, half-seriously, I want to refer to as the themes of reaction, liberal reform, radical reform, and neo-reaction.

The reactionary criticism is based on the premise that the defense of legal insanity provides a loophole through which those who deserve punishment can too easily manage to escape. Therefore, the protection of the public requires that the defense be eliminated altogether,[3] or at least be made so difficult to establish (for example, by placing the burden upon the defendant to prove his insanity beyond reasonable doubt[4]) that very few will escape.

The liberal reform criticism is that the M'Naghten test does not go far enough. Inconsistent with its own premise of exculpating the blameless, the test fails to cover classes of defendants who merit exculpation as much as those it does exculpate. The major class of such defendants comprises those whose ability to choose to conform is destroyed even though their cognitive capacity is sufficiently intact to disqualify them under M'Naghten. Another class consists of those who *knew* on a superficial intellectual level what they were doing and that it was wrong, but did not really understand with the full emotional affect that gives meaning to knowledge. This criticism produced a number of changes in the legal insanity defense in American jurisdictions, notably the addition of the irresistible impulse defense and a broadening in the conception of the requirement of knowledge.[5] It has also produced the increasingly influential proposal of the American Law Institute's Model Penal Code: "A person is not responsible for criminal conduct if at the time of such conduct as a result of mental disease or defect he lacks substantial capacity either to appreciate the criminality of his conduct or to conform his conduct to the requirements of law."[6]

The radical critique of M'Naghten is that it is wrongheaded, not simply inadequate, because it is based upon particular symptoms of mental disease in large part meaningless in the medical conception of mental illness. In short, it is a mistake to attempt to impose a legal definition upon what is inevitably a medical phenomenon. As a consequence of this criticism such proposals emerged as those of the Royal Commission on Capital Punishment in 1953, which put the test of legal insanity in terms of whether an accused was suffering from mental disease or deficiency to such a degree that he ought not to be held responsible.[7] It also produced the famous Durham test in 1954, which inquires whether the unlawful act of the accused was the product of mental disease or defects.[8] Such proposals have found virtually no acceptance either in England or in the United States.

The neo-reactionary criticism recommends that efforts to find improved definitions of the test of legal insanity be abandoned and that legal insanity as a defense be eliminated from the criminal law. The justification for this view differs from the reactionary case for abolition. Both end up proposing undiscriminating penalization of the sick and the bad. But the new criticism, or much of it, does so as a first step toward penalizing neither. This more sophisticated proposal for abolition has been advanced by a variety of persons for a variety of reasons.[9] Let me try to summarize what I understand to be the major arguments.

The first is that the administration of the tests of insanity—all tests—have been a total failure. It has proven impossible to administer the defense rationally and equitably. In the end the jury's determination is largely governed by the credentials and presentation of the psychiatric experts; and the defendant's ability to pay determines the quality of the psychiatric evidence he can present. Moreover, psychiatric testimony is worth little—it is the softest of the soft sciences; psychiatrists disagree on key concepts, and their conclusions and analyses turn on their own value judgments. Finally, the whole enterprise is an elaborate search after something that does not exist—there is not and cannot be a workable distinction between the responsible and the irresponsible, particularly when the distinction is drawn in terms of the issue of volitional capacity.

Second, it is argued that the defense of legal insanity is of little practical importance. To be sure, the defense has real bite in cases of capital punishment. But the death penalty has been abolished in England and is fast becoming otiose in the United States. In the United States legal insanity is pleaded in no more than about 2 percent of the jury cases that go to trial.[10] In England the situation is similar. With increasing frequency, issues of the mental abnormality of the offender are being taken into account after conviction rather than before. For example, mental abnormality questions in England are taken into consideration in probation orders with mental treatment as a condition, in hospital orders under section 60 or 65 of the Mental Health Act of 1959 and in transfers of prisoners from prisons to mental hospitals. As a consequence of these developments in recent years only in about 1 or 2 percent of cases is the mental abnormality of an offender taken into account by finding the defendant not guilty because of legal insanity.[11]

Finally, and of central importance, it is believed that the retention of the distinction between those to be punished and those only to be treated is unfortunate and invidious because in point of fact it is in all cases, not only in some, that persons who do harms should be treated and held in the interest of the public protection. The incidence of gross psychopathy among criminal offenders is enormous, ranging over the widest classes of offenders, and only the smallest fraction are covered by the legal insanity tests. The effect of maintaining the dichotomy between the sick and the bad (essentially a false one anyway) is to block public and legislative perception that in most crimes psychical and social determinants inhibit the capacity of the actors to control their behavior. As a consequence effective development and use of psychiatric therapeutic resources for the vast majority of offenders are thwarted.

In the last analysis this case for abolition makes two claims—the first, that the present situation is bad; the second, that abolition would make it better. My own view is that the first claim is supportable although somewhat overdrawn. The second claim I believe is unfounded.

I am ready to concede that the record of the administration of the legal insanity defense is very bad indeed. And to some extent I am inclined to believe that the softness of psychiatry as a science and the inherent difficulty of the issue which the defense presents are partly responsible. But several necessary qualifications tend to blunt the point made by this criticism. The insanity defense is scarcely the only feature of our criminal justice system that is badly administered in practice. For example, inefficiency and inequity are endemic to a system committed to an adversary process but not committed to supplying the resources of legal contest to the typically penurious who make up the bulk of criminal defendants. But I would hope that the lesson of all this would not be to abandon the adversary method on that score but to improve its operation. Likewise with the insanity defense, improvement of its operation rather than its abolition would seem the more appropriate response. The difficulty is not all produced by psychiatrists and the nature of the issue. To the extent that the difficulty is due to inadequate defense resources, to persistent, if not perverse, misunderstandings by psychiatrists of what the law's concern is, to unjustifiable restrictions on the scope of psychiatric testimony—and I believe it is due to all of these factors to some extent—it seems at least equally plausible to address those causes as to eliminate the feature of the law which allows them to operate. And even to the extent that the causes of the difficulty are incorrectible because inherent in the insanity defense, the case for abolition is not made out, any more than the case for abolishing the jury or the defense of unintentionality or ignorance would be made out by pointing to the grave problems of administration they produce. This dispositive issue is whether we would achieve a net gain in doing without the troublesome element in the law. And this I will come to shortly.

As to the argument founded on the infrequency of the defense, in one sense it cuts the other way. For to the extent that the case for abolition rests on the inequitableness and irrationality of its administration, the very infrequency of the invocation of that defense reduces the import of the criticism. But in any event the infrequency of a defense is not an argument for its elimination. The defenses of necessity or duress surely are invoked in a minute fraction of criminal cases. Yet few would regard this as a reason for abandoning them. The function of a legal defense is not measured by its use but by its usefulness in the total framework of the criminal justice system.

Finally, we face the claim that the perpetuation of the insanity defense has tended to reduce the flow of psychiatric and other resources for treatment of the great mass of offenders. Certainly the flow has been far too small. We need more research and more resources in the effective treatment of offenders. But whether the presence of the insanity defence has contributed to this situation (and substantially so, according to the charge) is a question of fact which I have not seen the slightest evidence to support. Indeed there is evidence to the contrary—witness the proliferation in England of alternative routes for the disposition of psychologically disturbed offenders[12] which abolitionists often use to show the otioseness of the defense of legal insanity.

Now for the second claim. Would we achieve a net advantage in eliminating the defense? As a start let us try to get clear what would follow if the defense of legal insanity were abolished. Certainly what would follow would depend on the formulation of the defense. But for present purposes we can confine ourselves to M'Naghten. Since other tests include the cases which it covers, what is true of eliminating the M'Naghten defense is true of eliminating the other formulations as well.

It will be remembered that M'Naghten authorizes the defense of legal insanity when the effect of the defendant's mental disease is to destroy his cognitive capacity, to make him unable to know the nature and quality of his act. When this is so the defence of legal insanity is made out and the defendant becomes subject to the variety of provisions governing commitment of the criminally insane. Now if this defense were eliminated what would be the position of a defendant charged with a crime? Apparently it would depend upon the *mens rea*, in the special sense, required by the definition of the crime. If the crime were one like attempt, requiring a purpose by the defendant to achieve an object; or if it were one like larceny, requiring knowledge of a particular matter of fact; or if it were one like manslaughter, requiring knowledge of a particular risk, would it not be the case that the defendant has a complete defense? A total inability to know the nature and quality of the act quite plainly precludes convicting a defendant of any crime whose definition requires that he have that knowledge. And any crime which requires intent, or knowledge or recklessness surely posits that knowing. If it were not for the special, preemptive defense of legal insanity, therefore, the defendant would have a complete defense on the merits to any such crime—namely, the lack of *mens rea*. What the insanity defense does is to deprive a defendant of his normal *mens rea* defense (which would be unqualified and lead to discharge) and to require that he be acquitted on this special ground with its consequences for indeterminate commitment.

If, on the other hand, the crime required only negligence, the absence of an insanity defense would leave the defendant with no defense at all, since all that is required is that the defendant has fallen substantially below the standard of the reasonable man, and this, by definition, a M'Naghten defendant has done. (Except, of course, to the extent that the subjective feature of the concept of negligence—requiring that *some* special characteristics of the defendant be considered in defining the standard, as, for example, his inability to see or to hear—were enlarged to embrace his special cognitive disabilities.)

Now precisely these consequences are apparently intended, or at least accepted, by some abolitionists.[13] But it is difficult to see the force of their case. The whole spirit of the proposal is to put social defense on a surer ground; to assure that those who constitute threats to personal and social security be effectively channeled into a preventive system which authorizes the state to subject them to restraint in the public interest and to provide them with a therapeutic regimen both in the public interest and in their own. The effect of eliminating the insanity defense is to do the opposite precisely for those offenders who have done the greatest harm—those defined by crimes requiring *mens rea* of intent, knowledge, or recklessness. (As for crimes of negligence, to which insane defendants might still be liable, this objection does not apply, of course. Here the difficulty created is the conviction of the innocent, a matter I will consider subsequently.)

This self-defeating consequence of eliminating the insanity defense simpliciter has moved other abolitionists to add another branch to their proposal. This entails enactment of a provision that would preclude all evidence bearing on the absence of *mens rea* which is founded on the mental abnormality of the accused.[14] This was the form, for example, that the earliest abolitionist enactment in the United States took. In 1909 the State of Washington amended its law to provide that it should no longer be a defense that the defendant by reason of his insanity was unable to comprehend the nature and quality of the act committed. But the statute then continued: "nor shall any testimony or other proof thereof be admitted in evidence."[15] In addition, it is interesting to note, the statute, consistent with the positivist premise and with more modern proposals, provided for indeterminate commitment in a state hospital for the insane or "the insane ward of the state penitentiary" for those convicted who are found by the judge to meet the M'Naghten test of insanity.

To the abolitionist proposal on this footing there are two principal objections—the first technical, the second fundamental.

The technical objection is this. For the reasons put earlier evidence of the defendant's mental abnormality may be directly relevant to the presence of the *mens rea* of the crime charged, without proof of which a conviction is not possible. If *some* evidence which is relevant to the issue of *mens rea* is excluded, the judge must have a standard to distinguish the admissible from the inadmissible evidence. This standard, of course, under the Washington statute as well as under similarly grounded formulations, would presumably be whether the evidence goes to establish the inability of the defendant, as the result of a mental disease, to understand the nature and the quality of his acts. The upshot would be, therefore, that the test of legal insanity having been ejected through one door would reenter through another, now presenting itself as a rule of evidence rather than as a substantive defense. And a good deal, if not all, of the messy and unsettling business of bringing psychiatrists into the courtroom and in exposing the guilt–innocent determination to those inherently inconclusive medical arguments over the operation of men's minds, which it is one of the important objectives of the abolitionist proposals to eliminate, would not be eliminated after all. For how else could the parties address themselves to the issue of whether certain *mens rea* evidence, somehow touching the defendant's mental abnormality, is or is not part of the forbidden case bearing on legal insanity?

And there is another consideration, which makes the picture even darker for the success of this proposal. That is the unlikelihood of finally working to screen out any substantial amount of psychiatric evidence from the trial on the issue of guilt or innocence. California's experience with the bifurcated trial teaches a dismaying lesson. In order to clarify and simplify the issues before the jury, the California law was amended in 1927 to require separate trials whenever the defendant raises defenses on the merits as well as the defense of legal insanity. At the first trial, the defendant's sanity is presumed, and evidence bearing on legal insanity is excluded.[16] The lower courts struggled for years in an attempt to distinguish between admissible and inadmissible evidence at the first trial. But it was hopeless. Evidence of mental insanity tending to establish legal insanity will usually do double service as also tending to establish the absence of the specific *mens rea* required. Finally the Supreme Court ended the agony by holding that any evidence of defendant's mental abnormality was admissible at the trial of the issue of his guilt, so long as it was relevant to the existence of a mental state required by the crime.[17] The experiment was a failure—issues of guilt and of mental condition proved to be inseparable.[18] Abolishing the legal insanity defense is no more likely to keep the trial free of psychiatry and its preceptors and their probing into the mental condition of the accused than is the requirement of the separate trial of the issue of insanity. You can change the name of the game, but you cannot avoid playing it so long as *mens rea* is required.

I turn now to what I referred to as the fundamental objection to this proposal. Essentially it is that it opens to the condemnation of a criminal conviction a class of persons who, on any common-sense notion of justice, are beyond blaming and ought not to be punished. The criminal law as we know it today does associate a substantial condemnatory onus with conviction for a crime. So long as this is so a just and humane legal system has an obligation to make a distinction between those who are eligible for this condemnation and those who are not. It is true, as has been argued,[19] that a person adjudicated not guilty but insane suffers a substantial social stigma. It is also true that this is hurtful and unfortunate, and indeed, unjust. But it results from the misinterpretation placed upon the person's conduct by people in the community. It is not, like the conviction of the irresponsible, the paradigmatic affront to the sense of justice in the law which consists in the deliberative act of convicting a morally innocent person of a crime, of imposing blame when there is no occasion for it.

This sentiment of justice has attained constitutional stature in decisions of the United States Supreme Court. Obviously I do not bring the Supreme Court into this for its legal authority in the United Kingdom. What is relevant is that in these decisions the Court was responding to a fundamental sense of justice, which, unlike the mandate of the Court, does not stop at national boundaries. The animating principal in several recent decisions was that to convict a person of a crime in circumstances in which it was impossible for him to conform violates a fundamental principle of justice. It was this principle which led the Court to hold that it constituted an unconstitutional imposition of cruel and unusual punishment to make it a crime for a person "to be" a narcotic addict.[20] The same principle persuaded the Court in another case to find a violation of due process of law in the conviction of a person for failing to register as a previously convicted offender upon arrival in Los Angeles in the absence of any circumstances calculated to give notice of her obligation to do so.[21] As observed recently by Mr. Justice Fortas: "Our morality does not permit us to punish for illness. We do not impose punishment for involuntary conduct, whether the lack of volition results from 'insanity,' or addiction to narcotics, or from other illnesses."[22]

Of course the spirit behind these proposals to abolish the insanity defense is humane rather than punitive: what is contemplated is that persons, once convicted, who are insane would then receive all the care and treatment appropriate to their condition, as indeed would all persons who commit crime. The answer was given by the Washington Supreme Court when it declared unconstitutional the abolition amendment to which I earlier referred: "Yet the stern and awful fact still remains, and is patent to all men, that the status and condition in the eyes of the world, and under the law, of one convicted of crime is vastly different from that of one simply adjudged insane. We cannot shut our eyes to the fact that the element of punishment is still in our criminal laws."[23]

A common rejoinder is that we convict and punish persons daily whose ability to conform is impaired by a variety of circumstances—by youthful neglect, by parental inadequacy, by the social and psychical deprivations of growing up in a grossly underprivileged minority subculture, or by countless other contingencies of life.[24] This is perfectly true, but I fail to see that it supports eliminating the insanity defense. First, the argument logically is an argument for extension of the defense of lack of responsibility, not for its abolition. It is never a reason for adding to injustice that we are already guilty of some. Second, confining the defense to patent and extreme cases of irresponsibility is not a whimsical irrationality. There may well be an injustice in it, but it rests upon the practical concern to avoid vitiating the deterrent impact of the criminal law upon those who are more or less susceptible to its influences. As Professor Wechsler has observed: "The problem is to differentiate between the wholly non-deterrable and persons who are more or less susceptible to influence by law. The category must be so extreme that to the ordinary man burdened by passion and beset by large temptations, the exculpation of the irresponsibles bespeaks no weakness in the law. He does not identify with them; they are a world apart."[25] We may accept as a necessary evil—necessary, that is, given our commitment to a punishment system—the criminal conviction of persons whose ability to conform is somewhat impaired and still protest that it is unacceptable for a society to fail to make a distinction for those who are utterly and obviously beyond the reach of the law.

At the heart of a good deal of the argument for abolition is, and must be, the rejection of the punishment system altogether. To the extent this is the case the rejoinder I have just been discussing makes more sense. The refusal to punish defined classes of offenders is an assertion of the propriety of punishing the rest. As Professor Morris has rightly observed, "one group's exculpation from criminal responsibility confirms the inculpation of other groups."[26] On this footing my reservations to the abolitionist proposal is twofold. In the first place it is far from self-evident that the best way to achieve the end of penalization is by penalizing all rather than by expanding the definition of the irresponsible. Second, and more fundamentally, the decline of guilt—which is what penalization is about—also means, and necessarily, the decline of innocence. This brings us squarely to the remaining major issue I want to deal with.

II

To this point I have been speaking of abolishing the insanity defense as a relatively conservative proposal that would leave the rest of the substantive criminal law intact. I turn now to more radical proposals, like those of Lady Wootton, which see this reform rather as one part of a larger radical transformation of the law which would tear up, root and branch, all manifestations of *mens rea* toward the end of extirpating blame and punishment from the criminal law.

Lady Wootton proposes (others have as well, but none so persuasively) that the entire body of qualifications to criminal liability embraced in the *mens rea* principle be eliminated.[27] She sometimes uses *mens rea* loosely, but it seems clear enough that she has in mind not only the defense of legal insanity but also *mens rea* in its special sense as denoting the mental state required by the definition of particular crimes. Under her scheme there would be two separate stages of determinations made in the case of a person accused of crime. At the first stage there would be decided only whether the defendant committed the act prohibited by the criminal law, without regard to whether he acted intentionally, knowingly, recklessly, and even negligently, or whether he had the capacity to conform to the law under the circumstances. His mental state would be altogether irrelevant. The second stage would arise if it were found that he committed the prohibited act. Now the issue would be to decide what ought to be done with the defendant considering all we know and can find out about him—from psychiatrists, from social workers, or from any other source—including, but not limited to, his mental and emotional state at the time he acted. The choice of the disposition would be governed by whatever is desirable to protect the public from his further criminality, whether what is required be medical or psychiatric treatment, training, a permissive or a rigorous environment, punishment or incarceration. Presumably if the offender did not pose a danger he would be released immediately. If he did, he would be held whether he was a villain or a helpless victim of his own incapacities, and for as long as he continued to pose the danger. Thus, according to Lady Wootton, a forward-looking approach would be substituted for a backward one we now use, a preventive system for a punitive one.

We should note at the outset what implications such a proposal would have for the whole body of substantive criminal law as we know it. Plainly it would not do to leave the criminal law as it is with only the mental element removed, because under our present law (the instances of strict liability apart) *mens rea* is crucial to the description of the behavior we want to prevent. Perjury without knowledge of the lie is simply making an incorrect statement under oath. An unlawful assembly without the intent to do unlawful acts is simply joining a group of people in a public place. An attempt to commit a crime without the intent to do so would be incoherent. It would follow under Lady Wootton's proposal that the substantive law of crimes would ultimately have to be rewritten to consist entirely in the specification of harms, somewhat on the order of the following hypothetical provision dealing with crimes against the person:

"A person commits a crime" (or perhaps "subjects himself to the compulsory régime of social prevention and personal betterment") "who engages in conduct (in the sense only of bodily movements) as a factual consequence of which:

(1) another person's life is lost; or,

(2) another person is physically injured; or

(3) another person's life or physical well-being is imperiled."

Now such a "criminal code" would eliminate many of the perplexities that confront the judge, the practitioner, and the student of the criminal law, but I venture to say that that would be its only redeeming feature. Let me try to indicate why I think this is so.

Presumably I am not allowed to say that the proposal would end up punishing innocent persons, because what is contemplated is the abandonment of punishment and of the significance of guilt and innocence in the criminal law. But what may be said is that the abandonment of the significance of that distinction can be accomplished more easily in legal form than in fact. The compulsory subjection of people to incarceration or other forms of restriction upon their liberty on account of their conduct is viewed by others and by the person as punishment despite all efforts of circumlocution. We have seen this happen in America with the juvenile delinquency laws. "Juvenile delinquency" in a very short time simply became another word for crime committed by youth.

Furthermore, as Professor Hart has observed, people in their own conduct and in relation to others do not view themselves as objects of circumstances but as responsible authors of conduct.[28] What often matters most in relating to others is the motivation and intention of the actors rather than the objective effects of their conduct. It would surely be damaging for the law to run counter to this pervasive human orientation to morality and social life in general.

And even if these basic human outlooks would in time be changed, the consequence would be even more damaging. Much of our commitment to democratic values, to human dignity and self-determination, to the value of the individual, turns on the pivot of a view of man as a responsible agent entitled to be praised or blamed depending upon his free choice of conduct. A view of men "merely as alterable, predictable, curable or manipulatable things"[29] is the foundation of a very different social order indeed. The ancient notion of free will may well in substantial measure be a myth. But even a convinced determinist should reject a governmental regime which is founded on anything less in its system of authoritative disposition of citizens. Whether the concept of man as responsible agent is fact or fancy is a very different question from whether we ought to insist that the government in its coercive dealings with individuals must act on that premise.

It is no answer that under the Wootton proposal *mens rea* would not be eliminated but simply taken into account, albeit with many other factors, after conviction rather than before. What is crucial is that it would cease to be relevant on the issue of guilt or innocence. That is the point at which it functions to distinguish the responsible from the irresponsible, the blameworthy from the blameless. To use *mens rea* simply as additional data in manipulating deviants is no concession at all.

There is also at stake the value of protection against crime. If the effectiveness of crime prevention through general deterrence, operating through the condemnation and conviction of offenders as a means of reinforcing habits and commitments of law abidingness, has never really been proven, neither has it been disproven. Given how little we really yet know of these matters it would be folly to abandon the traditional tools of social protection in favor of complete reliance on a system that works solely through the treatment of the actual offender and sacrifices the deterrrent possibilities of the penal system upon those who might, but have not, offended.

There are objections also on another level. The proposed reconstitution of the criminal law would create insecurity in the general community when the central function of the criminal law is to create that security. The Wootton fallacy is to see only the negative side of the criminal law—the punishment of persons found guilty of criminal conduct. But it is crucial to keep in mind as well the positive side of the criminal law. It not only provides for the punishment of the guilty, it also protects the rest of us against official interference in the conduct of our lives and does so primarily through the much maligned concept of innocence. Where a person has behaved as well as a human being can behave, the requirement of *mens rea,* in its special sense, protects him. To abandon *mens rea* and to substitute a Wootton code—in which, as I tried to show, the occurrence of the harm as a purely factual consequence of a person's physical movements suffices for conviction—removes this essential safeguard. Even the best of us may be swept into the net, for the test of our eligibility for sanctions is not our responsible acts and the consequences for which we may fairly be held responsible, but sheer accident; and accident, by definition, may befall us all. Nor is it any comfort that we will no longer be exposed to condemnation and punishment as such. Whatever it is called we will be exposed to coercive intervention by the state in our daily lives regardless of our most dutiful efforts to comply with what is required of us. Even if the proposal would more effectively deal with the threat of crime (which, as I said, there is no reason to believe) it would do so by substituting what most of us would consider a greater threat to our security and liberty.

Of course the police and the prosecutors usually would not prosecute and the judges would not convict (or whatever the word would be) and the dispositional authorities would promptly release—when convinced that the person presented no danger. But they would have an unfettered discretion to do so or not in the case of potentially every person in the community. Of so unfettered a discretion we have seen enough even in the way the law is administered under our present system. We do not have to guess at the dangers. We know them. The discretion would constitute an invitation to abusive and discriminatory exercise of authority against the disliked or the unpopular on political or other grounds. To speak only of my own country, ghetto blacks and long-haired hippies are singled out for police and prosecutorial reprisals even under our presently structured criminal law. Consider the rich possibilities for the play of prejudice a Wootton criminal law would provide.

Moreover, feelings of outrage and injustice over great wrongs are human. One may doubt how far a non-punitive law would go in eradicating such feelings. There would be no restriction on the expert dispositional authorities acting vindictively whenever the circumstances of particular crimes enraged them. At least our present criminal law serves in some measure to channel and confine the punitive sentiment.

Even when decisions of the dispositional experts were conscientious and enlightened, those decisions would rest entirely upon judgments of prediction of future behavior, a shaky foundation upon which to rest an entire system in the present imperfect state of our knowledge. The dispositional judgments would be based in addition upon the assumption that we have the ability to alter antisocial proclivities. This is an equally perilous premise in light of the substantial lack of knowledge, techniques, resources, and manpower to effect changes in people along these lines.

Moreover, the natural and logical implications of proposals like those of Lady Wootton would multiply further the evils I have tried to describe. Even if people, like Lady Wootton, stop short of those natural implications it is hard to see why. Why should there by any limit on the duration of the detention of persons brought within the system? The legislative gradations of maximum punishments are, after all, a product of the punishment-blame system and hardly serve the purposes of a preventive-therapeutic one. Why need there be any requirement to await some outward conduct which produces the harm? Surely it should be enough that experts find the seeds of antisocial behavior in personality tests and family relationships.

In the last analysis, what is entailed in the abolition of *mens rea* and the decline of innocence is only with slight exaggeration the conversion of the status of the entire population into that of persons on release on parole from mental institutions under an indeterminate commitment.[30]

In the criminal law of England and the United States today there are many small-scale enactments of proposals like those of Lady Wootton. We have strict liability in many offenses. Hospital orders in Britain and sexual psychopath laws in the United States, indeterminate sentence laws, and, to some extent, juvenile delinquency laws in the United States all exhibit some features of the Wootton *mens rea* proposal. One would hope that the direction of creative reform would not be to remake the criminal law after the model of these special and largely unsuccessful exceptions to the fundamental criminal law principles, but rather to devise legal principles and mechanisms for subjecting the process of treatment and social prevention to the restraints of law. But this is the subject of another paper.

6
EXCUSING CRIME

In both the criminal law and everyday moral judgments the concept of excuse plays a crucial role. This is because the practice of blaming is intrinsically selective. It cannot survive if all harm-doers are to be blamed, any more than it can if none are. Excuse is one of those central concepts that serve to draw the line between the blameworthy and the blameless and so make a blaming system possible.

In this essay I propose to examine the rationale and functioning of excuses in the legal system and to consider how far the law does and should follow ordinary moral conceptions in its definition of excusing conditions. Part I attempts to locate excuses in the network of rules and principles governing criminal liability, distinguishing them from other grounds of exculpation, such as justification, by their grounding in some disability of the defendant. Part II surveys the excuses allowed by the criminal law, grouping them into three categories of personal disability: involuntariness, reasonable deficiency and irresponsibility. Part III attempts to identify the principles that underlie the law's pattern of excuses, finding them in notions of voluntarism, both literal and metaphoric, that determine when blame is justified in ordinary moral discourse. Part IV then attempts a critical assessment of the legal excuses in each category, in an effort to determine how fully legal excuses conform to the requirements of just blaming, arguing, however, that not all departures from just blaming are necessarily unjustified.

I. EXCUSES AND OTHER DEFENSES

My first task is to locate excuses among the possible grounds of exculpation. This requires that I sketch a kind of map of the terrain of legal defenses, a common move among criminal law theorists looking for the unities in their subject.[1] There are many equally defensible approaches to this task. I offer mine only for its convenience in making the points I want to make.

We must start with the criminal prohibition itself. Roughly speaking, a crime is a description of certain actions in certain circumstances (the *actus reus*), the doing of which with designated mental states (the *mens rea*) is punishable. So, for example, assault is the use of force against a person with the intention to injure him; burglary is breaking and en-

tering a structure with intent to commit a felony; and so on. Sometimes
no mens rea is required; the action or result is enough. These are instances of strict liability. I will say more about them later.

Then there are the various grounds of exculpation. One ground is
simply that the person didn't do the acts constituting the crime, or didn't
act with the required mens rea. For example, "I didn't point the gun";
or "I did, but I had no intention of shooting it". We may speak of this
ground of exculpation as failure of the *prima facie* case. Another category
of exculpation is different. Here although I do not deny doing the action
prohibited, I claim I may not be punished even so because I have grounds
for exculpation. These grounds of exculpation I will refer to as defenses.

There are two kinds of defenses of this character. The first kind is
not grounded on notions of moral guilt or innocence, but rather on
policies of law enforcement—that the statute of limitations has run, that
the police obtained the evidence to be used against me by unlawful
methods. We may put this kind of defense aside. The other kind of
defense constitutes a claim of personal innocence, which I may assert
on one of two possible grounds.

One ground is justification. My claim here is that I did nothing
wrong even though I violated the prohibition. This is so, I argue, because
the crime's definition of the forbidden conduct was incomplete. The law
allows what the crime as defined prohibits where circumstances, specified
elsewhere in the law, make my action the right thing to do: I killed, but
only to keep an assailant from killing me or another; I entered another's
cabin in the wilderness, but only to obtain food and water to keep myself
alive.

The other ground for asserting my innocence is excuse. Here again,
I deny my culpability even while admitting the criminal harm, but not,
as before, because I did the right thing after all, but because some
disability in my freedom to choose the right makes it inappropriate to
punish me.

II. LEGAL EXCUSES DESCRIBED

The disabilities of choice that ground excuse in our law seem to fall into
one of three groups, depending on the particular disability of which
they take account.

A. INVOLUNTARY ACTIONS

The first group of excuses includes situations in which in the most literal
sense the person had no control over his bodily movements. Cases of
physical compulsion are obvious examples. Others are tumbling down-

stairs or being pushed. These are easy to deal with because we can see the external force being applied. But the law recognizes some excuses as belonging to this category even when the source of the lack of control is internal, as in the case of reflex movements or epileptic seizures.

If involuntariness is the touchstone or excuse, then literal involuntariness, of course, represents the paradigm case of excuse. But such extreme instances of involuntariness may also be viewed as raising a bar to liability more fundamental even than excuse; namely, that there is no *action* at all, only bodily movement, so that there is nothing to excuse. Under this view, which represents the conventional characterization of the involuntary act defense, the defense comes to an "I-didn't-do-it" defense, a failure of the prima facie case.

Thus, there are two ways to classify cases of physical compulsion or involuntariness. On the one hand, these cases can be interpreted as exculpatory because there was no *actus reus*, and hence no crime to excuse. This interpretation rests on the distinction between genuine human actions, which are susceptible to praise and blame, and mere events brought about by physical causes which happen to involve a human body. Such events can be harmful or harmless, but they are not human actions and therefore not subject to moral judgment. On the other hand, there is bodily movement in these cases, and it may have done harm. To that extent the involuntary act exculpation is not identical with the failure of the *prima facie* case. When a person denies doing the act the usual interpretation is that he didn't do it, someone else must have. When a person claims the involuntary-act defense he is conceding that his own body made the motion, but denies responsibility for it. Therefore, however we characterize the involuntary act exculpation, whether as a failure of the *prima facie* case or as a defense, the reason it exculpates belongs to the rationale of excuse—the defendant had no choice in the matter.

B. DEFICIENT BUT REASONABLE ACTIONS

In the second group of excusing conditions there is power to choose in a literal sense—nothing prevents the person from making a choice—but the choice is so constrained by circumstances that ordinary law-abiding persons would not have chosen otherwise. The constraining circumstances are of two kinds. In the first, the constraint arises from defect of knowledge; in the second, from defect of will.

1. COGNITIVE DEFICIENCY   The law's excuses based on reasonable lack of knowledge are commonly spoken of as cases of mistake or accident, the same terms that are used in blaming discourse outside the law. But

to constitute an excuse it is not enough that the person lacked knowledge of some relevant feature of his action—his lack of knowledge must itself be excusable, in the sense that it would be reasonable for any person in his situation not to have known.

For example, if I shoot at a firing range target and kill a person sitting behind it, who I have no reason to think is there, I have killed by accident. If I shoot at an object in the forest reasonably thinking it is a game animal, when in fact it is a person dressed in animal costume, I have killed by mistake. In both cases, I had the choice not to shoot at all. But once it is accepted that shooting in the circumstances, as I reasonably took them to be, was a proper action, the accidental or mistaken killing was effectively beyond my control. Aristotle, indeed, for this reason regarded an action taken under mistake as involuntary in the same sense that a compelled action is involuntary.[2]

Explaining accident and mistake as excuses is today somewhat unconventional. Like the involuntary-act defense, accident and mistake are more likely to be viewed as precluding liability not because of excuse, but because the elements of the crime have not been proven, thus resulting in failure of the *prima facie* case. After all, homicidal crimes are defined to require a *mens rea* of at least culpable negligence. Why, then, in my example, isn't reasonable mistake or accident a defense, not because they excuse what otherwise would be a crime, but simply because they negate the required culpable *mens rea*, without which there is no crime to excuse? The answer requires a brief explanation.

Some *mens rea* requirements are essential elements in the definition of the wrong made criminal. Take loitering with criminal intent, or reckless driving. Without the intent in the first case or recklessness in the second, there is only standing around or driving a car. Hence there is nothing to excuse, since we would not want the person to have acted otherwise. This is the case with all crimes whose definition, like that of loitering with intent and reckless driving, does not require occurrence of the ultimate harm the crime seeks to prevent. The concern of such crimes is the danger of further action or events that will produce the ultimate harm. The *mens rea* serves to identify that danger. This is characteristically true of all inchoate crimes, both these explicitly inchoate, like attempt and conspiracy, and those implicitly so, like burglary and larceny.

Other *mens rea* requirements, on the other hand, are excuses in *mens rea* clothing. They are excusing conditions because they serve to deny blame for a harm done. That they are cast in the form of *mens rea* requirements does not change their character. Thus, in my shooting example, my defense would not be put in terms of a formal excuse. It would be that I have not committed culpable homicide because that crime is defined to require that I intentionally or negligently kill, and I have not. Nonetheless, the reasons these particular *mentes reae* are required are the very reasons for excusing conditions—we could not expect a person to have chosen otherwise. This is why accident and mistake are excuses, despite their formal character as definitional *mens rea* requirements. Indeed, before the clarifying analysis of *mens rea* by the Model Penal Code, this was how accident and mistake were traditionally thought of.[3]

2. VOLITIONAL DEFICIENCY   The law's excuses based on defect of will are not as well developed as those based on defect of knowledge. Duress is the best established defense of this kind, and even its status is not free of doubt. Duress is generally established when a person commits a crime under the command of another backed by such threats of physical injury that even a person of reasonable fortitude would have done the same. It is often subject to restrictions; for example, in some jurisdictions it is not available as a defense to major crime, and in some there must be a threat of immediate and serious bodily injury.[4] There is also authority for the view that duress is not available as an excuse at all, but only where the choice to commit the crime is justified as the choice of the lesser evil.[5] Nevertheless, partly due to the influence of the Model Penal Code, duress in some circumstances is generally available as a defense, even when not justified by the lesser-evil principle.

C. IRRESPONSIBILITY

The excuses in my third category, unlike those in the first, do not involve involuntary actions. And unlike those in the second, they do not rest on circumstances which would lead a person of normal capacities to make the choice the defendant make. The grounds for excuse are simply that this particular person could not have been expected to act otherwise than as he did, given his own inadequate capacities for making judgments and exercising choice.

Our law is niggardly with excuses of this kind. The individual's difficulty in complying with the law is a common ground for mitigation, but it is rarely a ground for a total excuse. Infancy and legal insanity are the two excuses of this kind the law allows. And since the juvenile court laws have made the defense of infancy in practice redundant, legal insanity is the only significant defense remaining in this category.[6]

While the basis for excuses in the second category is that the actor has shown himself no different from the rest of us, the basis of the insanity excuse is that he has shown himself *very* different from the rest of us. But how different and in what respects? After all, those who commit atrocious crimes are certainly very different from the rest of us. That fact along scarcely excuses them.

The various competing formulations of legal insanity seek to answer this question. The M'Naghten and Model Penal Code rules are the most common today. Both rely on the concept of mental disease to distinguish the legally irresponsible person from the rest of us. M'Naghten asks whether as a result of mental disease the defendant was unable to know the nature of his act, or that the act was wrong.[7] The Model Penal Code expands M'Naghten to ask as well whether a mental disease prevented the defendant from conforming his conduct to the requirements of the law.[8] However formulated, the defense seeks to identify those who may not be regarded as moral agents, that is, persons not necessarily incapable of choice but incapable of making choices that count as such because of impaired reasoning and judgment. I will say more about the theory of legal insanity later when I attempt to assess the adequacy of the law's excuses.[9]

III. WHY EXCUSES

Why we have excuses is less obvious than why we have other defenses. Let's start with Jeremy Bentham's explanation.[10] He saw the point of excuses to be that they identified situations where conduct is non-deterrable, so that punishment would be so much unnecessary evil. For since only the non-deterrable are excused, withholding punishment offers no comfort to those that are deterrable. The trouble is, as is now widely appreciated, that this doesn't follow, for punishing all, whether or not they happen to be deterrable, closes off the hope that a deterrable offender might otherwise harbor that he could convince a jury he was among the non-deterrable.[11] Moreover, without excuses, prosecutions would be faster and cheaper, convictions more reliable, and the deterrent threat more credible. Indeed, we have in our law a class of offenses, strict liability offenses, that dispenses with *mens rea* requirements on just these grounds. Have we not given up something of value for the increased effectiveness that strict liability arguably provides, something that isn't captured in Bentham's rationale?[12]

Professor Hart, in one of his early essays,[13] offered a different account of excuses. He argued that by confining liability to cases where persons have freely chosen, excuses serve to maximize the effect of a person's choices within the framework of coercive law, thereby furthering the satisfaction people derive in knowing that they can avoid the sanction of the law if they choose.

This account is an improvement over Bentham, inasmuch as Hart gives us a reason why we might want to put up with the loss of deterrence caused by excuses. But does this account capture the full force of a system of excuses? Suppose we preferred the risk of accidentally being victims of law enforcement to the increased risk of being victims of crime.

That would be a plausible choice, particularly for a public in the grip of rising crime rates. Would we then feel there was nothing more problematic in giving up excuses than that we would be trading one kind of satisfaction for another? I think not. Something is missing in this account.

Hart's account focuses on the interests and satisfactions of the great majority of us who never become targets of law enforcement—our security in knowing we will not be punished if we do not choose to break the law. What is missing is an account of the concern for the innocent person who is the object of a criminal prosecution. Hart does refer in this essay to the satisfaction of the lawbreaker in knowing the price he must pay to get what he wants by breaking the law.[14] But it is doubtful that this is a satisfaction the law has any interest in furthering, for the point of the criminal law is surely to keep people from engaging in prohibited conduct, not to give them a choice between complying with the law or suffering punishment.[15] The law's concern is for the person accused who has not made a culpable choice to break the law, not with furthering the interests of persons who would like to.

To blame a person is to express a moral criticism, and if the person's action does not deserve criticism, blaming him is a kind of falsehood and, to the extent the person is injured by being blamed, unjust to him. It is this feature of our everyday moral practices that lies behind the law's excuses. Excuses, then, as Hart himself recognized in a later essay,[16] represent no sentimental compromise with the demands of a moral code; they are, on the contrary, of the essence of a moral code.

It may be argued that though this may be true of excuses in everyday moral judgment, it is not true of the criminal law, because it is not intrinsic to judgments of criminality in our society that they express a moral fault. But this is surely mistaken. Certainly not all criminal conduct is independently immoral. In some cases the law attaches criminal penalties as well to conduct that, apart from its being prohibited, is not immoral.[17] But in either case criminal conviction charges a moral fault—if not the violation of a moral standard embodied in the criminal prohibition, then the fault of doing what the law has forbidden. The same principle that compels excuses in moral criticism also compels them in the criminal law.

Of course, one might escape excuses altogether by withdrawing the element of blame from a finding of criminality. Indeed, there are some—though not so many as a generation ago—who would prefer that the criminal law reject all backward-looking judgments of punishment, blame and responsibility, and concern itself exclusively with identifying and treating those who constitute a social danger.[18] Whether it would be desirable to loosen punishment from its mooring in blame is a large and much discussed question.[19] I will confine myself here to two observations. First, such a dissociation would not likely succeed. People would continue to see state coercion as punishment, notwithstanding official declarations that the state's only interest is the individual's welfare and social protection. Second, it is very doubtful that we should want it to succeed, since blame and punishment give expression to the concept of personal responsibility, which is a central feature of our moral culture.[20]

The three categories of legal excuses that I described in the previous section suggest the common rationale behind excuses in both the law and everyday moral judgments—namely, that justice requires the preclusion of blame where none is deserved. In the first category, the person is not to blame because he has no control over his movements; in the second, because though be breached a legal norm, he acted in circumstances so constraining that most people would have done the same; in the third, because though there is action in breach of a norm in circumstances where most people would *not* have done the same, the person, because of a fundamental deficiency of mind, is not a responsible moral agent.

What principle lies behind these categories of excuse? I find it convenient to develop an answer to this question in the next section in the context of an assessment of legal excuses, but it may be helpful to state it briefly here. I suggest that the underlying principle is that of voluntarism, in two senses, literal and metaphorical. By literal voluntarism I mean the principle that requires choice as a condition of blame—the person must have chosen to do the action and had the capacity to have chosen otherwise. When this is not so there is no basis for attributing fault to the person, who is no less a victim of the event than those who have been injured by it.

This principle expresses the rationale of legal excuses of the first and third categories. This is most obvious in the first, because the very feature that marks these excuses is the absence of choice. But it is also true of the third, because there is here only the outward show of choice; the person's fundamental deficiency of mind makes it inappropriate to count his seeming choices as true choices.

Voluntarism in a metaphorical sense lies behind excuses of the second category. The sense is metaphorical because literally the actor has made a choice. But the choice to do an act that is criminal is nonetheless not blameable because of two considerations: first, he has acted either under ignorance of significant features of the situation or under constraining pressures on his will; and second, those circumstances would have led even a reasonable, normally law-abiding person to act in the same way. This being so his action does not merit blame because it fails to distinguish him from the common run of humankind. It may be said in these cases that the person had no *effective* choice or that no reasonable and upright person *could* have done otherwise.[21] But as I said, these usages are only metaphorically, not literally accurate.

IV. LEGAL EXCUSES ASSESSED

So much for the sketch of the excusing conditions in our law and what seems to lie behind them. But what shall we say of the excuses the law does not allow? Is our legal system too ungenerous with excuses? Are there excuses good in morals that should be, but are not good in law? Is the law always at fault in imposing blame where it is unjust to do so? These questions are the agenda for the remainder of my discussion of excuses. I will deal with the three categories of legal excuses in turn.

A. INVOLUNTARY ACTIONS

Legal excuses of the first kind, involuntary actions, generally parallel moral excuses. A problem arises only when one asks whether this category can fairly be limited to movements produced by external physical force and internal physiological reactions, or whether it should be extended to include conduct produced by psychological forces, like addiction, that seem to make resistance hopeless, or very difficult. I will return to this issue when I reach the subject of addiction in my last category.

B. DEFICIENT BUT REASONABLE ACTIONS

In the second class of excuses—those based on some deficiency of cognition or volition that is the common lot of humankind—we find significant gaps between what is legally and morally excusable. I will deal first with excuses based on lack of knowledge.

1. COGNITIVE DEFICIENCY—STRICT LIABILITY   Strict liability imposes guilt without regard to whether the defendant knew or could reasonably have known some relevant feature of the situation. The defendant does an act which, judged from his or her perspective, is blameless: she drove a car; she rented her home in another city;[22] he presided over a pharmaceutical company that bought packaged drugs and cosmetics and reshipped them under its own label.[23] But, unknown to each of these defendants, and not reasonably knowable by anyone in the circumstances, the facts were otherwise. The driver could not see a stop sign at the intersection, because it was obscured by a bush. The home owner's otherwise respectable tenants decided to throw a marijuana party. The drugs and cosmetics the defendant's company reshipped were mislabeled by the manufacturer and there was nothing the defendant could practically have done about it. These circumstances would surely be a defense to a charge of moral fault and usually, under the requirement of *mena rea* or the doctrine of reasonable mistake, they would be a legal defense as well. But in the three cases I described many jurisdictions would

disallow the excuse of reasonable mistake because, it would be explained, these are instances of strict liability. If a principle is at work here, it is the principle of tough luck.

Another gap is created by the rule that ignorance of the law is no excuse. This rule presents no problem where the law embodies a moral wrong. There is usually little injustice in the law turning a deaf ear to a defendant who claims that he didn't know it was against the law to mug a stranger or steal from his employer's till.[24] It is another matter to deny a defense to a defendant, engaged in an otherwise lawful activity, who claims unawareness of one of the numerous regulations governing the conduct of his business. If no reasonable person in the defendant's situation could be expected to know of the existence of the regulation (a big if, but still an if), he could not be morally faulted and neither, it would seem, should he be legally blamed. Yet, with few exceptions, the law gives the same answer: in the Latin the law often uses for lofty sentiments, *Ignorantia legis neminem excusat*. Or, in not very lofty English, tough luck again.

The injustice of blaming a person despite reasonable mistake or reasonable ignorance of the law does not derive from the principle of voluntariness in its literal sense. In these cases, unlike the cases of involuntary actions, the person's capacity to exercise choice is intact—literally he does choose to do what he does. And the fact that reasonable persons in his situation would have been as ignorant of the relevant facts or law as he was does not itself necessarily demonstrate a lack of opportunity to choose, rendering his act involuntary in the Aristotelian sense. This is because it is always (or, at least, usually) theoretically possible for him to have found out. This is the point sometimes made in defense of strict liability. So it has been argued, for example, that though a person may have acted in altogether reasonable ignorance of the factual circumstances or law that made his action criminal, nothing compelled her in the first place to engage in the activity during which she faultlessly committed the harmful action. She could have chosen another line of activity, and might well have if, as is often the case, she was aware that the general line of activity, like the food and drug industry, for example, was subject to a myriad of strict liability regulations.[25]

The reason this argument is inadequate is that the source of the injustice is not the violation of the voluntarism principle in its literal sense, but that the person did nothing meriting blame in originally venturing into the general line of activity.[26] Driving a car, letting a premises, running a drug packaging business, to recur to the examples just given, are lawful and socially useful activities; they are unlike leaguing oneself with a criminal group, for example. Engaging in these activities, therefore, cannot justly serve as a basis for blame. The defendant did only what it was reasonable to do. Later she did something harmful, but only in virtue of circumstances even a thoroughly reasonable person would have been ignorant of. We may say that holding her liable in these circumstances would violate the voluntarism principle, but only in the sense that the opportunity to know, which otherwise would make her choice voluntary, is not one we regard as genuinely open, because it is right and reasonable for her not to act on it.

In strict liability and conventional ignorance-of-law doctrine, therefore, there is a gap between legal and moral blaming. Can it be justified? The usual attempt to do so rests on the need to protect the public interest, which would be imperiled by allowing the normal excuse. In defense of the doctrine that ignorance of law does not excuse, Holmes wrote:

> It is no doubt true that there are many cases in which the criminal could not have known that he was breaking the law, but to admit the excuse at all would be to encourage ignorance where the law-maker has determined to make men know and obey, and justice to the individual is rightly outweighed by the larger interests on the other side of the scale.[27]

The defense of strict liability runs along similar lines. So Justice Frankfurter, upholding the conviction of the pharmaceutical company president in the drug mislabelling case I referred to, echoed the views of Holmes:

> [Strict liability] legislation dispenses with the conventional requirements for criminal conduct - awareness of some wrongdoing. In the interest of the larger good it puts the burden of acting at hazard upon a person otherwise innocent but standing in responsible relation to a public danger.[28]

I don't believe these responses are sufficient even on their own terms. It is not at all obvious that eliminating the defenses of non-culpable mistake is necessary for social protection. Other legal systems allow the defenses and seem to get along well enough.[29] Moreover, there are other ways to improve enforcement. One is to shift the burden of proving reasonable mistake to the defendant.[30] Another is to impose criminal liability for negligence in failing to be aware of the law or of the danger.[31] A third is to permit only civil sanctions.[32] These arguments are well known and well taken.

2. JUSTIFYING DEPARTURES FROM THE BLAME PRINCIPLE   But this is a natural place to raise a question that has more theoretical interest and that has to be addressed in an enterprise like this which attempts to assess legal blaming by the measure of moral blaming. Suppose these arguments were not right, that compromising the principle of blameworthiness was actually necessary to maintain a credible level of law enforcement. If this were the case, could punishment possibly be morally justified?

There are those who seem to say no, on the ground that no social gain can justify an injustice to an individual.[33] Again in lofty Latin, *Fiat justitia ruat coelum.* This response is appealing in many ways. It has the virtue of clarity and simplicity. All we need know to do the right thing is that some injustice will be done to an individual. But I doubt that the absolutism of this position is a part of our common intuitions of what morality requires.

Surely an individual's claim to a right not to be blamed in the absence of fault carries great weight, quite apart from its social uses. But it does not follow that this claim must prevail in all circumstances and whatever the costs. On one level, the very existence of a system of formal blame and punishment entails some compromise, since that system requires the establishment of the factual grounds for blaming. We know that a system of this kind will probably result in punishing some innocent people because of the inevitability of error. We can adopt procedures designed to minimize punishing the innocent, such as the requirement of proof beyond a reasonable doubt. But we know this will only reduce error, not preclude it, and we know that we could, if we chose, reduce the chance of error still further, by, for example, requiring proof beyond a doubt, always allowing retrial where further evidence is adduced, and so on. We don't because we think it necessary and right to accept some compromise with a commitment not to punish the innocent in the interest of the practical needs of a functioning criminal justice system.

Similar considerations govern the formulation of the substantive law of excuses. The criminal law, in contrast to social mores, must serve as a clear, explicit guide to lawful conduct. It must also discourage the belief that a "loophole" can always be found to escape prosecution. Further, it must be suited to fair and uniform application, and restrain as much as possible the biases of individual judges and jurors. Hence, instead of permitting any excuse that the court deems relevant, the law defines the elements of available excuses. It is the nature of such definitions that they cannot always accommodate subtle moral distinctions or novel situations. For these reasons the law sacrifices complete accord between moral and legal excuses.

Suppose that under a strict liability rule, the total amount of injustice would be slight, because it will be rare that an individual will have a good excuse for not knowing the law or for being unaware of some relevant factual feature of his action. Suppose also that the penalty is slight (a fine rather than imprisonment), and that a great deal is riding on compliance (e.g., the safety of foods and drugs). I suggest that in these circumstances there is a reasonable argument that disallowing the excuse would not merely be the practical thing to do, it would be the right thing to do as well.

The argument is that though justice to the individual has great and usually determinative weight, it need not not have absolute weight. We would expect John Stuart Mill, as a utilitarian theorist, to hold this view.[34]

But one need not wholly embrace utilitarianism to conclude, as Professor Feinberg has, that a "practice can be right even though to some extent unjust, and that we can sometimes be justified, all things considered, in treating some persons to some extent unjustly."[35] This represents a general moral intuition and a common ground for practical judgment. In this view, justice is regarded as one among other *prima facie* social values. As such it must be weighed against such other values as social peace and security, or the indispensable practical requirements of administering a system of law. While justice is a fundamental value, and hence usually paramount, it may on occasion be outweighed by these other values. What is right is what is right all things considered. This position finds support in constitutional adjudication, where even the fundamental guarantees of the Bill of Rights do not stand as absolutes.[36] In short, doing the right thing, all things considered, might justify ("rightify" would better convey the sense) some departure from the requirements of just blaming.

Another reason why justice for the individual is not an absolute is that it can conflict with moral claims of other individuals. Consider, for example, the claim of the law-abiding for some reasonable governmental protection against crime.[37] A legal system so scrupulous that nearly every defendant was acquitted would not only be inefficient and ineffective, it would be unfair to the citizens who rely on it to articulate and enforce standards of conduct. Thus, there are moral, as well as pragmatic, reasons why a perfect correspondence between an individual's moral fault and criminal liability is not an absolute value.

3. VOLITIONAL DEFICIENCY—THE NECESSITY-COERCION PRINCIPLE   I turn now to excuses based on reasonable deficiency of will. Here too there is an apparent gap between excuses allowed by the law and the requirements of just blaming. Professor Fletcher has done much to illuminate this gap,[38] which arises in situations where the law affords no excuse for a defendant's acts even though a person of reasonable, law-abiding capacities and inclinations would have chosen to violate the law. The common law and the law of most states excuse in only one situation of this kind—duress, where the coercive predicament facing the defendant arises from the threats of another; and even then, under the common law and the law of most jurisdictions, the act is excused only when the threat is immediate and the crime is not a homicidal one.[39] But, of course, coercive predicaments capable of breaking the will of persons of average fortitude can arise in other circumstances as well. To take familiar examples, consider the shipwrecked castaways who kill, reasonably concluding there is no other way to survive,[40] or a prisoner who escapes in the reasonable belief that it is the only way to avoid repeated sexual assaults and threats of violence.[41]

Our law, therefore, excuses only in some circumstances where persons of common fortitude would break the law. Even the Model Penal Code, while eliminating the common law restrictions on duress,[42] declined to establish a necessity-coercion defense[43] which would generalize the principle underlying duress,[44] as some foreign and a few American jurisdictions have done.[45]

I conclude, therefore, that the narrow recognition of the necessity-coercion excuse creates a gap between what the law allows and what just blaming requires. But what principle of just blaming is violated? It is not simply the principle that blame may not be imposed in the absence of voluntary choice, not at least without qualification. It is true that the defense of duress is often explained in terms of the threat overpowering the will, rendering the person unable to choose otherwise.[46] But the sense of disability of will present in duress situations is plainly not the same as when we say that a physically or physiologically compelled movement is beyond the control of the person.[47] Why, then, is it unjust to blame a person in this situation? The answer is parallel to the answer I offered in the case of reasonable mistake: in yielding to a threat to which most of us would yield the person has not shown herself to be more blameable than the rest of us. All that distinguishes her is the accident that produced her predicament. As the Model Penal code commentary observes:

> [L]aw is ineffective in the deepest sense, indeed . . . it is hypocritical, if it imposes on the actor who has the misfortune to confront a dilemmatic choice, a standard that his judges are not prepared to affirm that they should and could comply with if their turn to face the problem should arise. Condemnation in such a case is bound to be an ineffective threat; what is, however, more significant is that it is divorced from any moral base and is unjust.[48]

It is not, then that there is literally no choice in these cases, but that there is no effective choice, given the limits of moral fortitude, not just of the defendant, but of humankind generally. In another words, the choice exhibits no defect of character meriting blame.

The law, then departs from the requirements of just blaming by failing to include a general necessity-coercion defense. As with other such departures, however, it is potentially justifiable on an all-things-considered view of rightness. The case would have to be that a general necessity-coercion defense would open nearly every prosecution to the claim that even reasonable and lawful persons would have done the same in defendant's circumstances, and that this burden, with its potential for delay and jury mistakes, is too great for the criminal justice system to bear. Moreover, even when properly applied, the defense might be thought, as in the prison escape cases, to provide too great a weakening of the deterrent discipline of the criminal law.[49] The central issue is whether these considerations warrant condemning people who behave no differently than most of us would in the extraordinary situations in which they find themselves. I am not inclined to think so, but there is little ground for certitude.

4. THE ADEQUACY OF THE REASONABLENESS STANDARD   I turn now to a different challenge to excuses in this second category—not that the standard of common humanity is rejected, but that it is inadequate. The argument is that the standard of what most of us are capable of, or would do, is unjust, because it fails to take into account what the particular defendant was capable of.[50] The argument goes this way. Yes, in the situation in which I acted, the average reasonable person would have done otherwise. But it's not reasonable to expect it of me. So, for example, I raise the defense of duress. Yes, I argue, a person of reasonable fortitude would have stood up to the bully's threat to seek me out one day and bloody my nose if I didn't help him break into a premises. But not me, because I am a coward. I hate the sight of blood, particularly my own. I can't help it. That's the way with cowards. Weak we are, but not criminals.[51]

Or I claim self-defense. I concede that a person lucky enough to have normal judgment and nerves would never have mistaken the gesture of the deceased as the start of a deadly attack. I should have realized. But I didn't. I'm a nervous, fearful, apprehensive person and I always will be. I can't help it. I should be excused.

I fear these examples may not be sufficiently sympathetic. Let me try to do better with an actual case.[52] Defendants are charged with involuntary manslaughter in the death of their infant. Their lawyer argues: Yes, my clients should have realized their child was seriously ill and needed medical attention. It would have been obvious to you or me, but my clients are not like us. They are Native Americans, living on a reservation, with little formal education and little acquaintance with modern medicine. They loved the baby, staying up with it night after night trying to comfort it. They were crushed by its death. But they never realized how badly the baby needed medical attention. They thought it was only a toothache. If only they had known. Most people would have. But they didn't. They should be excused.

One response to these claims might be the all-things-considered view of what is right; namely, that allowing defects of self-discipline and judgment to excuse would cut too wide a swath through the criminal law, which has to coerce people of all degrees of capacities and varieties of inclination to conform. Indeed, this is the usual defense of the objective standard—the standard of what can be expected of reasonable persons—that our law imposes on excusing conditions.[53] But I want to take a different tack. I want to argue that in these cases the law does not commit injustice in imposing blame.

The first point to be made is that in applying its objective standard the law does not abstract all of the circumstances in which the defendant acted. To some extent it does individualize. A relevant physical defect of the defendant, that he was blind or deaf, for example, surely would be seen as part of the circumstances in which we imagine the ordinary person to be acting when the law asks what his or her response would be. So would some less obvious features of the actor's situation. Suppose in my duress case the defendant were in such poor health that the threat of a bloody nose took on more than its usual significance; or in the mistaken self-defense case, suppose that the defendant had recently received anonymous threats. These circumstances, presumably, would be seen as a part of the situation facing our reasonable person when we consider how he would act.[54]

Now the line is hazy between those special circumstances that are relevant and those that are not, but surely it is a very different thing to individualize completely. For that would be to abandon altogether the very point of excusing in the second category of excuses I have described. What could be expected of the ordinary run of individuals would be irrelevant. All that would count would be the behavior of this very person. But what, then, could be the reason for excusing him? That he is the kind of person he is? That, in duress case, the defendant is unnaturally cowardly? That, in the mistaken self-defense case, the defendant is unnaturally apprehensive? These are most peculiar excuses. Presumably to say that a person is cowardly, or apprehensive, or whatever, is to say that his actions tend to be deficient in certain ways. It is certainly not to say that the person has no choice but to act in those ways. That he has once again acted in this way is the very ground for blaming him. It could hardly serve as an excuse. Such defenses are not accorded in moral judgments any more than in legal ones.[55]

Nonetheless there is a case for considering the deficiencies of the particular defendant in one circumstance: where negligence is the basis of liability. So, for example, Professor Hart has argued that while punishing for negligence may justly rest on an objective standard (which he prefers to describe as an invariant standard of care) the law is obliged in justice to adopt an individualized condition of liability.[56] That is, while it is not necessary to show that the defendant was aware of the objectively unreasonable risk her action created to justify blaming her, it is necessary to show that she could have been aware and could have taken the necessary precautions. Only if this is so do we avoid the injustice of holding liable "unfortunate individuals who, through lack of intelligence, powers of concentration or memory, or through clumsiness," could not have acted in conformity with the required standard.[57]

This is an appealing argument. The case of the backward parents who failed to realize their child's need for medical attention vividly illustrates its force. Nonetheless, Hart's argument cannot easily escape the objection I just raised to a requirement of a completely individualized standard in all situations. If we excuse parents for ignorance of the medical needs of their child on the ground that they are ignorant people, must we not also excuse a person for yielding to a trivial threat of future harm on the ground that he is a cowardly person? If it is a defense to crimes of negligence that the defendant couldn't have known and taken care (because that's the kind of person he is) why would it not also be a defense to crimes of intention that the defendant couldn't help choosing to act as he did because that's the kind of person *he* is—aggressive, self-centered, brutal and so on?

If this objection is to be met it must be by distinguishing between incapacities of cognition and incapacities of volition. An argument for such a distinction would be the following. We can accept that some people can't help being deficient in intelligence, power of concentration, or memory, and that this, even with all the good will in the world, may keep them from being able to advert to a danger others would attend to. To excuse such people for actions they could not have helped does not seriously erode the concept of blame. On the other hand, we do not accept that otherwise normal people who are uncompelled cannot control their intentional actions. That would be incompatible with the way we view human actions. That the defendant is the kind of person who has yielded to his anti-social inclinations in the past does not show him to be incapable of resisting on this occasion. To hold otherwise would undermine the practice of blaming altogether, in common moral discourse as well as in law.

This distinction, then, would lead to the conclusion that the law commits no injustice by refusing excuses of incapacity for intentional crimes, but that it is a condition of just liability for unintentional crimes that the capacity of this defendant to have known and done otherwise be open to inquiry in every case. But before too quickly judging the law deficient in not allowing such a defense to unintentional crimes, we should understand the practical difficulties in administering it.

For example, in the infant neglect case, how could it be shown that the parents were unable to know enough to call a doctor? They didn't, this time. But in the actual case, they did some months before. And they knew their baby was sick. No doubt they didn't appreciate how sick the baby was. But what does it mean to say they couldn't have? Would the excuse simply function as a message to the jury to acquit in any case of criminal negligence when they sympathize enough with the defendants? And could the excuse be confined to sympathetic cases like the infant neglect case? Consider the case of unreasonably mistaken self-defense I put earlier. Would we be obliged to allow as an excuse that the defendant's abnormal fearfulness (which he would show, presumably, by a long record of such behavior) disabled him from discriminating a hostile gesture from a friendly wave?[58] We might want to say that such a defect of judgment in deciding to shoot and kill someone is blameworthy. But could it be distinguished from the infant neglect case? Isn't deficient judgment in appraising reality at issue in both cases?

These kinds of practical difficulties were no doubt in the minds of the Model Penal Code framers when they concluded that "the heredity, intelligence or temperament of the actor would not be held material in judging negligence."[59] Further, these practical problems reveal that the moral distinction between ability to know and ability to will is not entirely clear. Someone's purposes and concerns can influence how he develops and uses his cognitive abilities, and how hard he tries to overcome his intellectual shortcomings. In this sense, his intentions may be relevant even in unintentional crimes. In view of both the practical and moral complexities raised by an excuse of incapacity to know better, it is understandable that our law does not recognize it.

C. IRRESPONSIBILITY

This brings us to the last category of excuses, cases of irresponsibility, represented primarily by the defense of legal insanity. To assess the justification for and the adequacy of the excuse of legal insanity it is necessary to explicate further the principle of justice that lies behind it.

1. A RATIONALE OF IRRESPONSIBILITY   The modern tests of legal insanity are varied and controversial, but they all rest on the view that the claim of incapacity to comply with the law—because of defects of understanding or self-control[60]—is an excuse only if it is the result of a mental disease. Here, then, it is precisely the individual's personal incapacities that serve as the basis of the excuse, whereas, in other cases, saving cases of physical and physiological compulsion, the law declines to permit individualized inquiries into the capacities of the defendant. Why should the presence of mental disease make all this difference?

One answer is a wholly practical one. We can't allow personal incapacity as an excuse generally without unduly compromising the deterrent effectiveness of the law. Proof would be too speculative and uncertain, acquittals would be invited based on the jury's subjective attitudes toward the defendant, there would be too great a chance of erroneous acquittals, and less incentive would be given potential violators to make every effort to comply. Narrowing the excuse to those who can be identified as having a mental disease, through the testimony of the medical profession, helps to meet those practical concerns. There is support for this explanation in the efforts, from time to time, and certainly these times, to limit or abolish the defense precisely on the ground that the requirement of a mental disease is inadequate to meet these concerns.[61]

Without denying that this practical explanation plays a part, I suggest it is not the heart of the matter. The explanation seems to accept that the reason for disallowing an unqualified defense that the defendant could not understand or control his conduct is wholly a matter of expediency. But neither in moral judgments nor in legal ones do we ask of a person who wrongs another whether he could have helped choosing to do so. Being responsible for our characters means that we are responsible for our choices, even if in some sense they have their causes like any other events in the world.[62]

What, then, is different about a person whose disabilities result from mental disease? The answer, I believe, is that the concept of mental disease serves to identify such a breakdown of the normal, human capacities of judgment and practical reason that the afflicted person cannot fairly be held liable. That concept, it should be emphasized, is not synonymous with the varieties of mental illness identified for therapeutic purposes. Categories developed with regard to whether and how a person can be helped by psychiatry are not designed to determine whether a person may be justly punished. They have some, but only evidentiary relevance to the questions of judgment and moral responsibility, which are the law's concern.

Though the prevailing tests of legal insanity speak in one way or another of inability of the defendant (because of mental disease) to know the nature of wrongfulness of his action or (sometimes) to choose to comply with the law, it is apparent that "know" and "choose" in these tests mean more than what those terms signify in casual discourse. Many defendants acquitted on grounds of legal insanity, particularly those with psychoses, "knew" what they were doing and "meant" to do it, taken in a literal sense.

Consider the situation in a famous California case, *People v. Wolff*:[63] A schizophrenic teenager after previous failed attempts killed his mother with an axe, because he saw her as an obstacle to fulfilling bizarre sexual fantasies. He kept a list of seven girls he had not met whom he planned to chloroform and kidnap and bring back to his home where he would rape them and photograph them nude. In such a case, surely the defendant knows well enough what he is doing and acts with deliberate choice. But he may nonetheless be excused if his disease of the mind has so far impaired his rationality that he has ceased to be a moral agent.[64] As Professor Moore puts it:

> [S]everely diminished rationality preclude[s] responsibility . . . because our notions of who is eligible to be held morally responsible depend on our ability to make out rather regularly practical syllogisms for actions. One is a moral agent only if one is a rational agent. Only if we can see another being as one who acts to achieve some rational end in light of some rational beliefs will we understand him in the same fun-

damental way that we understand ourselves and our fellow persons in everyday life. We regard as moral agents only those beings we can understand in this way.[65]

Seen in this way it is apparent why the excuse of legal insanity is fundamental. No blaming system would be coherent if it imposed blame without regard to moral agency. We may become angry with an object or an animal that thwarts us, but we can't blame it.

Of course, being beyond the reach of moral responsibility, not being a moral agent, is not the same as being non-human. The acts of insane people are usually ambiguous between deliberate actions and pointless, unreasoned behavior; they are not mere events, like rocks falling. Insane people are *just* beyond responsibility, and that is why they are so disturbing. Nevertheless, blaming them commits an anomaly (we would say "injustice" as applied to people) similar to that entailed in blaming a rock for falling or a dog for barking.

This, then, explains the distinctive and fundamental character of the defense of legal insanity. It also explains the central objection to recently reviewed proposals to abolish the defense[66]—to do so would open a dramatic gap between moral and legal requirements of blaming. Whether abolishing the defense could nonetheless be justified by an "all-things-considered" view of what is right[67] is another question, though, for reasons that are beyond the purview of these comments, I doubt that the case can be made.[68]

2. VOLITIONAL DISABILITY   I have so far discussed the moral significance of the legal insanity defense without attending to its proper formulation, just as I have with respect to the other excuse defenses. But one long-standing and basic issue in defining the defense has received considerable attention as part of the current reassessment of the defense and therefore merits comment. This is whether the insanity defense should extend to cases where a mental disease has impaired a person's ability to control his conduct, as well as to cases where it has impaired his cognitive abilities.

One reason not to extend legal insanity to cases of volitional disability is the practical difficulty of administering an insanity defense so extended. It has been urged with force that there is no way objectively to establish that a person could not refrain from a criminal action, rather than would not,[69] and that therefore such a test "involves an unacceptable risk of abuse and mistake."[70] Those considerations may justify eliminating that feature of the defense, particularly if most cases of substantial volitional impairment are accompanied by cognitive impairment sufficient to establish a defense.[71] They do not, however, settle the question I am most concerned with here; namely, whether legal insanity would have to include a volitional disability feature in order to meet the moral requirement of blaming.

This question involves the defensibility of treating cognitive and volitional disabilities differently for the purpose of assessing blame. I considered this issue earlier in connection with Professor Hart's argument for an individualized standard of negligence.[72] He argued, it will be recalled, that the requirements of just blaming compel allowing an inquiry in each case into the cognitive capacity of the defendant. I concluded that this argument could not succeed without making the case for treating negligent and intentional conduct differently. While just blaming might require proof of the defendant's capacity to know, it could not require proof of his capacity to have intended other than he did without seriously threatening the whole concept of moral blame.

In the context of the legal insanity defense we again face the cogency of this distinction between cognitive and volitional capacity. In defining legal insanity are we equally constrained to disallow inquiry into the capacity of the person to control his intentional, uncompelled conduct? There is perhaps some support for an affirmative answer in the traditional formulation of the insanity defense, still vigorously defended in some quarters, which allows inquiry into the ability of the defendant to know what he was doing, but not into his ability to do other than what he chose to do. But there is ground to believe that for purposes of defining legal insanity an inquiry into volitional capacity has a special claim.

The idea that a normal actor, who commits a crime intentionally and under no physical or physiological compulsion, might have been unable to choose to act otherwise threatens to undermine blame at its foundation.[73] But the notion is less threatening as applied to those suffering from a mental disease,[74] not simply in the sense of a medically recognized psychological disorder, but as reflecting the common sense moral judgment that the person lacks the minimal capacities for rational action required to be a subject of moral agency.[75]

It seems apparent that distorted reality perceptions are not the only ground on which we may come to such a judgment. Bizarre, senseless and unintelligible motivations may manifest lack of moral agency even where the person is literally aware of what he is doing. The teenage schizophrenic in the *Wolff* case is an example.[76] Lack of the minimal capacity for rational action required for moral agency may be manifested not only by the inability to know the nature and wrongfulness of one's actions, but also by the performance of knowing and intentional actions that are motivated by bizarre and unintelligible purposes.[77]

In this sense volitional incapacity is a morally relevant element of a concept of legal insanity. I should want to distinguish it, however, from a different sense of volitional incapacity that is not grounded on the standard of general capacity to be a moral agent, but on the moral literal notion of a "psychic" compulsion, a desire so strong and urgent that the person is unable to resist it. Here is where the greatest difficulties lie in determining whether a person was unable to resist or simply did not resist, and, indeed, in even knowing what the distinction could mean. A jury can judge whether a person was physically compelled by another or physiologically compelled by a reflex. But (putting drug addiction aside for the moment) how can a jury distinguish between a psychic compulsion and a strong desire that the person lacks the character to resist? Indeed, how is the psychiatrist to know? Using Greek nouns to describe repetitive stealing or fire setting is hardly an explanation. I do not believe that the proper ground of excuse in these cases is the person's inability to choose not to steal or not to set fires. Such persons choose not to do such acts on many occasions. Nor in *Wolff* was it that the young man was unable to choose not to kill his mother. Indeed, he held back on an earlier occasion when it appeared too risky. The ground of excuse is not inability to choose, but rather the senseless and absurd character of the behavior—its bizarre repetitiveness in the first case, its wildly unrealistic motivation in the second. In other words, it is not that the defendant is not capable of choosing, but that his choosing is so irrational that he manifests a lack of moral agency.

3. EXPANSION OF IRRESPONSIBILITY—SOCIAL DEPRIVATION AND ADDIC- TION   I have so far tried to make the case for the fundamental impor- tance of the defense of legal insanity and against proposals to eliminate it. I turn now to arguments that take the opposite view: not that the defense should be abolished, but that the concept of legal irresponsibility must be expanded beyond legal insanity if legal and moral blame are to be brought into line.

One such proposal is to establish a defense of social deprivation.[78] The argument proceeds this way: If the law recognizes that mental disease can have the effect of so far interfering with the capacity of the defendant to conform that he is excused, why should it not recognize other influences that have the same effect? Consider a defendant who has, from birth, led a life of grinding poverty and deprivation, who suffered from defective parenting and little family support, who spent his childhood and youth mostly in the streets under the tutelage of older youngsters similarly situated, and who, naturally enough, turned to crime. This demonstrably criminogenic background, it is argued, itself should serve as the basis for an excuse, without a need to show that this history of cultural deprivation produced a mental disease. In short, a defendant who has been subjected to such a life may have as little effective control over his conduct as one with a mental disease.

Courts have resisted this line of argument,[79] and I think with good reason. One strong argument is practical. The defense would be difficult to administer, it would weaken the law's deterrent effect, and, once recognized, it would be hard to justify punishing anyone, for even evil has its causal roots somewhere. But I am here concerned with the defense as a matter of principle, that is, whether the principle of just blaming requires it.

Social deprivation may well establish a credible explanation of how the defendant has come to have the character he has. But it not does establish a moral excuse any more than a legal one, for there is a difference between explaining a person's wrongful behavior and explaining it away. Explanations are not excuses if they merely explain how the defendant came to have the character of someone who could do such a thing. If it were otherwise, there would be no basis for moral responsibility in any case where we knew enough about a person to understand him. And that would mean every case, because ignorance about a person could hardly stand as a justification for blaming him.[80]

The reason the argument fails to make out a moral excuse, as insanity does, is that it fails to establish the breakdown of rationality and judgment that is incompatible with moral agency. It may be conceded that cultural deprivation contributed to making the defendant what he is (though, of course, only some so brought up end up committing crimes). But what is he? He is a person with wrong values and inclinations, not a human being whose powers of judgment and rational actions have been so destroyed that he must be dealt with like an infant, a machine, or an animal. Those who propose this defense are plainly moved by compassion for the downtrodden, to whom, however, it is nonetheless an insult.[81]

The strongest case for the social deprivation defense is that a state which fosters or tolerates such deprivation forfeits its right to condemn its victims. But the question, "Who has the legitimate authority to judge and punish?" is a different question from, "Who should be blamed for individual crimes?" The social deprivation defense may be a fair vehicle for accusing the society responsible for the deprivation. But it is not a ground for excusing the deprived defendant, because by itself it fails to establish the defendant's lack of responsibility.

Other proposals to expand the concept of legal irresponsibility are tied to special conditions which, it is argued, substantially impair the capacity of the person to conform in certain ways. On this basis narcotics addiction has been urged as a defense to narcotics crimes,[82] and even to other crimes driven by the need to support the addiction;[83] chronic alcoholism has been raised as a defense to crimes involving public drunkenness;[84] and compulsive gambling has been raised as a defense to theft offenses.[85] Very rarely have courts been receptive.[86]

Courts have chiefly emphasized the threat to the social control functions of the criminal law that allowing these defenses would pose.[87] This is plausible enough, considering that drugs and alcohol figure prominently in the commission of many of the crimes the public most fears. Perhaps these concerns justify departing from the requirement of moral blame, as I said earlier. But the issue that concerns me here is whether denial of the excuse in those cases is indeed a violation of those requirements.

It has been argued that the principles of responsibility and blame underlying the legal insanity defense require a legal defense of addiction.[88] One defense of this view is that the crimes of an addict are symptoms of sickness and therefore require treatment, not punishment.[89] But this is surely a *non sequitur*. To find that criminal conduct is causally related to persistent patterns of behavior which are to some extent medically treatable (for this is what sickness here presumably connotes) does not establish that punishment is unjust. Being "sick" in this sense does not mean or imply that the person is irresponsible and not morally culpable.[90] Just as a psychiatric diagnosis of mental illness does not itself establish a defense of legal insanity, so a diagnosis of addiction does not establish that the addict is not responsible for his actions. The concept of disease of the mind as it functions in the insanity defense does not simply represent a medical treatment category. As I said before, it is rather a judgment that the person suffers from such a persistent distortion of his powers of judgment and practical reasoning that he lacks moral agency.

It is hard to see how addiction could qualify as a disease of the mind in the sense of negating moral agency. There is nothing irrational in the conduct of a person who engages in addictive behavior. Distortion of reality is not a necessary feature of addiction. Nor is there anything bizarre or unintelligible in the desire to achieve either the gratification the conduct affords (gratification that non-addicted people seek in large numbers, in drink, drugs or gambling) or the avoidance of the negative effects of not gratifying the desire. What distinguishes addiction is that it constitutes a powerful motivation to engage in certain kinds of conduct. The argument for a defense of irresponsibility is better seen, therefore, as a claim that the motivation of the addict goes so far beyond strong temptation, which itself can hardly constitute a full excuse in morals or law, that it must be thought of as utterly overwhelming behavior controls.

The argument that such overwhelming motivation should constitute an excuse could proceed by analogy to two well-established grounds of exculpation—the defense of an involuntary act, and the excuse of duress or, more generally, the necessity-coercion principle.

There is some looseness in the concept of an involuntary act. Even the Model Penal Code eschews a definition and resorts to an enumeration of examples, plus a general reference to other bodily movements that are not "a product of the effort or determination of the actor, either conscious or habitual."[91] But the characteristic actions of an addict could hardly be made to fit. They are movements he chooses to make to achieve his purposes and therefore have nothing in common with falling or being pushed or with reflexive or convulsive movements, or even with sleepwalking or hypnotic movements.[92] There is a substantial difference between those movements and the complex and varied activities involved in obtaining and using alcohol and other drugs. There are enough conscious, purposive actions in the characteristic behavior of addicts (including abstinence when the motivation is great enough) that it cannot possibly be considered involuntary. The same objections apply *a fortiori* to crimes, such as theft, committed to support addiction, which are even less like mere reflexes than crimes of possession and use.

A second possible argument is one which draws support from the principle of duress. Just as a defendant may be excused if he commits a crime under the imminent threat of bodily injury by another, so, it may be argued, should the addict be excused if he commits a crime in order to avoid the acute suffering of withdrawal. While duress is technically distinguishable because it is limited to threats by another person, in principle the excuse can hardly be so contained. Indeed, the defense of necessity-coercion, better recognized in other legal systems than our own, constitutes just such an extension.[93]

Nevertheless, the argument for an addiction defense based on the rationale of the necessity-coercion principle confronts significant difficulties. That principle, it will be recalled, does not excuse simply because the will of the defendant was overwhelmed by pressures he lacked the fortitude to resist.[94] There is always an objective qualification, which requires that in like circumstances a person of reasonable firmness would not have resisted, and that the defendant was not at fault in producing his predicament.[95] The addiction defense fails to meet either requirement.

As to the latter requirement, anyone can suddenly and without fault become the victim of a terrorist's threats. Not so the victim of addiction. Save in the rarest of cases, he must have voluntarily consumed narcotics over a period of time before becoming addicted. Therefore his problem is almost always in some sense of his own making. However powerful the pressures once the person becomes addicted, they were not present in the steps along the way.

Concerning the former requirement, the first difficulty is the same as that just discussed—persons of reasonable firmness do not become addicted. Therefore the standard would have to be construed to refer to the *addicted* person of reasonable firmness. But even if this much concession were made to an individualized standard, there is the further difficulty of demonstrating this standard is met. The evidence makes it appear doubtful that it could be.

The once popular view was that the addict was enslaved to his habit, irresistibly hooked in ways beyond his capacity to alter, and in the thrall of the body-and-soul-wracking experience of withdrawal. Recent reviews of what is known about narcotic addiction tell a different story.[96] The great majority of heroin addicts do not experience extraordinary suffering when they stop using drugs. And even in classic form, withdrawal symptoms seem closer to those of the one-week flu than to the horrors of the popular myth.[97] Further, the distress of withdrawal can be kept relatively moderate and bearable by gradual withdrawal under professional care, which is widely available.[98] Recent data concerning patterns of addiction and withdrawal also refute the bondage myth. Addiction is not an inevitable result of use. There appears to be a sizable population of non-addicted but regular heroin users who succeed in controlling its use and leading normal lives.[99] Nor does addiction appear to be either continuous or permanent. Many addicts succeed in giving up heroin at an early stage and never return to using it.[100] Finally, social and psychological inducements to begin and to continue using narcotics appear to have a large role in accounting for addiction patterns.[101]

Of course, to show that the theory of existing legal excuses does not support an addiction defense does not show that exculpating addicts is not a requirement of moral blame. That theory may be insupportable or wholly a reflection of practical requirements of law enforcement. But I believe neither is the case.

Sometime during the gradual process of conditioning himself to drugs—before the addiction reached its greatest force—the addict could have desisted, but didn't. These early voluntary actions constitute a sufficient predicate for blaming him. There may well be ground for mitigation in a long lapse of time between the voluntary action and the addiction, or in the unawareness of the defendant that his actions would lead to addiction. But this is not to say there are no grounds for blame.

As for the requirement of an objective standard, I have already tried to develop the case for it.[102] A wholly individualized standard would look only to the condition of the defendant-addict before the court. But what would be the question: Could this defendant have resisted committing the crime? But no one compelled him, and he was not incapable of choice. Was it too hard for this defendant to resist in light of his desires and fears? But absent some objective measure of "too hard," what could the measure be? Presumably it would have to be the capacity of this individual to prefer to choose doing the right thing, under varying conditions of temptation and pressure. But this is simply a way of talking about character, and it would lead to the paradoxical result that the worse the person's character the stronger the case for excusing his conduct. We need some standard of responsibility external to the make-up of the person to maintain our practices of blame. The law's objective standard, therefore, has significant roots in the very logic of blaming itself.

I must emphasize that I am speaking only of excuse as a complete negation of blame. Of course there is room for compassion and mitigation based on special elements in the background of the individual. The difference is that compassion and mitigation are not incompatible with blame. Excuse is.

CHAPTER FOUR

JUSTIFICATION

7
RESPECT FOR LIFE AND REGARD FOR RIGHTS IN THE CRIMINAL LAW

Life is a unique kind of good because it is the necessary condition for the enjoyment of all other goods. Therefore, every person by and large tends to value his life preeminently, and any society must place a high value on preserving it. As Professor Hart observed, "our concern is with social arrangements for continued existence, not with those of a suicide club."[1] But while the aim of survival affords "a reason why . . . law and morals should include a specific content,"[2] it obviously does not afford a reason why that content should include placing the survival of every person above all else. For although we value our own lives preeminently, it does not follow that we equally value other people's lives; their lives may conflict with rights we claim or with goods we value, including our own lives. Hence, any society must face the problem of deciding when the life of some should yield to the claims or interests of others.

On the one hand, our society, like all others, has, over the centuries, produced a substantial consensus as to how these issues should be resolved. On the other hand, that consensus tends continually to be shaken by new events and new challenges. So in recent years we have been divided and perplexed by such problems as bombing civilians in war, mass starvation elsewhere in the world, abortion, euthanasia, human medical experimentation, obtaining organs for transplant, and deciding who should be kept alive for how long by life-sustaining devices.

Having stated these issues, however, I shall not mention them again until the end, because my principal subject will be the received consensus itself rather than the current uncertainties about its application. I shall dwell, rather, on those relatively settled judgments and understandings concerning the taking of human life that we seem to have arrived at. My purpose in doing this is to try to get at what it is that lies beneath those judgments and understandings. I undertake this inquiry for its own sake—it will not not solve the hard questions I referred to. Still, insofar as it exposes what we agree on and why, it may, as a by-product, contribute something to the debate on the issues of the day that trouble us.

Where, then, shall we look for those settled understandings? I propose we look to the criminal law insofar as it deals with actions that result or tend to result in loss of life. For in its provisions that direct when life

109

should be taken, when it may be taken justifiably, and when taking it is prohibited and when permitted, we have a body of formulations that have evolved over time through reflective and tested examinations of what we regard as of greater or lesser value and of what we regard as right and what wrong. We have, in short, some kind of map of our sentiments with respect to life to serve as a basis for securing our bearings on where we have come to stand.

Before proceeding to draw that map, let me acknowledge that it cannot be a precise indication of our settled sentiments. One reason is that some problems of justified killing are, as we shall see, not clearly settled in the criminal law. Insofar as we shall have to speculate on what the law would be, we will be compromising with our model of drawing inferences from the settled consensus. Another reason is that there are considerations other than our attitudes toward the wrongness and undesirability of actions that affect how we shape the criminal law. Some conduct that tends to result in loss of life might be judged strongly undesirable and yet be unprohibited by law—either because it cannot be prevented by criminal threat, or, if it can, then in too small a degree in light of the undesirable consequences the attempt at prevention would entail. For similar reasons, some conduct that tends to preserve lives might be judged strongly desirable and yet be uncompelled by the criminal law. We will have to be careful, therefore, in drawing conclusions too hastily from what the criminal law does or does not prohibit, compel or tolerate.

It will be helpful to state at the outset one such instance of a need for caution. I refer to excused actions—those that are relieved of criminal liability out of regard not to a judgment of the nature and quality of the action (which would make them justified, rather than excused), but to the condition of the actor in the circumstances. So we should say of an excused action not that the actor was right to do as he did, but, for one reason or another, that more could not fairly be demanded of him, at least by the criminal law.[3] Although it may not always be clear whether some particular defense (even self-defense, for example) operates as an excuse or a justification, to the extent that it is the former it does not represent the kind of judgment that serves our purposes. The same is true, of course, of homicidal actions that are partially excused, in the sense that a lesser punishment is indicated, for here too the judgment turns on the situation of the actor rather than on the rightness of the action.

I. MAPPING THE RULES OF THE CRIMINAL LAW

In presenting the rules of the criminal law, I will start with actions intended or known to kill.[4] These are actions which are generally prohibited by the criminal law of our own and every legal system, and typically with the severest penalties. The victim's consent to an intended killing is not a defense. Taking one's own life was a felony at the common law. Today it is no longer a crime, although attempted suicide is sometimes criminal and aiding another person to commit suicide virtually always is criminal.

To these primary prohibitions, however, there are exceptions which have a special interest for us because they rest on a judgment that intentional killings in certain circumstances are right actions. These exceptional circumstances include cases in which the person killed is not a wrongdoer as well as those in which he is. The latter are more familiar, and I will start with them.

Capital punishment has been defended even by natural rights philosophers, like Kant and Locke, and has historically been the typical penal response to the most feared or serious crimes. Although its moral legitimacy has been challenged,[5] it is, on the whole, an accepted part of our jurisprudence.[6]

Law enforcement officials may kill in other circumstances as well. At common law, they may kill where reasonably believed necessary to prevent "violent" felonies, even those against property, and to apprehend any felon. Under some modern statutes, reflecting an enhanced regard for the life of the felon, they are limited to killing to prevent crimes that threaten death or serious bodily injury or to prevent the escape of a suspect who is armed or otherwise poses a threat to life if left at large.[7]

Private persons may justifiably take life largely in the same circumstances in which law enforcement officials may, though, unlike such officials, they are never duty-bound to do so. A person is also privileged to kill in an overlapping but more specifically defined class of cases: he may kill an unlawful aggressor where it reasonably appears necessary to avoid either the imminent loss of his life or the imminent infliction of serious bodily injury upon him (which need not necessarily threaten his life, as in the case of kidnapping and forced sexual intercourse). A person may use force to defend his property; but, except to the extent that the threat to his property also constitutes a "violent felony," he may not go so far as to kill. To this exception, however, there are further exceptions. At common law one could kill to prevent being unlawfully dispossessed from one's home or, indeed, to prevent any threat to property occurring through a forcible entry of his dwelling. The latter exception survives in modern statutes as well.

There is division on whether an obligation to run away, when one knows he can safely do so, qualifies the right to kill in defense of one's person. The common law permitted a person to hold his ground, as do most states today. Those that require retreat, however, do not require that one run from his home or place of business.

Killing by a private person in defense of another is today generally allowed in the same circumstances as killing in defense of self. The common law and a few old state statutes restrict this privilege to kill on reasonable appearance of necessity to cases in which the victim stands in a specified close relation to the defender. And some jurisdictions have required the defender in all cases to act at his peril, disallowing the defense if it turns out, contrary to appearances, that the apparent victim was really the aggressor.

Turning now to intentional killings to preserve one's own life or the life of one or more other persons, where the person killed is known *not* to be a culpable aggressor, we reach less certain legal ground. First, consider the case where the actor's choice is to take one innocent life in order to save multiple lives. The Model Penal Code found support in the common law for its proposal that one is generally justified in breaking the law where doing so is the only way to avoid an evil the legal system would regard as greater.[8] Although there is authority that denies the extension of this principle to homicidal conduct, the authors of the Model Penal Code meant it to extend here as well, on the footing that the death of two persons is a greater evil than taking the life of one, and there is authority that supports their view.[9]

Where the actor's choice is to take one innocent life in order to save one other, whether himself or someone else, so that reliance upon a numerical calculus of lives is unavailable, the law may not be stated with confidence. Laws and cases on the issues are scarce or nonexistent, and I will have to speak much more speculatively.

I should think we need to distinguish those cases where the person killed constitutes a part (although an innocent part) of the circumstances imperiling the actor, from those where he is a bystander whose life is conscripted in the service of the actor's or another's survival. The first set of cases, the "innocent threat" cases, are those typically in which the threatener is excused or is otherwise nonpunishable, and is known to be so by the defender. The threatener may at the time be acting under duress,[10] he may be legally insane, or he may be a small child. He may even be committing no "legal" action at all, as when one acts in his sleep or when one's body is used as a physical instrument by another. It is fairly clear that one who kills such a person in these circumstances, when necessary to save himself, is not punishable under Anglo-American law. It is probable, though by no means certain, that his action would be regarded as an instance of justifiable self-defense rather than simply as excusable, and that a third person would be equally justified in intervening on his behalf.[11]

The second set of cases, the "innocent bystander" cases, are those in which one creates a deadly peril to a person uninvolved in one's own peril in order to preserve oneself—seizing another to use as a shield against danger, for example. Here there is no authority for finding a justification.

We have so far spoken of actions intended to kill. But actions may take life even if not so intended. How does the criminal law deal with these? The key concepts are recklessness and negligence. Both denote a significant departure from a minimally acceptable standard of care: in the case of recklessness, in awareness of the risk being created; in the case of negligence, in culpable unawareness of it. Whether conduct will be so regarded, and hence be criminal, turns on whether the risk to life it portends is substantial—it need not be highly probable and whether creating the risk can be justified in terms of the otherwise socially de- sirable consequences of the conduct and the nonexistence of less risky ways of achieving them.[12] Hence, unintentional killing in the course of driving a car is a serious crime if the risk of killing was needlessly in- creased by highly unsafe driving. But though the mere action of driving a car creates a risk of life, the driver will not be criminally responsible for a resulting death simply on that account. This consequentialist as- sessment applies even where the risk to life is very great indeed, as in the case of constructing bridges and tunnels, as well as in that of many other routine and accepted activities of modern life. Here, though loss of a certain number of lives could be predicted in advance with very great statistical probability, there is no criminal liability for consequential deaths. Crime is committed only where the persons engaging in the activity can be shown to have created excessive risks, which were not inherent in such activity.

Risking just one's own life is another matter. Some statutes prohibit specified activities out of a concern for the risk to those who engage in them. But there is not and never has been any general prohibition against a person risking his life, as there once was against his taking it.

The final body of law I shall mention concerns omissions to act, which may, of course, be intentional or unintentional. At the common law one is not criminally obliged to save another's life, no matter how easily he could do so. The principal qualification arises where the law otherwise imposes a duty to act, as in the case of a close relative, or where one has agreed to act, explicitly or implicitly.[13] Specific statutes sometimes make punishable the failure to act to rescue a person in peril where one can do so without danger to himself.[14]

II. ACCOUNTING FOR THE RULES

So much for the map. We are now ready to consider what we can make of it. What underlying principles or patterns of thought can be perceived in this variety of legal rules that prohibit, require, justify, and permit actions that tend to cause death? In the following I will first consider whether and how far the several principles associated with the precept of the sanctity of life can account for the whole of the map of the rules.

I will then consider particular segments of that map and test the explanatory force of a variety of possible theories.

A. AN APPROACH THROUGH GENERAL PRINCIPLES: THE SANCTITY OF LIFE?

It is clear, of course, that we value life very highly. Most intentional killings are punishable with law's most severe sanctions, and even reckless and negligent killings are made criminal. But it is equally clear that we do not give the preservation of life all possible weight. One tradition of thought would give it this weight. I have in mind the sanctity-of-life principle in its strongest sense: the "good and simple moral principle that human life is sacred,"[15] either because it is the gift of God or because of some more general religious commitment, and that it therefore may never be taken by man. One finds these sentiments, for example, in Tolstoy, Schweitzer, and the Buddhist precepts of reverence for life. This absolute view may contribute something to understanding some of our laws, such as the law on suicide and consented killings. But its systematic contradiction by the variety of situations in which the law permits life to be taken and risked suggests that it cannot, at least without qualification, provide an understanding of what is beneath the law.

A variant of this tradition of thought would defend a somewhat weaker version of this principle—namely, that one may never intentionally choose to take the life of another, for whatever end. Thus, cases of justified killing have been accounted for on the ground that they do not constitute intentional killings. This argument has its source in the double-effect principle advanced by Saint Thomas Aquinas and other Catholic theologians. It distinguishes two effects of an action, the one consisting of what the actor intended, either as an end in itself or as a means to some end, and the other consisting of what he foresaw but did not intend in this sense. In all cases where killing is justified, so the argument runs, there is no intentional choice to take life, because the actor does not, strictly speaking, intend the effect of his action to cause death, but is simply aware that his action will have that effect. Thus, when one uses deadly force against an assailant to save one's own life, one's action in causing the death of the assailant is not the *intended* effect, but the *known* effect, of *that* action. The intended effect is to remove the threat and no more. The defender, therefore, is not choosing the death of his attacker as a means of preserving his own life, but is choosing the only means available to counteract the threat, though aware it will result in the assailant's death.[16]

The doctrine of double effect does not provide that knowing killings may not be serious crimes and wrongs, but only that this weaker sense of the sanctity-of-life principle is not necessarily violated when they occur. This weaker version, then, still leaves us uninformed of the *theory* on which killings are justifiable or acceptable when they are not intentional in the strict sense. Beyond that, however, the distinction is so alien to our intuitive common sense as to seem sophistical. For if I shoot a man between the eyes because he is assailing me with upraised dagger, it seems strange to allow me to say I did not choose to take his life, but that I chose only to prevent the attack. Although the former was not a logically necessary condition of the latter, it was actually necessary in the circumstances—or I, at least, acted on that assumption.[17] Only the ghost of an absolute ban on intended killing is left if it excepts such a killing as this. The double-effect doctrine seems to me much like a fiction in the law, serving to preserve appearances for a principle that has lost its sufficiency.

Although one may reject the sanctity-of-life principle in the two senses already discussed, an even weaker sense may still be defended. The principle may be taken to assert not an absolute priority of life or an absolute ban on intentional killing, but a presumption in favor of life and against killing, so that there can be exceptional circumstances in which the value of life is outweighed by other values or in which killing may be justified on other grounds. This explanation indeed is consistent with the rules of the law, but since it leaves us unenlightened as to what those exceptional circumstances are, it does not greatly advance us.

Another and still weaker sense, however, is not only consistent with the law, but is undoubtedly demanded by it. Specifically, this sense entails an aspect of the principle of equality; namely, that all human lives must be regarded as having an equal claim to preservation simply because life itself is an irreducible value. Therefore, the value of the particular life, over and above the value of life itself, may not be taken into account. In this sense the sanctity-of-life principle does not purport to say when life may be taken or risked, but only requires that in making the judgment certain considerations be ruled out. The life of the good man and the bad stand equal, because how a man has led his life may not affect his claim to continued life; the life of the contributing citizen and the dependent or even parasitic one stand equal, because knowing how a man will use his remaining life may not affect his claim; and the life of a child and the life of a nonagenarian stand equal, because it is irrelevant how much life a person has left.[18] In this sense, the principle reflects an important constraint on how we approach judging when life may be taken, which we must have in mind as we undertake to disentangle what lies beneath such judgments.

B. AN APPROACH THROUGH THE PARTICULARS

Let me now change direction in the search for these underlying judgments. Instead of further postulating encompassing principles, I propose to proceed in the tradition of the common law lawyer, who starts with the cases and sees what he can make of them. In this context, that tradition entails considering the particular categories of legal doctrine I put earlier and testing the explanatory force of various possible theories with respect to each.

1. INTENTIONAL KILLINGS OF AGGRESSORS.   I consider first the body of laws justifying the intentional killing of one threatening another. When the choice is between the life of the victim and the life of his assailant, the answer is unambiguous in every legal system: the victim may kill to save his own life.

It might seem plausible to explain the result in terms of excuse, on the view that however much we should prefer people to desist from taking life, even when their own is at risk, the law must take people as they are and no future criminal threat can deter people from acting to meet an immediate threat to their lives. It is very doubtful, however, that this rationale explains Anglo-American law. First, "people as they are" indeed do regard the response as justifiable. Second, the explanation is fatally inconsistent with the accepted rule allowing third parties to kill the aggressor, since they are not similarly unamenable to the threat of criminal punishment. One may argue that the excuse rationale is seen partially at work in the rule of some jurisdictions exculpating third-party killings only in cases of actual as opposed to apparent necessity—except when the third person intervenes on behalf of close relatives where, presumably, deterrence is less workable. But even putting aside that this rule is outmoded and that it was never applicable when the aggressor was committing a felony (which would be true in virtually all cases), what is entailed in this rule is a qualification of the terms on which mistake is available as an excuse (quite possibly out of regard to the enhanced risks of error when a third party intervenes) rather than a judgment that killing the actual aggressor is not justifiable.

Then if such intentional killings are justifiable, on what theory? One possible response is that, on the balance of utilities, it is better—if one person has to die—that it be the attacker rather than his victim. Why is it better? One reason might be that the life of the victim is of greater value than that of the attacker. There are, however, several objections to this explanation. First, it contradicts the equality principle that the lives of all persons must be regarded, as lives, of equal value. Second, the rule is not confined to life-against-life situations. As we have seen, defensive killings are justifiable when the interest protected is other than life: prevention of such crimes as kidnapping or rape or even lesser felonies, even when life is not imperiled; or prevention of crimes against property committed after a breaking into one's dwelling; or prevention of a deadly assault, where the victim can avoid the need to kill by availing himself of a safe retreat. Can the law really be based on a judgment that all such interests are of greater value than a man's life, even a wicked man's? One might reply that the law makes precisely this perverse judgment and that a more enlightened tradition has striven, with some recent success, to confine defensive killings more closely to life-preserving situations. Even conceding this explanation for the moment, one confronts the non-controverted extension of the rule to cases where several lives are balanced against the life of a single victim. Is it clear that the law's premise is that the lives of two attackers, or even 20, are in total of less value than the life of the one victim?[19] For surely the rule allows one attacked to kill all his attackers, however numerous they may be. Finally, we run again into the rule that justifies the killing of innocent threats to life as well as culpable ones. On what grounds can the law conceivably be saying that the value of the life of a mentally deranged attacker or of a small child is of less value than the life of the victim?

But one might try to give a more satisfactory answer to why a calculus of social utilities favors defensive killings. One need not say that the life of the victim is a greater good than the lives of his assailants, innocent or not. One can say simply that permitting the victim or a third party to kill in these cases is, in the long run, "justified as a means to preserving life,"[20] since such action will operate as a sanction against unlawful assaults. Certainly this rationale is plausible, at least if we put aside as perverse legally justified killing in defense of interests other than life.[21] Even so, it seems to me to miss the target. First, it proves too much. For if the deterrent threat of deadly preventive force by the victim or an intervenor explains our justifying such killings, it would also support deadly *retaliative* force after the attack was thwarted; yet, this extension is plainly not justified under the law. Second, the deterrence rationale proves too little. The argument rests on the contingent fact that justifying deadly defensive force will, in the long run, save more lives by deterring deadly assaults. But suppose this were not the case. Suppose in some jurisdiction law enforcement techniques were so perfected that every wrongful attacker would certainly and promptly be convicted and punished with sufficient severity, even perhaps with capital punishment, to exact the maximum deterrent effect possible. In such a jurisdiction preventive killing by the victim or another could not serve the end of preserving life by adding to the deterrent threat against wrongful attacks. Yet, is it not inconceivable that deadly defensive force against an attacker would for that reason be denied justification? Surely it would be thought unfair to deny the threatened person the use of justified deadly force against his assailant, no matter what was indicated by any longrun, life preserving calculus, because it is *his* life that is at stake.

This intuitive sense of what fairness requires suggests a quite different approach to understanding what may lie behind the law's justifying intentional killing of aggressors—an approach through the identification of moral rights, which require recognition no matter what policy is indicated by a calculus of utilities.

One such approach focuses on the right of the aggressor. Starting with a general right to life possessed by all human beings, the argument is that the aggressor, by his culpable act, forfeits his right to life. This analysis, however, is unsatisfactory on a number of counts. If forfeit means that by his wrongdoing the aggressor allows his life to be taken, it is a Pickwickian sense of "allow" that must be contemplated, since the aggressor would hardly agree that he had any such thing in mind. And even if this difficulty were resolved, there would still be conflict with the accepted principle that one may not, even by an explicit surrender, give up his life or authorize another to take it.[22] On the other hand, forfeit may mean that, wholly apart from what the aggressor may think about the matter, his wrongful act deprives him of any claim he could otherwise make on the basis of his right to life. But to say that his wrongful act deprives him of his right to life is to restate the legal conclusion, and one may question how much it illuminates. First, the theory, in resting forfeiture on wrongdoing, does not explain why the aggressor forfeits his right to life during the attack, but regains it after the attack has unsuccessfully ended. Second, the theory addresses only the liberty of the victim to kill the aggressor in self-defense. It does not deal with any *right* the victim may have to do so. Suppose, for example, the law did prohibit defensive killings. One's sense of the matter is that such a law would be unjust. But the forfeiture theory, as far as it goes, would not impugn such a law or explain why it would be wrong. In other words, the theory tells us why (or rather, that) the aggressor has no moral claim against the deadly force of the victim; it does not tell us why (or even, that) the victim has a right not to be hindered in his use of deadly force against the aggressor. Third, the theory posits that a person does have the general right that others should act in ways that do not imperil his life—a right that the aggressor yields by his action. But such a general right to life is inconsistent with the pattern of the relevant criminal law I have described. Finally, the whole concept of forfeiture by wrongdoing collapses in the case of a threat to life by one who acts without blame— the legally insane attacker, for example, or a very small child. For, as I pointed out earlier, it likely is the law with us, and certainly is the law in many Continental systems, that the person attacked may kill such an attacker to the same extent he may kill a culpable aggressor.

As a way of accounting for the law of justified killing of a deadly attacker, a more satisfactory rights approach than the forfeiture concept, which derives only a liberty of the victim to kill from the loss of the aggressor's right to live, is one that derives the liberty from a right against the state. That right, I suggest, is the right of every person to the law's protection against the deadly threats of others. For whatever uncertainty there may be about how much protection must be afforded under this right, it must at least, if it is to have any content, include maintenance of a legal liberty to resist deadly threats by all necessary means, including killing the aggressor. There is, after all, no novelty in positing such a right. The individual does not surrender his fundamental freedom to preserve himself against aggression by the establishment of state authority; this freedom is required by most theories of state legitimacy, whether Hobbesian, Lockeian or Rawlsian, according to which the individual's surrender of prerogative to the state yields a quid pro quo of greater, not lesser, protection against aggression than he had before.[23] This liberty to resist deadly aggression by deadly force, and the moral right against the state from which it derives, I will refer to as the right to resist aggression.

The recognition of this right accounts for the law of justified killing of aggressors more satisfactorily than other attempts we have considered. The legal right of the victim to kill an aggressor or any number of aggressors when necessary to save his life clearly follows. The explanation requires no concept of forfeiture of the aggressor's rights through his wrongdoing, which, as we saw earlier, was subject to several serious objections. An account of why the aggressor's rights are overridden need not be given, because under the theory he has none against his victim. The social and personal value of his life is not diminished by his actions; indeed, when there are multiple aggressors, the good of maximizing lives preserved argues against the victim's defensive actions. But since under this explanation the victim has a right to kill, justice requires that his action be legally justified. Neither has the aggressor any right of his own which is being violated. To say he has a right to life in the circumstances would be incoherent, since it would contradict the theory that gives the victim the right to kill him. What the aggressor has, as well as any person, is the right to resist aggression against his life, but that right is not violated by the victim who is only defending against the other's aggression.[24] Neither does the theory fail where the person threatening the actor is innocent, as when his action would be excused by the law, because the justification of the victim's defensive action does not arise from the wrongdoing of the threatener but from the right of the victim to preserve his life against a threat to it. The theory is also consistent with the lapse of the right to kill after the threat has ceased, for the right hinges on the presence of the threat. And it is consistent as well with the legal right of a third person to kill the aggressor. In this case, however, the underlying right is not that of the third person, but that of the victim, since the right of the victim to the law's protection would be violated as much by denying a third person's liberty to intervene as by denying the victim's liberty to defend.

But what would this right to resist aggression imply for threats short of the deadly ones I have so far been considering? Is the right limited to deadly threats, or does it include the right to kill to prevent lesser ones?

Two contending principles afford different answers to the question of the extension of the right to resist aggression: the principle of autonomy and the principle of proportionality.[25] According to the first, there should be no limit on the right to resist threats to the person of the actor or interests closely identified therewith. The unrestricted character of the right follows from the corollary of the principle of autonomy of persons—that no one may be used as the mere instrument of another—for the essence of physical aggression is that the aggressor seeks so to use the life (taken in this larger sense of personhood) of the victim. Insofar, then, as the autonomy principle determines the scope of the right to resist aggression, the kinds of interests of personality that may be protected by deadly force are unlimited. It suffices that so much force is necessary to protect the interest. The cost to the aggressor of the victim's exercise of his right so to resist carries no weight. A judgment that the victim could not employ all necessary force to protect personal interests within his autonomy—on the ground that the force needed (killing his aggressor, for example) is excessive—means that the victim's right to defend against aggression is to that extent violated, for he then should be obliged to suffer his being used as a means for the benefit of another against his will.[26]

According to the second principle, the principle of proportionality, the moral right to resist threats is subject to the qualification that the actions necessary to resist the threat must not be out of proportion to the nature of the threat. In compelling this qualification the proportionality principle acknowledges various interests within one's personality and discriminates among them according to degrees of importance. Because the victim has a right to kill his aggressor when necessary to preserve his life, it does not follow that he may do so to protect lesser interests. If killing the aggressor is the only way to save a significantly lesser interest, he must yield it to the aggressor. This qualification is commonly regarded as a principle of justice and is similarly manifested in the range of protective sanctions used by the state to protect various invasions of one's personality. Not all offenses against the person, let alone offenses against his property, carry the severest sanctions. Punishment for offenses generally are scaled in some rough proportion to the enormity of the harm done. It would be thought a basic wrong to the offender, for example, to take his life for a minor theft; and no less a wrong even if it were demonstrable that any lesser punishment would afford less protection against such threats to persons in the community.

I suggest that both of these principles bearing on the extension of the right to resist aggression are reflected in the rules of Anglo-American law. It is the uneasy tension between them that underlies the perennial controversy and changing shape of the law with respect to defining the interests for whose protection one may kill. The proportionality principle is widely in evidence. It is strongly seen in the reform efforts of recent years, such as the proposals of the Model Penal Code, to confine the right to kill generally to cases where killing is necessary to avoid a danger to life.[27] It is also evidenced in more settled provisions of law which, while not so strictly defining proportionality, draw the line at some point on what interests deadly force may be used to protect—for example, the various restraints on killing to protect property, the obligation in many jurisdictions to yield one's ground if, by so doing, one can avoid the need to kill to save one's life, and even the denial of a right to kill to prevent an unaggravated battery.[28] At the same time, however, the autonomy principle has its influence. Even under recent statutes one may kill to protect one's property where the threat occurs through a forcible entry of one's dwelling. The duty to retreat as a condition of using deadly force has traditionally been a minority rule, and even today many jurisdictions reject it. Indeed, when it is required, there is never a duty to abandon one's home or (in many jurisdictions) similar places, like one's place of business. Moreover, despite efforts to confine the use of deadly force to prevent felonies threatening the life of the person, the law of most states continues to permit its use in a much wider range of situations, such as whenever any degree of force is used by the aggressor.

Now it may be argued that these latter rules are reflections not of the autonomy principle, but of varying judgments of what interests are proportional to taking the life of the aggressor. The argument has force in cases of killing to prevent crimes like kidnapping and rape, for one may plausibly argue that the interests protected are comparable to that of the victim's life. But one cannot say the same of the interest in remaining where one is, or in protecting one's property from an intruder into one's home, or in preventing any felony whenever some force is used. The strong current of sentiment behind such rules can be understood best as a reflection of the autonomy principle, which extends the right to resist aggression broadly to cover threats to the personality of the victim. It is hard to see from where the force behind the elevation of these distinctly lesser interests can come other than from the moral claim of the person to autonomy over his life.

In summary, so far as deadly threats are concerned, the best explanation of the pattern of law governing defensive killing of aggressors is the recognition of the moral right of the victim to kill his aggressor, a right deriving from the right of every person to the fullest protection by the state against such threats. So far as lesser threats are concerned, two contending moral principles are at work: the principle of autonomy, which would extend that moral right to resist aggression to the protection of all facets of the personality of the victim; and the principle of proportionality, which would qualify the extension of that right to interests of the victim commensurate with the life of the aggressor.

2. INTENTIONAL KILLING OF BYSTANDERS.   The remaining category of justified intentional killings I will consider[29] comprises killings committed in the interest of preserving life when the person sacrificed is not a culpable aggressor or even an innocent one, but a non-threatening bystander. The one circumstance in which the law arguably justifies killing such a person is that in which killing him is necessary to avoid the certain death of several. This represents the lesser-evil principle we discussed earlier, in which killing one person is deemed a lesser evil than the death of more than one.

It is apparent that the right to resist aggression cannot account for the justification of this type of intentional killing. Neither the actor nor those on whose behalf he acts are threatened in their rights by the one whose life is taken. To use the example of the Model Penal Code itself, the families whose lives are imperiled by the deflection of flood waters to their homes to avoid the death of a greater number who live in the normal path of the waters are totally uninvolved in the threat to the latter persons. Moreover, the deflection of the waters to their homes is itself an aggressive act against them, which violates their rights not to be used as a means for the benefit of others.[30] When the law justifies this action it therefore violates the right we earlier posited to the state's protection against aggression.[31] That this category of killings is usually explained in terms of the choice of the lesser evil suggests its theory of justification: on a judgment of end results it is better that the fewer number of lives is lost. In the case of the non-threatening bystanders, therefore, a balance of utilities becomes determinative, in which the preservation of several lives justifies the intentional taking of a lesser number, even at the cost of violating a fundamental right the law otherwise recognizes they possess. That is to say, within this category of killings a force is at work manifesting a very different notion of right: rightness in the sense of the desirable social consequence of an action—whether it will produce a net loss or savings of lives.

But stories tell more than propositions. Suppose a terrorist and her insane husband and 8-year old son are operating a machine gun emplacement from a flat in an apartment building. They are about to shoot down a member of the diplomatic corps, whose headquarters the terrorist band is attacking. His only chance is to throw a hand grenade (which he earlier picked up from a fallen terrorist) through his assailants' window. Probably under Anglo-American law he will be legally justified in doing so. His right to resist the aggressors' threat is determinative.

The value of preserving even the lives of the terrorist, her legally insane husband and their infant son carry no weight on the scale of rights.

Add to the facts that the victim knows there is one person in an adjoining flat who will surely be killed by the blast. Now he would *not* be legally justified in throwing the grenade (though he might be excused), for his action will not result in a net saving of lives. The right of the person in the adjoining flat (who is no part of the threat against him) not to be subjected to his aggression is, therefore, determinative.

Finally, assume in addition that the machine gun is being directed against a companion as well as himself. Under the lesser-evil doctrine the victim will be legally justified in throwing the grenade. The right of the person in the adjoining flat is the same, but that person's claim of right yields to the social valuation that the two other lives are to be preferred over his one life.

This last case reveals the anomaly in the law: that rights prevail over lives in the aggression cases, even multiple or innocent lives, but that lives prevail over rights in the bystander cases like this one or the flood deflection case. As suggested above, we must conclude that, to the extent this is the law, a bystander's right against aggression yields to a utilitarian assessment in terms of net saving of lives. Yet, it should be added, this is not always so, for there are some killings fairly within the net-saving-of-lives, lesser-evil doctrine that it is very doubtful courts would sanction—for example, killing a person to obtain his organs to save the lives of several other people, or even removing them for that purpose against his will without killing him. The unreadiness of the law to justify such aggression against non-threatening bystanders reflects a moral uneasiness with reliance on a utilitarian calculus for assessing the justification of intended killings, even when a net savings of lives is achieved.[32]

3. UNINTENTIONAL KILLINGS.   I turn now to actions neither intended nor known to cause death, which nonetheless create a risk (of which the actor may or may not be aware) that death will result. The law turns the criminality of these actions entirely on a calculus of utilities: how great the probability that life will be lost, how socially important the purposes served by the action, and how feasible the use of less risky measures to achieve the same purpose. While the criminality of intended killings only exceptionally (and, even then, controversially) turns on comparable assessments—that is, in the case of the lesser-evil doctrine—these utilitarian assessments are the standard factors in judging unintended killings. Moreover, this approach to unintended killings is uniformly accepted as sound. It is hard to see how risks to life in the normal processes of living could otherwise be handled by the criminal law, if they are to be handled by it at all.[33] Yet why is it so obviously commonsensical? Why

is there so relatively little tension, so few qualms about actions that create unintended threats to people's lives?

There are differences, surely, between intended and risked killings. Professors Wechsler and Michael, in their classic study of homicide law, pointed them out:

> [A]cts that are intended to kill and capable of causing death are usually highly likely to do so; and they rarely serve ends other than those to which the homicide itself is a means. On the other hand, acts not intended to kill are not, in general, likely to cause death; and even when they are likely to do so, they necessarily serve some other end, which, frequently enough, is desirable.[34]

Perhaps this rationale is adequate when risks are moderate; for it is consistent, given a set value on preserving lives, to intervene more protectively against an action, like an intended killing, which carries an extremely high risk, than against actions not so intended, which pose a much lesser risk.

Yet I doubt that this rationale is sufficient. As for the first distinction—the likelihood of causing death—so long as an action is intended to kill it counts for nothing that the chance of success in the particular case is not great. The chances of my being struck and killed by a poor marksman with bad eyesight and a crude weapon many yards away are not large. Yet that unlikelihood in no way impairs my right to use deadly force if there is no other way to eliminate that risk. Moreover, some unintended killings create risks as high as most intended ones. When elaborate construction projects are planned—like the Golden Gate Bridge, the Boulder Dam, a tunnel under the English Channel—it can be predicted with a statistical accuracy approaching certainty that a certain number of deaths will result. Nevertheless, we accept the prospect with equanimity and no qualms. We may know that a variety of safety precautions will reduce the number of deaths and, indeed, we often require them—but not always, not when they will cost so much money or time that the effort is deemed disproportionate.[35]

These utilitarian considerations raise the other part of Wechsler and Michael's answer—the social desirability of the bridge or the tunnel or the dam justifies the predicted loss of lives. But this answer generally does not suffice to justify intended killings. Although it is true that intended killings rarely serve ends other than those to which the homicide itself is a means, that is not to say that they may not serve socially desirable ends. When we do justify them on utilitarian grounds—for example, the intentional killing of bystanders—we insist on social goods of an order (usually saving lives) far more compelling than we require to justify risking life, even when the risk is statistically near certain.

Another story will illustrate this last point. An underwater tunnel

has been started despite an almost certain loss of five to 15 lives. Presumably the expected loss is a calculated cost that society is prepared to
pay for having the tunnel. At one point a workman is trapped in a
section of the partially laid tunnel. A fitting must be lowered into place.
If it is laid it will surely crush the workman to death. If it is not laid
within an hour—too short a time to effect a rescue—the whole tunnel
will have to be abandoned indefinitely, perhaps permanently, due to
changing river conditions. I expect that it would nonetheless be a form
of criminal homicide to lower the fitting. Even if it were justified under
a lesser-evils formula, which is doubtful, the decision would be a soul-
searching one. Yet attaining the very same social good—the construction
of the tunnel—readily justified its construction despite the predicted loss
of multiple lives.

I do not believe, therefore, that the difference in the law of intended
and unintended killing can be accounted for in the differences Wechsler
and Michael point to. I suggest, rather, that the explanation is to be
found in the fundamentally different perspectives we have toward intended and unintended killings. Generally, the former, as I tried to show,
are seen as violative of a basic personal right against the state to be
protected against the deadly threats of another person. The latter, on
the other hand, are not so perceived. Accidental risks to life deriving
from the actions of others tend to be accepted in the same way as risks
to life deriving from natural events—as a natural and inevitable contin-
gency of living. We do not have a right against the state to protection
against unintended killings, as we do against intended killings. The fundamental urge which animates the claim of right is security against threats
directed by others against us, not security against the perils of living.
Intentional killings are moral assaults. Risks to life are a part of nature
which, under any contractarian view, the state has no duty to protect
against.

We do not, of course, regard these risks indifferently. They are
undesirable and to be avoided, and they are often made criminal; but
only when it appears on a utilitarian calculus that the risk is not worth
bearing—not at all costs. It is not the degree of risk and the degree of
social justification of the respective actions that make the difference. It
is that there are not the same moral side-constraints on actions that create
risk as there are on actions that are seen as aggression. Hence, the
principle of optimizing end-results on a utility calculus has the field
entirely.

Yet, how can this explanation apply where it is known to a statistical
certainty that accidental deaths will result from a course of action, like
building a bridge or a tunnel? I have not, after all, argued a distinction
between intended and known killings for purposes of defining the extent
of the right against acts of aggression. Indeed, I took pains to reject the

distinction in discussion the double-effect doctrine. Hence, how can it be that the victims of an unintended killing do not have a right against the state to protection from this present risk of certain death to some of them? One possible answer is that the statistically certain risk created by the construction project is to the workmen who, by agreeing to work on it in return for wages, have consented to the risk. The point has force; yet, it seems insufficient. First, while consent to the risk of death may negate the criminality of a subsequent homicide, it may not do so in cases of intentional killings. Why, then, given our rejection of the distinction between intended and known killings, should consent negate the criminality of homicide in the cases of known killings in these examples? Some further explanation is needed. Second, the absence of consent does not appear determinative in these cases. The statistically certain risk of death produced by the widespread use of the automobile and attendant services, for example, is not confined to those who choose to drive.

The further necessary explanation, I suggest, lies in the nature of statistical knowledge. It is known that some people will be killed; it is not known who they will be. If statistical analysis demonstrates that 10 out of a thousand will die, no individual person can claim that his death is a known consequence of the action. His own risk, indeed, is relatively modest—in this case one percent. So it is that in these cases the known deaths need only be regarded as a regrettable cost and not as the perpetration of an injustice.

4. OMISSIONS.   I turn finally to the omission cases, the last piece in the puzzle. Though failing to act while knowing that a death will thereby result might be justified or not as affirmative actions are, the law treats omissions differently. Affirmative actions which cause or tend to cause the death of a person are culpable or not depending on an inquiry into their justification (putting aside excuse). With omissions to act, no such inquiry arises until a duty to act is first established. Hence, a person is at liberty knowingly to permit another to die, without regard to any consideration of whether his omission is justified, unless the law otherwise imposes a duty to act—as it may, for example, because of a status, contractual or equitable relationship between the parties. On what theory can the law be explained?

One view is that the criminal law is unable to formulate a rule commanding when a person must act without being so indefinite as to render its administration uncertain and unjust. For how could one formulate a rule that would say just how far a person need alter his life or burden himself and those dependent upon him in order to save the life of a person in need? And how could the rule distinguish those who must do so out of the many who could, at varying costs, do so as well? This emphasis on indefiniteness is the classic justification for requiring action only when the law otherwise imposes a duty to act.[36]

Certainly this explanation has some merit. In addition to its intrinsic plausibility, it tends to be borne out by occasional general statutes that require the non-dangerous rescue of a person in distress and those that require action in a variety of particular situations (like registering for the draft and filing income tax returns), for in these instances a sufficiently definite rule is practicable. Yet one may doubt that it represents the whole story. To be sure, any general formulation of a requirement to act—for example, one based on an appeal to common decency—would be indefinite; but, as has been persuasively argued,[37] it would be no more indefinite than the standard of criminal liability for reckless or negligent killings, which also turns on an assessment of such imponderables as necessity of means, desirability of ends, probability of death, and the like.[38]

An additional possible explanation is the undesirability of people sacrificing their own interests, no matter how slight, to aid another person, even where that person otherwise will die. We need not pause over this view. It obviously contradicts the elemental humanitarianism that permeates our culture. A lesser version of this view is that while it is desirable for people to act to keep another alive, it is not desirable for the criminal law to seek to make them do so. But one wonders why not. One possible reason is that a general affirmative duty to act would necessitate unacceptably indefinite standards of conduct. I have already said why I think this consequence would not necessarily follow. Another possible reason is that such an affirmative duty could not affect people's conduct. But surely deterring inaction is not intrinsically more difficult than deterring acts, even acknowledging the greater difficulty of proving the mens rea—the state of mind—that accompanies an omission.[39] Another reason might be the general undesirability of using the criminal law to coerce virtuousness.[40] But compelling actions to save life is hardly using punishment to exact private conformity to virtue or to standards of good conduct that are at all controversial.

What, then, is the further explanation of the law's traditional reluctance to criminalize omissions? I believe an approach through a rights analysis casts light on the question. On the one hand, the moral right to resist aggression hardly provides the basis for a claim on others to their help,[41] the failure to assist another in need is not the type of aggressive threat to personality that gives rise to a claim against the state for protection. Hence one finds the pervasive distinction, in the law as elsewhere, between killing a person, which does violate his right, and letting him die, which does not.[42] On the other hand, the right to resist aggression rests to some extent, as we saw above when dealing with deadly defensive force against non-deadly threats, upon the notion of autonomy, which posits a person's right not to be used coercively in the service of another. Requiring actions of bystanders to save others tends to collide with the autonomy principle. For to accord to a stranger a claim upon me that does not flow in any sense from my own actions conscripts the uses of my life to his.[43] This explanation, it may be observed, is consistent with the exceptional cases in which the common law does traditionally compel action—cases of status, contractual or equitable relationship between the parties. In these cases the putative helper, by his actions, has implicated himself in the predicament of the person in need, and he cannot make the same claim of autonomy.[44]

Of course, this autonomy principle does not have the field to itself. We saw earlier how the principle of proportionality contends with it in cases of resistance to non-deadly threats to the person. The proportionality principle does so also in cases of omissions where, in a variety of situations, usually statutory (for example, the statutes requiring the giving of aid to one in distress where there is practically no risk to the aider), the demands of the principle of autonomy are compromised on a judgment of gross disproportion between what is demanded of the aider and what is at stake for the person in need.

C. SUMMARY

So much, then, is the map of the criminal law and what I suggest to be some of the moral sentiments and the perceptions of actions and events that explain its contours. The sacredness of human life is an important ingredient of the humanistic ideal. Insofar as it asserts the equality-of-lives principle, it constitutes a significant influence on the law. In any other sense, it does not. We have to look elsewhere to comprehend the determinative influences on the shape of the law.

One predominant and persistent theme is the conception of the rightness of actions—rightness measured not by what most effectively preserves lives or by what best serves the social interest of all, but by what a person may claim as his due equally with all other persons. The right, in this sense, to resist aggression, embracing the liberty to use defensive force and the right to the law's protection against aggression, from which the liberty derives, plays a central role in explaining the shape of the law. When the victim must take the life of one threatening his own in order to survive, his action is justifiable, whether the persons he must kill are one or many, guilty or innocent, so long as they are part of the threat. But other principles of right manifest themselves in other situations where life is at stake. Where interests other than the victim's life (or interests closely identified with it) are threatened, two competing principles affect his right to kill: the principle of autonomy, which would extend the right to resist aggression to all threats to the personality of the victim, and the principle of proportionality, which would draw the line at preservation of life and closely identified interests. Neither principle governs entirely in the law. Further, in cases of omissions to act to avoid the death of another, there is a similar tension between these principles operating in the law.

But explanations in terms of rights and principles fail to account for the whole shape of the law. Another force is at work, manifesting a very different notion of right: rightness in the sense of the desirable consequence of an action—whether it will produce a net loss or saving of lives, whether it will serve or disserve prevailing estimates of social goods other than saving lives. This competing standard, turning solely on evaluation of consequences, is manifested in the lesser-evil doctrine. When taking the life of an innocent, non-threatening bystander will result in a net saving of lives, the law justifies an actor in doing so, notwithstanding the invasion of the bystander's own right to the law's protection against aggression. As we saw, the doctrine, when carried to its logical conclusion, is controversial, further reflecting the tensions in the impulses that shape our law.

This consequentialist standard is most firmly in evidence when unintended killing is involved, for here no individual rights are perceived which must be subordinated or qualified. It is in these cases that the value we place on life as against other goods and interests may be most clearly seen, since no competing principle of right exists to complicate its assessment. It is revealing that the judgments in this area that appeal most immediately to our common sense permit life to be yielded when the costs of saving it, in terms of the comforts, conveniences and satisfactions of many, seem too high.[45] The nature of the action that takes life commands our concern far more than loss of life itself.[46]

These, then, appear to be the underlying principles and controlling patterns of thought that govern the law's judgments of life-taking actions. The principles and patterns I have identified do not all fit into a harmonious pattern; inconsistencies and tensions, reflecting a variety of impulses and perceptions, appear to me a major feature of our experience. Whether, to that extent, what I have concluded is defective as a theory of the criminal law depends on what constitute the governing criteria of a proper theory of this kind. Although I could not properly address that issue here, I would venture two brief comments. First, I recognize that it may well be possible to discern a rationale underlying our criminal law tradition that achieves a more logically consistent explanation of the whole than what I have produced. I offer only my best effort. Second, I am dubious that any single, self-consistent theory is likely ever to comprehend the whole of our experience. I venture the intuition that the essential stuff of our moral judgments and perceptions in complex matters like the taking of life is tension and contradiction that may be identified but never dissolved.

CONCLUDING OBSERVATIONS

I should like to conclude by saying a few words on how this pattern of principles and perceptions bears on some of the controversial issues of the day I mentioned at the outset. Since my focus throughout has been on the law, I will confine myself to those issues that pose a problem for the criminal law and ask no more than how those principles and perceptions that I have argued underlie the shape of our criminal law bear on those issues.

Human medical experimentation seems to me, as it has to others,[47] not readily distinguishable from other cases where life may be legally risked to achieve some greater social good. Indeed, if a bridge justifies the predicted loss of life its construction entails, surely the saving of countless lives through medical discoveries does so as well. Since loss of life is risked, not intended, no right is invaded in either case. And since the subject consents to a risk of death rather than to being killed, there is no ground for denying the efficacy of the consent. The key problem for the law is not intrinsic but administrative—how to assure that risks are minimized, that consent is freely given, that the competence of the experimenter and the promise of the experiment justify the risk, and that abuses are avoided.

The criminalization of abortion is a different matter. Whether a fetus must be regarded as a person and at what stage are threshold questions little illumined by the themes we have found dominant in shaping the law. But once that threshold is passed and personhood recognized in a fetus at some stage, the abortion debate turns quite centrally on a number of those themes. How cogently may the dependent fetus be analogized to a person requiring affirmative aid from another to survive—aid to which it has no claim of right? Even if so analogized, has the mother's participation invested her with a duty not to let it die? How far may the answer turn on whether she at first sought the child, whether she was just careless, or whether she had been raped? Is the whole analogy to letting die by failing to aid misconceived because abortion entails affirmative action to stop life-sustaining aid already flowing? In other words, is it more like turning off a machine that is keeping a person alive than failing to attach the person to it in the first place? Even if so, how much does it weigh that it is *her* person—her "machine"—over which she has autonomy? Where the pregnancy is endangering her very existence, may the fetus be regarded as an innocent threat against which she may defend herself with whatever means are necessary? Where the fetus poses a threat "only" to her psychological well-being, does the principle of proportionality argue against taking the fetus' life, or should her interests of personality be defined broadly, so that the principle of autonomy would control? Finally, whatever the claims of justice in recognizing rights, how far do consequentialist considerations of achieving some optimal set of socially desirable results require their subordination? I am not so foolhardy as to venture answers at this point. My purpose is only to point out what is apparent in much of the abortion literature[48]— that the underlying themes we found at work in doctrines of the criminal law bear centrally on the current controversy over the criminalization of abortion.

The human transplant problem also raises several of these themes. In a suitable case, may the organs of a unique donor be removed against his will to save the lives of several? Probably, as I suggested earlier, the rights principle would be strong enough to resist legalizing such an action, but the lesser-evil principle, in its broadest reach, would point the other way. Where the donor consents at some risk to his life, the legal problems again, as in the case of medical experimentation, would be administrative. Where removing his organ would kill him, one faces the engrained reluctance to sanction taking one's own life or permitting another to do so. Where the donor is moribund, two main problems emerge. The first is whether one with virtually no life left may be treated as dead, as no longer a person, for purposes of the criminal law. An affirmative answer would entail a serious breach of the equality-of-lives principle. The second problem is determining when a person is dead, just as the abortion issue raises the problem of when a person begins to live. Here again legal experience offers little guidance, since the beginning and ending of life were generally regarded in the law as unproblematic events. Only recent scientific sophistication has fully revealed the gradualness of the process both of man's coming into being and his ceasing to be, and therefore has exposed the troubling choices that the law cannot eventually escape making.[49]

Euthanasia also involves the equality-of-life principle: may life be treated differently when it becomes unwanted and unbearable by the person; or must life, as life, always be treated equally, so that a judgment of its worth, even by the person himself, may never enter into a justification for taking it? May the lesser-evil rationale justify some qualification of the equality-of-life principle when death is certain and imminent in any event, and killing would save the person from the evil of a few moments of agonizing pain and terror?[50]

A FINAL COMMENT

Using the rules of the criminal law as a guide, I have tried in this essay to identify some of the underlying principles and controlling patterns of thought that govern our judgments of life-taking actions and to suggest their relevance to a number of controversial problems involving the taking of life. I took my task to be descriptive and analytical, not judgmental; to state, that is, what the controlling principles and patterns are in fact, not whether they are sound (whatever sound might mean) or whether some are sounder than others. But, of course, these judgmental issues are the ultimate ones. Should the sanctity-of-life ideal prevail over rights and calculus of other utilities, or does it represent a religious commitment that may not be given primacy in a secular, or at least pluralistic society? Should rights always prevail because they express a commitment to justice, or is the notion of justice they express a product of man's primordial fears, conditioning and genetic structuring over time, which a rational order should seek to overcome?[51] Is a consequentialist principle to be preferred because it nondogmatically opens the assessment to embrace the widest range of social utilities at any time and place, or is the final commitment to socially desirable consequences itself a dogma that should be rejected insofar as it denies the primacy of life and the claims of justice? I have not ventured to say, mainly because I do not know. These questions are, after all, at the core of the great controversies in moral philosophy. I have to be content with having shown how it is that even a criminal lawyer reaches them at the end.

CHAPTER FIVE

ACCOUNTABILITY

8
COMPLICITY, CAUSE AND BLAME: A STUDY IN THE INTERPRETATION OF DOCTRINE

This is a study of a body of doctrine, the doctrine of complicity, that determines when one person is liable for a crime committed by another. Doctrine may be studied in several ways depending on the question asked. One question asks what the doctrine is in some jurisdiction. This is the question primarily addressed by treatise writers. Another question asks whether the doctrine serves the purposes of the law and, to the extent it does not, how it should be altered. This is the question addressed by those engaged in revising the law. I do not mean that these questions can be answered independently of one another, only that they are different questions. In any event, the question this study addresses is distinguishable from both. It asks how the doctrine of complicity can best be interpreted as a coherent concept. This entails articulating the relationships between different parts of complicity doctrine and between complicity and other doctrines that are related to it, particularly causation, and identifying the general propositions that give logical and conceptual unity to the rules of liability. In short, the task is to develop the analytical framework that gives the doctrine of complicity its distinctive character. I make no claim that what is here proposed is the only defensible interpretation of the doctrine of complicity. I offer it only as the best account I have been able to produce.

While the question of interpretation is distinguishable from the questions of what the doctrine is and what it ought to be, it is apparent that it cannot be addressed apart from these other questions. Consider first the question of what the law is. One can hardly undertake an interpretation without describing, in some sense, what it is that is being interpreted. This essay, therefore, presents a description of the law of complicity in common law jurisdictions to serve as the empirical basis of the interpretive enterprise.

At the same time, my description of the law differs in several ways from what one would expect to find in a hornbook or treatise. First, it

does not attempt to depict the state of the law in any particular jurisdiction at any particular time. I have selected cases, commentary, and
statutes from a variety of common law jurisdictions in order to identify
the central problems of complicity and the dominant resolutions of those
problems. Second, my principle of selection was not photographic faith-
fulness. While I hope I have neither distorted what courts have done
nor omitted what did not suit my purpose, I cannot claim that my description is purely neutral. Interpretation and description are not wholly
separate actions. They inform one another. My description of the law
is inevitably affected by my interpretation of it. There is no escape.
Finally, since my thesis is that the concept of complicity, reflected in the
main body of common law decisions, entails some conclusions and fore-
closes others, I have felt free to conclude that certain propositions "must"
represent the law, even where few, if any, cases have had occasion so to
hold. Similarly, I have sometimes concluded that other propositions do
not belong to the doctrine of complicity, even where some courts have
announced them.

I must also qualify my statement that I am not concerned with either
judging the doctrine of complicity or proposing ways to improve it. I
do not mean to imply that doctrine may be understood as some disem-
bodied thing that exists independent of social purposes or moral constraints. It is true that doctrine tends to have a life of its own. Considerations of consistency and coherence lead toward certain conclusions
and away from others, quite apart from judgments of the social desirability of holding the defendant liable in particular cases. At the same
time, no doctrine could long survive if it worked at cross purposes to
the social objectives of the system of law in which it functioned. Unless
the system were static and unresponsive, it would soon be replaced by
new doctrine with new starting points. In the long run, the demands of
consistency and coherence serve to give doctrine an independent life
only to the extent that doctrine continues to serve the purposes of law.

A further and deeper relationship between doctrine and normative
considerations should be emphasized at the outset, because it suggests
why doctrines of criminal liability are worth taking seriously despite the
traditional American skepticism of doctrine.[1] The decision to impose
criminal liability is not governed solely by the social purposes of punishment. It is governed as well by the moral justification of punishing
people for both their conduct and the results of their conduct. Indeed,
criminal liability is best understood as responding primarily to considerations of the latter kind; the attainment of social purposes is confined,
at least in most cases, to punishment for actions for which the defendant
can be justly blamed. It follows that doctrines of criminal liability, being
generalizations of the conditions in which punishment is proper, are
primarily statements of normative import. Therefore, the kind of doc-

trinal interpretation attempted in this study—an analysis of the general propositions that give coherence to the body of rules governing liability in one area of the criminal law—necessarily entails an attempt to identify the nature of the pervasive intuitive judgments that render criminal liability acceptable in some circumstances, but not in others.

In his lecture *The Path of the Law*,[2] Holmes argued that the law is best understood from the lawyer's point of view by studying its actual operation, rather than its response to the influence of logic and morality. To this extent the focus of this study is distinctly un-Holmesian, since it is centrally concerned with the force of logical coherence and morality on the shape of doctrine. On the other hand, Holmes observed in the same lecture that the "law is the witness and external deposit of our moral life."[3] If that is true of the law generally, it is surely true of legal doctrines of criminal liability. My purpose in this essay is to see what we can learn, about the law and about ourselves, from a study of the moral deposit discoverable in the law of criminal complicity.

It may be useful at the outset to present the read with a brief summary of the major points of the argument.

Part I describes the conceptions of blame, responsibility, and causal responsibility inherent in our linguistic usages, social practices, and legal institutions. What is described, however, is not offered as the philosophically correct or most sophisticated analysis of those concepts. For present purposes, it is enough to determine what the concepts of blame, responsibility, and causation that underlie the criminal law are; we need not take a position on whether the concepts presupposed by the criminal law are, in the final analysis, true.

Central among the beliefs that underlie the criminal law is the distinction between nature and will, between the physical world and the world of voluntary human action. Events in the physical world follow one another with an inevitability, or natural necessity, that is conspicuously absent from our view of voluntary human actions. Voluntary human actions are not seen as the product of relentless forces, but rather as freely chosen expressions of will. Thus, the conception of causation appropriate to physical events is out of place in the human realm. Voluntary actions cannot be said to be caused in the physical sense that imports the images of relentless forces and necessary conditions.

These distinctions influence our conception of responsibility, including, of particular significance for this essay, attributions of blame for untoward consequences of actions. The criminal law accommodates these distinctions by employing two separate bodies of doctrine to determine responsibility for results: causation, for the realm of nature, and complicity, for the realm of will. Causation applies where results of a person's action happen in the physical world. Complicity applies where results take the form of another person's voluntary action.

Complicity emerges as a separate ground of liability because causation doctrine cannot in general satisfactorily deal with results that take the form of another's voluntary action. Causation doctrine encounters difficulties here because of the distinction between nature and will: the voluntary action of the principal actor cannot appropriately be said to have been caused (in the physical sense of cause) by the action of the secondary party (or accomplice). A voluntary action is treated as the terminal point of a causal inquiry beyond which the inquiry does not proceed. No one and nothing caused the principal's action. He freely and voluntarily chose to act.

Part II explores complicity doctrine. Section A describes the derivative character of complicity liability. That is, the liability of the accomplice depends upon the commission of an unlawful act by the principal. This dependency follows from the distinction between nature and will. Where the principal's actions are fully voluntary, the accomplice cannot be said to have caused the principal's actions, and thus cannot be held liable for the crime on the basis that he caused those actions. Complicity doctrine makes the accomplice liable for the unlawfulness of the principal's action. Absent that unlawfulness there is no basis for complicity liability.

A difficult question is what the legal status of the actions of the principal must be for the accomplice to incur liability. The obvious suggestion that the principal must be liable is shown to be incorrect by cases where the principal has a defense based upon policies extrinsic to his guilt (such as diplomatic immunity or entrapment), or where the principal's behavior is excused. The guilt of the principal would suffice to ground the liability of the accomplice where the principal has a policy-based defense (extrinsic to his guilt) but will not suffice where the principal is excused. Two theories that can handle cases where the primary party is excused are considered (each of which will play a prominent role later in the essay). First, one can resort to causation doctrine, as the early common law did, and hold the accomplice directly liable as a principal who uses the primary party as a tool—an innocent agent—to commit the crime. Second, the accomplice's liability may be said to derive from the *wrongful act* of the principal, even though that act was excused.

Section B explains why it is that essentially only two forms of action suffice for complicity—aid or influence—while, by contrast, any action that produces the result suffices for causation: only those two forms of contribution to the principal's actions are consistent with the volitional character of those actions.

Section C develops the requirement that the accomplice act intentionally. This Section explores the meaning of the intention requirement, and the ways in which courts and legislatures sometimes depart from it. It is suggested that the intention requirement can be explained by the concept of the autonomy of human actions.

Section *D* considers similarities and differences in the way causation and complicity doctrine hold a person accountable for what happens in consequence of his conduct. While both require a result, the relationship between act and result differs. Where the result is a physical event, causation requires at least a but-for relation. But where the result is a further action of another, complicity doctrine does not require that the sine qua non relation hold. The exploration of this paradox leads to the conclusion that in complicity the possibility of a but-for relationship is the analogue of the but-for relationship in causation. The inapplicability of necessary and sufficient conditions to the realm of the will, it is argued, explains this difference between causation and complicity.

Part III considers situations where causation doctrine complements complicity by serving as a ground of liability where complicity cannot. This occurs mainly in two kinds of cases, in both of which causation doctrine applies because the primary party's action is not wholly voluntary. First, where the primary actor has a defense that negates culpability, complicity doctrine has difficulty because there is no basis for derivative liability. Insofar as the factors that negate the primary party's culpability also negate the voluntary character of his action, causation doctrine applies. Second, complicity doctrine fails where the secondary actor does not intend the criminal conduct of the primary party. Once again, causation complements complicity insofar as the primary party's action is not wholly volitional, since that fact allows tracing the result of the primary party's act back to the secondary party.

Part III also explains the limits of causation and complicity. In some cases, neither doctrine succeeds in explaining a liability that otherwise appears appropriate. This occurs, for example, where the nature of the prohibited actions, or the class of persons to whom the prohibition applies, precludes holding the secondary party directly liable where he uses the primary party as an innocent agent. Arguably, it occurs also where the secondary party unintentionally contributes to a wholly voluntary act by the primary party.

I. THE CONCEPT OF BLAME

Any attempt to account for the doctrine of complicity must begin with the concept of blame. Attributing blame is a pervasive human phenomenon. It is one way in which we order and make sense of social experience and it is reflected in our language and social practices. But it is also a concept that reaches so deeply into the jurisprudence of the criminal law that no account of the law can succeed without explicating its meaning and its role. The doctrine of complicity is founded on a particular sense of blame. However, it will be helpful in elucidating that special sense to consider the concept of blame in its broader context.

Blame and its correlative, praise, serve as expressions of our disapproval or approval of some human action or quality. We occasionally
blame things other than human actions, as when we blame an earth
tremor for the fall of a picture from the wall. But these are only metaphorical usages—we often use a concept appropriate for a human action
to vivify our account of why something happened. We also sometimes
praise an event or an object, as when we praise a painting of a sunset.
But in this case, we are inferentially praising the actions of the painter.
We would express approval of the sunset itself by speaking of its beauty,
but we could not appropriately praise it.

There are important differences between praise and blame. First,
praise can be given only when it is expressed, because it is intrinsically
an expressive action. The sentiment of approval, experienced privately,
becomes praise only when it is bestowed on someone. Blame is different.
It is not intrinsically an expressive action, but a judgment of disapproval.
It is an internal evaluation that need not be expressed. Blame is the
sentiment of disapproval itself.

Second, significant differences exist between those actions suitable
for praising, and those suitable for blaming. We are freer with our praise
than with our blame. Praise is appropriate for any human action, achievement, or quality of which we approve. We praise people for their virtue,
but also for their beauty, strength, or special talent. Indeed, we praise
people for any kind of action of which we approve, including acting
rightly, but also including running a race, painting a picture, or solving
a puzzle. Blame, on the other hand, is more restricted. For example,
beauty may be praiseworthy, but lack of beauty is not necessarily blameworthy. Similarly, we may praise a runner for winning a race, but it does
not follow that we may properly blame him for losing it.

The reason for these differences is that blame entails a judgment
of responsibility, while praise does not. One who presents a poor appearance is not blamed for it unless he is responsible for it, as by poor
judgment or lack of care in dress or grooming. The runner who loses
a race may be blamed if he failed to train properly, but not if he did
the best he could.

The notion of responsibility that underlies the concept of blame is
an elusive one. Without attending to a variety of subtle complications
that inhere in the concept, or arguing any particular philosophical position, we may say generally that blame imports the notion of choice.
We perceive human actions as differing from other events in the world.
Things happen and events occur. They do not occur anarchically and
haphazardly, but in sequences and associations that have a necessary
quality about them. We express this quality in terms of causation and
we understand it in terms of laws of nature that are beyond our power
to alter. Human actions stand on an entirely different footing. While

man is total subject under the laws of the natural world, he is total sovereign over his own actions. Except in special circumstances, he possesses volition through which he is free to choose his actions. He may be influenced in his choices, but influences do not work like wind upon a straw; rather, they are considerations on the basis of which he chooses to act. He may also be the object of influence in the larger sense that he is the product of the forces that shaped him. But his actions are his and his alone, not those of his genes or his rearing, because if he had so desired he could have chosen to do otherwise. This is the perception that underlies the conception of responsibility which, in turn, is central to the conception of blame. We blame a person for an action that violates some approved norm of conduct. We not only disapprove of the conduct, we blame the person for it because he is a responsible agent with the power to choose to do otherwise.

The justification for this view of human action is the subject of the controversy over free will and determinism. The incompatibilists argue that this view of human action requires a conception of the will as uncaused—a singular exception to an otherwise determinate world. On the other hand, some compatibilists argue that this view of responsibility may adequately rest on our certain knowledge that we can do as we choose so long as no physical force compels our action. Is freedom of the will grounded in reality, or is it an illusory by-product of our prejudices and ignorance? Is it enough that it is rooted in our subjective experience of ourselves not as straws in the wind, but as agents with our own identities who define and act to achieve our own purposes? Since my task is to identify and trace the effect of this perception on legal doctrine, I need not enter this controversy. However these questions are answered, it is enough for my purposes to observe that the view of persons as responsible and autonomous agents is a central feature of the concept of blame; that without this concept of responsibility, moral judgment loses its essential character. The questions we must address are what blame entails and how far it helps account for the doctrines of the criminal law.

Blame has several senses, both in common usage and in the criminal law. In one sense, we may blame a person for his actions. There are two prerequisites for fixing blame in this sense. First, the act must be subject to disapproval. If I am blamed for appearing late for an appointment, I may defend my action by explaining that I took time to help an injured friend get to the hospital. There is no doubt that I am responsible for what I did. My defense, indeed, rests on it, because it asserts that what I did was the right thing to do, even if it meant being late. In short, I am not to be blamed because what I chose to do was not blameworthy. This is the aspect of blame at issue in any legal defense of justification, such as self defense, defense of another, enforcing the law, or the generalized defense of the choice of the lesser evil. This aspect of blame is also at issue when one tries to justify an action in moral norms outside the law, as in defending an action of civil disobedience.

A second prerequisite of this sense of blame turns on responsibility for the action, rather than justification for the action. Even if what the person did cannot be justified, he still may not be blameworthy if his action, for a variety of possible reasons, was not a product of that freedom to do otherwise that the notion of blame imports. So, if my latecoming could not be justified, I might still question my blameworthiness by appealing to this other aspect of blame. I might, for example, explain that I was locked into my building and it took time to find someone to let me out. My defense here is excuse, which asserts that my freedom to have acted otherwise was totally or partially impaired.

The law provides for excuse through a variety of defenses. Some defenses embrace situations in which the actor was without power to choose in the most literal sense—his movement was a reflex, or he was physically compelled or prevented. The law expresses this notion by requiring an act, taken to mean a voluntary act, as the indispensable requirement of any liability. In other situations the power of choice is not literally foreclosed but is so constrained that the action is excused. The law precludes liability in these cases as well, just as common usage would preclude blame. Typical circumstances of this kind include those in which the actor was coerced by threat of injury (duress), or through no fault of his own, mistook the situation such that his action would have been unexceptionable had he taken it correctly (mistake), or where he was unable to exercise rational choice at all because of mental disease and was therefore beyond blame (legal insanity).

We may also use blame in a different sense by blaming a person for something that occurs as a consequence of his action—that is, fixing blame for a result. An action may be blameworthy in the first sense as an unjustified and unexcused action. But this would leave unanswered the different question whether the actor should be blamed for what follows from his action. In this latter sense, responsibility is also involved, but not that sense of responsibility that turns on whether the person's power to act otherwise was impaired. Rather, it is a sense of responsibility for what follows from a freely chosen action. Thus, the issue of excuse is inapposite. If I insult my guest, who leaves in high anger and, distracted by the incident, walks into the path of an oncoming car, my responsibility for his injury will not turn on whether I should be excused for the injury. It would not make sense to speak of being excused for something that happens; we may be excused only for what we do. Here the question is whether the injury may be attributed to my action, whether it can fairly be regarded as "belonging" to the action I chose to do. In common usage, as well as in the law, whether we may be blamed for something that results from our actions turns on whether we may be said to have been the cause of that result, or to be blameable for it on some related ground.

A consequence of a person's action may be of two general kinds. It may consist of subsequent events. If I light a match in an area containing explosive vapors that ignite, starting a fire that burns down a building, I may be blamed for the burning of the building because I can be said to have caused it. I started a chain of events that led to the burning of the building through cause and effect relationships governed by laws of nature.[4] But a consequence of a person's action may also consist of the actions of other people. I may have persuaded another responsible person to light the match or helped him by giving him a match for the purpose. The other person then caused the burning of the building. But whether I am to be blamed for the other person's action would not be assessed by asking whether I caused his action in the same sense that his lighting the match caused the fire. Rather, my responsibility would be determined by asking whether my persuasion or help made me accountable for the other person's actions and what they caused.

Responding to these common perceptions of the relationship between actions and consequences, the criminal law has developed two separate doctrines for fixing blame. The doctrine of causation deals with fixing blame for natural events. The doctrine of complicity deals with fixing blame for the criminal action of another person. While the doctrine of complicity is the subject of this essay, the doctrine of causation cannot be put aside. For though there are significant contrasts between causation and complicity, there are also important similarities deriving from the common function of both doctrines to fix blame for consequences. In comparing and contrasting these doctrines, I shall draw heavily on the classic treatment of causation by Professors Hart and Honoré.[5]

At the outset, it is important to develop more fully why both in common usage and in law we use different concepts to determine when a person may be blamed for things that happen and when he may be blamed for what other people do. The explanation lies in that singular view of human action that underlies blame. That same view of human action that entails freedom to choose obviously applies to the actions of one who is responding to the actions of another. In the same sense and for the same reasons that a person's genes, upbringing, and social surroundings are not seen as the cause of his actions, neither are the actions of another seen as the cause of his actions. We regard a person's acts as the products of his choice, not as an inevitable, natural result of a chain of events. Therefore, antecedent events do not cause a person to act in the same way that they cause things to happen, and neither do the antecedent acts of others. To treat the acts of others as causing a person's actions (in the physical sense of cause) would be inconsistent with the premise on which we hold a person responsible.

There are exceptions to this general perception of human action that need to be noted here because they figure in the play between the doctrines of complicity and causation. Certain kinds of actions are in fact treated as caused by a prior action of another because we deem them lacking that quality of unconstrained free choice that generally characterizes human actions. Following Hart and Honoré, we may refer to these as nonvoluntary (or nonvolitional), or not wholly voluntary (or not wholly volitional) actions.[6] Of course, an involuntary action, which in law is not regarded as an action at all, is of this character. But the class of nonvolitional actions, in the sense developed by Hart and Honoré, includes actions that are not literally involuntary. It includes all actions that are not wholly unconstrained or that are done without knowledge of those relevant circumstances that give the action its significance. There are two principal circumstances in which we treat human actions as nonvolitional: where they are excusable and where they are justifiable. Actions of persons who are legally irresponsible, actions where the actor acts without a required mens rea or where other factors betoken absence of free choice (for example, duress), constitute excusable actions. Actions required by duty (i.e., a police officer's attempt to enforce the law) and actions constrained by the predicament of self-defense are examples of justifiable actions. As Hart and Honoré have shown, there are a variety of other circumstances as well where actions are not regarded as sufficiently volitional to warrant treating them the way human actions are normally treated.[7] But since they are rarely relevant to the kinds of problems discussed in this essay, they may be put aside.

I do not mean to say that the language of causation is inappropriate when dealing with one person's influence on the actions of another even when the latter's actions are entirely volitional. We commonly speak of one person occasioning the actions of another or of one person's action being the result of what another person says or does. This is appropriate because causation, broadly conceived, concerns the relationship between successive phenomena, whether they have the character of events or happenings, or of another person's volitional actions. The point I mean to stress is that in dealing with the influence of one person upon the actions of another, we refer to a different kind of causal concept than that involved in physical causation.[8] However philosophers may dispute the point,[9] as far as the law is concerned, the way in which a person's acts produce results in the physical world is significantly different from the way in which a person's acts produce results that take the form of the volitional actions of others. The difference derives from the special view we take of the nature of a human action. In the course of this essay, therefore, I will use causation restrictively to refer to relationships in which succeeding events take the form of happenings, exclusive of individuals' volitional actions.

This view of volitional human action has two relevant implications for understanding the doctrine of complicity. First, when we examine a sequence of events that follows a person's action, the presence in the sequence of a subsequent human action precludes assigning causal responsibility to the first actor. What results from the second actor's action is something the second actor causes, and no one else can be said to have caused it through him. This is expressed in the familiar doctrine of *novus actus interveniens*.[10] Second, when we seek to determine the responsibility of one person for the volitional actions of another, the concept of cause is not available to determine the answer. For whatever the relation of one person's acts to those of another, it cannot be described in terms of that sense of cause and effect appropriate to the occurrence of natural events without doing violence to our conception of a human action as freely chosen.[11]

These two implications of how we conceive of human actions give rise to the doctrine of complicity in the following way. Criminal prohibitions take two principal forms. Most prohibitions threaten punishment for particular kinds of actions (of course, with defined mens rea), sometimes only when some harm eventuates from the action, but sometimes whether it does or not. Examples of this form of prohibition include appropriating another's property, receiving stolen goods, breaking and entering defined structures, obtaining property by false pretenses, having sexual relations with another against her will, and killing a person in the course of operating a motor vehicle. On the other hand, we may punish a person for causing some defined harm, with no further description of the action prohibited: causing the death of a human being (killing) is the most common example. To be guilty of the first kind of crime (action crimes) the person charged must engage in the particular kinds of activity prohibited. To be guilty of the second kind (result crimes), he must be found to have caused the result, by any actions that suffice to do so.

How then can the law reach those whose conduct makes it appropriate to punish them for the criminal actions of others—a person, for example, who persuades or helps another to commit a crime? Such persons do not commit action crimes, since they do not engage in the prohibited action. Some general doctrine is required through which such persons may be found liable. But what form should the doctrine take? If it were not for the very special way in which we perceive human actions, causation doctrine might serve this purpose, on the view that one who causes another to commit certain actions falls under the prohibition against committing those actions. But our conception of human actions as freely chosen precludes this analysis. Some alternative doctrine is needed, therefore, that imposes liability on the first actor who is to blame for the conduct of another, but that does so upon principles that comport with our conception of human actions. This is the office of the doctrine of complicity.

What then of result crimes? It again follows from our view of human actions that causation doctrine cannot make the first actor liable for a prohibited result caused by a volitional act of the second actor. As Hart and Honoré put it, the latter's action serves as a barrier through which the causal inquiry cannot penetrate to hold the first actor liable.[12] To hold the first actor for the crime, we need an alternative doctrine that is consistent with our conception of human actions. The doctrine of complicity also fills the doctrinal gap for result crimes.

II. THE THEORY OF COMPLICITY

For the reasons just presented, the doctrine of complicity (sometimes referred to as the law of aiding and abetting, or accessorial liability) emerges to define the circumstances in which one person (to whom I will refer as the secondary party or actor, accomplice, or accessory) becomes liable for the crime of another (the primary party or actor, or the principal).[13] To develop the theory of complicity further, it is necessary now to consider: (A) the nature of the liability imposed on the secondary party; (B) the kinds of actions that create this liability; (C) the intention with which those actions must be committed; and (D) the relevance of the success of those actions in achieving their objective.

A. THE DERIVATIVE NATURE OF THE LIABILITY

The nature of complicity liability follows from the considerations that called it forth. The secondary party's liability is derivative,[14] which is to say, it is incurred by virtue of a violation of law by the primary party to which the secondary party contributed. It is not direct, as it would be if causation analysis were applicable. That is ruled out by our concept of human action, which informs much of complicity doctrine. Volitional actions are the choices of the primary party. Therefore they are his acts and his alone. One who "aids and abets" him to do those acts, in the traditional language of the common law, can be liable for doing so, but not because he has thereby caused the actions of the principal or because the actions of the principal are his acts. His liability must rest on the violation of law by the principal, the legal consequences of which he incurs because of his own actions.

It is important not to misconstrue derivative liability as imparting vicarious liability. Accomplice liability does not involve imposing liability on one party for the wrongs of another solely because of the relationship between the parties. Liability requires action by the secondary actor—as we shall see, intentional action designed to persuade or help—that makes it appropriate to blame him for what the primary actor does. The term "derivative" as used here merely means that his liability is dependent on the principal violating the law. What is at issue is the responsibility of the secondary actor for the principal actor's violation of law. Unless the latter occurs there can be no accomplice liability. Perhaps "dependent" would be a better term. I choose derivative because it has gained some currency.

So understood, the notion of derivativeness can be expressed as well in terms of the requirement of a result: just as causation doctrine requires that the prohibited result occur before there can be an issue of the actor having caused it, so in complicity doctrine there must be a violation of law by the principal before there can be an issue of the secondary party's liability for it.

The most troublesome aspect of the concept of derivative liability is defining the legal status of the principal's actions required to impose liability on an accomplice who aids or encourages him. So far, I have defined it loosely as a violation of law by the principal in order to avoid prejudging the question of how that legal status should be more precisely defined. That question must now be pursued.

The traditional formulation of derivative liability finds the source of secondary party liability in the liability of the primary party. On this view, the liability of the secondary party derives from that of the primary party. The former shares the latter's liability because he contributed to the actions of the primary party that gave rise to the latter's liability. This has become a central axiom of complicity liability. As the Second Circuit recently stated, "It is hornbook law that a defendant charged with aiding and abetting the commission of crime by another cannot be convicted in the absence of proof that the crime was actually committed."[15] An English court gave the principle pungent expression in reversing a conviction of a bus conductor for aiding and abetting the bus driver's careless driving. The conductor had carelessly signaled the driver (who could not see to his rear) that it was safe to back up. In fact, it was not, because passengers were disembarking, and several were struck. Since the driver had been acquitted of negligent driving—because his reliance on the conductor was not negligent—the conviction of the conductor as his aider and abetter became insupportable: "In one breath [the trial justices] say that the principal did nothing which he should not have done, and in the next breath they hold that the bus conductor aided and abetted the driver in doing something which he had not done. . . ."[16]

The derivative nature of the secondary party's liability explains a variety of outcomes in the law of complicity. It is well settled that a secondary party is liable as an accomplice for influencing or aiding another to commit a crime that the secondary party is not himself capable of committing.[17] An unmarried man, for example, cannot himself commit bigamy, because that crime extends only to those who, already married, marry again.[18] But he can be convicted of bigamy as an accomplice for aiding or influencing a married person to commit the crime.[19] Where a husband is incapable of raping his own wife, he may nonetheless be liable for her rape by another if he helps or encourages the other to do the act.[20] Liability in these cases follows logically from the premise that the liability of the secondary party rests on the liability of the primary party. Since the secondary party could not be held for violating the law himself, his liability must be derivative.

The conventional derivative liability principle is also evident in cases in which one person helps another commit a crime, not realizing that the other is only feigning for the purpose of ensnaring him. For example, suppose a person boosts an ostensible principal into a window and the latter, having previously arranged for the police to arrive, and acting without the intent to steal required for burglary, passes out property to his helper. The helper is not liable as an accomplice so long as the feigning principal has incurred no liability by his actions,[21] since the secondary party's liability derives from that of the primary party.

The relation between the degree of liability of the secondary party and that of the primary party likewise evidences the principle that an accomplice's liability derives from that of the primary party. It is widely accepted that the secondary party's liability need not be as great as that of the principal,[22] who may have acted with a mens rea that makes him more culpable than the secondary party. The latter, for example, may, in the heat of provocation, induce the primary party to kill, while the primary party may act with cool deliberation.[23] But this does not contradict the conception of the secondary party's liability as derivative. The accomplice's liability derives from that of the principal no less because it may derive from some and not all of his liability. These cases do not require attributing to the accomplice the volitional actions of the principal, only his (or some of his) liability. They are therefore consistent with the basic premise of complicity liability.

On the other hand, if the accomplice's liability derives from that of the principal, the liability of an accomplice could not exceed that of the principal.[24] However, there are situations in which a secondary actor's liability surely should exceed that of the primary actor. Suppose the instigator with cool deliberation provokes another person to kill in hot blood. The classic instance is Iago coolly whipping Othello into murderous rage. One way to justify a higher liability for Iago is through the doctrine of causation, as we shall later see.[25] Another way to sustain liability in this situation is to reconceive the traditional theory to rest the accomplice's liability on some ground other than the liability of the principal. I will consider shortly what ground that might be. But it is helpful first to consider the extent to which the traditional theory is otherwise in need of repair.

The theory that accomplice liability is altogether controlled by the principal's liability was once taken quite literally. In an early day the common law required the principal to have been convicted before his accomplice could be convicted. This was abandoned by Blackstone's time.[26] It was enough that the principal be proven liable in the trial of the accomplice; his liability need not have been previously established. Subsequent decisions and statutes determined that the accomplice may be liable even when the principal had been tried and acquitted in an earlier trial.[27] This result is consistent with the traditional theory on the view that the principal's acquittal establishes his innocence only in the sense that he may not be punished. The acquittal may have been the product of difficulties of proof at his trial or of the vagaries of jury fact-finding. Double jeopardy precludes trying him a second time. But there is no reason why it should preclude proof of his guilt in a subsequent trial of his accomplice.[28] These developments require a change in formulation, if not in concept, of the traditional view. It would seem more accurate to say that what grounds the liability of the accomplice is the liability of the principal at the time he acted, even though it was not and could no longer be imposed upon him.

This is a minor change, but it is not quite enough to account for accomplice liability in a somewhat different class of cases. Sometimes the principal, though having violated the law with the required mens rea and without excuse or justification, enjoys some special defense that would have precluded his conviction at any time. The principal, for example, may enjoy a defense of diplomatic immunity[29] or entrapment.[30] There seems no reason not to impose accomplice liability upon a person who helps him. The legal defense precludes convicting the primary party for reasons of policy that are inapplicable to convicting the secondary party. But to hold the helper as an accomplice requires an even greater modification of the traditional theory. The reason the principal cannot be held liable is not evidentiary, but substantive; since the law gave him a defense, he never was subject to liability. If the theory of derivative liability is to be preserved, therefore, it must rest not on the principal's liability or potential liability, but on a sense of guilt divorced from liability. The principal must be regarded as guilty because he violated the law with the required mens rea and without excuse or justification, and his guilt in this sense is not negated by the legal defense. In other words, the principal's *guilt* is what the accomplice shares because he contributed to the principal's actions. As one court put it, the principal's defense of entrapment " 'is made available not because inducement negatives criminal intent and thus establishes the fact of innocence, but because Government agents should not be permitted to act in such a fashion. The defense does not so much establish innocence as grant immunity from prosecution for criminal acts concededly committed.' "[31]

But even this modification of the traditional theory may be inadequate where the principal is not liable because he is excused, rather than because he has some defense based on policies extrinsic to his guilt. Suppose, for example, the primary actor acted under the duress of a third party, was legally irresponsible, or, because of a reasonable mistake, believed he was doing something harmless. Under the theory of accomplice liability that derives liability from the *guilt* of the principal, one who culpably helps or instigates such a principal would apparently not be liable as an accomplice because the principal is not guilty. And yet, if it were not for these defenses, which are not as such available to the secondary actor, the actions that he helped the principal perform would be criminal. The secondary actor's culpability is surely unaffected by the fact that the principal has an excuse. Therefore, some doctrinal adaptation is needed to avoid the absurdity of acquitting the defendant in these cases.

The common law's early response was to resort to causation doctrine. Since the acts of the primary party are excused and hence not fully volitional, they can be treated as caused by the actions of the secondary party. Liability is justified by regarding the secondary party as a principal and the primary party a tool—an innocent agent—that he uses to commit the crime. I will deal more fully with the innocent-agency doctrine later in this essay, as one of the several ways in which causation doctrine is used to supplement accomplice doctrine when it fails to inculpate culpable actors.[32] I mention it at this point in order to call attention to the possibility of an alternative move that has not been taken in Anglo-American law. In some foreign jurisdictions, the secondary party is treated as an accomplice notwithstanding the absence of a guilty principal. The theory is that though excused, the primary party did a wrongful act prohibited by the law; the liability of the secondary party derives from the principal's innocent wrongdoing.

This sounds strange to common law ears, and one may wonder why it even needs to be considered in light of the availability of the innocent-agency doctrine. The reason is that the innocent-agency doctrine may prove less than fully adequate to solve the Iago problem.[33] Moreover, it may fail entirely in some cases where the innocence of the principal precludes accomplice liability on traditional grounds. I will tell that story subsequently and, in the course of it, consider further the case for modifying accomplice liability in a way that makes it sufficient for a primary party to have done a wrongful act, even though he is excused and therefore innocent.[34]

B. THE ACTION

Two kinds of actions render the secondary party liable for the criminal actions of the primary party: intentionally influencing the decision of the primary party to commit a crime, and intentionally helping the primary actor commit the crime, where the helping actions themselves constitute no part of the actions prohibited by the definition of the crime. These commonly overlap, because knowledge that aid will be given can influence the principal's decision to go forward. Moreover, the legal consequences are the same whichever mode of participation is involved. Nonetheless, an analytic difference remains: in cases of influence, the secondary actor's liability derives from his contribution to the principal's decision to commit the crime; in the other, his liability is based on the assistance he gives him in executing the crime.

Various terms are used to capture the central notions of assistance and influence. Assistance is sometimes expressed as helping, aiding, or abetting. Liability never turns, however, on the choice among these terms. All embrace ways in which one person may help another commit a crime, including furnishing means, whether material or informational, providing opportunities, and lending a hand in preparation or execution. Influence is expressed in a greater variety of terms, sometimes with overlapping meanings, sometimes with different connotations. *Advise*, like counsel, imports offering one's opinion in favor of some action. *Persuade* is stronger, suggesting a greater effort to prevail on a person, or counseling strongly. *Command* is even stronger, implying an order or direction, commonly by one with some authority over the other. *Encourage* suggests giving support to a course of action to which another is already inclined. *Induce* means to persuade, but may suggest influence beyond persuasion. *Procure* seems to go further, suggesting bringing something about in the sense of producing a result. *Instigate* as well as *incite* suggest stirring up and stimulating, spurring another to a course of action. *Provoke* is roughly equivalent to incite, with the added sense of producing a response by exploiting a person's sensitivities. *Solicit* is generally equivalent to incite in legal usage, although in common usage it suggests simply asking or proposing.

These differences in emphasis and connotation rarely have legal significance. All of these terms describe ways of influencing a person to choose to act in a particular way and therefore constitute a ground of complicity. Occasionally, however, the precise form of influence affects the legal conclusion, most often where statutes employ one or more of these terms restrictively. I shall use the term "influence" compendiously, to cover all these ways of affecting another person's decision to act.

1. INFLUENCE. Holding a secondary party liable for influencing the principal's decision to act is plainly compatible with the premise that the

latter's acts are determined by his own choice. Recognizing that a person is influenced by what other people say and do, just as a person is influenced by all his experiences, does not imply that volitional actions are caused, in the physical sense, the way natural events are determined by antecedent conditions. The choice of the principal is what ultimately determines the effectiveness of the influence.

As Hart and Honoré have pointed out, the characteristic form of influencing another is the giving of reasons for an action. This differs from causal influence in that the influence operates not as a determining condition, but as a consideration that renders a particular course of action more desirable to the primary actor.[35] If one persuades or encourages another to commit a criminal act by appealing to some consideration that moves him, by giving him emotional support and approval, by offering a rationalization for the action, or by similar means, one has not caused the principal to act in the physical sense of cause. These influences did not make the principal act, for he was free to act as he chose. Nonetheless, since the secondary party intentionally initiated the influences in order to induce the principal to act, he may be held liable. This is a commonplace ground for blaming a person in ordinary experience and is reflected in the legal doctrine of complicity.

2. ASSISTANCE.   Liability for helping another commit a crime is likewise compatible with the concept of a volitional action. To say that one may assist another to carry out his intended actions is, of course, not to imply that he caused those actions. Again, the acts the principal does toward commission of the crime represent his own choices. What, then, are the kinds of helping actions that make a person liable as an accomplice?

In some cases where two or more actors contribute to a criminal act, the problem of secondary party liability does not arise. For example, when each of the parties does all the acts constituting the crime, each has committed the crime and is liable as a principal in his own right. Nor does the issue of secondary party liability arise where one does all and the other some of the acts constituting the crime—as where two men hold a victim at gunpoint and one of them takes his wallet. Both are primary parties committing the crime of robbery. The same is true where neither of the parties commits all the acts constituting the crime but together they do, as where one holds a victim at gunpoint while the other, unarmed, takes his wallet. So long as each person commits some of the actus reus of the crime and, acting jointly, they succeed in committing the crime, each is liable as a co-principal.[36]

The problem of the secondary party's liability does arise where one of the parties commits all the acts necessary for the crime and the other does none of these acts but renders some assistance, typically by providing the means or opportunity. The secondary party may serve as lookout, or drive the getaway car, or hold a ladder, or perform numerous other tasks that help the primary party execute the crime.[37] He may also help at the preparation stage, for example, by providing the primary party with some needed material or information.[38] These cases require a special concept of complicity in order to make the helper liable, since his role in each is altogether secondary—he himself does none of the acts constituting any part of the crime.

In both these modes of assistance, preparation and execution, there is usually an element of encouragement to the primary actor. The primary actor's knowledge that he is receiving this assistance constitutes a reason to go forward. Without it he might not choose to engage in the criminal undertaking in the first place, or he might choose to abandon it once started. Insofar as the secondary actor is intentionally providing this encouragement, he could be held liable for influencing the primary party to commit the crime. Nonetheless, providing assistance is a distinct mode of accomplice liability. The secondary party is liable even if the primary party was unaware of the help being provided and, consequently, was not influenced by the aid in his decision to commit the crime or continue his efforts.[39]

C. THE INTENTION

1. THE BASIC REQUIREMENT. Whether the mode of involvement in another's criminal act is influence or assistance, the law of complicity generally requires that the secondary actor act intentionally; that is, he must act with the intention of influencing or assisting the primary actor to engage in the conduct constituting the crime. Thus, courts have held that if a person spontaneously shouts approval to one committing an assault, without really intending to encourage him, he cannot be held as an accomplice in the crimes committed.[40] We can also assume that a person could not be held as an accomplice for recklessly disclosing how a safe could be opened within the hearing of a known safecracker, unless he intended to further the subsequent burglary.[41] Giving disinterested advice on the pros and cons of a criminal venture is closer to the line, and there is sometimes doubt about whether it should suffice to establish liability.[42] But in principle, if it was the purpose of the one giving the advice to influence the other to commit the crime, he is an accomplice; if that was not his purpose, he is not liable.[43] Here again complicity doctrine differs from that of causation, which permits a person to be held liable for a result even if he did not intend it.[44]

The intention requirement, however, does not preclude holding a person for complicity in a crime for which recklessness or negligence suffices for liability, so long as the secondary actor *intended* to help or persuade the primary actor to do the reckless or negligent act. When a

person does an act that recklessly causes the death of another, he is liable
for manslaughter as a principal offender. That he did not intend the
death is irrelevant. Likewise, when another person intentionally helps
or influences the principal to do a reckless or negligent act, he shares
the criminal liability of the principal.[45] Thus, one who knows a boiler is
defective, but nonetheless encourages another to fire it, is an accomplice
to the crime of manslaughter if the boiler explodes and kills someone.[46]
The requirement of intention for complicity liability is satisfied by the
intention of the secondary party to help or influence the primary party
to commit the act that resulted in the harm.[47] These cases, therefore,
mark no exception to the principle that a secondary actor must act
intentionally in influencing or assisting the primary party.[48]

It is important to distinguish these cases from those in which the
criminal liability of the principal arises from actions that go beyond those
that the accomplice intended. The accomplice may have been reckless
as to those further actions. They may have been probable and foreseeable. But on a strict view of the intention requirement (which, as we shall
see, is not always followed), the fact that the further actions result in
death makes only the primary party guilty of manslaughter. The secondary party is not liable for these consequences because he did not
intend the actions that caused them. So, for example, a defendant who
lends his car keys to a driver he knows to have just had several drinks
is an accomplice to the driver's crime of driving under the influence of
alcohol.[49] But strictly, he would not be liable for manslaughter as an
accomplice of the driver if the driver's liability arises out of particular
acts of reckless driving—for example, driving in the wrong direction on
an expressway and colliding with an oncoming vehicle—that the defendant did not intend.[50]

It is important to observe that the intention requirement is independent of the mens rea requirement for the underlying crime. The
latter requirement means that to be liable as an accomplice in the crime
committed by the principal, the secondary party must act with the mens
rea required by the definition of the principal's crime.[51] Thus, if the
principal commits larceny by taking another's property with the required
intention of permanently depriving its owner of it without consent or
claim of right, the secondary party cannot be held as an accomplice
unless he influenced or helped the principal intending (or knowing) that
the principal would so deprive another of his property. If he believed
the principal had a rightful claim to the property, for example, he could
not be held for larceny.

It might seem, therefore, that the requirement that the secondary
party act intentionally to influence or assist the principal is a consequence
of the mens rea requirement of the substantive crime. This view appears
plausible, however, only when we focus on cases where the mens rea of

the underlying crime is knowledge or purpose. But consider the case described in the paragraph before last where recklessness satisfies the requirement for the underlying crime. In lending his car keys to the inebriated person, the lender acted recklessly, and that is all that is required for the crime of manslaughter committed by the driver. Yet the lender's recklessness about the likelihood that the driver would drive the car in the wrong direction is not enough to make him an accomplice. The lender must have *intended* the very acts that gave rise to the liability.[52] It may be seen, therefore, that the intentionality requirement is not the same as the mens rea requirement. In addition to having the mens rea for the underlying crime, the accomplice must intend that the principal commit the acts that give rise to the principal's liability.[53]

2. STRAINS IN APPLICATION. While the requirement that the secondary party intend the criminal action is a conventional feature of complicity doctrine, it is not always rigorously applied and occasionally it is abandoned altogether. This occurs where there is a strong pull toward viewing the actions of the primary party as in some sense fairly attributable to the secondary actor, even though he did not intend the primary actor to commit them.

One class of cases where the intention requirement is not always rigorously applied is that in which the primary party commits a crime in response to the influence or with the aid of the secondary party, but in doing so departs in some way from what the secondary party intended. In some such situations the courts apply the intention requirement straightforwardly. So, for example, if the principal commits a crime wholly different from the one the secondary party intended robs a person he was instructed to assault, for example[54]—the secondary party cannot be held as an accomplice to the crime committed.[55] The same is true even if the unintended crime furthers the general purpose of the secondary party, as where the primary party uses a knife when all the secondary party intended was an unarmed assault.[56] On the other hand, it is not always required that the secondary party intend the very crime he helps the principal to commit.[57] For example, a person who drives a gang of terrorists to their destination knowing they intend some terrorist activity is liable for any crime of terrorism they commit, even if he did not know the particular crime they would commit.[58] It is enough that what they eventually did was within his contemplation as one of the possibilities; it is enough that in this sense he intended their action.[59]

Some modification of the intention requirement also occurs where the principal uses unintended *means* to commit the intended crime. May it be said that the secondary party intended the principal's actions in such a case? Suppose, for example, that contrary to Iago's explicit instructions, Othello had poisoned Desdemona rather than strangling her in her bed. The courts have found no difficulty in finding liability in such cases.[60] The intention required is that the principal should commit the acts constituting the crime, not that he should use the means intended by the accomplice.[61]

The intent requirement must be somewhat more seriously qualified to hold the accomplice liable if the principal makes a mistake regarding the identity of the victim or the targeted property. Consider, for example, a principal who assaults X, mistaking him for Y, whom the secondary party instructed him to assault. Or suppose the principal burglarizes a garage, thinking it was the warehouse the secondary party intended him to burglarize. Under these facts, the principal's acts were not intended by the secondary party, assuming that the relevant acts are characterized as those constituting the crime committed. The accomplice did not intend the principal to assault X or to burglarize the garage. Indeed, he might have had strong reason for not wanting him to do so. Unlike the situations where an unintended means is used, in these instances an unintended crime is committed. The few cases that have faced the issue hold the secondary party liable.[62] These courts view the identity of the victim as irrelevant so long as in all other respects the crime intended by the accomplice is committed. This approach is consistent with the principle of transferred intent, according to which a person who commits a criminal harm is no less guilty because the person or property harmed was not that which he intended to harm.[63] Disregarding the identity of the victim, therefore, is not unique to accomplice liability.

The cases that most clearly challenge the intent requirement are those in which no reasonable construction of the secondary party's intent can embrace the course of action of the principal. Courts sometimes nonetheless hold the secondary party liable, on the ground that the criminal action of the primary party was a probable consequence of the action of the secondary party.[64] Stephen, for example, took the common law to be that "[i]f a person instigates another to commit a crime, and the person so instigated commits a crime different from the one which he was instigated to commit, but likely to be caused by such instigation, the instigator is an accessory before the fact."[65] It is impossible to make this proposition consistent with the usual requirement of intentionality. Indeed, it is inconsistent as well with the related requirement that the accomplice act with the mens rea required of the principal's crime. For it would seem to allow holding the accomplice for a crime of knowledge or purpose committed by the principal as long as he should have anticipated the principal's actions.[66]

Consider, for example, a principal who commits a burglary with the encouragement and planning of a secondary party. Deciding not to climb through a second-story window as planned, he carelessly starts a fire while heating a lock to make it easier to open. As a result, the building is set afire and someone in it is burned to death. It is clear that the secondary party is liable for the burglary. That the primary party used unintended means to commit the intended crime is irrelevant to the secondary party's complicity in the intended crime. It is a different matter, however, to hold him liable for arson or murder. First, his negligence as to the principal's actions of heating the lock do not satisfy the mens rea requirements of arson or murder. Second, since he did not intend those actions, he would not be liable for them under the normal doctrine of complicity. He can be held liable only under an extension of complicity to include crimes that are a probable consequence of the acts intended. It is noteworthy that this occurs primarily in cases involving the felony-murder rule, a rule notorious for its anomalies.

Under the felony-murder rule, the principal is himself guilty of murder if he kills in furtherance of (sometimes only in the course of) a felony, even if his action was only negligent or wholly accidental. Contrary to the principles that normally apply, the mens rea for the felony does service for the mens rea for murder, which otherwise requires an intent to kill, or at least very great recklessness. That being so of the principal, it might appear plausible to treat an accomplice to the felony in the same way.[67] To make the secondary party strictly liable for murder because he has the mens rea for the felony is to treat him no differently than the principal. Holding him for any probable criminal acts committed by the principal in the course of the intended felony surely extends the ground of complicity liability. But in this situation, the ground for murder liability has already been relaxed.[68]

To rationalize the probable consequence rule in this way is to view it as an exception to the normal complicity doctrine produced by the felony-murder rule. Yet this explanation is not wholly satisfactory, for it does not account for the courts' willingness to loosen the requirement of intentionality in contexts other than felony murder. Nor does it account for the occasional abandonment of the requirement by statutes that make a secondary actor liable in all cases for probable, as well as intended, actions of a primary actor.[69] Where the fault of an action is that it increases the chances that another will commit a crime, even though it is not intended to do so, there is an understandable pull to regard the first actor as responsible for the action of the second. If this could be accomplished by the doctrine of causation there would be no need to extend complicity liability. But, as we shall see, though causation doctrine provides a solution in some cases, it does not do so in all.[70] Just as we shall later see a strain in causation doctrine to accommodate these cases, so here we see a strain in complicity doctrine to do so. The complementary doctrines of complicity and causation leave a gap for cases of this sort. I will return to this issue after we have had a chance to see the limits of causation doctrine in these cases. For the moment, let us look more closely at the feature of complicity, the intent requirement, that gives rise to the problem.

3. THEORY OF THE INTENTION REQUIREMENT.   The theory of the intentionality requirement is not obvious. One possible explanation is social policy; namely, that it would be undesirable to draw the circle of criminal liability any wider. A pall would be cast on ordinary activity if we had to fear criminal liability for what others might do simply because our actions made their acts more probable. This has been the dominant consideration in recent debates over proposals to extend liability to those who know their actions will assist another to commit a crime but who act for reasons other than to further those criminal actions—the supplier of materials, for example, who knows that a buyer plans to use them to commit a crime.[71] The argument that people otherwise lawfully conducting their affairs should not be constrained by fear of liability for what their customers will do[72] has tended to prevail over the argument that it is proper for the criminal law to prohibit conduct that knowingly facilitates the commission of crime.[73] The prevailing argument would seem to have even greater force in the case of a person who was only reckless as to the risk that his actions would lead another to commit a crime.

These policy considerations, however, may not be the whole story. If they were decisive, they should preclude extending criminal liability to knowing, reckless, and negligent actions that *cause* another to commit a criminal harm, as well as to actions that influence or assist another to commit a crime. But in those special situations where causation doctrine applies to interpersonal relationships (because the actions of the primary actor are not regarded as fully volitional), courts have shown no disposition to restrict the reach of causation doctrine, which ordinarily extends to unintended as well as intended consequences.[74]

The explanation for the intention requirement must be found elsewhere. It may reside in the notion of agreement as the paradigm mode by which a principal in agency law (the secondary party in the terminology of the criminal law) becomes liable for the acts of another person. The liability of the principal in civil law rests essentially on his consent to be bound by the actions of his agent, whom he vests with authority for this purpose.[75] Under the prevailing objective approach of contract law, it is the principal's manifestation of consent, rather than his subjective state of mind, that determines the authority of the agent and the rights of third parties.[76] But this is attributable to the policy of facilitating business transactions by protecting people who reasonably rely on appearances the principal creates.[77]

Insofar as manifesting consent to be bound by the acts of another is a general requirement for holding one person liable for the actions of another, the requirement of intention for complicity liability becomes more readily explicable. Obviously, in the context of the criminal law, literal consent to be criminally liable is irrelevant. But by intentionally acting to further the criminal actions of another, the secondary party voluntarily identifies himself with the principal party. The intention to further the acts of another, which creates liability under the criminal law, may be understood as equivalent to manifesting consent to liability under the civil law.

This theory would also explain why intention is not required where the ground of accountability for a result is causation.[78] In causation cases, the actor's liability does not derive from the criminal acts of another. Either there is no other person intervening between the actor's action and the result or, in cases of interpersonal relations, the acts·of the later actor are not regarded as volitional because they are excused, and hence are treated the same as any other event that the first actor causes. His liability does not depend on the unlawfulness of the actions of another, but on his own actions, as principal. Intention is therefore not necessary to establish criminal liability.

Assuming this account is correct, there remains a deeper question: why should consent be a general requirement for liability for another's actions? The reason may again involve the characteristic way we view the actions of persons as opposed to events. Persons are autonomous agents, governed by self-determined choices. We are responsible for ourselves and for what our actions cause in the physical world, and we may cause things to happen unintentionally as well as intentionally. However, what other people choose to do as a consequence of what we have done is their action and not ours. Our actions do not cause what they do in the sense that our actions cause events. We become accountable for the liability created by the actions of others, therefore, only when we join in and identify with those actions by intentionally helping or inducing them to do those actions; in other words, by extending our wills to their action.

I am not suggesting that this is a good and sufficient reason for not holding people responsible for the voluntary acts of others that they may recklessly or negligently occasion (though whether this is more suitably accomplished through a causation analysis remains to be considered).[79] I am only proposing that the strong attraction to consent as the necessary condition of accomplice liability may be explained by the law's adherence to the premise of the autonomy of human action.

D. THE RESULT

By its nature, the doctrine of complicity, like causation, requires a result. It is not a doctrine of inchoate liability. If the primary party does not act in violation of the law, there is no unlawfulness for which to hold the secondary actor accountable.[80] We saw this earlier in considering the derivative (or dependent) character of complicity. But there is another feature of the result requirement: not only must there have been an unlawful action by the principal; in addition, the action of the secondary party must have succeeded in contributing to it.[81]

In this way complicity functions like causation; it fixes blame upon a person for a result. Causation determines when a person is responsible for a subsequent event; complicity determines when he is responsible for the subsequent unlawful action of another. The doctrines of causation and complicity are to this extent cognate.

This is not to suggest that it would be incongruous to apply the concept of attempt to complicity, thereby converting it into a doctrine of inchoate liability.[82] Indeed, a number of American jurisdictions, following the lead of the Model Penal Code, have made it punishable as an attempt to try (even unsuccessfully) to help or influence another to commit a crime (though only where the other does commit a crime).[83] This modification is equivalent to expanding the liability for a result crime to reach those who attempt to cause the result. The fact that a person may be liable for attempting to cause a result does not mean that he may be found liable for causing the result on a finding that he tried. The same is true of complicity and attempted complicity. Complicity cannot be established if the acts of the secondary actor were unsuccessful in influencing or assisting the principal to commit the crime.[84] To this extent, the secondary party's liability depends on his own success.

1. SUCCESSFUL CONTRIBUTIONS AND SINE QUA NON CONDITIONS.   If these claims are to hold, however, it is necessary to account for some well-established propositions of complicity doctrine that at first blush seem to undercut the requirement of a successful contribution.

The common notion of success is captured in the ordinary locution of something having mattered, of it having made a difference. In causation, the requirement of a condition sine qua non assures this sense of success, since the requirement means that without the act the result would not have happened as it did. In complicity, however, a sine qua non relationship in this sense need not be established. It is not required that the prosecution prove, as it must in causation cases, that the result would not have occurred without the actions of the secondary party. The commonly accepted formulation is that to establish complicity, any influence or help suffices for liability.[85]

Two familiar cases illustrate these propositions. In *State v. Tally*,[86] Tally's responsibility for a killing committed by two others turned on his attempted aid. Tally had sent a telegram that instructed a telegraph operator not to deliver a telegram previously sent by one of the victim's relatives warning the victim of the killers. The operator did not deliver the warning telegram, and the killers were unaware of Tally's attempt to help them. The court found these facts sufficient to establish Tally's liability as an accomplice, stating:

> The assistance given . . . need not contribute to the criminal result in the sense that but for it the result would not have ensued. It is quite sufficient if it facilitated a result that would have transpired without it. It is quite enough if the aid merely rendered it easier for the principal actor to accomplish the end intended by him and the aider and abettor, though in all human probability the end would have been attained without it. If the aid in the homicide can be shown to have put the deceased at a disadvantage, to have deprived him of a single chance of life, which but for it he would have had, he who furnishes such aid is guilty, though it cannot be known or shown that the dead man, in the absence thereof, would have availed himself of that chance; as where one counsels murder, he is guilty as an accessory before the fact, though it appears to be probable that murder would have been done without his counsel. . . . [87]

In *Wilcox v. Jeffery*,[88] the publisher of a jazz magazine was found guilty of aiding and abetting an illegal public performance by buying a ticket and attending the concert in order to report on it in his magazine. The court upheld the conviction, stating: "The appellant clearly knew that it was an unlawful act for [the saxophonist] to play. He had gone there to hear him, and his presence and his payment to go there was an encouragement."[89]

The doctrine illustrated in these cases[90] raises a question of what it means for the secondary actor's contribution to have made a difference. For in what sense can the contribution be said to have mattered if it was not a necessary condition of the primary party's decision to commit the crime or of his committing it as he did? Should we conclude, after all, that complicity does not require a successful contribution?[91] I think not, for the following reasons.

In at least one class of cases, the same requirement of a sine qua non that prevails in causation also prevails in complicity. There is no accomplice liability where the attempted contribution demonstrably failed to achieve its purpose because it never reached its target.[92] So, for example, if an individual shouts encouragement to another to attack a third person and the attacker is deaf or otherwise unaware of the encouragement, the putative accomplice could hardly be held liable for the assault as a secondary party. He might be held for the independent crime of incitement or solicitation, which by definition does not require success of the inciter's efforts.[93] But he is not liable for the assault because his contribution could not possibly have been effective. The same conclusion applies to demonstrably futile attempts to aid another. The secondary party may be liable if the principal is aware of the proffered aid, since knowledge of the efforts of another to give help may constitute sufficient encouragement to hold the secondary actor liable.[94] But it is well accepted that the secondary actor may not be held liable where his demonstrably ineffective effort to aid is unknown to the primary actor. For example, suppose a person unlocks the door of a building in order to facilitate a burglar's entrance. Unaware of this, the burglar breaks and enters through a window. The secondary actor could not be held as an accomplice to the burglary; he tried but failed to be of assistance. This conclusion would seem necessarily to follow from cases absolving defendants of accomplice liability when their aid arrived after the principal had been apprehended.[95] In these cases, then, the absence of a sine qua non relation between the acts of the primary and secondary actors precludes liability, just as the absence of that relation between the act and a subsequent event precludes liability in causation.

In order to make sense of the apparently conflicting indications the cases give of the requirement of a successful contribution, we need an interpretation of success that accommodates both sets of cases. An interpretation that would do this is one that takes a successful contribution to be one that *could have* contributed to the criminal action of the principal. By "could have contributed," I mean that without the influence or aid, it is *possible* that the principal would not have acted as he did. In complicity cases, unlike causation cases, the prosecution need not prove a but-for relationship. But that does not mean accomplice liability can be imposed if the secondary party fails to influence or aid the principal. When he could not have been successful in any case, there is no liability. But it is enough if the facts establish a possibility of success.

Nevertheless, we are still left with a puzzle. In causation, proof of a but-for relationship is required; in complicity, the possibility of a but-for relationship suffices. How should we account for this difference?

Perhaps the answer follows from the fact that the concept of a sine qua non condition belongs to the natural world of cause and effect, and has no place in accounting for human actions. Physical causation deals with natural events in the physical world. Experience teaches us that natural events occur in consequence of some antecedent events, whether those antecedent events are the conduct of persons or other natural events. Barring miracles, so long as we know the causal laws we can speak with certainty. This permits of the concept of sufficient conditions, enabling us to conclude that if those conditions are present, a certain result has to occur. It also permits of the concept of necessary conditions, enabling us to conclude that if some conditions are absent, the result cannot occur. In cases of causation, therefore, once the facts are established, we can determine with certainty whether a condition was a sine qua non of a subsequent event. We can say in every instance either that the event would not have happened if that condition were not present, or that it would have occurred even if the condition were absent. Of course, the facts may be in dispute or be unascertainable, and we may have to find them on the level of probability. But the future is latent in the past; if we knew all the facts (and all the relevant laws) we could determine what would happen with certainty. The laws of cause and effect permit no other conclusion.

Cases of influencing another to commit an act are different. We do not view a chain of events that includes volitional human actions as governed solely by the laws of nature. In complicity, the result at issue is another volitional human action, which we perceive as controlled ultimately by that actor's choice, not by natural forces. No matter how well or fully we learn the antecedent facts, we can never say of a voluntary action that it had to be the case that the person would choose to act in a certain way.

In a word, every volitional actor is a wild card; he need never act in a certain way. He responds as he chooses to influences and appeals. It may be in a given case that the principal would not have chosen to act without the influence of the accomplice. But this is never necessarily so, in the sense, for example, that my tilting my chair was a necessary condition of its tipping over. Since an individual could always have chosen to act without the influence, it is always possible that he might have. No laws of nature can settle the issue. Sine qua non in the physical causation sense, therefore, does not exist in any account of human actions. On the view of human action I have been postulating, there are no sufficient conditions for an act of will; nor are there any necessary conditions, save those like knowledge and nonconstraint, without which there can be no free act of will at all.

In dealing with the meaning of a successful contribution, I have thus far dwelled mainly on contributions that take the form of influence. Only a few further points need be made where the contribution takes the form of aid. If the principal is aware of the aid, as he is in most cases of complicity, the possibility of influence (through reliance and encouragement) is always present. Apart from this, in most cases where aid has been successfully given, it can be said that without that aid, the crime would not have been committed as it was; in this sense the secondary party's aid is a but-for condition of the crime. That is the very meaning of successful aid in contrast to attempted aid. So, for example, if I provided the crowbar that the principal uses to gain illegal entry, my assistance was a but-for condition of the entry. To be sure, he might have entered anyway—with his own crowbar or by other means. But he did not. My aid was necessary for what actually happened.

This is not the case, however, if the aid is unknown to the principal and takes the form of influence upon a third person to do (or not to do) an action designed to aid the principal. The *Tally* case is an example.

It cannot be demonstrated that the deceased's life would have been spared if Tally had not instructed the telegraph operator to withhold the warning telegram.[96] This is because human actions intervened. Hence, all one could demonstrate is that the aid might have made a difference. These cases of aid, therefore, are subject to the same analysis as all cases of influence.

I have argued that the concept of the sine qua non condition is one that involves results occurring as a matter of necessity, and that it therefore has no application to acts of will. Nonetheless, whether the principal would have committed the crime if the secondary party had not acted as he did is determinable as a historical surmise on the basis of a probabilistic inference from the proven facts. Why should the mere possibility that this was the case be enough, rather than some higher showing? This involves the issue of the required extent of the influence or aid, to which I now turn.

2. MINIMAL CONTRIBUTIONS.   It is often said that any amount of influence or aid suffices, no matter how slight.[97] Is this evidence that a successful contribution is not required after all? Again, not if the liability requires only the possibility of success. Except where it never reached the target, any influence or aid could always have made a difference, even if it took such trivial form as giving the principal moral encouragement,[98] or lending him a covering to protect his clothing.[99] Therefore, when it is said that any aid or influence will suffice, no matter how slight, it must mean that any such contribution that might have made a difference will be enough.

This analysis bears on the controversy over conspiracy as a proper ground of complicity. An implicit or explicit agreement to participate in a criminal venture is commonly regarded as an independent basis for holding every party liable for any criminal action committed by coconspirators in furtherance of the agreement, even if the party does nothing more. This doctrine has been much criticized as an unjustified extension of liability to persons who would not be liable under the normal doctrines of complicity. Even those who defend the doctrine concede that it is an extension.[100] Yet it is important to see to what extent it constitutes an extension and to what extent it does not.

Conspiracy apparently became an independent basis for complicity liability on the theory of agency that figures so prominently in conspiracy doctrine generally: that each conspirator is an agent of the others and each is therefore liable for what the others do. This theory extends liability for the acts of another beyond what complicity doctrine permits in two circumstances. First, to the extent that complicity doctrine requires that a secondary party intend the criminal actions of the principal, it imposes a narrower liability than conspiracy. Under conspiracy theory, one conspirator is liable for all actions of his coconspirator, whether intended by the conspirator or not, so long as the acts were committed in furtherance of the common goal of the conspiracy. Second, conspiracy theory imposes a broader liability insofar as it has extended the concept of an agreement to embrace any kind of participation in an organized activity united only by an abstractly defined common purpose.[101] If, however, agreement were given its normal meaning the scope of conspiracy and complicity liability for the acts of another would appear coterminous, since agreement is as much encouragement as complicity doctrine requires.

So the Supreme Court concluded in *Pinkerton v. United States*,[102] where it applied conspiracy doctrine to hold the defendant liable for the acts of bootlegging of a coconspirator even though the acts were unknown to the defendant, who was in prison for another offense at the time. The Court said:

> The criminal intent to do the act is established by the formation of the conspiracy. Each conspirator instigated the commission of the crime. The unlawful agreement contemplated precisely what was done. It was formed for the purpose. The act done was in execution of the enterprise. The rule which holds responsible one who counsels, procures, or commands another to commit a crime is founded on the same principle.[103]

In a case like this, the contribution of the secondary party is exceedingly attenuated. But this result is no more than the doctrine of complicity would technically permit, since the degree of likelihood that the contribution made a difference is irrelevant, so long as there is a chance that it did.

These cases seem excessive because they hold a secondary party liable for the acts of a principal in circumstances where the possibility that the secondary's actions mattered at all is remote. In sentencing, we would expect a judge to give weight to the extent of the accomplice's contribution. Certainly it would not be contrary to the theory underlying the doctrine of complicity to require a substantial contribution.[104] Nor would it be contrary to complicity doctrine to create a separate and lesser punishment classification for those whose contribution is less than substantial.[105] If it is a fault to impose liability at all for a highly attenuated contribution, it belongs to complicity, not conspiracy.

3. CONTRIBUTION UNKNOWN TO THE PRINCIPAL. There is one remaining issue to be considered on the meaning of the contribution requirement: must the principal be aware of the influence or assistance the accomplice is intentionally furnishing? Certainly in the case of aid the law is clear enough: it is well settled that one who intentionally aids

another in committing a crime is liable for the crime whether or not the principal is aware of his aid. The *Tally* case[106] is a clear example.

Some uncertainty lingers, however, when the secondary actor influences the principal without the latter's knowledge. There is little to go on in the reported cases, but the considerable authority of James Fitzjames Stephen stands against liability in such cases. He argued:

> Suppose, for instance, A. tells B. of facts which operate as a motive to B. for the murder of C. It would be an abuse of language to say that A. had killed C., though no doubt he has been the remote cause of C.'s death. If A. were to counsel, procure, or command B. to kill C. he would be an accessory before the fact to the murder, but I think that if he had stopped short of this A. would be in no way responsible for C.'s death, even if he expected and hoped that the effect of what he said would be to cause B. to commit murder. In Othello's case, for instance, I am inclined to think that Iago could not have been convicted as an accessory before the fact to Desdemona's murder, but for one single remark—"Do it not with poison, strangle her in her bed."[107]

Stephen appears to have in mind cases in which a secondary party truthfully reveals facts to another, with the effect, intended by the secondary party, of motivating the other to commit a homicide. He treats *Othello* as a case of this kind, though, of course, in the play Iago stages an elaborate lie. On this footing, the reason he gives for his conclusion— that though the secondary party was the remote cause of the victim's death, he could not be said to have killed the victim—is inapposite. Complicity, as we have seen, does not rest at all on the secondary party having himself killed the victim, but on actions of his that make him liable for the killing by the primary party.[108]

The real question in this hypotheticals is whether it is any part of the requirement of a successful contribution through influence that the principal be aware that he is being influenced. There would not appear to be any reason why this should be so. That rendering aid unknown to the principal suffices for accomplice liability should make this evident. The theory of complicity liability is satisfied so long as influence succeeds, as intended, in contributing to the decision of the principal to commit the crime. That the latter is unaware of the secondary party's intention appears quite irrelevant, for one may influence another just as powerfully by giving him reason, in the sense of giving him cause, as by giving him reasons presented as such—witness the Othello case, even if the facts had been that Iago was telling the truth.[109]

The difficulty with these cases lies elsewhere. It has to do, I suggest, with concern over proof of the requisite intent. Furnishing aid to an unwitting primary party evidences, or at least corroborates, the secondary party's intent. Volunteering the truth to another is different. It is as consistent with an innocent state of mind as with a culpable one. Consider

Othello's case on the assumption that Iago was telling the truth: a lieu-
tenant discloses to his leader that he is being cuckolded by another of
his lieutenants. To make this the basis of accessory liability invites judicial
examination of how far the disclosure was motivated by Othello's expected reaction rather than duty or friendship. Making the telling of
the truth an element of criminal liability casts a long shadow over proper
social behavior.

This concern largely disappears, however, where the instigator's
action takes the form of lying and deceit. Iago's actions leave no doubt
what his game is. It is played out when Othello kills Desdemona, and
there is no reason why Iago should not be held accountable as Othello's
accessory.[110] There is the problem of whether Iago can be convicted of
a greater crime than Othello, but that raises a different question that
we shall come to later.[111]

4. REMOTE AND PROXIMATE RELATIONSHIPS BETWEEN CONTRIBUTION AND
RESULT.   Cause requires a strong relationship between an act or event
and a consequence, the relationship of sine qua non. But that relationship
is never enough to fix blame for a result, either in ordinary usage or in
the law. The sine qua non condition must be an adequate, proximate,
or legal cause. The definition of these terms is the central problem of
the law of causation. The legal requirement rules out relationships bro-
ken by intervening volitional actions and rules out cases where the result
is remote, occurring through coincidence, abnormality, or accident.[112]
Hart and Honoré have made a notable contribution to understanding
these concepts in *Causation in the Law*. I raise them here to show their
relevance to complicity.

Complicity and causation are cognate concepts. They fix blame for
a result characterized by a but-for relationship to the actor's contribution,
although complicity allows a weaker version of that relationship. Since
that relationship is not sufficient to establish legal causation when the
result is too remote or accidental, or too dependent on the volitional act
of another, we should expect the same to be true of complicity. In fact
it is, although the considerations analogous to legal cause in causation
theory are often obscured by mens rea issues.[113]

We encountered one set of cases that instance these considerations
in the discussion of the intentionality requirement. Variations between
what the primary party did and what the secondary party intended him
to do can affect complicity liability. Where the variation takes the form
of the principal committing an entirely different crime than that intended by the secondary party, the latter is not liable.[114] The absence
of the required mens rea—the intent that the primary party should
commit the act, as well as the mens rea for the crime committed—suffices
to explain this conclusion. There is, however, an alternative explanation

for these cases that rests upon the same considerations underlying the concept of legal cause in causation. In *Regina v. Anderson & Morris*,[115] for example, the defendant joined another in a simple assault. In the course of the assault, the other attacker unexpectedly killed the victim with a concealed knife. In reversing the secondary party's conviction for manslaughter, the court said:

> [A]s a matter of common sense . . . the death resulted or was caused by the sudden action of the adventurer who decided to kill and killed. Considered as a matter of causation there may well be an overwhelming supervening event which is of such a character that it will relegate into history matters which would otherwise be looked upon as causative factors.[116]

The independent force of these considerations appear most clearly in cases in which the liability does not attach even though the mens rea requirements are met. A common example is the case of a principal who deliberately chooses a different victim than the one intended by the secondary party. If the principal *mistakenly* burglarizes the wrong premises or robs the wrong person, the courts hold the secondary party liable.[117] They regard the intent requirement as satisfied if the secondary party intended the primary party to commit a burglary or a robbery, and the primary party committed that crime. It should follow, then, that the intent requirement is equally satisfied where the principal *deliberately* chooses to burglarize a different building or to rob a different person. Yet in this situations, it is clear that the secondary party is not liable.[118]

The explanation for this result cannot be the absence of mens rea or the absence of the kind of sine qua non relationship required for complicity, for both are present. The explanation lies in the same kind of consideration that precludes a but-for cause from being treated as a proximate cause in the law of causation. In the above hypotheticals, the determining factor is the force of the intervening volitional act of the principal in choosing a different victim. When he intentionally does so, his independent choice, not shared in or contributed to by the secondary party, precludes liability, just as it would in causation cases.[119]

There is nothing in principle to confine these considerations to cases involving the principal's deliberate departure from the agreed plan. One may presume that similar considerations would operate in any situation where, though the crime intended is actually committed, the contribution of the secondary party worked out in unanticipated, abnormal, or co-incidental ways. Suppose a foreigner, *A*, witnessing a fight between two persons, tells one of them, *B*, that he can find a knife in a nearby desk drawer. *B* pays no attention because he does not understand the language in which *A* is speaking—Hindustani, let us assume. If, quite by chance, another bystander, who does happen to understand Hindustani, conveys the information to B, who then uses the knife to kill his adversary, would A be guilty as an accomplice to the deadly assault?[120] Or assume that A, without B's knowledge, leaves a battery-operated radio transmitter in B's apartment for B to use to send secret information to the enemy. But instead of using the transmitter to transmit, B uses the light it emits to read a secret memorandum he then transmits by other means, the power suddenly having failed in his apartment. Would A be liable as an accomplice? These examples are arguable, but the point is that they would have to be argued in the same terms that would be apposite if the issue were causation rather than complicity; namely, whether the unintended and abnormal way in which the aid was received precluded liability.

III. CAUSING ACTIONS

I have presented complicity thus far as a doctrine designed to cover the liability of one party for the volitional actions of another. Causation, I have argued, cannot serve to impose liability because the volitional acts of another are not perceived as caused in the full sense of physical causation. There are situations, however, where the complicity doctrine fails, or at least falters, though the case for inculpation is strong. I had occasion earlier to call attention to these situations. They arise where the primary party is not culpable and therefore incurs no guilt that the accomplice can be made to share;[121] where the principal is guilty, but of a lesser crime than the secondary party deserves to be held for;[122] and where the secondary party risks but does not intend the unlawful actions of the primary party.[123] In each of these situations, causation doctrine has been pressed into service to fill the gaps in complicity doctrine. The justification for doing so is that special features of the situations permit it to be said that the primary actor's conduct was caused by the secondary actor. The successes and failures of this doctrinal rescue mission are the subject of this Part of the essay. I will consider in Section A the situations where the principal actor is innocent, and in Section B those where the principal actor is less culpable than the secondary actor. I will then consider in Section C the situations where the secondary party unintentionally occasions crimes committed by another.

A. NONCULPABLE ACTIONS

Since the liability of the accomplice derives from that of the principal, the former cannot be held liable unless the latter has acted in violation of the law.[124] Normally, this conclusion is consonant with our conceptions of blame. If the action of a primary actor is not blameworthy, there is no basis for blaming the secondary actor for influencing or helping that action. There are cases, however, in which the actions of the principal constitute a criminal harm even though he may not be blamed for them. When this is so, the instigating actor may sometimes be held accountable for the innocent actor's conduct on the view that he caused it. The innocent actor is treated as the innocent agent of the party who culpably aided or influenced him. In this Section I will consider (1) the theory and function of the innocent-agency doctrine and (2) the problems created when the innocent-agency doctrine does not apply because of the way the crime is defined.

1. THEORY OF THE INNOCENT-AGENCY DOCTRINE. This doctrine is grounded on the premise that in some circumstances it is appropriate to rely on causation analysis to hold the secondary actor liable for the actions of the primary actor. When the primary actor is not blameworthy, even though his actions inflict a criminal harm, the reason is that his actions are not regarded as volitional. This will be principally for one of two reasons. Either his actions will be excusable—because he acts without mens rea, is legally irresponsible, or otherwise excusable—or they will be justifiable, as in the case of a police officer performing his duty, or a victim acting in self-defense. For purposes of causation doctrine, excusable and justifiable actions are not seen as completely freely chosen.[125] In this Section, I will deal with cases of the first kind, that is, those where the primary actor is excused. Cases of the second kind, where the primary actor is justified, typically involve actions by the primary actor that the secondary actor did not intend.[126] They are therefore properly dealt with in Section C.

Where the defendant intentionally manipulates an innocent person to commit what would be a crime if the innocent person were not legally excused, the defendant is seen as causing the other's act in the same way he would be seen to cause a physical event. The primary actor becomes "merely an instrument" of the secondary actor.[127] When the former's overt acts are prohibited by law, or cause a result prohibited by law, the secondary actor becomes liable, not derivatively, but directly as the principal. "In point of law, the act of the innocent agent is as much the act of the procurer as if he were present and did the act himself."[128] So one who induces a child below the age of discretion to take money from his father's till is guilty of larceny,[129] one who deliberately induces another to administer deadly poison to a third person in the belief that it is medicine is guilty of murder,[130] and one who passes a fraudulent document to another knowing that the latter will innocently place it in the mails is guilty of mail fraud.[131]

It is quite natural to conceive of the secondary actor as causing the actions of the primary actor in these cases, and, therefore, of causing the results of the actions of the primary actor.[132] It is less natural to conceive of the actions of the primary actor as those of the secondary actor himself, as if the former were literally a machine or a physical instrument. Conduct of some kinds of irresponsible persons—those, for example, with a psychosis so severe that they resemble automatons—may plausibly be thought of as that of the person who instigated it, rather than of the irresponsible person himself. By contrast, consider a child just below the age of responsibility, or a responsible person who is laboring under a reasonable mistake. Their conduct may be thought of as the product of the secondary actor's manipulation, but much less easily as the action of the secondary actor and not of their own. Surely there is an element of metaphor, if not fiction, at work here, owing its provenance to the need to provide for the liability of the secondary actor for action crimes, as well as for result crimes.[133]

One feature of the doctrine of innocent agency bears noting at this point. The fact that the induced actor is innocent of a crime does not itself make him an innocent agent of the actor who induced his action. We saw earlier that where A helps or encourages B to commit a crime that B has no intention of committing, B's purpose being only to ensnare A, A cannot be held as an accomplice.[134] This follows from the derivative character of accomplice liability—there is no liability or guilt of the principal actor for which A can be held accountable. But neither may A be held as a principal under the innocent-agency doctrine. The practical reason is surely as Professor Williams suggests: "It would be unjust to allow [B] in these circumstances to manufacture a consummated crime on the part of [A] by conduct of his own."[135] The doctrinal explanation is equally clear: B is not acting as the instrument of A at all; he is a responsible and fully aware actor, making wholly volitional choices. Hence his actions may not be said to be caused by A.

The doctrine of causation through an innocent agent has been widely applied in a great variety of situations.[136] It has become the prevailing doctrinal move for holding a culpable secondary party liable where accomplice liability would fail because of the absence of a guilty principal. However, there are cases without a guilty principal that are not properly resolved by this move, resulting in a potential doctrinal hiatus. I now turn to these cases.

2. THE LIMITS OF THE INNOCENT-AGENCY DOCTRINE. Crimes defined to prohibit a result, with no requirement that the result be achieved by particular kinds of actions or by particular classes of persons (result crimes, as I earlier called them), can always be handled by causation doctrine. For example, a person "kills" another when his action causes the death of another. It is irrelevant whether he does so with his hands, with an instrument, or through the actions of another, which, because they are not fully volitional, he may be said to cause.[137] Action crimes,

on the other hand, sometimes create formidable difficulties for the doctrine of causation through innocent agency. These are crimes whose definition includes engaging in specified kinds of actions, whether or not a result is required. Sometimes the action can be committed only by a defined class of persons.

It is easy to see the difficulties in applying the innocent-agency doctrine to crimes so defined that they can only be committed by designated classes of persons. If a statute prohibits an officer or employee of a bank from entering false records of transactions, then one who is not an officer or an employee cannot commit the offense. If he helps or encourages a culpable officer or employee to do so, he can be held as an accomplice. As such, his liability is derived from that of the culpable officer or employee. If, however, he dupes an innocent officer or employee into doing so, the absence of a guilty principal precludes accomplice liability. The usual recourse, therefore, is to apply the innocent-agency doctrine on the theory that the instigator has done the prohibited act, using the officer or employee as his instrument. But because the instigator is not an officer or employee, he cannot violate the statute. Thus, in this case, the innocent-agency doctrine would not serve to make him liable.

A second, more elusive difficulty derives not from a legislative judgment to limit the proscribed action to defined classes of persons, but from the nature of the action proscribed. Most criminal actions can readily be committed through the instrumentality of another person: breaking and entering (burglary),[138] taking another's property (larceny),[139] obtaining property by deception (false pretenses,[140] or making and uttering (forgery).[141] But some actions can be done by the actor only with his own body and never through the action of another. I will call these nonproxyable actions. A sober defendant may cause an insensate and disorderly drunk to appear in a public place by physically depositing him there. But we could hardly say that the sober person has, through the instrumentality of the drunk, himself committed the criminal action of being drunk and disorderly in a public place. A defendant may cause a married person to marry another by falsely leading the married person to believe his prior marriage was legally terminated. But the defendant could hardly be held liable for the crime of bigamy, since one does not marry simply by causing another person to marry.[142] A defendant may cause a man to have intercourse with a nonconsenting woman, perhaps by duress or by inducing him to misinterpret the resistance of the woman. But we cannot properly say that the defendant (who might in fact be a woman) has, through the agency of another man, committed rape by having sexual intercourse with a woman against her will. Or, to take a final example, a visitor to a prison who abducts a prisoner could not be said to have committed the crime of escaping from prison by forcing a prisoner to do so.[143]

That certain actions cannot be committed through the agency of another person does not, I think, reflect any moral considerations. It reflects, rather, our understanding of those actions. What it means to be drunk and disorderly, to marry, to have sexual intercourse, or to escape from prison, is to do these things through one's own person. Personal conduct is a necessary element simply because that is what these actions import in common usage and understanding.

Thus, the limits to the reach of the innocent-agency doctrine are wholly technical, both in the case of nonproxyable actions and actions limited to a defined class of persons.[144] They derive from definitional considerations rather than moral or policy ones. If a defendant may fairly be held liable when he aids or encourages a *guilty* principal to commit the crime (even where the defendant is not within the defined class or where the criminal action is nonproxyable), there is no moral or policy reason why he should not be similarly treated if he causes the prohibited actions of an *unwitting* primary actor.

Technical impasses of this kind are of interest because they are part of the natural history of doctrinal developments. Criminal law doctrine functions to give general expression of the circumstances in which liability may be imposed consistent with penal policy, but limited by judgments of moral blameworthiness. Sometimes, however, situations arise in which the logical implications of the doctrine, resisted only at the expense of consistency and coherence, produce conclusions that are anomalous. In short, doctrine sometimes fails us. Let us see how courts have responded to the predicament created by the limitations of the innocent-agency doctrine.

The problem of the nonproxyable action has arisen principally in cases involving sex crimes. Only rarely, however, have courts felt obliged to deny liability on the ground that having sex is a nonproxyable action. *Dusenbery v. Commonwealth*[145] was such a case. An armed guard, coming upon a teenage boy and girl preparing to have sex, threatened to tell their parents if they did not continue while he watched. They attempted to do so, and at one point the defendant used physical force upon the boy to cause him to achieve penetration. The court reversed the guard's rape conviction, holding the innocent-agency doctrine inapplicable to rape, which required that penetration be achieved by the person of the defendant himself.

Generally, however, the courts have manifested less regard for the niceties of doctrine. A number of American cases raise the issue of liability of a husband's liability for rape when he threatens deadly force to compel his wife and another to have intercourse. The courts have upheld the husband's conviction, although on varying grounds. In one case,[146] the other man's actions were held not to be excused, thereby permitting the husband to be held as an accomplice on conventional grounds.[147] In another, where the innocence of the other man was assumed, the court upheld the husband's conviction of assault with intent to commit rape (the other man having failed to achieve penetration), concluding that the law "couples the act of the instrument with the felonious intent of the instigator."[148] In still another case the court upheld the conviction without giving a reason.[149]

A similar case was decided in California, with the difference that it was the wife who used an armed threat to compel her husband to have sex with a nonconsenting woman.[150] The court of appeal upheld the wife's rape conviction on what it termed the "innocent conduit theory," finding nothing extraordinary in the application of this theory to the facts. The court also noted that it was well established that a woman could be held as an aider and abettor of a rape by a man, and saw no reason why the same should not be true where the man was excused on grounds of duress.[151] Otherwise, said the court, "the law . . . would create a crime without a punishable perpetrator."[152]

Each of the cases involving a defendant husband and a victim wife was further complicated in that the defendant was not a member of a class capable of committing the offense. Under the prevailing definition of rape a husband could not rape his own wife. Unlike the issue of the nonproxyable nature of the action, which is rarely perceived, this issue was squarely faced in these cases. The difficulty was overcome, however, by a plausible redefinition of the husband's exclusion as a "privilege that is a personal one only" with no application to a husband who forces another to have intercourse with his wife.[153] This solution was not open to the court in the case where the woman was convicted of raping another woman through the instrument of her husband. What, after all, could one do with the statute's limitation of the crime of rape to males? The court's non sequitur—that if a person can be held as an accessory she can be held as a principal—did service here as well.[154]

These cases attracted nothing like the attention English writers have given two English decisions. The first was *Regina v. Bourne*,[155] where the court upheld the defendant's conviction as an accomplice to his wife's act of buggery with a dog, even on the view that he had terrorized her into submitting, thereby giving her a defense of duress to the crime. The absence of a guilty principal did not, in the court's view, preclude finding the defendant liable as an accessory. Her defense of duress, the court held, did not mean that she did not commit the crime, only that "she prays to be excused from the punishment for the consequences of the crime by reason of the duress."[156] The court did not speak at all of the innocent-agency doctrine, which would have had to rest on the notion that the man had sex with the dog by compelling his wife to do so.

The second English case was *Regina v. Cogan & Leak*.[157] Leak induced Cogan, while both were drunk, to have sex with Leak's wife by persuading Cogan, contrary to the truth, that she was willing. In fact he had compelled his wife to submit. Cogan's conviction of rape was quashed on appeal under a then-recent holding of the House of Lords[158] that a man who believes a woman was consenting is not guilty of rape even if his belief is unreasonable. But Leak's conviction of rape was nonetheless affirmed.

The court appeared to rest its decision on two independent grounds. First it seemed to suggest that accomplice liability would lie because the crime was actually committed: "The fact that Cogan was innocent of rape because he believed that she was consenting does not affect the position that she was raped. . . . [N]o one outside a court of law would say that she had not been."[159] Second, the court reasoned that Leak could be regarded as a principal who, by causing Cogan to have forced sex with the victim, himself raped her, using Cogan's "body as the instrument for the necessary physical act."[160] As in the American cases, the court avoided the incapacity of a husband to rape his wife by limiting the rule to a husband who accomplishes sexual relations through his own person.[161]

The solutions the courts have reached in the preceding cases are not, in the end, satisfactory. It is sensible and doctrinally unexceptional to solve the problem of the exclusion of a husband from the class of those capable of committing rape by interpreting the exclusion as not extending to a husband who forces another man on his wife. But this limitation will not solve the general problem of statutory definitions of crimes restricting potential offenders to those belonging to a particular class. The solutions to the problem of crimes defined in terms of nonproxyable actions, on the other hand, would solve the general problem, but are based on doubtful reasoning.

Of course, the innocent-agency theory may be made to work if the concept of nonproxyable actions is simply rejected, so that any criminal action may be committed through the instrumentality of another person. The price of doing so, however, is to depart from the commonsense understanding of these actions. While this may create only a minor oddity in cases of rape by a male instigator, it would present more jarring anomalies in cases such as those in which a woman is an instigator. Professor Williams' comment makes the point tellingly:

> [I]f the duress is applied by a woman it would need an even greater degree of hawkishness than that displayed by the court in *Cogan* to call her a constructive man. Yet it is highly illogical that a man can commit rape through an innocent agent when a woman cannot, because if the notion of innocent agency is held to be applicable, so that the bodily acts of an innocent agent are attributed to the instigator, the sex of the instigator (the fact that the instigator lacks the sex organ of the innocent agent) becomes irrelevant.[162]

We have seen one California case where this remarkable conclusion was accepted with equanimity, but only under the reassuring delusion that it was no different than holding a woman liable as accessory to the crime of rape committed by a man.[163]

The argument for accessorial liability is also problematic. The statement in *Bourne* that the husband's liability as accessory can rest on that of his wife because her defense of duress is only an appeal to be excused from punishment is plainly incorrect. The wife could not be punished because she was not guilty of the crime, not because special circumstances would justify the court in withholding punishment.[164] No more persuasive is the strange argument in *Cogan* that the wife was raped because nonlawyers would think so.[165]

The purpose of these comments is not to show that judges sometimes falter. It is rather to draw attention to the predicament in which doctrine can place judges when, in unusual cases, it fails to inculpate blameworthy defendants. How should a court respond? In all but one of the above cases in which the courts faced this predicament, they found a way to uphold the conviction of culpable actors, though without producing a persuasive doctrinal justification for doing so. Whether that is a lesser evil than reversing the convictions of reprehensible defendants seems readily answerable in these cases where all would agree on the defendants' culpability. Indeed, the doctrinal arguments to the contrary have the distinct smell of the lamp. It may be more worrisome, however, in other cases where we are less content to permit guilt to be determined by the judge's view of who is culpable rather than by the consistent application of legal doctrine. I will not consider this dilemma further; it raises a familiar and frequently studied issue, and it would take us afield. Instead, I want to consider if it is possible in these cases to sustain liability on doctrinally acceptable grounds.

One proposed solution is to rest the secondary actor's liability as an accomplice on his having aided and abetted the actus reus committed by the innocent principal. This is a possible interpretation of the alternate ground advanced in *Cogan & Leak* for holding the defendant liable for rape as an accomplice,[166] and it has received the approval of Smith and Hogan.[167] The theory is most explicitly articulated in a comment to *Cogan & Leak* appearing soon after the decision:

> The principle . . . is that when a man causes the *actus reus* of a crime with the *mens rea* of the same crime he is guilty of the offence either as the principal offender or as an aider, abettor, counsellor or procuror, according to the facts. Where the facts can be brought within the innocent agency principle, there is no difficulty—the accused is the principal offender. Where they cannot be brought within that principle there is no difference in substance—the harm proscribed by the law has been brought about with the degree of fault required as a condition of guilt.[168]

In the above cases, there is no problem in treating the actions of the principal as caused by the secondary actor. But this only justifies applying the innocent-agency doctrine, which, for the reasons discussed, does not establish liability in these cases. On the other hand, there is a real difficulty in concluding that since the culpable instigator caused the actions of the primary actor, he may be held as an accomplice. For this amounts to adopting the causation analysis, and then labeling the inducing party an accomplice to avoid the difficulties created by treating him as a principal.

A person may be an accomplice to a crime committed by another even if he is not within the class of persons to whom the criminal prohibition is explicitly and solely directed. And, of course, it is never an objection to accomplice liability that the crime can be committed only by the personal actions of the actor. But it must be remembered why these consequences follow. It is because of the premise that the liability of the accomplice is derived from the guilt of the principal. The basis of the accomplice's liability is not that he himself has committed the crime, but that the principal has. The crime of the accomplice is that he helped or persuaded the principal to do so.

But on the theory that one can be an accomplice to the mere actions of the principal party there is no basis at all for any of these consequences, since the "accomplice" himself commits the crime (albeit through the primary party's actions); the primary party does not. The theory uses the accomplice label without its substance, a kind of doctrinal patchwork. It yields the sound result in these particular troublesome cases, but by fiat rather than by logic. Taken seriously, the theory would unsettle sensible results that traditional doctrine has achieved in other cases. Consider the feigning principal we discussed earlier. He lets the defendant help him perform the actus reus of a crime, burglary, for example, that he has no intention of committing (although the defendant believes otherwise).[169] If it suffices for accomplice liability that a culpable actor aids and abets the actus reus of a crime, then the defendant would be an accomplice to the crime the primary actor was only feigning.

The difficulties with this theory highlight the appeal of another, which escapes some of the major flaws of the first by a subtle but significant change in formulation. Professor Fletcher first drew attention to this option in the English literature,[170] and it has since attracted the attention of several English writers.[171] It derives from the German law's distinction between justification and excuse. When a person is exculpated because his act is justified (or because what he did is not prohibited), there is no wrong committed. But where a person is exculpated because he is excused, the wrong has been done, although the defendant is, for reasons that apply only to him, not guilty. It is to the commission of this wrong that the secondary party is an accomplice, rather than to the actus reus (not every actus reus entails a wrong); his liability derives from the wrong done by the primary party. (I will refer to this as the innocent-wrong theory.)

We saw earlier in the Section on derivative liability the difficulty in identifying the feature of the principal's conduct from which the liability of the accomplice derives.[172] The actual liability of the principal provides no basis in cases where the principal was previously acquitted. Nor would the principal's liability do in cases where he enjoyed a personal immunity, such as diplomatic immunity or entrapment. It was necessary, therefore, to conceive of the crucial feature of the principal's conduct as the guilt of the principal, taken to mean the mens rea and the actus reus of the crime, but excluding procedural and policy defenses that prevent his guilt from being established against him. The question raised by the innocent-wrong theory is the acceptability of a further refinement of the feature of the principal's conduct that grounds the accomplice's liability. That feature would be described not as the principal's guilt, but rather as the wrongfulness of his action.

This theory would solve the problem caused by the inadequacy of the innocent-agency theory where the crime is defined to include a non-proxyable action or to exclude from its scope a class of persons to which the defendant belongs. At the same time, it would not disturb the network of rules constituting complicity doctrine, since it embraces a derivative, not a direct, theory of accomplice liability. It would, indeed, make the innocent-agency doctrine redundant in every case where the principal is excused. Still, this might not be a loss, in view of the strained character of some applications of the innocent-agency doctrine.

A major difficulty with this theory is its conceptual implausibility. It is perfectly straightforward to say that an accomplice shares the liability of the principal. And it seems acceptable to say that he shares the guilt of the principal where the latter's liability cannot be established because of defenses unrelated to his guilt. We can easily see a principal as guilty of the crime he committed even though he enjoys a defense of diplomatic immunity or entrapment. But where the primary actor has a defense that serves to excuse him, it is less convicing to speak of the primary actor as having done a wrong. He may have done a harm, but while all harms are regrettable, they are not all necessarily the result of wrongdoing.

This objection has somewhat less force where the primary party is excused on grounds of duress. Duress does not deny that the person did the prohibited act with the required mens rea. It is his volitional disability in the circumstances that excuses him. Perhaps the same argument would apply to a primary actor not guilty by reason of insanity, at least where his mens rea is not negatived. In these cases, the concept of innocent wrongdoing is quite plausible.

Where, on the other hand, the defendant's excuse involves lack of the mens rea required for the crime (and cases of lack of mens rea would, of course, have to be regarded as cases of excuse if this doctrine were to solve the problems in this area[173]) the concept of innocent wrong-doing runs into trouble. In these cases the primary actor may be not guilty for the simple reason that he did nothing wrong. Consider a case where a conductor signals to the bus driver that it is safe to back up when it is not, and someone is killed as a consequence. If the conductor was negligent in failing to see the danger, but the driver acted reasonably in relying on the conductor, could the conductor be found liable as an accomplice for a crime of causing a death through negligent driving?[174] It has been argued that he could since he encouraged the wrongful but excused act of the driver.[175] But it is hard to see how the driver can be said to have done a wrongful act when he simply backed up in reasonable reliance on the conductor, his driving being perfectly prudent and proper. Far from having done a wrong, he did what we want him to do.[176] One might argue that his action could just as adequately be described as backing his bus into a group of alighting passengers. Even so, this would describe an action that caused a harm, not one that is wrongful, because wrongfulness, in contrast to harm, implies responsibility.

A similar analysis applies to *Cogan & Leak*. When the primary actor had sex with Mrs. Cogan he inflicted a harm, since she in fact did not consent. But did he do a wrongful act? He had sex with a woman in the honest but unreasonable belief that she consented. But while this act was careless and may have been immoral, it was, under the English law, not criminal misconduct. Here we could not say that he did no more than what the law approves of his doing. Still what he did was not prohibited by English criminal law. It is therefore hard to justify describing his action as wrongful conduct in the sense required by the innocent-wrong theory.

The conception of innocent wrongdoing may seem implausible because it is unfamiliar to the common law mind. After all, it has enjoyed general acceptance in Germany. Moreover, the reasoning of several of the English and American cases that have imposed accomplice liability based on the actions of an excused principal can be construed as an attempt, however unartful, to state just such a theory. Finally, this theory, even with its drawbacks, appears to be the best doctrinal move to justify liability that a court could make without statutory changes.

There is one last doctrinal ground to consider for imposing liability on the defendant. These cases all present the situation in which an instigator causes an excused person to commit what would be a crime if he had lacked the excuse. The innocent-agency doctrine operates to allow the instigator to be treated as a principal, but because of the way these particular crimes are defined the instigator cannot be held liable as a principal. A straightforward solution is to make it a crime to cause an excused person to commit the actus reus of a crime—an "action causing" theory of liability. Causing an innocent person to perform the prohibited actus reus is an accurate description of what the defendant does in these cases. And resting liability on this ground would avoid the difficulties confronted by existing doctrine, since liability would not rest on either the defendant himself having committed the prohibited action, or on the guilt of a principal. Yet it is questionable that a court could properly rest liability on this ground since, at least technically, it amounts to creating a new crime.[177] It may be worth pausing to make clear why this is so.

The action-causing analysis is not simply an extension of the innocent-agency doctrine. It rests upon a distinguishable basis of liability. Action crimes proscribe certain actions. They do not, like result crimes, prohibit merely causing a defined result by any actions. And they do not, except for certain statutory offenses, proscribe causing another to engage in the prohibited action. How, then, can there be a successful prosecution of a culpable person who influences or assists an innocent person to commit those actions? Not through complicity, because, under the analysis of the doctrine previously developed, if the primary actor is innocent there is no criminal guilt for the culpable secondary actor to share. He must somehow be found to have committed the actions himself. This is what the innocent-agency analysis accomplishes. Since he intentionally uses the innocent person to commit the proscribed actions for his culpable purposes, there is a degree of plausibility in portraying those actions as his own, as though he committed the action by the use of an instrument. Thus, the conditions of the crime as defined are satisfied.

The action-causing analysis differs significantly. It does not ground the defendant's liability on his commission of the acts through the innocent actions of another. That would not do in the cases we have been considering, either because the action is nonproxyable or because the defendant is not a member of the class prohibited from committing the action. It grounds the liability of the defendant simply on the fact that he caused the actions of the innocent person. But this would not suffice to hold a defendant liable for crimes defined in terms of a specified action. It would be necessary to redefine those crimes to include causing others to commit those actions. The effect of doing so would be to render the traditional innocent-agency analysis redundant, since it would no longer be necessary to attribute the innocent person's actions to the defendant to make the defendant liable.

American statutory solutions to the problem have taken precisely this form. An early example is Section 2(b) of Title 18 of the United States Code, which has been interpreted as effecting such a change in the law. Apparently, it was not the problem of nonproxyable actions that led to this change (these situations have apparently not arisen in federal prosecutions), but the problem of the liability of a person who, though himself not a member of the class capable of committing a particular crime, causes an innocent person who is a member of the class to commit the prohibited actions.[178] This is because a number of federal crimes are limited, for jurisdictional reasons, to officers and employees of the government, judges, judicial officers, witnesses, and officers, employees, or persons connected with national banks or member banks.[179] Section 2(b), enacted in 1948 as part of a consolidation and reorganization of federal criminal statutes, was amended in 1981 to read: "Whoever willfully causes an act to be done which if directly performed by him or another would be an offense against the United States, is punishable as a principal."[180] Though the legislative history of this provision[181] as well as its drafting[182] leave some doubt that the problem was perceived with perfect clarity, most federal courts have interpreted it as encompassing a defendant who causes an innocent person to do acts prohibited by law where the defendant is not within the class designated by the statute as being capable of committing the crime.[183]

Another example of an action-causing theory of liability, and one less subject to the drafting perplexities of the federal statute, is Section 2.06(2)(a) of the Model Penal Code. That section, which has served as a model for a number of state provisions,[184] provides: "A person is legally accountable for the conduct of another person when: . . . acting with the kind of culpability that is sufficient for the commission of the offense, he causes an innocent or irresponsible person to engage in such conduct."[185] There is no indication in the comments that this provision was designed to overcome the limitations of the innocent-agency doctrine that we have been considering. Yet in formulating that doctrine as an independent ground of liability, rather than as one way in which a person may be said to perform acts in violation of law, the effect is to establish an action-causing ground of liability to which the limitations of the traditional innocent-agency doctrine do not attach.[186]

B. PARTLY CULPABLE ACTIONS

The partly culpable principal presents the same problems for complicity doctrine as the wholly innocent principal: since the accomplice's culpability is derived from that of the principal, the limit of the accomplice's culpability is determined by that of the principal. Thus if the principal is not guilty, the secondary actor cannot be held liable as his accomplice; and if the principal is culpable of a given crime, the accomplice cannot be held for a higher one.

For a case, we may once again resort to *Othello*. Iago deliberately influenced Othello to kill Desdemona by making him erroneously believe that Desdemona had been unfaithful and by otherwise inflaming his jealousy and vengefulness. Othello would be guilty of a culpable homicide, but perhaps only of manslaughter in view of the circumstances. Iago, however, acted with greater culpability, since he coldbloodedly engineered the killing. Could he be held for the crime of murder? The answer would appear to be no under the standard complicity doctrine, and it is clear that the text writers thought so. For example, Hawkins concluded that the accomplice's crime could rise no higher than the principal's: "it seeming incongruous and absurd that he who is punished only as a partaker of the guilt of another, should be adjudged guilty of a higher crime than the other."[187]

Incongruous yes; absurd no. What would be absurd is to convict Iago of no more than manslaughter because Othello was carried away by a storm of jealousy. Here is another instance of doctrinal logic defeating itself. The dilemma could be avoided under common law rules in one situation—where the secondary actor was present giving aid or encouragement at the time of the principal's crime.[188] In these circumstances the secondary actor would be a principal (of the second degree), rather than an accomplice, and as such his liability would be direct and not derivative.[189] While the distinction has been reaffirmed in a recent English case,[190] it is widely regarded as anomalous,[191] since whatever the difficulties of complicity doctrine in these situations, they are only worsened by a distinction turning on where the aid was given.

Notwithstanding these doctrinal constraints, later cases have sometimes imposed greater liability on the accomplice than on the principal. These cases are comparable to *Othello*, in that the accomplice is held to a higher homicidal crime than the principal is.[192] The opinions, however, do little to justify the result in terms of complicity doctrine, or any other, leaving us with the question of whether it can be defended.

It is tempting to reason that the liability of the parties is determined by the culpability of each, and that the actus reus of the principal may be attributed to the secondary party so that it may be considered with the secondary party's mens rea to determine his liability. The flaw in this, as we have seen, is that complicity doctrine affords no justification for attributing the actions of the principal to the secondary party. A natural move, then, is to the one major instance in which the actions of the principal, and not imply his guilt, may be attributed to the secondary actor. This is the doctrine of innocent agency.

The question that arises, however, is whether that doctrine is applicable in the *Othello* hypothetical. After all, Othello is a culpable, not an innocent actor. The argument that the doctrine is applicable is that Othello is, after all, Iago's tool, and not less so because he was maneuvered into committing a crime. On the facts in the play this is readily apparent—through deceit and misrepresentation Iago led Othello to believe the situation to be radically different than it was. Had the misrepresentation been that Desdemona had committed the capital offense of treason, leading Othello to order her execution, Othello would presumably be innocent. But in that case, Iago plainly could be held for murder on the innocent-agency doctrine: since Othello was acting on a false view, his action was not fully volitional, and Iago, in deliberately inducing it, could be held to have caused the killing. It should make no difference that Iago's fabrication served only to mitigate Othello's guilt rather than to exculpate him. As Professor Williams observed, "If a person can act through a completely innocent agent, there is no reason why he should not act through a semi-innocent agent. It is wholly unreasonably that the partial guilt of the agent should operate as a defence to the instigator."[193]

The common sense of this conclusion is clear enough, but the conceptual difficulty remains that Othello acted culpably and responsibly in intentionally killing his wife. There is, to be sure, some rhetorical force in speaking of him as Iago's tool, maneuvered into doing what Iago wanted him to do. But since Othello committed an action for which he himself is responsible, it is straining to say in the same breath that, on the theory of innocent agency, his act was (also) the act of Iago. Professor Williams coins the phrase "semi-innocent agent" to describe the situation, and suggests that the primary party be regarded as "an innocent agent in respect of part of the responsibility of the secondary party."[194] However, the ideas of a "semi-innocent agent" and of responsibility as a composite of parts seem only to add to the conceptual mystery.

Perhaps a better doctrinal explanation of what is obviously the sound result in these cases is simply to regard the secondary party as causing the death of the victim. As Hart and Honoré have shown, it is quite consistent with the law of causation to trace the causal inquiry through an intervening actor to the end result in those cases where the action of the intervening actor is not wholly voluntary.[195] Cases applying this concept to hold a secondary party liable for a result caused by a primary party usually occur in situations where the secondary party did not intend the principal's action.[196] The analysis would appear to be no less appropriate where the secondary actor intended the principal's action, so long as the latter's action was not fully voluntary. In the *Othello* example this is plainly the case. That Othello's actions are not excused is not an obstacle to this analysis. The intervening action need only be less than wholly voluntary to permit tracing the causal inquiry through the intervening actor; it need not be so nonvoluntary as to be fully excused.[197] Once it is established, of course, that Iago caused the death of Desdemona it follows that the nature of his crime is determined by the culpability with which he acted.[198]

It follows that the greater liability of the secondary party can be supported only where some feature of the primary party's action is not volitional in the full sense, so that the former can be said to have caused it by using the latter as his instrument. This limitation is illustrated in *Regina v. Richards*.[199] Mrs. Richards hired two men to beat her husband severely, but the men instead (so the jury apparently found) chose to inflict only a minor assault. The jury convicted the men simply of unlawful wounding, but convicted Mrs. Richards of the offense of wounding with intent to cause grievous bodily harm. The appellate court reduced her conviction to unlawful wounding, on the view that as an inciter, her guilt could not be greater than the principal. The case has been criticized,[200] and insofar as the decision rested on the distinction between whether the secondary party was present or not, the criticism is well taken.[201] But the decision is supportable, it would seem, on the ground that Mrs. Richards did not *cause* the actions of the men.

Critics of the *Richards* decision have taken a different view. Smith and Hogan, for example, argue by analogy to a person, *D*, who gives poison to another, *E*, to administer to the deceased, telling *E* it is an emetic that will cause only discomfort. They argue that if *D* had told *E* that the poison was medicine the deceased needed, *D* would unquestionably be guilty of murder. It should make no difference that *D* told *E* the poison was an emetic, which, since *E*'s action would then have been an intentional assault, would have made *E* guilty of manslaughter. They conclude: "The true principle . . . is that where the principal has caused an *actus reus*, the liability of each of the secondary parties should be assessed according to his own *mens rea*."[202]

Their conclusion that *D* is liable for murder is sound, but the generalization they adduce to support it is questionable. It is not a "true principle" that the secondary party's liability is assessed according to his own mens rea when the primary party "has caused an *actus reus*." This is true only when the secondary party can be said to have caused the actions of the primary party, thereby bringing into play the doctrine of causation which, unlike the doctrine of complicity, does not rest on a derivative theory of liability. In Smith and Hogan's hypothetical this is the case, since *D* used *E* as his unwitting instrument. But it is not the case with Mrs. Richards. She made no misrepresentation to the men she hired. They were not her unwitting instruments, but freely chose to act as they did. Hence their actions, as such, could not be attributed to Mrs. Richards. The innocent-agency doctrine is inapplicable because she did not cause their action.[203]

It is a further question whether Mrs. Richards *should* be liable for assault with intent to do grievous injury, even if I am right that existing doctrine precludes that result. Surely the strongest argument for liability is that the culpability of her hirelings is irrelevant to *her* culpability. But that argument proves too much. If her hirelings committed no assault, but instead went to the police, it is incontrovertible that Mrs. Richards could not be found liable for any assault, let alone an aggravated assault.Yet whether her hirelings chose to do as she bade them or to go to the police is also irrelevant to her culpability. The point would be that however culpable her intentions she could not be blamed for an assault that did not take place. The same retort is applicable on the facts of the case: an actual assault took place (and Mrs. Richards is liable for it) but an aggravated assault did not take place. It did not take place because those committing the assault did not intend to inflict grievous bodily harm. She could properly be held liable for solicitation to commit an aggravated assault, not for aggravated assault.

Even critics of the decision would probably find this reasoning appropriate in a case where the pseudo-principal was only feigning.[204] A secondary party may be culpable of seeking to help a principal commit a burglary, by boosting him through a transom, for example, but as we have seen, if the principal has no intention of committing a felony, but is acting solely to ensnare the secondary party, the latter cannot be held as an accomplice to the burglary.[205] This follows because the pseudo-principal has committed no burglary, and his actions, being wholly volitional acts done with his eyes wide open, cannot be attributed to his misguided helper. The identical reasoning precludes holding Mrs. Richards liable for an aggravated assault: her hirelings committed no aggravated assault. The only difference is that there is no evidence that her hirelings were motivated by a desire to ensnare her. But could it be argued convincingly that if there were such evidence the case should come out differently? It is hard to see why the ultimate motive of the primary actor should require a different result. It is rather his mens rea as to the action that is decisive.

So much, then, for the uses and limits of causation in justifying holding an accomplice liable for a greater crime than the principal. The last question I want to raise is whether there is an alternative doctrinal move for accomplishing the same purpose. The one that immediately suggests itself is the doctrine discussed in the preceding section on the nonculpable principal.[206] If it is plausible to base an accomplice's liability upon the "wrong" committed by an "excused" primary actor who is thus guilty of no crime, it is equally plausible to base an accomplice's liability on the wrong of a partly culpable primary actor. Thus, in our *Othello* hypothetical, Iago's liability for murder would be justified on the view that what is imputed to the accomplice is the legal wrong Othello committed. Othello committed the crime of manslaughter, not murder. But the basis of the accomplice's liability is not the crime of which the principal is guilty, but the legal wrong the principal committed, here the unlawful killing of Desdemona. The derivative nature of Iago's liability having been thus respected, it is possible to assess his actual legal guilt for sharing in that wrong in terms of his own mens rea.

How would Mrs. Richards fare under this analysis? Would it require that she be held liable as an accomplice to aggravated assault? On the one hand, it is clear that the hirelings committed the legal wrong of an ordinary assault on her husband. Perhaps this would be enough to permit her guilt to be determined by her intention that her husband should be severely beaten. On the other hand, it does not appear accurate to say that that the hirelings did the wrong of an aggravated assault but are innocent because of an excuse personal to them. It seems more apt to say that they are innocent of the aggravated assault because they did not commit the crime as defined, specifically because they did not assault with intention to inflict grievous injury. On this view the "innocent wrong" theory would not sustain Mrs. Richards' liability for the aggravated assault.

C. UNINTENDED ACTIONS

The doctrines governing the liability of one person for the crimes or acts of another that we have canvassed to this point require that the secondary actor have intended that the primary actor act as he did. This is plainly the case for complicitly liability as a general proposition. It is no less true in cases of complicity to manslaughter, where the intent requirement is satisfied by the intent that the principal should do the reckless act that caused the death. We saw one instance where the intention requirement was in doubt, namely, those occasional cases and statutes that make it sufficient that the principal's criminal act was a probable consequence of the action the secondary party intended. But even those instances were subject to the limitation that the actions of the primary party further the ends of the secondary actor. The requirement of an intentional action also applies to the innocent-agency doctrine, since it rests on the notion of agency as a basis for attributing the acts of the innocent party to the instigator.

The doctrines we have so far examined, therefore, leave uncovered situations in which the fault of the secondary actor lies in engaging in conduct that creates the danger (which in fact materializes) that some other person will engage in criminal conduct, whether or not that conduct serves the purposes of the secondary actor. In order to deal with these cases, courts have sometimes invoked the concept of causation, not in the sense of the innocent-agency doctrine, which makes the actions of the innocent party the actions of the intentional instigator, but in the sense that allows the instigator to be treated as having caused the result of the actions of some other person. The problem raised by this use of causation follows from the characteristic ways in which human actions are conceived as taking place. Actions are seen not as caused happenings, but as the product of the actor's self-determined choices, so that it is the actor who is the cause of what he does, not one who set the stage for his action. For purposes of considering this and related problems of the use of causation in these cases it will be helpful to consider separately cases where the action of the second actor is not wholly volitional and those where it is.

1. NONVOLITIONAL ACTIONS.   Consider, first, cases like the following: A person leaves his car keys with a legally irresponsible person known to have a penchant for wild driving, who kills another person while driving the car.[207] A person shoots at police, inviting return fire that kills a bystander or another felon. A person creates a justifiable apprehension of danger in his victim, who kills another accidentally while defending himself.[208]

A special feature of these cases is that the primary actor's conduct is not wholly volitional. This was the feature of the situations treated in the preceding Sections on nonculpable and partly culpable actions that permitted application of the causation concept to hold the secondary actor liable. Because in addition to the nonvolitional character of the primary actor's actions, the secondary actor intentionally used the primary actor to achieve his purposes, it was possible to apply the doctrine of innocent agency to hold the secondary actor to have caused the actions of the primary actor. In consequence, the innocent agent's actions could be attributed to the secondary actor (so that he becomes liable if those actions are prohibited), and he could properly be said to have caused the result of those actions (so that he becomes liable also if the crime consists of causing that result).

However, in the cases now under consideration the secondary actor does not intentionally help or instigate the acts of the primary actor. On the generally accepted view, therefore, the innocent agency doctrine is inapplicable[209] and the primary actor's actions cannot be attributed to the secondary actor. But the nonvolitional character of the primary actor's actions makes it possible to treat the secondary actor as having caused the result of those actions. This is so because nonvolitional actions, unlike volitional ones, do not serve as a barrier to tracing a causal inquiry through those actions to those of an antecedent actor.[210] To this extent the nonvolitional action of the primary actor is treated as a natural event for purposes of finding the cause of some result. For convenience we may refer to this as the "result causing" analysis.

Decisions that have held a person liable for recklessly risking criminal harms inflicted by others appear to rest on just such an analysis. This is most helpfully seen in a class of felony-murder cases where the action of a person resisting the felony results in a homicide—sometimes of a co-felon, sometimes of a bystander or another victim. The artificialities of the felony-murder doctrine tend to obscure the force of an analysis in these terms, since that doctrine holds a felon for murder when his precipitating acts may have been done with recklessness or some lesser mens rea insufficient for murder. Thus, in a number of cases where a bystander or a co-felon was killed by the victim or a policeman resisting the felony, courts have held a surviving felon for felony murder, without attending to anything more than that the victim died as a proximate result of the felony committed by the defendant[211]—the so-called "proximate cause theory."[212] Reacting against those cases, recent decisions have rejected the applicability of felony murder in these situations, holding that the doctrine may not be used to convict a felon of felony murder unless the killing was committed by the felon or one who is his accomplice acting in furtherance of their common design[213]—the so-called "agency theory" of felony murder.[214]

At all events, we are not now concerned with the liability of the actors in these cases for murder under the very special rules of the felony-murder doctrine, but their liability under standard doctrine for some appropriate category of homicide. (This would normally be manslaughter since the fault of the actor, so far as the homocide is concerned, is recklessness.) Therefore, we need to examine these situations apart from the distortions of the felony-murder doctrine.

The agency theory (which is to say, the standard doctrine of complicity) plainly cannot, apart from the special force of the felony-murder doctrine, justify imposing liability on a felon for killings committed by those who are not his accomplices. Likewise, the proximate-cause theory cannot, apart from felony murder, justify holding the felon for murder when such killings occur, unless recklessness or some lesser mens rea is deemed sufficient for murder, and certainly cannot justify holding him for first-degree murder, which requires an intentional killing.[215] But the causation theory, wholly apart from the felony-murder doctrine (though, of course, subject to the usual limitations of remoteness),[216] can justify holding the felon liable for causing the homicide committed by a nonfelon in resisting the felony. What level of homicide depends, of course, on the extent of the felon's recklessness in the circumstances.

The California cases offer useful illustrations, since they have most clearly articulated the rationale for holding a felon liable for causing a killing done by a nonfelon in resisting the felony, quite apart from the felony-murder doctrine.[217] The theory for holding the felon in these cases was expounded shortly after the applicability of felony murder had been rejected. In *People v. Gilbert*,[218] the court reasoned:

> When the defendant or his accomplice, with a conscious disregard for life, intentionally commits an act that is likely to cause death, and his victim or a police officer kills in reasonable response to such act, the defendant is guilty of murder. In such a case, the killing is attributable,

not merely to the commission of a felony, but to the intentional act of the defendant or his accomplice committed with conscious disregard for life. *Thus, the victim's self-defensive killing or the police officer's killing in the performance of his duty cannot be considered an independent intervening cause for which the defendant is not liable, for it is a reasonable response to the dilemma thrust upon the victim or the policeman by the intentional act of the defendant or his accomplice.*[219]

Subsequent decisions have not had occasion to decide whether the felon may be liable for manslaughter when his acts lack the mens rea required for murder, although the court's analysis would seem to support the possibility. Instead, the decisions have focused on the kinds of provocative actions that manifest the "conscious disregard for life" necessary for murder.[220] This attention to mens rea is irrelevant to our concern here, which is causation. The decision in *Gilbert*, however, is germane because it indicates that in some circumstances—where the killing is committed by a policeman performing his duty or a victim exercising his privilege of self-defense—the action of the intervening actor does not constitute an intervening cause, and therefore permits the cause of the death to be traced to the initiating action of the felon. The court has not explicitly spoken of the actions of the policeman or the victim as being less than wholly volitional, but it characterized those actions as "a reasonable response to the dilemma" thrust upon them, which seems to imply restricted volition. The constrained character of the policeman's or victim's actions distinguishes the usual case where the independent action of an intervening actor blocks tracing the cause of the result to another person's earlier action.[221]

A recent English decision[222] puts the matter quite explicitly. The defendant was convicted of manslaughter of a girl who was in fact shot by a policeman. The defendant, who had already shot and injured others, held the girl as a shield against the policemen and opened fire upon them. The policemen returned his fire and accidentally killed the girl. In affirming the conviction, the court of appeal rejected the reasoning of a number of American cases that hold the defendant not liable for murder in these situations, on the ground that those cases were interpretations of the felony-murder concept, which had long since been abandoned in England. The court rejected as well the argument that the shooting by the policemen was a *novus actus interveniens* that severed the defendant's causal relationship to the girl's killing. It held that, under ordinary principles of causation, the acts of the policeman were not *novus actus interveniens*, since they were done either out of self-defense or in the execution of duty, and hence were not voluntary actions in the sense required to make them, rather than the defendant's prior actions, the cause of the girl's death.[223]

The Model Penal Code's approach to these matters is worth noting

because it constitutes something of a departure from traditional causation doctrine. It plainly accepts the liability of the defendants in the
kinds of hypotheticals and cases under consideration,[224] but formulates
the principle in terms somewhat wider than the traditional result-causing
analysis. The relevant provision is the same one discussed earlier, Section
2.06(2)(a), which substitutes an action-causing doctrine for the innocent-
agency doctrine. We may repeat it here: "A person is legally accountable
for the conduct of another person when . . . acting with the kind of
culpability that is sufficient for the commission of the offense, he causes
an innocent or irresponsible person to engage in such conduct."[225]

In dispensing with the requirement of intention, the Model Penal
Code departs from traditional causation analysis. There is no doctrinal
obstacle to holding a person for unintentionally causing a prohibited
result, even though an action of an innocent or irresponsible person
intervened. This is because our conception of causation permits tracing
the cause of some result through a nonvolitional actor to an antecedent
actor. The latter's action may be found to be the cause of the result even
if he did not intend the action of the nonvolitional actor. As Hart and
Honoré's review of the causation cases reveals, however, it is different
with causing actions, even nonvolitional ones. Actions, like results, can
be caused, but only by acts intended to cause them.

> [A]n element of intention (intending the other to act in a specified way)
> is essential if one person is to be said to 'cause' another to act but not
> when he is said to cause some event to happen. This is . . . not an
> independent legal requirement of a certain state of mind in the accused
> person, but part of the meaning of 'causing' in the sense of providing
> a reason for the non-voluntary act of another.[226]

The Model Penal Code eliminates this distinction and treats nonvolitional
actions as capable of being caused accidentally as well as intentionally.[227]

Professor Williams early criticized this feature of the Model Penal
Code. Positing the case of a victim of an armed assault who accidentally
shoots a bystander while justifiably resisting the assault, he questions the
theory under which the Model Penal Code would find the author of the
assault guilty of manslaughter,[228] namely by treating him as negligently
causing the lethal act of the innocent person. Williams prefers to treat
the author of the assault as having directly caused the death, subject to
the normal limitation that the death is not too remote a consequence of
his action.[229]

The Model Penal Code approach would not produce a different
outcome in most cases. Where the crime is a result crime, as it normally
is, both approaches would hold the first actor liable, since they would
both conclude that he caused the result. Under the Model Penal Code
approach he would cause it by causing the actions of the innocent person;

under the traditional result-causing approach he would cause the result directly by his own act. Perhaps, as Williams suggests, the direct-causation analysis would allow more room for argument about remoteness than the Model Penal Code analysis would. Still, remoteness considerations would appear relevant as well to finding the defendant to have caused the action of the innocent person.

Many action crimes would also come out the same way, although the underlying analysis would be different. Under the Model Penal Code the issue of liability would be resolved in terms of mens rea, while under the result-causing approach it would be resolved in terms of causation. Consider a hypothetical involving an action rather than a result crime. Suppose a guard at a mental hospital recklessly leaves the keys to the drug room unattended. An irresponsible inmate finds the keys and uses them to gain access to an annexed building that contains restricted drugs. Would the guard be guilty of the crimes of burglary and illegal possession of restricted drugs? Not under the traditional causation approach, even if causing prohibited actions is a crime, since the crimes require defined actions which he did not commit and which he could not be said to have caused, not having acted intentionally. Nor would he be liable under the Model Penal Code provision—not because he did not cause the actions, but because he did not act with the culpability required for those crimes: he did not intend to steal (or for the inmate to steal), and he lacked the knowledge necessary for possession.

The one case in which the outcome could be different is where the prohibited action can be committed recklessly or negligently, or without mens rea at all. We have already seen that under both the result-causing analysis and the Model Penal Code approach, a person may be held accountable if an irresponsible person with whom the defendant intentionally left his car keys causes the death of another person through reckless driving. But under the Model Penal Code the defendant could also be held liable for reckless driving since he acted recklessly, which is the culpability sufficient for the offense. Consider also the hypothetical of the guard at a mental hospital in the preceding paragraph, with the change that the crime of possession of restricted drugs is one of strict liability. Thus, the person who had the drugs within his control would be guilty of illegal possession whether or not he was aware that they were drugs or that he had them. Under the traditional causation analysis the guard would not be guilty of possession of the drugs since, not having intended that the inmate have possession of them, he could not be said to have caused the inmate's action of possessing them. However, it would seem that under the Model Penal Code provision the guard might be guilty, even if he were faultless in leaving the keys—if, for example, the keys fell out of his pocket accidentally while he was struggling with an unruly patient.[230]

Whether the Model Penal Code innovation is a desirable substitute for traditional causation doctrine in dealing with unintended actions of another is unclear. One problem is that it compels courts to resolve questions of causation without regard to a factor, the intention of the actor, that has become part of the meaning of cause in these cases. Another problem concerns the desirability of expanding criminal liability. Absent a requirement of intent that would confine liability, a substantial range of actions is put at risk, perhaps a broader range than is wise. The strict liability example I just put is a case in point. Perhaps courts could confine the scope of liability through restrictive interpretations of when one action causes another. With intention no longer a consideration, however, this may be difficult to accomplish.[231]

2. VOLITIONAL ACTIONS.   The second set of cases involving the liability of an actor for creating the danger of a primary actor's harmful actions is more difficult to deal with in terms of causation, because the action of the one who directly causes the harm may be wholly volitional. The cases I propose to use as examples are these: The defendant lends his car keys to a person he knows to have been drinking[232] or to one he knows has never driven, who kills another in an automobile accident. The defendant engages in a road race on a public street in the course of which his competitor collides with another car, resulting in the competitor's death[233] or the death of the driver of the other car.[234] We may include also the case of a defendant who engages in a game of Russian roulette with another, in the course of which the other shoots and kills himself.[235] Here, while the defendant may be said to have intentionaly encouraged the deceased to fire the revolver at himself, to the extent the deceased committed no crime there is no liability in which the defendant may be said to participate. Barring a special statute, causation offers the only plausible ground for holding him responsible.

It may be thought at first blush that complicity liability is possible in these cases (putting the Russian roulette example aside), for as we have seen, there is no conceptual barrier to holding a person as an accomplice to a crime of recklessness, like involuntary manslaughter. Where a secondary actor influences or helps another to commit acts that are sufficiently reckless that if death results, the other is guilty of manslaughter, the secondary actor shares his liability as an accomplice. While he does not intend the resulting death, he does intend that the principal do the acts that turn out to cause it.[236] This analysis does not apply, however, to the cases we are now considering. As we saw earlier, this is because the deaths were not caused by those actions of the other party that the secondary actor intended (in the way, for example, the heating of a defective boiler causes it to explode[237]), but by actions of the other party that, while perhaps probable and foreseeable, were not intended by the secondary actor. The defendant who lends his car keys to a person he knows has been drinking intentionally aids him to drive, but not to drive in a way that causes death. A party to an automobile race on a public street may be said to intend (or at least to know) that his competitor will speed, but not that he will, for example, try to pass another car on a two-lane road at the crest of a hill. Therefore, the defendant cannot normally be held as an accomplice under standard complicity doctrine.

The failure of traditional doctrine to provide for liability in these situations, where the culpable consequence of defendant's action is some unintended but voluntary action of another, has produced a tension in the law. We saw this earlier in the cases and statutes that seem to reject the requirement of intentionality for complicity liability in favor of a standard of recklessness.[238] So in causation we may observe an analogous pressure to depart from the view that voluntary actions are not caused in order to provide a ground for imposing liability.[239]

This tension is apparent in the decisions. In *Commonwealth v. Root*,[240] for example, the defendant and deceased engaged in an automobile race on a rural highway, reaching speeds of ninety miles per hour. At one point, in seeking to pass defendant, deceased pulled out in a no-passing zone where the road narrowed as it approached a bridge and collided with a truck coming from the opposite direction. He was killed in the crash and the defendant was convicted of involuntary manslaughter. The majority of the Pennsylvania Supreme Court reversed the conviction in recognition of the inappropriateness of tracing through the voluntary actions of the deceased to find the cause of the death in the defendant's prior actions.[241] The court regarded the defendant's recklessness as having been established. More was required, however: for liability to attach he must be shown to have been the direct cause of the death.[242]

> [T]he action of the deceased driver in recklessly and suicidally swerving his car to the left lane of a 2-lane highway into the path of an oncoming truck was not forced upon him by any act of the defendant; it was done by the deceased and by him alone, who thus directly brought about his own demise.[243]

The deceased's voluntary actions were an "intervening cause," sufficient to bar the defendant's liability for causing the death. The court took note of several tort cases that had expanded proximate cause to include the foreseeable actions of others, but regarded it as inappropriate to apply them to criminal cases.[244] The policies of tort law may justify expanding the concept of cause in order to permit an injured party to recover compensation from a tortfeasor, but it did not seem to the court to follow that a similar expansion is justified when the stakes are criminal liability for homicide.[245]

The dissent, on the other hand, was more persuaded by the soundness in penal policy of holding the defendant liable than by the strictures of causation analysis:

> If the defendant did not engage in the unlawful race and so operate his automobile in such a reckless manner, this accident would never have occurred. He helped create the dangerous event. He was a vital part of it. The victim's acts were a natural reaction to the stimulus of the situation. The race, the attempt to pass the other car and forge ahead, the reckless speed, all of these factors the defendant himself helped create. He was part and parcel of them. That the victim's response was normal under the circumstances, that his reaction should have been expected and was clearly foreseeable, is to me beyond argument. That the defendant's recklessness was a substantial factor is obvious. All of this . . . makes his unlawful conduct a direct cause of the resulting collision.[246]

Cases involving the liability of a person who lends his car to a person he knows to have been drinking, where the latter kills another by his reckless driving, are usually concerned solely with whether the lender may be held as an accomplice to manslaughter. We have seen the difficulties with concluding that he may be.[247] There is little evidence of courts resorting to causation as an alternative stratagem,[248] but Professors LaFave and Scott have proposed that solution. They argue that the mens rea of manslaughter is satisfied if the lender's action in lending his car to an intoxicated driver was criminally negligent, and the actus reus is satisfied if that action is found to be the legal cause of death.[249] The difficulty is this last—finding the lending of the car to be the cause of death. The driver's actions in causing the fatal accident would have to be found sufficiently nonvoluntary to allow the causal inquiry to trace through this intervening actions in driving the car. This may be possible if the driver were drunk enough, but it may not be possible in many cases of driving under the influence.

The Russian roulette case differs from those we have been discussing, since the deceased's action of discharging the revolver at himself was precisely the act intended by the secondary party. But since complicity is unavailable so long as the deceased committed no crime in shooting himself, the issue presented is comparable to those we have been discussing: may the voluntary act of the deceased not be treated as an intervening cause because it was a probable consequence of the defendant's action? In the Russian roulette case,[250] the court upheld a conviction of manslaughter, relying on a plausible view of penal policy: "[T]he Commonwealth had an interest that the deceased should not be killed by the wanton or reckless conduct of himself and others."[251] Indeed, it makes little sense from the standpoint of penal policy to hold the surviving player liable (as he certainly would be) if the game took the form of the players discharging the revolver at each other in turn,[252] but not to hold him liable if each player fired at himself. But the case is not really distinguishable from *Root,* despite the court's argument that it was,[253] because both cases presented the same obstacle to causation liability, namely, the intervening volitional act of the deceased.

It is apparent that the grip of the conception that a voluntary human action bars assigning causal responsibility to an earlier actor, pervasive as it is in the law, is loosened by the pull of the policy of holding people liable for recklessly providing others with an occasion to do harm. It is the same policy that produced the pull to loosen the requirement of intentionality and to allow such persons to be held as accomplices. There is no way to extend liability in these cases through either doctrine in a way that does not require a significant departure from doctrinal premises, and, indeed, some courts have done just that.

Removing the requirement of intentionality for complicity has the major drawback of exposing a reckless actor to liability for a crime committed by another which requires a higher mens rea. While it is possible to confine the secondary party's liability to crimes of recklessness, there is the ever present danger of the doctrine spilling over beyond such limits.[254] A further drawback of making complicity applicable in these cases is the very weak but-for showing that suffices (the mere possibility of a but-for relationship),[255] as compared to the showing required to establish causation liability.

Developments in the law of torts, on the other hand, offer a well-established precedent for modifying proximate cause principles to impose liability on a defendant for harm caused by another where the defendant negligently provided him with the opportunity to do the harm. In torts the *novus actus interveniens* principle has yielded to the principle of foreseeability. If the voluntary and intentional action of another was one of the risks in virtue of which the defendant's conduct was negligent, it is regarded as foreseeable and not, therefore, as a superseding cause.[256] Under this principle it is plain that tort liability for damages could be imposed on the defendant in each of the situations discussed in this Section: on the defendant who lent his car to a driver he knew to have been drinking or to be incompetent, on the road race survivor, and on the Russian roulette game survivor. Many will regard it as quite appropriate that criminal liability for manslaughter should also be imposed.[257] Indeed, one legislative proposal sought explicitly to adopt the tort standard for criminal cases by establishing causal responsibility when the result was within the risk of which the defendant should have been aware, "whether that risk extends to natural events or to the conduct of another."[258]

An arguable difficulty with this approach is that it could extend the reach of the criminal law to include cases where the justification for criminal punishment might seem less compelling than in the cases we have discussed in this section.[259] On the other hand, the significantly greater culpability requirement for criminal negligence might serve to keep criminal liability within bounds. And in any event, causal responsibility has already been extended in accordance with the tort principle when the primary actor's act is not wholly volitional, as we saw in the previous Section, and the problem of the reach of the criminal law is hardly different depending on the volitionality of the primary actor's conduct.[260]

CLOSING COMMENTS

I have tried to show in Parts I and II of this essay that the variety of rules and principles constituting the Anglo-American common law doctrine of complicity manifest a conceptual unity. That is to say, to a significant degree they follow from certain fundamental propositions.

These propositions are not arbitrary. They flow from central features of the way we experience the external world and our part in it. In that experience, as reflected in our social practices, our language, and our intuitive perceptions, there is a dichotomy between nature and will. Connections between events in nature are subject to relentless forces. Whether explained as the work of the gods or as the physical laws of the universe, the sense of their being beyond human power is the same. We inhabit the natural world and are therefore subject to it. But we also stand outside it. As persons, with our individuality, we confront the natural world with our own selves. In what we choose to do, as opposed to what happens to us, we are free and autonomous actors.

These perceptions have a shaping influence on our conception of responsibility, including, of principal interest for this essay, the assignment of blame for untoward results that happen as a consequence of our actions. Responding to these perceptions, our law has developed two separate bodies of doctrine to determine responsibility for results: causation, for the realm of nature, and complicity, for the realm of will. Causation deals with results of a person's action that happen in the physical world. Complicity deals with results that take the form of another person's voluntary actions.

The reason why complicity emerges as a separate ground of liability is that causation doctrine cannot generally deal satisfactorily with results that take the form of another person's voluntary action. This is so because the voluntary action of a primary party cannot appropriately be said to have been caused (in the physical sense of cause) by the action of the secondary party. As Hart and Honoré's study has shown, a voluntary action is treated as the terminal point of a causal inquiry beyond which the inquiry does not usually proceed. The primary party's voluntary act is his own action. No one and nothing caused him to act as he did. He chose to act. Thus the basic premise of the concept of responsibility itself is the ultimate ground for the distinction between causation and complicity.

This account of the provenance of complicity doctrine serves to explain a number of its central features, as well as its contrasts with and similarities to causation doctrine.

First, a person may be held accountable for a result under the doctrine of causation on the basis of any action that satisfies sine qua non and proximate cause requirements. A person may be held accountable for the unlawful action of another, however, only for two kinds of action—actions that influence the decision of the principal to commit the crime or that help him to do so. This is because only these forms of affecting the conduct of the principal are consistent with the notion of the principal having freely chosen to act as he did.

Second, since the principal has committed a crime through his own voluntary conduct, that conduct cannot be attributed to the secondary party, who may have influenced or helped, but did not cause the principal's action. Therefore the secondary party cannot be regarded as having committed the substantive crime. The principal has committed the crime and the secondary party becomes legally accountable for it by virtue of the doctrine of complicity. If the principal has committed no violation, there is no ground for imposing liability on the accomplice. In this sense accomplice liability is derivative, or dependent, rather than direct, as causation liability always is.

This derivative character of the accomplice's liability explains a variety of outcomes in the law of complicity. It explains, for example, the liability of an accomplice for a crime committed by a principal where the crime is so defined that the accomplice is incapable of committing it, the nonliability of the secondary party where the primary party is feigning involvement, and the difficulties encountered by courts in holding the accomplice for a crime greater than that of the principal.

The most problematic feature of the theory of derivative liability is determining the legal status of the principal's action required to impose liability on an accomplice who aids or influences him. The classic common law position is that the principal's action must incur liability. But, as we saw, the requirement has been loosened to make it sufficient that the principal committed a culpable violation of law, though he could not have been held criminally liable for it. A further loosening, arguably not yet part of common law doctrine, but adopted in German law, would dispense with the requirement of a culpable principal so long as the principal committed a wrongful act. None of these modifications, however, contradicts the premise of derivative liability.

Third, in contrast to causation doctrine, which allows for liability for negligent (even accidental) as well as intentional actions, the normal principle of complicity doctrine requires that the accomplice intend the culpable conduct of the principal. It is not completely clear that this requirement is entailed in the core suppositions of complicity doctrine. I have surmised that intention may serve as the analogue of consent, which in the law of agency is the standard mode whereby a principal is made accountable for the obligations incurred by his agent. This would explain the absence of the intent requirement in causation. The standard requirement of consent (or intent), it may be further surmised, has its roots also in the conception of the autonomy of human action: what another freely chooses to do is his doing, not mine. It cannot be seen as a part of my action the way a natural physical consequence would be. Only if I chose to identify with his action may I incur the liability that action creates.

Fourth, complicity and causation are cognate concepts in the sense that they both govern when a person's actions may be blamed for a consequence. Both require at a minimum that the person's conduct succeed in contributing to the result, that it make a difference to what happened. In causation this is expressed in the requirement that the action be a sine qua non condition of the result. In complicity, however, this need not be established. The reason is not that an accomplice may be liable for the crime of another even if his action made no difference. The reason is rather that the requirement of a sine qua non condition becomes attenuated in complicity to the requirement of a possibility that it was a sine qua non condition, because in cases of influence, in contrast to aid, that is all that can be established.

This follows again from the different ways we conceive of physical events and voluntary actions. While events in the physical world are governed by laws of nature that imply the existence of necessary and sufficient conditions, voluntary decisions to act are not. They are controlled by the choice of the actor, a "wild card," for whose action no set of conditions is sufficient and no condition is necessary, save the condition of a free act of will. Therefore, though it may be in any particular case that the principal would not have chosen to act without the influence of the accomplice, it is never so as a matter of necessity, since the principal could have chosen otherwise. All we can say as a matter of necessity is that in the one case where the influence fails to reach its target it could not possibly have made a difference and hence may be ruled out as a sine qua non condition.

In other respects, where differences are not compelled by the nature-will distinction, causation and complicity inquiries run parallel courses, as their cognate functions would lead one to expect. In order to attribute causal blame to an actor more is required than a but-for relationship between his action and the result; his action must be a "legal" or "proximate" cause, meaning that the result must not be accidental or abnormal or one directly produced by intervening voluntary actions of others. Similar restrictions preclude complicity liability even if the possibility of a but-for relation exists. This is evident most clearly where the principal voluntarily departs from the conduct the secondary party intended, but it would also be true where the contribution of the secondary party, even to what was intended, works out in abnormal or accidental ways.

Part III considered the complementarity between complicity and causation. Complicity is not the exclusive ground for determining the liability of one person for what another does. Causation may also serve that purpose. It does so where the action of the principal is not fully voluntary, such actions being seen as belonging sufficiently to the realm of nature to permit analysis in terms of causation. Causation therefore serves to complement complicity, whose function is to govern cases of fully voluntary actions.

Causation is relied on to perform this complementary office mainly in two situations. One is where the principal has a defense that negates his culpability. The absense of a basis for derivative liability makes complicity doctrine inappropriate. However, causation doctrine becomes appropriate to the extent that the factors that negate the principal's culpability also negate the voluntary character of his action. This suffices to establish the secondary party's liability for a result crime. He may be held liable for an action crime as well where the instigator intentionally uses the principal to commit the crime, on the theory that he commits the proscribed action through the instrumentality of the innocent principal (the innocent-agency theory).

The other situation where causation complements complicity is that in which complicity fails because the secondary party does not intend the criminal conduct of the principal. So long as the action of the principal is not fully volitional, causation doctrine allows tracing the results of his conduct through him to the secondary party, whose culpable act in some sense invited the criminal conduct of the principal, even though he did not intend it.

But the fit between causation and complicity turns out to be imperfect. In some cases neither doctrine suffices to impose a liability which seems otherwise appropriate, and courts quite naturally may be observed striving to impose liability.

One such situation is where the nature of the prohibited action (nonproxyable actions) or the limitation of the class of persons capable of violating the prohibition precludes holding an instigator liable for the crime under the innocent-agency theory. Courts have often had to exceed doctrinal limitations in imposing liability in these situations. The source of the difficulty may perhaps be regarded as a defect in causation or complicity doctrine, but it is more accurately stated as the absence of a general ground of criminal liability based on causing another to do a prohibited act. Legislative provision of such a ground (as the Model Penal Code has proposed) entails no inconsistency with complicity or causation doctrines as I have interpreted them. Another case of this kind occurs where the secondary party tries but fails to contribute to the criminal action of the primary party. No inconsistency with the theory of complicity is created in providing for liability based on attempt (as again the Model Penal Code has proposed) any more than one is created with causation doctrine by the traditional provisions for liability based on attempting to cause a result.

The other main situation where the fit between causation and complicity is arguably imperfect is that in which the secondary actor unintentionally contributed to a wholly volitional criminal action of a primary party. This differs significantly from the situations treated in the preceding paragraph because the discrepancy arises from the character of complicity and causation doctrines. Imposing liability would have to entail some inconsistency with these doctrines, as I have suggested they be understood. An exception would need to be made either to the requirement of intentionality for complicity liability, or to the principle that a fully voluntary action cannot be regarded as caused by a previous actor. This obviously raises a problem for the theory of these doctrines as I have presented it.

If the sense behind imposing liability in these cases is that public policy requires it, regardless of the inappropriateness of blaming the defendant, there is no difficulty. Nothing I have proposed is inconsistent with public policy judgments overriding the constraints of appropriate blaming. If, on the other hand, it is deemed consistent with those constraints to impose liability, then I am presented with a counterexample to my interpretations: either intent is not always a requirement of complicity, or a voluntary act can sometimes be caused.

There is a strong case to be made that in some situations it is both sound in policy and conformable to our intuitions of just blaming to hold a person liable for recklessly facilitating the criminal action of another. Some courts have made that case and some legislation rests on it, the judgment being expressed either by a doctrine of reckless complicity or by one that accepts the principle that voluntary actions can be caused. This is an important challenge to the doctrinal interpretation I have offered, particularly when expressed in the latter way. But it is not necessarily a serious one for the following reasons.

First, there is strong resistance to the case for extending liability in these situations and much law is the other way. It is fairer to say, therefore, that the law reflects ambivalence on the issue, rather than to say flatly that voluntary actions can be caused. Second, that we are sometimes prepared to treat another's voluntary action as having been caused is not inconsistent with a general reluctance to do so, or with the view that that reluctance is reflected in the provenance and shape of complicity doctrine.[261] Third, the strong evidence in support of that premise, to be found in its power to explain many features of complicity doctrine, is not seriously undermined by evidence that we sometimes find it acceptable to blame a person for unintentionally causing another's voluntary action. There is reason to expect that our social experience in blaming for results should be broadly responsive to several fundamental propositions. There is no reason to expect that anything so human and subjective should exist without some tension and even contradiction.

Let me now conclude with a general perspective of the character of the enterprise I have undertaken.

The notion that law has an existence independent of the society of which it is a part—a "brooding omnipresence in the sky"—is no longer thought at all credible, if it was ever really believed. People who worry about such things entertain strongly differing views of the nature of law, but few doubt that law, and assuredly the criminal law, is an instrument for attaining certain purposes. Some see it more or less neutrally as an instrument for maintaining the conditions of social living; others see it less neutrally as an instrument for furthering the interests of the powerful. Some see its purposes fulfilled by positive enactments designed to achieve preferred states of affairs; others see it as a working out of fundamental moral principles whose roots are to be found either in the nature of things or in the mortality embedded in particular political structures and practices. But that the law is man-made for man's purposes is not an issue in serious dispute, nor could it be.

But to concede so much is not to deny that law may have other important features as well. Law is the product of deliberate decisions, but it is also a product of our culture, through which we express our deepest preoccupations with the world in which we live and our perceptions of its nature and of our own. It is familiar to regard our literature, art, legends, ceremonies, religion, and other cultural forms as vehicles of expression of this kind. But it is no less true of law; of the law's institutions, structures and practices, no doubt in many ways, but also of its bodies of substantive doctrine. Doctrinal law is a cultural product as worthy of being interpreted from the perspective of the social anthropologist as the cultural forms conventionally studied for this purpose. In this essay, I have tried to make this claim good for one small segment of legal doctrine, the doctrine of complicity in the criminal law.

CHAPTER SIX

REFORM

9
CODIFIERS OF THE
CRIMINAL LAW

For my contribution to this Festschrift for Professor Herbert Wechsler I have chosen a subject suggested by one of his spectacular achievements, the Model Penal Code, for which he was Chief Reporter and guiding spirit. In that role he was the latest in a tradition of Anglo-American criminal law codifiers going back to Jeremy Bentham, who launched the nineteenth-century codification movement in the English-speaking jurisdictions of the world. There were many who contributed significantly in one way or another to statutory reform—people like Romilly, Brougham, Peel, and Greaves.[1] But I have in mind those few figures, of whom Wechsler is the preeminent twentieth-century representative, who produced original, comprehensive codes of criminal law in the Benthamite style—Edward Livingston in Louisiana; Thomas Babington Macaulay in India; David Dudley Field in New York; and Sir James Fitzjames Stephen in England. In the following pages I propose to sketch something of the circumstances of their codification efforts, the spirit that motivated these men, the philosophy and outlook they brought to the task, the character of the codes they produced, and the significance of their work.

A word, first, about Bentham. Though in a sense the greatest codifier of all, he was, in the end, a codifier *manqué*. While he wrote far and wide to obtain a codification commission—to the English Home Secretary,[2] to President Madison (twice),[3] to the Governor of Pennsylvania,[4] to all the American governors[5] and to the Russian Emperor[6]—he never obtained one; nor did he ever produce a completed code, penal or otherwise (which might have been just as well, to judge from the specimen of part of a penal code he did leave behind).[7] What he did contribute to the movement for codification, however, was nothing less than its intellectual energy and content. He devoted much of his life to writing detailed plans for a variety of codes in the course of which he opened new fields of philosophical, moral, and legal inquiry. Moreover, he created a distinctive style of codification—codes drafted by learned "philosophes," removed from the political process, proceeding systematically from basic principle to practical corollary to the construction of an internally harmonious and philosophically grounded system—and left a deposit of thought that made him the intellectual father of codification generally and of penal codification in particular.[8] Still, since it is not Bentham and his code-writing epigone who are the subject of this essay, the force and content of his thinking may be more appropriately noted in the course of reviewing their work.

EDWARD LIVINGSTON

Edward Livingston, the draftsman of the proposed Louisiana Penal Code, was nearest in time and spirit to the Benthamite revolution in thought. A lawyer learned enough to meet the Benthamite standard—he was versed in French and Roman law, as well as in the common law[9]—he was also a man of affairs before, during, and after his penal code efforts, a characteristic shared in varying degrees by each of our codifiers and one whose significance for reform apparently escaped the cloistered Bentham.[10] Before moving to Louisiana, he served as congressman, U.S. attorney, and mayor of New York. In Louisiana he became a state legislator (where he engineered the act providing for the appointment of a person "learned in the law" to prepare a criminal code[11]), United States congressman, and senator; later he served as secretary of state and minister to France in Jackson's administration.[12]

Livingston was a reader and admirer of the works of Bentham that Dumont's labors had made available in French.[13] He embraced quite totally the utilitarian philosophy and its commitment to codification of the law.[14] His law reform efforts began early. As a congressman from New York he had a committee appointed, which he later chaired, to explore the revision of the United States penal laws.[15] In Louisiana he was involved in drafting not only a Penal Code, but also a Civil Code and a Code of Practice, both of which were successfully enacted, as well as a Commercial Code.[16] His Penal Code, though never enacted, was his most significant achievement, representing the first complete view of what a penal code built on Benthamite principles would look like.[17]

Livingston was preoccupied not just with the reform of the criminal law, but rather with the goal of comprehensive codification of all law that followed from the general Benthamite philosophy, which he shared. According to this view, government had a proper role in shaping society and its institutions in accordance with the master principle of utility. Precedent and tradition were never good reasons for a law; all law should be reappraised in light of contemporary judgments founded on the science of legislation.[18] Unclear, unsettled, and discordant laws were a needless curse. The legitimacy of law depended upon its being readily knowable and known by those it purported to govern. An integrated and self-contained body of written law that embraced all the law needed to decide cases, without resort to other sources, was essential to a rational system. The common law was to be deeply distrusted because it violated all these principles and because it constituted a charter to the judges to govern, and to govern in the worst way—through ex post facto laws grounded on the judges' own preferences masquerading as the product of legal logic and precedent.[19] These ideas are now familiar, since they represented, in a somewhat diluted form, the core of the case for codification throughout the codification controversy of the nineteenth century. Livingston stood at the beginning.

The Penal Code Livingston submitted in 1826 to the Louisiana legislature bore the imprint of his Benthamite utilitarianism.[20] He was well aware of it. Writing to Bentham in 1829 he said, "In laying before you this work [the Penal Code], I offer you little that you have not a legitimate title to; for, hereafter no one can in Criminal Jurisprudence, propose any favourable change that you have not recommended, or make any wise improvement, that your superior sagacity has not suggested."[21]

Livingston's Penal Code consisted of four separate codes covering over 650 pages—a Code of Crimes and Punishments, a Code of Procedure, a Code of Evidence, and a Code of Reform and Prison Discipline. None of the penal codes we shall be considering approached it in scope. That this vast project was completed in two years almost entirely by one man preoccupied with law practice and other codes and then, when the first completed draft was destroyed by fire, was redone from scratch after another two years, speaks volumes of the extraordinary spirit and ability of the author.[22]

Livingston's commitment to making the Code readily knowable and understood gave the Code a distinctive style. The definition of crimes sometimes entailed a unique blending of command and explanation.[23] For example, before defining the circumstances in which persons might kill in executing judicial orders, the Code explained that since the public interest in executing judicial orders was so great that officials were obliged to risk their lives, justice required that they be permitted to defend themselves in performing this duty.[24] The prohibition of conspiracies to fix prices or wages followed a statement of the right of an individual to set the price of his own goods or the wages for his own services.[25] Even more often, the prohibitions were followed by illustrations. For example, article 484 of his draft declared one who voluntarily permits another to cause his own death to be guilty of homicide and added as an example of such homicide the case of a person who sees a blind man walking to a precipice and declines to inform him of the danger; article 519(5) explicated the meaning of prudent caution with several illustrations involving the use of firearms and quarry-blasting.

Livingston further attempted to make the Code more fully understood through an early general statement of the motives and basic principles of the legislature in enacting the Code. Livingston was particularly proud of this accomplishment. "In no other code that I have seen," he wrote, "has the legislator entered into a full and frank explanation with the people; told them what he intended to do, and for what reason; marked out the limits of the right course, and bade them observe whether he exceeded them. In no other has he treated them, in short, like reasonable beings, and told them to reflect as well as obey."[26]

It is in these general provisions that the Benthamite creed appears quite unobscured.[27] Thus, the Code stated: "Vengeance is unknown to the law." The only object of punishment is prevention which the law achieves by special deterrence of the delinquent and general deterrence of the rest of the community. Acts injurious to the state and to persons should be made criminal; but to avoid multiplication of penal laws without "evident necessity," such acts should not be made criminal when private suit is sufficient to repress them; neither should such acts be made crimes which cannot be enforced, whether because of public opinion or otherwise. Laws should be written in plain, unequivocal language so that all can understand, and concisely so that all can remember; moreover they should be taught in schools and publicly read on stated occasions.[28]

Other Benthamite reflections appeared throughout Livingston's Code. One remarkable feature of the Code was its elimination of capital punishment. In his earlier writings Bentham was apparently prepared to accept capital punishment for aggravated murder.[29] Not so Livingston who, in his Introductory Report to the Code of Crimes and Punishment, developed a long and powerful case to which little has since been added.[30]

Perhaps the most pervasive Benthamite theme to be found in the Code is the distrust of judges.[31] Common-law crimes, reference to common-law terms, and all means through which judges might infuse their own moral views into the definition of crimes were eliminated.[32] Where the language of the Code proved uncertain in application despite the Code's attempt at clarity through unequivocal language, definitions, and illustrations, judges could not punish simply because they viewed the conduct as within the spirit of the provision. To Livingston, better that evil acts go unpunished than that judges assume legislative powers.[33] Only one concession was made to statutory uncertainty—when the judge believed that the statute included conduct the legislature did not intend to penalize, he should acquit and should then report the case to the legislature.[34] Judicial discretion in sentencing was harder to deal with. Livingston responded with a very large number of statutory punishment discriminations (at least ten different maximum and ten different minimum gradations, with numerous fractional increments for aggravating circumstances) and a detailed specification of aggravating and mitigating circumstances to guide the judges' sentencing discretion,[35] an innovation which was largely ignored until its use by the Model Penal Code.

The Code sought to guard against judicial abuse in other ways as well. The power of a judge to hold a person in contempt for acts committed in court was eliminated. Instead, specific crimes of interfering with judicial proceedings were defined, triable through the ordinary criminal processes rather than summarily by the offended judge applying his own standard of offensiveness.[36] The Code did not just remove the power to enjoin libelous or seditious writing from the judge; it made any judge who granted such an injunction punishable by fine and suspension of political rights for two years.[37] Criminal penalties were provided for a range of judicial improprieties: receiving bribes or "maliciously" doing a legally unauthorized act; receiving a gift (other than a legacy) from anyone but close relatives;[38] advising another judge or participating in cases of possible conflict of interest.[39] After a case had been tried no one could be punished for arguing against "the legality or propriety" of the decision.[40] A judge (also an executive officer) who through official action interfered with freedom of speech or of the press was punishable by imprisonment for sixty days to six months and four years loss of his political rights.[41]

There is another side to the ideology underlying Livingston's Code, one not at all incompatible with Bentham's thought, but more identified with the Jeffersonian ideas of revolutionary America and those of the Jacksonian democracy that were on the rise.[42] In the area of the criminal process, for example, the Code went beyond the Bill of Rights formulations of the times: the accused was entitled to counsel at every stage of the proceedings, and if he was unable to provide one, the court was to appoint a lawyer to represent him;[43] no confession was admissible against the accused unless "it be given freely."[44] The Code employed the criminal law to protect the civil liberties of persons: it made it a misdemeanor to attempt to prevent a person from exercising his freedom of speech[45] or his freedom to engage in his own religious worship[46] through violence or threats to his person or his property. Striking another modern chord, Livingston's Report stated that "[p]ublicity is an object of such importance in free governments, that it not only ought to be permitted, but must be secured by a species of compulsion."[47] Hence the judge was required to pronounce the reasons for his final judgment in criminal cases, which had to be available for public scrutiny and criticism.[48] Even true statements could constitute criminal defamation when not made for justifiable cause, but true statements about the conduct of officials were never illegal;[49] mistaken comments about official actions or the motives of officials could not be prosecuted, so long as they did not falsely allege criminality.[50] A modern recognition of the importance of privacy was shown in Livingston's treatment of "epistolatory correspondence": it was punishable to open a letter addressed to another and more severely punishable maliciously to publish its contents.[51]

These provisions exhibited the libertarian spirit of Livingston's Code.

Others reflect a broad humanitarianism and social liberalism. His proposed abolition of capital punishment itself expressed these impulses.
For though he argued its ineffectiveness and general disutility, in the
end Livingston confessed his "firm religious belief . . . [in] the truth of
the doctrine" of total abolition.[52] His humanitarianism is most vividly
revealed in the fourth part of his Code, the Code of Reform and Prison
Discipline.[53] In his Introductory Report to the Code he wrote with el-
oquence and feeling of the crime-spawning nature of prisons, and provided in the Code for segregated confinement of young people, those
awaiting trial for misdemeanors and those awaiting trial for more serious
offenses.[54] He provided for separate places of imprisonment after conviction, as well, for juveniles and those who committed misdemeanors
of no great moral wrong.[55] The conditions of imprisonment of such
offenders were set out in the Code, and made subject to the discretion
of the judge, "not according to the caprice of a turnkey."[56] For serious
offenders, separately housed in the penitentiary, the conditions of imprisonment were to be directed to reformatory discipline and punishment at the same time, with as little suffering to the offender as was
necessary to accomplish both objectives.[57] Here too, the discretion of a
jailer was limited. Labor, education, moral instruction were to be provided systematically so that the reform potential of imprisonment itself
would be enhanced.[58] Deprivation of wholesome food and drink was
not to be an instrument of punishment, although variations in quality
of food and conditions of housing and labor could be used as a means
of reforming the offender.[59]

Livingston regarded punishment and reform of offenders as only
part of the proper social response to crime, however. These responses
would be inadequate unless accompanied by efforts to strike at the "great
sources of those offenses which send the greatest number to our prisons,"
which he believed to be "pauperism, mendicity, idleness, and vagrancy."[60] Therefore, in addition to prisons for those who committed
crimes, his Code provided for a House of Refuge and a House of Industry. The House of Refuge would provide employment for those
unable to support themselves on their own, as well as for discharged
convicts who needed employment on the way back into society. The
House of Industry would house beggars and vagrants who refused labor
in the House of Refuge. In the words of the Code, the object of the
House of Refuge was "to afford the means of voluntary employment to
those who are able and willing to labour, and gratuitous support to those
who are not"; the object of the House of Industry was "to coerce those
who, although capable of supporting themselves, prefer a life of idleness,
vice, and mendicity, to one of honest labour."[61]

Responding to the arguments against his scheme, Livingston articulated themes suggesting a social-democratic philosophy. The duty of

private charity was not to be preferred over "that social duty which every nation owes to the individuals which compose it; which duty is not only protection, but mutual support."[62] Society owed protection to individuals from famine as well as the sword. The protection of property was secondary to the protection of life. Thus, the imposition of burdens on the property of some so that others might survive was an obligation of society. "[C]an it be supposed that any just contract," Livingston wrote, referring to the notion of the social contract, "could stipulate that one of the contracting parties should die of hunger, in order that the others might enjoy, without deduction, the whole of their property? The obligation, then, if derived from the only source to which we can look for its conditions, includes support as well as protection."[63]

The state of the criminal law in Louisiana at the time of Livingston's Code—remnants of French and Spanish law, overlaid with a variety of statutory enactments and the common law itself—would seem to have made it ripe for a codification victory. Yet the effort failed, both in Louisiana and as a direct model elsewhere.[64] The reasons are many and complex.[65] But Livingston's vehement attack on the judges and his proposals to limit their authority, as well as his other radical ideas, such as his attempt to make the problem of unemployment part of the problem of crime, probably alienated the commercial, slave-holding society of Louisiana in that day.[66] Livingston's triumph lay not in enacted codes, but in the judgment of his peers, one of whom, Sir Henry Maine, thought him to be "the first legal genius of modern times."[67]

THOMAS BABINGTON MACAULAY

Thomas Babington Macaulay, the draftsman of the proposed Indian Penal Code of 1837, followed next in the line of codifiers. Like Livingston, Macaulay was a man of affairs. He held a variety of administrative positions in government and served as a member of Parliament on and off for much of his career. Unlike Livingston (and unlike all the codifiers discussed here), he was barely a lawyer. As a young man he was called to the bar, but his practice, as he said, was "extremely small."[68] Moreover, his principal career was devoted to historical scholarship; it is as the author of the *History of England* and other historical and literary books and essays that he established his renown. It is sobering indeed for legal educators to realize that one of the great codes of law was written by a historian and man of letters with a mere smattering of legal training.

As a member of Parliament, Macaulay played an important part in the debates leading to the enactment of the India Charter Act of 1833.[69] He and others succeeded in incorporating a provision that laid the basis for Indian law codification. This provision declared that a general judicial system and common body of laws applicable to Europeans and natives should be enacted, with due regard to the "rights, feelings and peculiar usages of the People," and that to that end existing laws and customs should be ascertained, consolidated, and amended where required. It directed the Governor General in Council (constituting the British Government in India and sometimes also referred to as the Supreme Council of India) to appoint a body of experts, known as the Indian Law Commission, to make reports and recommendations to carry out these objectives.[70]

Macaulay was soon appointed to the Supreme Council and later became Chairman of a four-man Indian Law Commission, appointed by the Supreme Council as directed by the Charter Act.[71] The task of the Commission was to prepare "a code of laws common (as far as may be) to the whole people of India, and having its varieties classified and systematized. . . ."[72] Thus was Macaulay provided with a key role in a plan for the comprehensive codification of laws for India. He embraced the task with enthusiasm, impelled by a plan for codification and reform that probably exceeded the terms of his commission.[73]

Unfortunately, for a variety of reasons best told in Professor Stokes's study,[74] the plan was never accomplished. The Indian Penal Code—though without the accompanying Codes of Procedure and Prison Discipline that Macaulay thought essential[75]—was the only significant success of the codification movement in India during this period (and even that lay unenacted for over 20 years after its completion). Because of illness and other reasons, the three other members of the Indian Law Commission participated very little in the work of preparing the Code. Virtually the entire burden of drafting the Code, therefore, fell on Macaulay;[76] he accomplished the job within two short years, 1835 to 1837, while attending to other governmental and legislative duties, continuing his essay writing, and keeping up with his Greek in the evenings.[77]

Three features of Macaulay's thought and personality affected the style and substance of his Code. Like Livingston, Macaulay was a utilitarian in the Benthamite tradition, an influence imparted early as a member of the "Clapham sect" at Cambridge.[78] He shared fully the premises of the tradition with respect to the unacceptability of judge-made law; the desirability of a root-and-branch legislative remaking of the law responding to what it ought to be, judged by the utility ethic;[79] the distaste for small, piecemeal reforms; and the high regard for clarity, brevity, and simplicity in legal statement as the means of enhancing the knowledge of the law by those it affects.[80]

At the same time, Macaulay was an unremitting Whig in politics; he departed from those implications of the Benthamite creed (quite fully embraced by Livingston) that favored a large role for the state in redressing social evils and dislocations. Comprehensive codification in the style of Bentham he favored fully, but only to render the administration of law more efficient and rational, not to restructure society.[81] Moreover, while he was a libertarian, Macaulay did not share Livingston's passionate democratic impulses and was unsympathetic to undermining the status of governmental authority.

In addition, Macaulay was not a man of speculative, philosophical bent.[82] As a historian he was an elegant and gripping story-teller, whose power arose from the virtuosity of his prose, his command of facts, and his erudition; as a politician he was hardheaded, pragmatic, and expedient—a man of "sturdy common sense" with "a very hard kernel of business in him."[83] As a draftsman-codifier he combined both sets of qualities.

Turning now to how these three aspects of Macaulay—his Benthamism, his Whig preferences, his practical-mindedness—are reflected in his Penal Code, I start with his Benthamism. The chaotic condition of the criminal law in India at the time presented an extraordinary opportunity for a Benthamite codification, as Bentham had earlier perceived.[84] The variety of overlapping laws of different provenance and indeterminate authority that characterized Livingston's Louisiana also characterized India. Muslim and Hindu law, the East India Company's regulations, and the common law itself, all competed in uncertain application. The criminality of a person's actions often depended on who he was—his caste, his religion, whether English or native—and on which of the presidencies he happened to be tried in. Much of the Muslim law was cruel, bizarre, and arbitrary to English eyes.[85] All this afforded Macaulay the justification for largely ignoring the existing Indian law in framing a fresh Penal Code.[86]

Macaulay stated that no other system of penal law provided even a "ground work" for his code.[87] This is an arguable issue. He acknowledged assistance from the French Code and the French decisions, and "still more valuable" assistance from Livingston's Code, but it is clear enough that these were not his groundwork.[88] A number of commentators, however, seeing the many parallels with English law in concept and structure, if not in language, have concluded that the Code in substance embodied (if unconsciously) the English common law.[89] Fitzjames Stephen, for example, described the Code "as the criminal law in England freed from all technicalities and superfluities, systematically arranged and modified in some few particulars . . . to suit the circumstances of British India."[90] No doubt there is much of the English criminal law in the Code, but Professor Fitzgerald has probably come closest to the nub in observing, in reference to Stephen's statement: "Is it irreverent to suggest that English Criminal Law, 'freed from all technicalities and ambiguities and systematically arranged', has undergone such a metamorphosis as to be an entirely new thing?"[91]

Macaulay's general outlook on British rule in India obviously bears on any inquiry into his position on the uses of English law in Indian codification. For Macaulay, what England could best do for India was to serve as the instrument of its modernization, which Macaulay took as tantamount to its Anglicization, or at least its Europeanization. This can fairly be viewed as an instance of arrogant British provincialism[92]—the notion that native cultural values and forms were inferior to Western ones—and as a strategy of imperialism, involving the destruction of an indigenous national and individual identity.[93] That sentiment is plain in Macaulay's famous 1835 Minute on Indian Education, which was influential in establishing the English language as the principal means of instruction in the new national system of education.[94] But though Macaulay was a colonialist, it must be remembered that the existing alternative to his approach was not one built on the anticolonial values of self-determination and autonomy. These values had yet to emerge in British politics. The approach that Macaulay opposed was the typical approach of British colonial administrators for much of the 19th century—one founded on a paternalism that sought to maintain Indian backwardness in the interests of British rule and that was justified by a glorification of inherited tradition and a distrust of all social change.[95] Macaulay sought to further British interests differently—through a far-reaching Europeanization that would lead to a modern India, one that would make the benefits of a modern state available to the Indians.

Macaulay's assimilationist colonial policy, therefore, does suggest a strong reason for him to have looked to English law for his "ground work." One might, nonetheless, find some evidence that he did not in the many concessions his Code made to local customs, conditions, and sensibilities. For example, transportation was retained because native fear of it made it a powerful sanction;[96] the privilege of self-defense was drawn liberally because he believed Indians to be too meek in the face of aggression;[97] and, offenses dealing with religion were drawn in deference to the peculiar religious sensibilities of Indians.[98] But these concessions do not refute the argument that Macaulay's Code assimilated English law. The Charter Act itself required "due Regard . . . to the Rights, Feelings, and peculiar Usages of the People" in drafting legislation.[99] More significantly, the instances of deference were marginal and did not greatly affect the overall structure of the Code; they represented the kind of accommodation to local conditions that sound colonial government of the times saw as transitionally necessary. To be sure, Macaulay did say in his covering letter to the Governor General that he would have been inclined simply to digest Indian law and only moderately correct it if the law had found favor with the people.[100] But this was written as an excuse for not adhering to the Charter Act's direction to have regard to the existing law and may, especially viewed in light of Macaulay's philosophy, be fairly regarded as a diplomatic preemptive defense.

The strongest argument against the view that Macaulay's Code resembled his Minute on education in imposing English mores on India is that, in marked contrast to English culture and language generally, he held the English law as it stood in contempt. Modernization of the Indian criminal law he certainly sought, but not a modernization which involved the transplanting of English law. Instead, he sought for England as well as for India a wholesale redoing of the criminal law, rooted in a "universal science of jurisprudence." As Professor Stokes observed, "to neglect this universality of outlook, this cast of mind that was of the 18th century *philosophe,* is to lose the historical atmosphere in which the Code took shape."[101]

The style of presentation of a code was of great concern to Bentham. But he sought to achieve through that style objectives that, in practice, are difficult to achieve together. The code should speak in the language of command and yet integrate statements of reasons to serve both as a means for popular accountability of the legislature and for greater understanding by the citizen of why he should comply.[102] The language should be clear, brief, and simple for ready understanding even by the less sophisticated, yet it should draw lines between the permitted and the prohibited with such elegant precision as to leave no room for judicial lawmaking.[103] Macaulay, though least the lawyer, was much the most accomplished stylist of the Benthamite codifiers, and came closest to achieving those prescriptions. Of precious few legal works, let alone a code of law, it is imaginable that a perceptive scholar could credibly say what Clive said of Macaulay's Code: "[I]t . . . turns out to be at one level what Bagehot called *The Wealth of Nations*—an amusing book, imbued with the knowledge, learning, and stylistic vigor of its author."[104]

Unlike Livingston, Macaulay did not interweave the legislative reasons with the proscriptive features of the code, as Bentham proposed.[105] He did append a set of Notes containing the reasons for those provisions that seemed to require explanation or defense.[106] But the Notes were addressed to the legislature as reasons to adopt rather than to the public as reasons to comply, as Bentham contemplated; they were not part of the Code Macaulay proposed for adoption and were not so adopted in 1860 when the Penal Code was finally enacted.

The clarity and vigor of the Code's style was largely a product of Macaulay's peculiar talents. He followed a technique, however, that no doubt strengthened the effect. Stephen identified its elements as follows: "In the first place the leading idea to be laid down is stated in the most explicit and pointed form which can be devised."[107] Thus, in dealing with "mischief," article 399 first stated that whoever causes the destruction of any property or any change in it that diminishes its value, intending wrongful loss to any party, commits mischief. "Then such expressions in it as are not regarded as being sufficiently explicit are made the subject of definite explanations." The "Explanation" stated a person cannot commit mischief to his own property. "This is followed by equally definite exceptions. . . ." The "Exception" in this article was that mischief did not include anything a person did openly with the good faith intention of saving anyone from death or hurt or of preventing a greater loss of property than that which he occasioned. "[A]nd in order to set the whole in the clearest possible light the matter thus explained and qualified is illustrated by a number of concrete cases." The article on mischief concluded with nine illustrations (with "A" invariably the actor and "Z" the victim) consisting of short hypotheticals to exhibit the law in application. For example, illustration (g) stated: "A, having joint property with Z in a horse, shoots the horse, intending thereby to cause wrongful loss to Z. A has committed mischief."

Macaulay put great stock in these illustrations as a way of making unmistakable to the unprofessional reader what the use of unfamiliar terms and locutions, unavoidable in the interests of precision, would otherwise make perplexing. In this way "the Code will be at once a statute book and a collection of decided cases: . . . cases decided not by judges but by the legislature. . . ."[108] Macaulay was not "the first to use them in practical legislation,"[109] as has often been said.[110] Livingston before him used illustrations in the body of his Code and for much the same reasons later advanced by Macaulay,[111] though Macaulay used them far more elaborately and extensively. These illustrations met with great success in India. They were carried into the version of Macaulay's Code later adopted; they are still to be found, though much attenuated, in modern versions of the Penal Code[112] and in the other Anglo-Indian Codes as well;[113] they are even today frequently used by the Indian courts,[114] and their use has been applauded "as an instrument of new constructive power, enabling the legislature, to combine the good points of statute-law and case-law . . . while avoiding almost all their respective drawbacks."[115] Nonetheless, the use of examples has not found favor in subsequent codification efforts. The American Restatements contain the only instance of their use of which I am aware, but these are not codes, model or otherwise, or even laws. Perhaps the most common reason for not using examples was given by the English Commissioners on Criminal Law in their Fourth Report.[116] They reasoned that if the illustration falls clearly within the rule there is no need for it as part of the law; and if it is needed to remove some doubt then the terms of the rule are thereby shown to be imperfect and should themselves be redrawn.[117]

One of the leading goals of Benthamite codifications like Macaulay's was to set forth the whole of the penal law with such simplicity and clarity that the average citizen would be able to understand it and the average judge would be unable not to. Stephen's comments, therefore, written in 1883, some twenty years after the enactment of Macaulay's Code, are a remarkable tribute to its success: "Till I had been in India I could not have believed it to be possible that so extensive a body of law could be made so generally known to all whom it concerned in its minutest details. . . . After twenty years' use it is still true that any one who wants to know what the criminal law of India is has only to read the Penal Code with a common use of memory and attention."[118]

So much, then, for Macaulay's Benthamism. His Whig proclivities were most evident, and the contrast with Livingston greatest, on the large issues of the relation between the individual and the state. There was, for example, no suggestion of anything comparable to Livingston's plan to have the state undertake a large program of unemployment relief as part of the attack on crime. Since he shared fully the traditional Whig libertarianism and dislike of large government,[119] Macaulay did not accept those elements of Benthamism that cast on the state the duty to establish large bureaucratic enterprises to ameliorate social and economic conditions.[120] This is not to say that Macaulay believed that the penal law might not be used to nudge some social change. He proposed that there be no immunity of a master for crimes he committed against his slaves because the absence of such an immunity would help to end slavery.[121] He also proposed excluding the crime of adultery for women in part to counter the unjust subjugation of women in India.[122] These instances were far removed, however, from governmental undertakings to remake the social structure.

Macaulay was surely no anti-civil libertarian. Contrary to the laws prevailing at the time, and to Livingston's Code as well, he proposed that the truth of a prejudicial imputation be a full defense to criminal defamation in all cases.[123] He also included provisions penalizing actions that insulted religious sensibilities or that interfered with the exercise of religious worship,[124] not only because they reflected a principle expedient for conditions in India, but because the principle was one "on which it would be desirable that all Governments should act."[125] Nonetheless, his Code did not reflect the same passion for democratic freedoms one finds in Livingston. For example, there were no provisions criminalizing actions that interfered with freedom of speech and the press. Where Livingston restricted the crime of sedition to enlisting men or making other preparations to subvert the state, or to utterances designed to counsel to such actions,[126] Macaulay made punishable the use of words to "excite feelings of disaffection to the Government."[127]

Particularly revealing on the issues of state authority and individual freedom were the provisions concerning a citizen's duty to comply with official orders that might be illegal. The Code gave no right of private defense against an action by an official that the official was legally competent to undertake, even if that action was illegal and itself constituted an offense.[128] Thus, resistance to an illegal arrest was not permitted. No action was an offense that was done by a person who believed "in good faith" that he was either compelled by law or authorized by law to do it.[129] Since "good faith" as used by Macaulay in various portions of the Code[130] as well as in these articles[131] appeared to posit only a subjective standard (*i.e.*, the absence of bad faith)[132] the weighting was heavy on the side of authority in the balance between the state and the individual. Consistent with Whig political values, the state had a limited role but within that role its authority was great.

Macaulay's treatment of omissions was also consistent with his Whig outlook. He was not prepared to join Livingston in imposing a criminal duty on all persons to act to save others; that duty should extend only to those who otherwise have a legal duty to act.[133] Only in part did this view result from the practical difficulty of legislating an acceptable line that would protect the individual when the burdens of actions were too great. More important was Macaulay's position, frequently reiterated, that private virtue should be left to other instrumentalities and that the coercive sanctions of punishment should be restricted to preventing men from doing positive harm to others.[134]

Though distinguished commentators have found in the Code evidence of Macaulay's humanitarianism,[135] I do not myself find it heavily displayed. He did restrict capital punishment to murder and treason, but his reasons were practical, not humanitarian.[136] Similarly, he favored the elimination of corporal punishment because it fell unevenly and most heavily on those with higher sensitivities, and not because it was inhumane.[137] Much the same may be said of Macaulay's proposals for the treatment of offenders. Though no Code of Prison Discipline was completed, a report of the Law Commission on this subject, in which Macaulay participated, was submitted.[138] Nothing can be found of Livingston's sympathy for the social unfortunates that are led to a life of crime, nor any programs for their rehabilitation, but only a stern special deterrence program built on "solitary confinement," "monotonous, uninteresting labour within doors," and deprivation "of every indulgence not absolutely necessary to health."[139] Indeed, Macaulay explicitly advanced the view that prison conditions should be as severe and intense as public sensibilities would tolerate—on the premise that the same amount of deterrence could thereby be obtained with shorter prison terms.[140]

Finally, there is Macaulay's nonideological and pragmatic side. It is evident in several of the Code's provisions already mentioned, but certain other features of the Code reveal these qualities with particular sharpness. Livingston, a very different sort of man, thought that his ringing statement of fundamental principles with which he opened his Code were among his most constructive innovations.[141] Macaulay had no use for them. As a tough-minded, practical man, he had little taste for grand pronouncements of penological philosophy and no more confidence in their utility for solving concrete problems. If statements of general principle were drawn tightly enough to have meaning they could prove embarrassingly tight for practical adjustments and compromises. If, on the other hand, they were loose enough to allow adjustments they were likely to be aphoristic and empty. A man of Macaulay's turn of mind avoids them.[142]

Macaulay quite thoroughly disapproved of judicial lawmaking, as did all codifiers in the Benthamite tradition.[143] He was prepared, however, far more than Livingston, to tolerate a judicial role when the alternative appeared impractical or productive of worse evils. Where Livingston tried to construct legislative solutions to some typical problems of causation in homicide (e.g., neglect or maltreatment of slight wounds resulting in death),[144] Macaulay, after showing that these formulations could be both over- and underinclusive, concluded that causation issues should best "be left a question of evidence to be decided by the Courts, according to the circumstances of every case."[145] Where Livingston sought to control judicial discretion in imposing prison terms by providing an extremely large number of punishment gradations for different offences,[146] Macaulay's Code included considerably fewer maximum gradations and used a minimum only for a few crimes.[147] Livingston sought to prevent judicial excesses in fining the poor by prohibiting a fine greater than one-fourth of the offender's property.[148] Macaulay reasoned that this prohibition would be impractical, in requiring lengthy and unsatisfactory investigations into the offender's wealth, as well as unwise, in preventing the court, where appropriate, from requiring the offender to disgorge the whole of the profit made from his wrong. He concluded that judicial discretion over fines was an evil that had to be endured if fines were to be used.[149] Where Livingston sought, in the provisions on theft offenses, to deal definitively with the problem of defining "possession,"[150] Macaulay, after deftly poking a few holes in Livingston's formulation, concluded that it was better to "leave it to the tribunals, without any direction, to determine whether particular property is at a particular time in the possession of a particular person, or not."[151] Livingston's adherence to the primacy of life led him to the doctrine that verbal insults could not constitute sufficient provocation.[152] Macaulay, aware of the impracticality of such a rule, especially in light of the high Indian sensitivity to injuries to feelings, provided otherwise.[153]

Two other provisions that show Macaulay's sense of the practical are noteworthy because they represent innovations that have been adopted in subsequent legislation. One is his provision for dealing with what he regarded as the ineradicable indistinctness of the lines separating theft, criminal misappropriation of property not in possession, and criminal breaches of trust.[154] Since these distinctions were irrelevant to whether a person was punishable, Macaulay provided that in doubtful cases it need not be resolved which provision the offender violated so long as

he was sentenced to a punishment common to the mooted penal provisions.[155] The other was a provision explicitly exempting from punishment actions technically punishable if the harm caused was "so slight
that no person of ordinary sense and temper would complain."[156] He
reasoned that judges would sensibly exclude such cases in any event, but
without the clause could do so only by one of two equally pernicious
practices: "by making law, or by wresting the language of law from its
plain meaning."[157]

I have already lingered longer over Macaulay than the principle of
equal time would permit. But the competing principle of doing him
justice leads me to stay a moment more in order to try to convey what
is perhaps the most remarkable thing about his Code—its freshness of
thought and perspicuity of analysis. I have already alluded to his departure from existing law in making truth a defense to criminal defamation in all cases;[158] in extending provocation to include verbal insult;[159] in omitting the crime of adultery;[160] and in enlarging the privilege
to kill in self-defense,[161] which he accomplished by the daring move of
making it enough, as I read it, that the defendant honestly believed that
justifying circumstances existed.[162] To these should be added his treatment of mens rea questions.

The constructive crimes of felony murder and misdemeanor manslaughter found no place in his Code. "It will be admitted," he wrote,
"that, when an act is in itself innocent, to punish the person who does
it because bad consequences which no human wisdom could have fore-
seen have followed from it would be in the highest degree barbarous
and absurd."[163] That the same accident occurred while the actor was
otherwise committing a crime, say, safely making a fire to burn a will,
adds nothing to the offense he committed and punishing him for murder
adds nothing to the security of life.

> The only good effect which such punishment can produce will be to
> deter people from committing any of those offenses which turn into
> murders what are in themselves mere accidents. It is in fact an addition
> to the punishment of those offenses, and it is an addition made in the
> very worst way . . . that, besides the ordinary punishment, every of-
> fender shall run an exceedingly small risk of being hanged.[164]

In these cases, therefore, the offender was punishable only for the offense he committed, with nothing additional for the accidental death.[165]

The use of the constructive-crime theory to raise a crime of negligent
killing to murder was, to Macaulay, no more defensible, since it violated
a "distinction which more than any other it behooves the legislator to
bear constantly in mind"—that "between harm voluntarily caused and
harm involuntarily caused." Negligence often deserved punishment, but
it was intolerable "to punish a man whose negligence has produced some

evil which he never contemplated as if he had produced the same evil knowingly, and with deliberate malice."[166] Thus, where a man negligently killed in the course of committing a crime, he was punishable only for that crime plus the ordinary punishment for negligent killing ("involuntary culpable homicide").[167]

The same sensitivity to considerations of culpability was manifested in the way Macaulay defined the mental element component of crimes—with unusual particularity and without the confusing epithetical qualifiers not uncommon in the common law.[168] Strict liability was rarely imposed, and then only where the punishment was minor and the offense regulatory in character. An example is having command of a vessel for hire so loaded as to endanger life.[169] One knows strict liability was intended because in contiguous clauses Macaulay employed the Code's standard formula for negligence—an act or a manner "so rash or negligent as to indicate a want of due regard for human life."[170] In other provisions, Macaulay opted for a higher standard of culpability, awareness of the danger, and used language to make this self-evident—selling food "knowing the same to be noxious,"[171] or adulterating a drug "intending or knowing it to be likely" that the drug will be dispensed as if not adulterated.[172] These examples were all regulatory provisions, but it is in this area that law makers are most likely to stumble over mens rea questions. Macaulay displayed the same sensitivity in other portions of the Code. Voluntary culpable homicide occurred when one acted "with the intention of thereby causing, or with the knowledge that he is likely thereby to cause the death of any person."[173] Negligent homicidal liability occurred through an act "so rash and negligent as to indicate a want of due regard for human life."[174] Mischief was the destruction of another's property "intending thereby to cause wrongful loss to any party."[175] Making a counterfeit property mark was criminal when done "intending or knowing it to be likely" that the mark may be used as genuine to the injury of another.[176] The term "fraudulently" was used to denote the mental element for some crimes,[177] but it was clearly defined in the General Explanations.[178] It is indeed regrettable that so enlightened and clear-headed an approach to the definition of crimes had so little effect on later statutory and judicial lawmaking in the criminal law.

Macaulay's Penal Code was adopted in 1860,[179] twenty-two years after its submission and one year too late for Macaulay to have lived to see his work bear fruit (though he turned so precipitously and finally from law and codification on his return to England that, by then, he might not have cared). The proposed Code was subjected to revision by several commissions, but lay dormant even after the major revisions were completed.[180] Stephen thought the changes improved the original.[181] He may, however, have only been paying tribute to the chief revisor,

Sir Peacock Barnes, who sat on the Judicial Committee of the Privy Council at the time Stephen wrote. Omitting the provisions for negligent homicide;[182] reinstating the crime of adultery;[183] and awkwardly complicating the homicide provisions[184] were distinctly not improvements. Still, as Stephen noted, to compare Macaulay's Code with English criminal law was "like comparing cosmos with chaos."[185] As he later noted: "the Penal Code has triumphantly supported the test of experience for upwards of twenty-one years during which time it has met with a degree of success which can hardly be ascribed to any other statute of anything approaching to the same dimensions."[186]

JAMES FITZJAMES STEPHEN

Chronologically, David Field is the next of the codifiers to be considered, but his temporal priority is not great and it will be best to delay crossing the ocean so as not to lose the thread between Macaulay and James Fitzjames Stephen. Stephen, whose 1878 Criminal Code (Indictable Offenses) Bill was said to be the first serious effort in England to codify completely any branch of the law,[187] was a prominent barrister, essayist, journalist, and judge who was born into and worked among the intellectual aristocracy of Victorian England. His professional career as a barrister was accompanied by outpourings of essays in the intellectual journals of the times through which he participated in the social, moral, and literary debates of the day.[188] To the modern generation he is known, if at all, as the Devil's Advocate (pro se, in this case) who, in his book, *Liberty, Equality, Fraternity,* ventured a sustained rebuttal to the libertarian arguments in John Stuart Mill's *Essay on Liberty.*[189] In the tradition of his predecessor codifiers, he was a public servant, having succeeded Sir Henry Maine as law member of the India Supreme Council. Unlike his predecessors, he was a scholar of the criminal law whose three-volume *History of the Criminal Law in England* still stands as a major contribution.

Stephen's active involvement with codification began, like Macaulay's, with his Indian service, although, unlike Macaulay's, it did not end with it. As the law member of the Supreme Council, on which he served for over two years (1869–1872), his task was to continue the work of codification in India that had been given a fresh impetus in the aftermath of the Indian Mutiny.[190] He took an important role in drafting the Limitation Act and the Contract Act and a determining role in drafting the Evidence Act.[191] His work as an Indian codifier drew mixed reviews. Lord Bryce's subsequent interviews with people in India led him to conclude that Stephen's "capacity for the work of drafting was deemed not equal to his fondness for it. He did not shine either in fineness of discrimination or in delicacy of expression."[192] A more recent observer, however, thought that the Evidence Act of 1872 was Stephen's "crowning personal achievement."[193]

Stephen returned to England with the desire to continue there the codification efforts that had engaged him in India.[194] An opportunity arose when he was asked to prepare a homicide bill. His draft—the Homicide Law Amendment Bill of 1874—got to a select committee but not out of it. One ground of oposition that Stephen took seriously was that the Bill codified only a part of the criminal law. Stephen thereupon promptly set himself to "performing, as a private enterprise, the work of making a Digest of it [the criminal law] which might serve as a first step towards a Code."[195] Following the appearance of the Digest, he was commissioned, as he had hoped, to prepare a draft code of criminal law and procedure. The Criminal Code (Indictable Offenses) Bill of 1878, his first effort, was not enacted, but it led to the appointment of a Royal Commission, composed of Stephen and three High Court judges, which in the following year, 1879, presented a Draft Code (Indictable Offenses) that consisted of a revision of the earlier Bill, together with supporting commentary.[196]

Stephen's Code is far more conservative and less ambitious than Macaulay's, and certainly than Livingston's. At least three major differences in the circumstances of its drafting made that contrast inevitable: the fact that it was written for the developed legal system of late nineteenth-century England; the maturing of the Benthamite codification effort; and the deeply conservative political and moral philosophy of its author.[197]

As we have seen, Livingston and Macaulay drafted their codes for jurisdictions whose laws were unsettled, foreign, and lightly rooted. It was far easier to venture a radical, Benthamite codification in those circumstances than in those prevailing in England in Stephen's time. As Perry Miller has pointed out, one significant function of the codification of a country's laws is to draw a society together by establishing a national identity.[198] This need was great in Livingston's Louisiana (though, as we have seen, not great enough to carry the day) and equally great in India, where colonial policy (at least in Macaulay's view) was to remake the nation in the image of a modern, Western state. No such need existed for England in Stephen's time. English law was deeply engrained. For all its defects, it worked. Despite what the Benthamite reformers saw as its bizarre and irrational legal system, England had emerged as the leading commercial, industrial, and colonial nation of the world. In these circumstances, mild legal reform in the spirit of even further progress would be a credible enterprise; a root and branch reconstruction of a nation's laws would not. The bulk of the legal profession, lawyers and judges alike, tend, in most conditions, to resist the radical upsetting of legal institutions. Their power of resistance was substantial in Louisiana (enough to win) and in India (enough, with support of a paternalistic colonial policy, to delay for over two decades). In late nineteenth-century England it was far stronger, in part because of the legal establishment's entrenchment in society and in part because the drive for radical reconstruction of the laws had so much less power behind it.

A second and related major difference in circumstance was the maturing of the Benthamite codification spirit; maturing in the sense of growing old, certainly, but also probably in the sense of growing up as well.[199] Criminal law reform had been a cause in England for decades by the time Stephen returned from India. Even before Macaulay's Indian venture the drive to reform the criminal law of England had begun with the work of Romilly, Bentham's disciple, and others, and had continued with the work of Sir Robert Peel, under whose leadership several statutes were enacted which digested and consolidated a massive number of laws.[200] These were not the kind of codifications that Bentham had urged[201] and that Livingston and Macaulay had undertaken, but they established the English tradition of codification to which fresh life was given by the liberalizing electoral changes of the Reform Act of 1832. The following year the India Charter Act was passed, with its provision for Indian codification that eventually led to Macaulay's Indian Penal Code.[202] In addition, and far more consequential for English reform activity, a Royal Commission on Criminal Law was appointed and was charged with digesting the statutory and unwritten criminal law of England and with producing a single comprehensive statute.[203] Over the next ten years, this and successor Commissions systematically and exhaustively reviewed the substantive and procedural criminal law of England and produced thirteen reports, containing drafts of proposed laws and extensive commentary,[204] culminating in the production in 1845 of a "Draft of the Bill for consolidating into one statute the written and unwritten law relating to the definition of Crimes and Punishments."[205] This draft was not enacted, nor were later versions of it, nor the parts of it that were introduced in subsequent years. The "stupendous efforts" yielded only the Criminal Consolidation Acts of 1861, relating to offenses against persons and property, which were mild and vague restatements of common-law rules and nothing like a codification, even in the attenuated tradition of a digest and consolidation.[206]

The third major factor affecting the conception and nature of the Draft Code was the basic outlook of its draftsman. Livingston was a radical; Macaulay a Whig. Stephen, by contrast, was a profound conservative in politics and a social Darwinian in morals.[207] As his brother, Leslie Stephen, put it, "[i]n philosophy he was a disciple of Mill and the utilitarians,[208] but in the application to political questions rather followed Hobbes, and was in sympathy with Caryle's approval of strong government."[209] His predilections appeared early. As an eighteen year old confessed that the 1848 revolutions in Europe excited in him "feelings of zeal against all popular aspirations and in favour of all established institutions."[210] His attack on the ideals of "Liberty, Equality, and Fraternity" was a part of his general anti-democratic thinking, which he expressed with breathtaking dogmatism and ferocity. The result of dividing political power into bits through universal suffrage and other electoral reforms was "simply that the man who can sweep the greatest of them into one heap will govern the rest. The strongest man in some form or other will always rule. . . . In a pure democracy the ruling men will be the wire-pullers and their friends. . . ."[211] He further believed: "The essence of life is force."[212] "Equality [is] a big name for a small thing"[213] and in America it "tends to invert . . . the natural relation between wisdom and folly,[214] producing "the rapid production of an immense multitude of commonplace, self-satisfied, and essentially slight people. . . ."[215]

His rejection of the possibility of any disinterested moral sentiment was profound. "Humanity is only I writ large, and love for Humanity generally means zeal for MY notions."[216] The world was better off with people eschewing grand altruistic pretensions and engaging in their ordinary pursuits.[217] Since one man's happiness was another man's unhappiness the principle of greatest happiness as formulated by Bentham and Mill could not be a precept for social action. "A legislator may regard a meat diet as an element of the happiness which he seeks to promote, but sheep, oxen, and pigs can hardly look on the butcher as a friend."[218] Therefore the utilitarian standard was not overall happiness maximized, but "the widest possible extension of the ideal of life formed by the person who sets up the standard."[219] The object of promoting virtue and preventing vice was good and intelligible for legislative purposes[220] and using compulsion for that object was sound so long as it was likely to be effective at a reasonable cost.[221] The purpose of punishing vice when these conditions were met was not only to prevent crime, but to "gratify the feeling of hatred . . . which the contemplation of such conduct excites in healthily constituted minds."[222] Indeed, this was true of criminal punishment generally, since it is "highly desirable that criminals should be hated, that the punishment inflicted upon them should be so contrived as to give expression to that hatred, and to justify it so far as the public provision of means for expressing and gratifying a healthy natural sentiment can justify and encourage it."[223]

These three circumstances, then—that the Code was meant for Victorian England, that the codification movement had matured, and Stephen's cast of mind—combined to give the Draft Code its character. When Stephen returned from India resolved to carry on with codifying the English criminal law, it was natural for him to see as a preliminary task the creation of a digest of criminal law to serve as the basis for a new code (a task made feasible by the extensive studies of the various Royal Commissions).[224] In the introduction to his Digest he revealed an approach markedly different from those of Livingston and Macaulay. The Digest was meant to state the existing law by condensing the statutes and articulating the principles of the cases, so that it might serve a "first step" toward a penal code which "must, of course, consist of the existing Criminal Laws of England re-arranged and amended."[225] The 1879 Draft Code carried forward that rationale—"the reduction of the criminal law of England, written and unwritten, into one code."[226] As he later said, a code "ought to be based upon the principle that it aims at nothing more than the reduction to a definite and systematic shape of results obtained and sanctioned by the experience of many centuries."[227] Codification aims at eliminating "the needless technicalities, obscurities, and other defects which the experience of its administration has disclosed," but its essential object is "merely the reduction of the existing law to an orderly written system."[228] Changes in the law were also involved, but such changes only as a systematic restatement of the law required.

Stephen's Draft Code, therefore, contains none of the groundbreaking Benthamism of Livingston's or Macaulay's codes. It deliberately left untouched a variety of obsolete crimes that would have made Bentham turn in his grave in posthumous disgrace.[229] The same may be said of his refusal even to deal with the existing law of sedition,[230] and of his retention of myriads of separate offenses when one generalization would have done.[231] The Benthamite principle of achieving popular "cognoscibility" disappeared. Stephen said as much,[232] but it went without saying in a Code that stated: "Every one who undertakes to do any act the omission to do which is or may be dangerous to life, is under a legal duty to do that act, and is criminally responsible for the consequences of omitting without lawful excuse to discharge that duty."[233]

Stephen did not find law-making by judges, the great Benthamite *bête noir,* to be a serious problem. Judges had no discretion anyway since they were firmly bound by precedent to the common-law rules. The restatement of common-law rules in statutory form by the Draft Code took nothing from the judges, since they were bound equally by common law as by statutory rules[234] The Code did clear up doubts and technicalities, "but," Stephen asserted, "it neither increases nor diminishes to any material extent, if at all, any discretion at present vested in either judges or juries."[235] Moreover, discretion was sometimes desirable. "Thus for instance," Stephen's Report explained, "it is declared to be a question of law whether a particular order given for the suppression of a riot is 'mainfestly unlawful'; whether the occasion of the sale . . . of certain classes of books . . . is such 'as might be for the public good,' and whether there is evidence for the jury of 'excess.'"[236] "Blasphemous libel" was made criminal,[237] but it was thought "inexpedient to define [it] otherwise than by the use of that expression."[238] So also the crime of "obscene libel."[239] Common-law offenses were eliminated because parliamentary responsiveness sufficed to deal with newly developed evils,[240] but all common-law defenses were retained[241]—to restate them in statutory terms would have frozen their shape since judges would have had to apply them "according to the[ir] words," while to have left them as common-law defenses would have kept them fluid because judges would be able to apply them "according to [their] substance."[242] (So much for his argument two pages earlier that no greater restraint is imposed upon judges by statutory formulation of common-law rules than by the common-law rules alone!) Further, the Code recognized that a number of situations where defenses might be appropriate simply are not dealt with adequately under the common law and that new rules would have to be created by the judges: "It is far better to decide such cases as and when they arise, and with the light which may then be thrown upon them both by circumstances and by the ingenuity and research of counsel, than to attempt to lay down rules beforehand, for which no definite materials exist."[243]

The Draft's approach to punishment bore Stephen's mark. Unlike Livingston, whose Code declared that, "Vengeance is unknown to the law," Stephen regarded vengeance as the central object of criminal punishment. As for capital punishment, it was for him, as Sir Leon Radzinowicz has observed, "the keystone of all moral and penological principles."[244] His Code retained the death penalty in all cases in which it was provided for under the existing law.[245] Stephen later admitted that but for opposing popular sentiment he would have enlarged the mandatory death penalty to include repeating property offenders: "I suspect that a small number of executions of professional receivers of stolen goods, habitual cheats, and ingenious forgers . . . would do more to check crime than twenty times as many sentences of penal servitude."[246] Corporal punishment, in the form of flogging and whipping was retained,[247] Stephen's only criticism of existing law being that it was not severe enough— "little, if at all, more serious than a birching at a public school."[248] Finally, Stephen's major reason for urging his Code was characteristic. It was not that crime was rampant. He thought it had been more active and mischievous at other times and places. What struck him was that

> there has never been an age of the world in which so much and such genuine doubt was felt as to the other sanctions on which morality exists. . . . In such circumstances it seems to be specially necessary for those who do care for morality to make its one unquestionable, indisputable sanction as clear, and strong, and emphatic, as words and acts can make it.[249]

It would, however, be misleading and unjust to leave these comments on Stephen's Code at that. Within the codification tradition in which he worked, the Code was a significant achievement. His Code was to the English criminal law as—to paraphrase what he said of Macaulay's Code—cosmos to chaos. It drew together, systematized and pruned the English law, not radically, but still not trivially and made of it a more manageable whole. Just to advert, by way of example, to some of the many useful features of the Code: it adopted from the Indian Penal Code Macaulay's provision for dismissal of de minimis cases;[250] abolished the distinction between felonies and misdemeanors for purposes of determining a variety of procedural consequences;[251] precluded mandatory minimum punishments;[252] eliminated the requirement of materiality in perjury;[253] tried to articulate the situations in which homicidal omissions were culpable;[254] formulated the law of murder without the common-law concepts of malice aforethought and implied malice;[255] narrowed felony murder to cases where the defendant either did an unlawful act that he should have known would be likely to cause death, or intentionally inflicted great bodily injury in the commission of designated heinous felonies;[256] established insult as a possible legal provocation;[257] made an illegal arrest only evidence of provocation rather than an automatic basis for reducing the offense to manslaughter;[258] eliminated the defense of impossibility in attempt;[259] provided for the punishment of nonhomicidal negligent injuries;[260] allowed the privilege of self-defense even where the victim's aggressive acts initiated the encounter;[261] and eliminated the distinction between second degree principles and accessories before the fact.[262]

To be sure, even as a technical document the Code had limitations. For example, as one of its strategies for meeting the danger of mistakes, it made the unfortunate move of turning the criminality of conduct into a gamble for the actor. So in dealing with killing in defense of dwelling, if the killing took place in the nighttime, the Code made it a defense that the accused reasonably believed the victim to be a criminal intruder and that his action was necessary to stop him,[263] but in the daytime a defense was made out only if the action was in fact necessary for the purpose.[264] More generally, the Draft stopped short of generalizing where, at least from today's perspective,[265] generalization would have been desirable. For example, Stephen retained the dozen or so separate provisions on mischief to different kinds of property[266] and the numerous separate specifications of the crime of theft depending on the object stolen—wills,[267] post letter bags,[268] post letters,[269] cattle,[270] and so on. Further illustrations were his unwillingness to generalize a defense of necessity;[271] and his treatment of omission and causation solely by specifying particular instances.[272]

Still, as Sir Leon Radzinowicz has said,[273] Stephen's Draft Code was a significant advance. Undoubtedly, had Parliament enacted his Code, generations of lawyers and students might have been spared a huge corpus of tortured case law, and the judges might have found more useful outlets for their analytical ingenuity. In any event, Parliament did not pass it. Given the strong conservative influences of the period, so large a piece of criminal law reform was too much for Parliament to bite off and too important to be swallowed whole.[274] But despite its failure in England, the Code had a fair measure of success in other Commonwealth countries. The Draft Code served as a model for a number of newer jurisdictions, including New Zealand,[275] Western Australia, Queensland and Tasmania,[276] and Canada,[277] for which the chaos of the common law of crimes was less of an old shoe than it was for the English.

DAVID DUDLEY FIELD

Bentham, our first penal law codifier, never drafted a code. David Dudley Field, our last, never drafted a penal code. His dominance of the New York codification efforts is not in doubt.[278] But the first report of the Commission that eventually produced the substantive Field Codes states that the Penal Code was being prepared by another of the Commissioners, Curtis Noyes, a former district attorney.[279] This represented a plausible division of labor since Field had no professional or scholarly competence in the criminal law and had been assigned the lion's share of the burden—drafting the Civil and Political Codes.[280] Moreover, Field's biographer, his brother, not otherwise given to minimizing his subject's activities, tells us quite explicitly that Noyes prepared the preliminary analysis of the Penal Code and then drafted the Code itself with the assistance of B. V. Abbott.[281] Nonetheless, Field was one member of the small group of three that produced the Penal Code[282] and his intellectual domination of the codification effort in New York was unquestionable. For present purposes, therefore, the Penal Code may be taken, as it is generally, as one of the Field Codes.

Field was one of a notable family of men of achievement in nineteenth-century America. His brother, Stephen, became Chief Justice of the Supreme Court of California and later a Justice of the United States Supreme Court. Another brother, Cyrus, was a successful entrepreneur who had much to do with laying the first trans-Atlantic cable. David Dudley Field had a prominent career at the bar in New York, but he is remembered today because of his singular devotion to the cause of reforming the administration of justice through the codification of the laws, which he pursued as an unpaid public service for most of his life.[283]

Field was the dominant figure in the movement for codification of American law that spanned approximately the middle fifty years of the nineteenth century. Livingston was the major figure at its inception. Field presided over its rise and modest successes and witnessed its ultimate decline.[284] A number of more fundamental and related controversies of the period became involved in the great codification controversy. There was, first, the rise of populism associated with Jacksonian democracy, a movement which, at it inception, seized upon Benthamite iconoclasm for its basic orientation in matters of law.[285] In their contest with the Federalists and the Whigs, the Jacksonian Democrats advanced the causes of the producing classes—farmers and workingmen—against the business community, especially monopoly capitalism; of individual human rights against property rights; of greater equality in the distribution of wealth; of popular political participation in all phases of government against aristocratic privilege.[286] Codification, then, was a natural battleground for these ideas, for it represented an attack on the power of lawyers and judges to make and declare law without democratic participation. It offered a plainly articulated body of laws accessible to and understandable by all in place of the oracular, mysterious incantation of doctrinal technicalities by lawyers and judges. And it placed the power over the law squarely in the hands of the people's elected representatives in the legislature.

Another controversy, related to the first but more rarified, was the controversy between positivism and historicism in accounting for the shape of law. In this controversy Field was the leader of the Benthamite cause.[287] His most articulate challenger was another New York lawyer, James Carter, who, as a disciple of the Savigny school flourishing in Germany,[288] provided a theoretical basis for resistance to codification as well as to innovative legislation generally. Carter argued that law could not be produced new and whole by legislative fiat because law reflects the experience and life of a culture, which projects a social standard of what is right. The discovery and explication of the precepts and principles constituting this standard required the ministrations of a professional class of lawyers and judges employing the method of juristic science in the processes of litigation and decision.[289] These doctrines have long since ceased to be influential in American jurisprudence, but in Field's day they constituted a serious challenge to codification.[290]

A third, more basic, issue involved in the codification controversy, as Perry Miller has pointed out, was the "contest between nationalism and cosmopolitanism"—provincial codifiers versus the cosmopolitan adherents of the common law.[291] As against the judges and lawyers who worked with the materials and in the traditions of the English common law, the codifiers offered an opportunity for the virtually instantaneous creation of an American body of law, responsive to purely American circumstances and sentiments.

Fields's entrance into the center of the storm coincided with the ascendancy of Jacksonian populism in New York. Reflecting a revulsion against lawyers and judges, a Constitutional Convention in New York in 1846 leveled the existing court structure, established elective judges with limited tenure and entitled any male over twenty-one years of age of good character and in possession of the requisite learning and ability to be admitted to the bar.[292] In substantial measure due to Field's pamphleteering,[293] it also directed the legislature to appoint two commissions, each with three commissioners, one to propose reforms in the law of practice and proceedings,[294] and the other "to reduce into a written and systematic code the whole body of the law of this State," specifying such changes they thought proper.[295] This led to the appointment of the Commissioners of Practice and Pleading and the Commissioners of the Code in 1847. Field was shortly thereafter made a member of the former Commission and in that capacity did the pioneering work on procedural reform[296] that resulted in the Field Code of Procedure.[297] The latter Commission, on which Field did not serve at first, made little progress, producing only a limited statutory revision, until a newly created Commission of the Code, with Field as one of the three Commissioners, was established by statute (drafted by Field) in 1857.[298] It was this Commission that produced drafts of the famous substantive Field Codes—a Political Code, a Civil Code, and a Penal Code,[299] the last in 1864 and again in 1865, after recommendations of the judges, prosecutors and others had been taken into account.[300]

The Field Penal Code[301] gives no evidence of a radical, Livingstonian spirit at work, any more than do the other Field Codes. Though his codes may have "represented the culmination of the Jacksonian demand for reform,"[302] Field's demands for reform were less fundamental. He was, after all, despite occasional radical rhetoric,[303] an establishment New York lawyer all his life.[304] His views on property rights were in the correct conservative tradition[305] and his views on the training of lawyers were certainly not populist. He deplored loose apprentice systems as perpetuating "transcriber[s] of legal formulas" and "promotor[s] of neighborhood litigation"; he felt that a good lawyer must be learned in the wholeness of the law and the relationship of its parts,[306] and that strict examinations following a prescribed course of study in school or office should precede admission to the profession.[307] Field's paramount concerns were those of the professional lawyer, not radical reform of the law or broad social reform generally.[308] In particular, the outpouring of judicial decisions was becoming an unmanageable avalanche. The "wilderness of single instances" of which "the lawless science of our law" consisted, called for one remedy: "It is to reduce the bulk, clear out the refuse, condense and arrange the residuum, so that the people, and the lawyer and judge as well, may know what they have to practice and obey."[309] He meant his Penal Code as a remedy of this kind.

Field's Code yields little joy or instruction to the contemporary reader. Livingston's Code had passion and originality; Macaulay's had perspicuity and style; and Stephen's had high professional competence. But Field's is plain pedestrian. That quality is not among the profession's cardinal sins. But what makes its presence in the Code so painful is the sense that one has discovered the headwaters of a tradition that dominated criminal law-making until fairly recent times. That sense is heightened as one recognizes in many of its provisions the baleful prototypes of formulations that have burdened American criminal law for generations: murder by "any act imminently dangerous to others and evincing a depraved mind, regardless of human life,"[310] or "[w]hen perpetrated without any design to effect death, by a person engaged in the commission of any felony";[311] conspiracy "to commit any act injurious to the public health, to public morals, or to trade or commerce, or for the perversion or obstruction of justice . . .";[312] excusable homicide "[w]hen committed by accident and misfortune in the heat of passion, upon any sudden and sufficient provocation, or upon a sudden combat."[313]

One major defect of the Code arose from what the Commissioners identified as its first objective: "To bring within the compass of a single volume the whole body of the law of crimes and punishment in force within this state"—in short, to produce a comprehensive compilation of existing law.[314] Although the terms of the Act creating Field's Commission[315] seemed to require as much, it is also true that he was the draftsman of this statute, which, we are told, he drew up "with the greatest care."[316] Moreover, there are ways of approaching restrictions in the terms of a commission. Macaulay, as we have seen, found reason to go well beyond the terms of his. And even Stephen managed a number of important improvements in English law in the course of consolidating it. Field and Noyes were apparently content with their bonds, whether out of conviction or political necessity one cannot be sure.

The objective of encompassing all actions carrying a criminal punishment was carried through with unremitting thoroughness. The Code drew within its scope every instance in which a New York statute imposed the criminal penalty—and by 1864, that penalty was well on its way to becoming the major regulatory sanction. So one finds included such subjects as intoxicated physicians,[317] overloading passenger vessels,[318] mismanagement of steamboats,[319] trade mark infringements,[320] refilling mineral bottles,[321] omitting to mark packages of hay,[322] running ferries without authorization,[323] using nets unlawfully in the Hudson River,[324] misconduct by auctioneers,[325] and removing beacons in New York harbor.[326] Even Stephen, faced with a similar charge, omitted provisions of this genre from his Code on the ground that they are "so closely connected with branches of law which have little or nothing to do with crimes, commonly so called, that it seems better to let them stand as a class than to introduce them into a Criminal Code."[327] Field's Code, on the other hand, carrying the spirit of codification to its ultimate conclusion, saw "[t]he value of the Penal Code" as depending "upon its containing provisions which embrace every species of act or omission which is the subject of criminal punishment."[328]

Related to this regrettable choice is the decision to retain in separate provisions the variety of crimes that had emanated separately from the ad hoc legislative process. The draftsmen themselves recognized this, pointing out that "the bulk of the Code may be materially reduced without impairing its clearness and efficiency, by a rigid exclusion of particular provisions which are capable of being combined in general ones. . . ."[329] But caution led them to defer to legislative revision to accomplish this with the result that the Code, even more than Stephen's, looks more like a hoarder's accumulation than a code, or even a consolidation.

Regarding the crimes "commonly so called," the tendency was to reproduce existing statutes virtually whole. There was some effort "[t]o supply deficiencies and correct errors in existing definitions of crimes," one of the Commission's stated goals.[330] For example, noting that the many special statutes governing perjury in a variety of proceedings were unnecessary in view of the general perjury statute, which abandoned the common-law restriction to judicial proceedings, the draftsman omitted the unnecessary statutes.[331] But the examples of such revision were few and usually no more daring.[332] Indeed, when changes were made they were often misconceived. Though degrees of murder had been introduced precisely to allow juries to withhold capital punishment, the Code eliminated them on the ground that "[t]he practical result of introducing such a distinction will be that jurors influenced by unwillingness to unite in a capital conviction, will always find the prisoner guilty of the second degree only."[333] While provocation properly conceived serves to reduce an intentional killing to manslaughter,[334] the Code made it serve to reduce an *un*intentional killing to manslaughter[335] and to contribute to excusing an accidental killing.[336]

Consistent with one of the fundamental tenets of codification, the Code eliminated common-law offenses[337] on the ground that "[a]s long as the criminality of acts is left to depend upon the uncertain definition or conflicting authorities of the common law, uncertainty must pervade our criminal jurisprudence."[338] Similarly, common-law terms were avoided, "because it is deemed essential to the usefulness of the Code that its definitions should not be dependent upon a recourse to the common law to render them intelligible."[339] Yet in defining some important crimes the Code invited back precisely what it purported to eliminate. Larceny, for example, was minimally defined as "the taking of personal property accomplished by fraud or stealth, and with intent to deprive another thereof."[340] The Note then identified the issues that had produced the most difficulties: "[w]hat property may be the subject of larceny"; "[w]hat is an intent to deprive another of his interest in the property taken"; "the distinction between a taking originally, and which is therefore larceny, and a possession acquired without intent to steal, and followed by a wrongful appropriation . . . ." But instead of legislating solutions to these problems, the Note in each instance simply directed the reader to the scores of English and American cases responsible for the chaos.[341] Similarly, in dealing with burglary, the Note explained that "[i]t has not been thought best to insert any definition of 'breaking' or of 'entering', but rather to leave the meanings of these words, now well settled [sic], to adjudication" and then cited over thirty-five English and American cases.[342] In the Field Code, the codification spirit had not simply matured, it had died. Having begun with Bentham as, in Sir Arthur Maine's phrase, "the clearing of the brain,"[343] it became at the end a rearranging of the attic.

It is remarkable that so tame a treatment of the existing law should have aroused the opposition it did. It may have been the victim of the heavy lawyer resentments generated by Field's other codes and by his many caustic attacks on the bar.[344] Submitted to the New York legislature in 1865, it was not enacted until 1881,[345] an earlier enactment having been blocked several times by failure of passage in one house or the other or by gubernatorial veto when passed by both.[346] The Draft Code, either directly or indirectly through the New York Penal Code, which substantially enacted it, had a remarkable influence on American law,[347] taking root, as did Stephen's Code, in recently established jurisdictions. It was enacted in Dakota in 1865[348] and in California in 1872,[349] where the local Commissioners further injured an already marred product by reintroducing the concepts of malice aforethought and express and implied malice in the homicide provisions.[350] Both states enacted the other Field Codes as well.[351] California's adoption of the Penal Code was significant in the further success of the Code in a number of other Western states—Arizona,[352] Idaho,[353] Montana,[354] Oregon,[355] Utah,[356] and Wyoming[357]—where the California model was influential. None of the codes we have considered had a larger measure of influence. None deserved it less.

CONCLUSION—WECHSLER AND THE MODEL PENAL CODE

Between the Field Penal Code and the first stirrings of criminal law reform by the American Law Institute before World War II there is a yawning emptiness. Those stirrings, however, led eventually, under the leadership of Herbert Wechsler, to the Model Penal Code, and it is appropriate to conclude this piece with a few comments on that Code viewed from the perspective of this account of its predecessors.

By the time the idea of a Model Penal Code emerged, the codification controversy of the nineteenth century was over. The legislatures had long since asserted their dominance as lawmakers, though through statutes in particular areas, rather than through comprehensive codes, which the increasing complexity of law rendered quite futile. Since the role of courts in common-law adjudication and statutory interpretation had been settled as subordinate, curbing an arrogant judiciary no longer figured as the driving reason for legislation.[358] Gone also were such codification aspirations as writing the law so simply that any citizen could read and understand all his rights and obligations. The Benthamite precept—"every man his own lawyer"—had become quaint.

Much of this was true by the time of Field's and Stephen's codes and one finds no rekindling of the old codification flames in the Model Penal Code. But the similarity ends there. For what is most notable in Professor Wechsler's Model Penal Code enterprise is its affinity with the fundamental reformist zeal of the early Benthamite codification movement. Moving the principal lawmaking power to the legislature was not, after all, the simple cure that the early codifiers imagined it would be. Though many states had adopted criminal codes and virtually all had adopted substantial bodies of statutory law, the law represented in these statutes was scarcely less entitled to the Benthamite scorn than was the common law. As Professor Wechsler observed early in the work of the Model Penal Code, "[a]s our statutes stand at present, they are disorganized and often accidental in their coverage, a medley of enactment and of common law, far more important in their gloss than in their text even in cases where the text is fairly full, a combination of the old and of the new that only history explains."[359] To this challenge Wechsler and his colleagues rose with a reformist legislative spirit Bentham would have cheered. Seeking wisdom in the law and armed with collaboration from other disciplines, the draftsman would act as a "legislative commission, charged with construction of an ideal penal code"[360] in order to induce the legislative process "to determine the contents of the penal law, the prohibitions it lays down, the excuses it admits, the sanctions it employs, and the range of authority that it confers, by a contemporary reasoned judgment," heeding "Lord Radcliff's counsel that 'every system of jurisprudence needs . . . a constant preoccupation with the task of relating its rules and principles to the fundamental moral assumptions of the society to which it belongs.'"[361]

Several circumstances proved favorable to realizing this ambition. First, the undertaking was a private one, conducted by the American Law Institute under a grant from a private foundation. This allowed the draftsmen to proceed, as Wechsler observed, "free, as legislative commissions rarely are, to take account of long range values as distinguished from immediate political demands."[362] Second, they were not preparing a criminal code for a particular jurisdiction where the momentum tends to favor rearranging the existing law, rendering drastic change always an uphill battle. Instead, they were preparing a criminal code that the draftsmen thought ought to be, leaving to the particular jurisdiction the decision of what to adopt and what to reject. Third, the varying and often inconsistent approaches to particular problems reflected in the criminal law of the states demanded evaluation and choice in a code that purported to be a model for all states. A restatement approach was plainly unfeasible as well as undesirable.[363] Fourth, the venture had time, talent, and organization. None of the earlier codes took more than two or three years to complete, most under pressure to produce. The Model Penal Code moved at a relatively leisurely pace, taking ten years, 1952–1962, to produce a final draft. Moreover, this Code was a collaborative project in a more thoroughgoing way than any of the others were. The venture conscripted scores of law professors from all over the country as Reporters and Consultants in particular areas—a striking contrast to the largely solo performances represented by the earlier codes. Also, where the earlier codifiers had only a few judges and prosecutors to whom to submit their drafts, the Model Penal Code had the benefit of the elaborate and well established system of review of the American Law Institute.[364] Finally, and probably of decisive importance, the work was led by Professor Wechsler who, for over a decade, had pioneered legislative rethinking of the substantive criminal law[365] and who combined some of the best qualities of his predecessors— Macaulay's perspicuity and insight, Stephen's mastery of the subject matter, and Bentham's reformist dedication.

One important circumstance did not favor the Code's reformist ambitions: the ground had not been prepared by treatise writers. As Wechsler observed, "[n]o Williston or Wigmore has undertaken to chart the contours of the subject, ordering its doctrines, rules and practice in the light of underlying policies and bringing critical intelligence to bear upon the whole."[366] We may forgive Wechsler for failing to note that in one important area this task had been done—by his own and Professor Michael's classic two-part article on the *Rationale of the Law of Homicide*.[367] Still, the great bulk of the subject had not been rethought in this way and the labors of Wechsler and his colleagues had to include the preparation of "rationales" of the whole of the law of crimes as part of the drafting of the Code. While this was an additional burden to the draftsmen, it resulted in a unique benefit to the field of criminal law. The extensive commentary to the thirteen tentative drafts of the Model Penal Code, far more probing, comprehensive, and integrating in analysis than the more narrowly focused supporting commentary of the earlier codes, furnished a text that revitalized criminal law scholarship, provided a new starting point for writing in the field and profoundly influenced the materials and direction of criminal law study in American law schools.

The Code itself was stunningly successful in accomplishing the comprehensive rethinking of the criminal law that Wechsler and his colleagues sought. An adequate demonstration of this assertion is beyond the scope of an essay devoted to Wechsler's predecessors, but a few comments on the subject may properly serve to conclude it.

The Code, despite its reformist spirit, is in no sense an anti-establishment document. It takes the institutions of the criminal law within society as given, with none of the radical critique reflected in Livingston's Code. Society needs a system of punishment to protect it against major harms, and it needs the criminal law to order and control the use of public force against individuals in the process of administering the system of punishment.[368] The Code's ideology is the conventional one, which Wechsler described as a "moral sentiment," that so much being "at stake for the community and the individual, care has to be taken to make law as rational and just as law can be."[369]

Rationality for Wechsler and his colleagues meant the prevailing law must be thoroughly reexamined for flaws and gaps, measured by an instrumentalist standard of serving the purpose of the criminal law, and for logical solecisms. Reckless conduct is no less worthy of deterrence when harm does not occur than when it does; hence the Code creates a general crime of recklessly endangering another person.[370] Whether a mistake is factual or legal is beside the point; the point is whether the mistake does or does not negative the mental element in the definition of the crime.[371] Drawing the line between attempt and preparation at the point of proximity to success excludes liability for persons who have sufficiently identified themselves as dangerous; requiring a substantial step that strongly corroborates the intention gives the needed protection to innocence.[372] Liability for the crime of another which is defined as requiring purpose or knowledge cannot be imposed logically unless the aider shares the required purpose or knowledge.[373]

Another dimension of the rationality sought by the draftsmen is their reaching toward specialized areas of expertise where logic and general policy fell short. This is illustrated in the collaboration with psychiatric experts in approaching the problem of legal insanity[374] and with correctional experts in dealing with sentencing and correction.[375]

A third component of the rationality sought by the draftsmen is exhibited in the unremitting effort to locate and state the governing principles in areas traditionally dealt with on an ad hoc particularity. This confidence in the capacity to generalize legislative formulations evokes the early codification spirit, though in the execution the for mulations emerge with a degree of generality that would have disappointed Bentham. While in the earlier codes, causation provisions are drawn to cover particular cases, typically medical maltreatment, the Model Penal Code for the first time essays a comprehensive formulation. The provision builds on the insight that the traditional problems of "proximate causation" are basically problems of determining the culpability required for conviction,[376] and reduces the hard questions to an inquiry whether the result is too accidental to have a just bearing on liability or degree of punishment.[377] Perceiving that the defense of necessity has often confused cases of excuse and justification, the Code disentangles the threads, and deals separately with duress and necessity, the latter constructed on a broad lesser-evil principle (eschewed on practical grounds by Macaulay and Stephen) applicable across the board to all offenses.[378] Negligence as a basis of liability runs all through the law—in particular crimes, like homicide, and in defenses, like mistake and self-defense. The Model Penal Code for the first time identified the unitary character of the concept and provided an integrative definition of negligence that governs in whatever guise that standard appears as the basis of liability.[379]

For Wechsler and his colleagues, making the law just meant at bottom that the preventive purpose of the criminal law must be sought within the constraints of the principle that punishment may not be imposed in the absence of blameworthy conduct or in disregard of the degree of blameworthiness reflected in the mental state accompanying the conduct. The standard of just blaming tends to be the conventional common-law standard, which finds blame sufficiently established "if the actor knew or should have known the facts" that give his conduct its offensive character,[380] rather than an individualized standard which requires searching the ability of the particular actor to know and to conform.[381] However, that conventional standard is applied with a fidelity quite unconventional in prevailing law.

Strict criminal liability is eliminated both in regulatory offenses, where only a fine or other civil penalty may be imposed without a finding of fault,[382] and in those serious offenses in which it was to be found in the law under doctrinal disguises—the felony murder and misdemeanor manslaughter rules, the exclusion of even a resonable mistake as a defense in such crimes as bigamy and rape, the rules that justified defensive force in certain cases solely in terms of actual, rather than reasonably apparent necessity.[383] The Code's concern with justice is manifested also in the provisions dealing with justified force against the person, for here too the central value is protecting faultless conduct from punishment.[384] The Code carefully articulates the norms governing the use of such force, particularly, deadly force, in a variety of circumstances[385] and, as previously noted, formulate an innovative principle of justification in the form of the lesser-evil principle. Another illustration, and one of the major contributions of the Code, is its general treatment of mens rea questions. The prevailing law had failed notoriously to distinguish varying degrees of blameworthiness reflected in the mental element of crimes. Both statutory law, when the matter was attended to at all, and case law confused the issue with moralistic epithets like willful, malice, wantonly, corruptly, or with spongey concepts like specific and general intent. The Model Penal Code, in a remarkable tour de force of analytical precision, formulated a set of definitional tools with which the entire code of specific crimes could be fashioned. Four mental states were identified and defined—purpose, knowledge, recklessness, and negligence—and three objective elements in the definition of crimes were identified as to which the appropriate mental state had to be specified—the nature of the conduct, the attendant circumstances, and the result of the conduct.[386] The contribution of this set of tools was to spotlight the mens rea questions in defining crimes, to bring thought and order to the resolution of these questions and to dispel the obscurantist cloud that hung for so long on the central mens rea issues in criminal law.

Having said that justice and rationality, in the senses described and exemplified, constitute the Code's ideology, it is important to add that Wechsler and his colleagues proceeded with a wholly non-ideological sense of the practical.[387] Capital punishment, though obviously disapproved, was left in as an option, with constraints suggested to render it less objectionable.[388] Felony murder was eliminated. But a sense of the strong pressures to retain it led the draftsmen to retain at least a shadow of its former self in the form of a presumption that a homicide in the course of a dangerous felony creates a presumption of extreme indifference to human life.[389] With characteristic logic the Code treats the absence of the purpose or knowledge required for conviction of a particular crime as decisive of non-liability for that crime, whether the cause is intoxication or any other circumstance. But with uncharacteristic illogic it makes an exception for the absence of recklessness where the cause is intoxication,[390] in recognition "of the political necessity of dealing specially with drunkenness."[391] Another illustration appears in confining the standard of excuse, expressed in terms of compelling circumstances irresistible to a person of reasonable firmness, to cases of physical duress of one person by another, excluding cases where a like irresistibility is produced by some other circumstance. Presumably the fear that so doing would open potentially every case to an exploration of reasonable willpower led the Code to stop short of the logic of its premise.[392]

It may be that these modest dosages of accommodation to politics and practicality made the medicine of reform go down. It seems likely. What is certain is that Wechsler and his colleagues were as successful in influencing law reform as they were in producing a model code. Its formulations of entrapment and obscenity affected the course of constitutional adjudication and its treatment of the defense of legal insanity has been adopted by almost every United States court of appeals.[393] More significantly the Code stimulated a movement for legislative criminal law reform of unprecedented scope.[394] The latest Annual Report of the American Law Institute reveals that over thirty states have adopted revised criminal codes since the Model Penal Code started reporting its drafts; six states and Congress have revisions completed awaiting enactment; and three states have revisions under way.[395] In very few instances has any jurisdiction adopted the Code substantially whole. But in virtually no case has the revision escaped the impact of the Code's formulations. As a result the Model Penal Code has by now permeated and transformed the substantive criminal law of the country. None of the codes we have considered, including Field's, had a greater influence. None deserved it more.

CHAPTER SEVEN

LAW AND DISCRETION

10
LEGAL NORM AND DISCRETION IN THE POLICE AND SENTENCING PROCESSES

The administration of criminal justice is marked at the same time by as elaborate a structure of limitations upon the exercise of governmental power and as free an exercise of discretionary judgment as will be found in our legal system. In that part of the criminal process from accusation to conviction and appeal, the two root principles of the rule of law, legality and due process, have their historical origins and their fullest expression. The principle of *nulla poena sine lege* imposes formidable restraints upon the definition of criminal conduct. Standards of conduct must meet stringent tests of specificity and clarity, may act only prospectively, and must be strictly construed in favor of the accused. Further, the definition of criminal conduct has largely come to be regarded as a legislative function, thereby precluding the judiciary from devising new crimes. The public-mischief doctrine and the sometimes overgeneralized "ends" of criminal conspiracy are usually regarded as anomalous departures from this main stream. The cognate principle of procedural regularity and fairness, in short, due process of law, commands that the legal standard be applied to the individual with scrupulous fairness in order to minimize the chances of convicting the innocent, protect against abuse of official power, and generate an atmosphere of impartial justice. As a consequence, a complex network of procedural requirements embodied variously in constitutional, statutory, or judge-made law is imposed upon the criminal adjudicatory process—public trial, unbiased tribunal, legal representation, open hearing, confrontation, and related concomitants of procedural justice.

On the other hand, principally prior to accusation and after conviction, these two principles become subordinated in favor of a wide-ranging freedom of the official to make decisions within the area of his competence. Before accusation the criminal process is marked by an extensive *de facto* if not *de jure* police and prosecutorial discretion to determine what laws to enforce against what individuals and in what circumstances. After guilt has finally been ascertained, the system is marked by a *de jure* discretion of the sentencing judge, parole agencies, and correctional institutions to determine the treatment the offender will receive.[1]

The purpose of this paper is to examine in a preliminary way the character of the problems presented by the rejection in those stages of the criminal process in which law has been subordinated to official discretion of the values implicit in the principles of legality and due process. However, in view of the exemplificative purposes of this paper only two of the stages of the criminal process which raise this issue will be considered, namely the stages in which police and sentencing discretion are required to be exercised.[2] These two areas have been selected because, although in both the problem is raised of the compatibility of a wide reservoir of discretion for public officials with the values implicit in the rule of law in situations in which the discretion is basically ameliorative, *i.e.,* a discretion to impose upon individuals less restraint than the law authorizes,[3] there are significant differences in the prevailing approach to the operation of the discretionary judgment in these areas. So far as the police function is concerned, the official assumption of the system seems to be that there is no place for expert administrative discretion; police are supposed to enforce all the laws against all offenders in all circumstances. In the exercise of the sentencing function, the official assumption seems to be that there is little place for the legal norm and that the judgments to be made call exclusively for the discretionary judgment, free of legal restraints. Thus the policeman attracts the image of a ministerial official with talents and authority solely to follow the law's precise commands,[4] while the sentencing decider is regarded as the expert professional with talents to make crucial decisions where the law meets the limits of its competence. A comparison of the origin and rationale of these divergent approaches may afford some illumination of the nature of the common problem.

I. POLICE DISCRETION

The ideal of full enforcement by the police is preserved officially in formal law as well as in popular conception.[5] Statutes, mostly of nineteenth century vintage, tend to speak in terms of the duty of the police diligently and faithfully to enforce all the penal laws.[6] Decisions of appellate courts dealing with the legality of arrest commonly assert that the officer had not only the right but the duty to arrest or face charges of recreancy to that duty.[7] A recent decision exemplifies the common hostility to selectivity in police law enforcement.[8] In a proceeding to enjoin police enforcement of the Sunday Blue Law against a large retailing operation, the police department admitted (remarkably) a policy of selective enforcement against the larger retailers because of limitations on police personnel available. While recognizing that "to enforce [the law] . . . against all retail merchants would necessitate the transfer of large numbers of police personnel from other important duties,"[9] the court granted the injunction, concluding that the policy of selective enforcement constituted unconstitutional discrimination.[10] In informal sources as well, one finds a conception of the duty of full enforcement. Thus police manuals, when they address themselves to this question at all, either speak with some ambiguity or expressly instruct the police officer that it is his duty to enforce all the laws against everyone without exception.[11] The common reaction of police chiefs queried by the press concerning their attitude to enforcement of controversial laws is revealing. On the record, it is that the duty of the police is to enforce all the criminal laws of the state; off the record it is that to say otherwise would create hostility in some segments of the public and expose the police to nonfeasance charges by grand juries.

In terms of fact, of course, the practice reduces this ideal to a myth, and the need to preserve the existence of the ideal in these mythological terms has tended to divert attention from the nature of the problem presented: Is it subversive of the principle of legality that the police in fact exercise a wide discretion in their enforcement of the criminal law, even though what is involved is the withholding of prosecution? Is this discretion practically inevitable? Is it desirable? Should it be eliminated or controlled? How should it be controlled?

It is not helpful in approaching these problems to insist either that all selective police law enforcement is an intolerable compromise with the principle of legality, or, contrariwise, that it is all a legitimate and necessary means of making the law act soundly and in accordance with common sense.[12] The discretionary judgment to arrest or not is made in a wide variety of circumstances, for a wide variety of reasons, raising considerations which are not the same in all cases.[13] The point of what follows is to select a few of the circumstances in which arrest judgments are made in order to explore the particular kinds of choices called for in evaluating rule and discretion at the police level.

The most obvious kind of discretionary judgment involves the police deployment of forces for patrolling and for investigation.[14] Such judgments clearly affect the persons who will be subject to the criminal process and to some extent the crimes which will be sanctioned. There may nonetheless be some force in the view that such decisions are essentially professional in nature, involving ways of making maximum use of limited men, equipment, and resources, and that the consequences for the principle of legality are not major. In any event the necessity for judgments such as these is created by limitations on the amount of resources a community is prepared to invest in police enforcement and the refusal of the public to accept the consequences of a garrison-type community entailed in a program of saturation law enforcement.

The more difficult cases are those in which the policeman declines to make an arrest of an apparently guilty suspect on the ground that it is better for some reason that the criminal process not be invoked against him. To some extent, of course, every decision of this kind, despite its ameliorative character, is inconsistent with the rule of law in the occasion it creates for inequality in official action, arbitrariness, discrimination, and abuse,[15] let alone in its potential for thwarting the legislative goals of crime prevention usually implicit in the substantive definition of the crime.[16] There are, however, considerable differences in the degree of danger posed and in the desirability and feasibility of eliminating such discretionary judgments.

One kind of systematic nonenforcement by the police is produced by criminal statutes which seem deliberately to overcriminalize, in the sense of encompassing conduct not the target of legislative concern, in order to assure that suitable suspects will be prevented from escaping through legal loopholes as the result of the inability of the prosecution to prove acts which bring the defendants within the scope of the prohibited conduct. A prime example are laws prohibiting gambling. Such laws are frequently drawn by the legislature in deliberately wide terms purporting to make unlawful, without material exception, all kinds of gambling, whether of a commercial character or of a private social character and even where used as part of a charitable or religious fundraising project. The task then devolves upon the police (and prosecutor, in the second instance) to determine whether a particular violation falls within the real vice with which the legislature was concerned.[17] Therefore, private social gambling among friends in their own homes, church bingo games, and the like are typically left alone. Where however the police believe sufficient elements of commercialization to be present, the decision to arrest is made. There are of course other instances of this deliberate overcriminalization, *e.g.*, automobile homicide and strict liability statutes.[18] In these, however, it is generally the prosecutor who tends to assume primary responsibility for the discriminating judgment through his power to charge, rather than the police through their power to arrest.

Insofar as such laws purport to bring within the condemnation of the criminal statute kinds of activities whose moral neutrality, if not innocence, is widely recognized, they raise basic issues of a morally acceptable criminal code.[19] Moreover, these laws are in effect equivalent to enactments of a broad legislative policy against, for example, undesirable gambling, leaving it to the police to further that policy by such arrests as seem to them compatible with it. From one point of view such statutes invite a danger cognate to that of defining crime by analogy, augmented by the fact that it is the policeman who is defining criminal conduct rather than a court.[20] That no actual abuse has been demonstrated in police administration of an overdrawn statute,[21] such as gambling, would not seem to answer the moral and precedential objections to this tactic, any more than the fact that courts in states where the doctrine of common law crimes exists have not in recent years abused it would answer the objections to this doctrine. Doubts concerning such practices have their source too deep in history to be swept aside because of a fortunate experience. Nor are abuses of these powers likely to be sufficiently visible and demonstrable to permit the inference that all is well from the absence of affirmative evidence of their existence. It may be concluded of this genre of police discretion, therefore, that it is deliberately created by the legislature, that it holds primary dangers, and that it is, to a large degree, avoidable by substantive law reform, although with some loss to law enforcement.

A second category of substantial police discretion is the product of criminal legislation which, either in practical effect or in actual purpose, involves the use of the criminal law for social objectives other than crime prevention. A well known example is legislation prohibiting consenting extramarital or deviant sexual behavior among adults. That these laws only rarely result in criminal arrests and prosecutions is well known. And the studies of Dr. Kinsey have not let us believe the lack of enforcement is due to an absence of violations.[22] Thurman Arnold has neatly put the final justification of such unenforced laws: They "survive in order to satisfy moral objections to established modes of conduct. They are unenforced because we want to continue our conduct, and unrepealed because we want to preserve our morals."[23]

Their existence, however, casts the same shadow of potentially arbitrary and abusive law enforcement as that cast by purposely overdrawn legislation. It has been suggested that here, as in overdrawn gambling laws, the lack of adequate demonstration that harm results from this legislation weakens the case against it.[24] The point carries no greater weight here than there. Moreover, it does not seem convincing to argue, as it has been argued,[25] that the objection loses further force in view of the broad discretionary power which exists elsewhere in our legal system, such as the power to use the income tax penalty against gangsters where gangster activity cannot be proved. If sex legislation and tax legislation are meant to be enforced equally and are in fact generally enforced equally, the point is well taken. In that event the problem, if it be one, is the use by the police or prosecutor of a generally enforced criminal statute, intended to be enforced, when the authorities are really concerned with the accused because of other criminal conduct. The point is less convincing, however, if the starting point is that much sex legislation, unlike criminal tax penalties, is not enforced except for other reasons, nor, in a sense, meant to be enforced, and that violation is general and known. In this case the problem is prosecution for conduct which is criminal in name only, as it were, in order to convict a defendant whom the police, for reasons sufficient or insufficient, regard as otherwise worthy of imprisonment.[26]

A group of criminal laws plainly not meant, as well as in practice not used, for purposes of crime prevention is constituted of those designed to perform essentially social service functions. The bad-checks laws, insofar as they include insufficient-funds cases, are an instance of this kind; another are the nonsupport laws. In the former, the criminal law is designed as a means of enforcing payment of debts; in the latter it is used in order to ensure payments by defaulting husbands. The rationale of these laws, therefore, invites, if it does not require, judgments by the police to arrest not simply where there has been a violation, but only where the arrest will tend to serve the end of ensuring that the debt is paid or the payment made. As with sex legislation, the problem to be faced here is a legislative one of determining whether the cost of adding to discretionary judgments by the police is worth the assumed social value of using the criminal law for noncriminal purposes.[27]

A third category of discretionary police nonenforcement differs from the previous two in that the responsibility for its existence is not primarily a legislative choice and it is not amenable to resolution by broad policy formulations. In these cases, the discretionary judgment is the product of the inevitable need for mediation between generally formulated laws and the human values contained in the varieties of particular circumstances in which the law is technically violated. For example, should the police arrest for assault where the dispute which gave rise to the incident occurs in connection with a matrimonial difference and the victim declines to sign a complaint? Should the police arrest where a customer is bilked of his money by a defaulting prostitute? Should they arrest a wife for falsely reporting a felony, where under interrogation she admits to claiming she was raped in order to conceal her infidelity from her husband? Should a respected citizen be arrested for a homosexual accosting when he is already under psychiatric care? In cases of this kind the need for some kind of amelioration is plain. The issue is whether that function should be confined to the sentencing and dismissal powers of the court, where it is normally vested by statute, or on the other hand, whether it is worth the cost of adding to police discretion to save the stigma, embarrassment, and general destructiveness to a man's life often entailed in the very preliminary act of arresting.

The foregoing examples of circumstances calling for free police judgment in the arrest function suggest, as counterbalancing the gains of maintaining the police choice, the potential losses in inequality, arbitrariness, and abuse. That there are losses of subtler dimension even in the conscientious arrest decision is suggested by two kinds of police practice recently brought into sharp focus.[28] At least in one large city with a sizable black population, the black press commonly exploits the charge that the police are harder on blacks than on whites, a charge that finds apparent support in the far greater percentage of blacks arrested. The facts, however, suggest a subtler kind of discrimination, insidious rather than invidious. Rather than overly strict enforcement against blacks, what commonly is involved is a calculated nonenforcement of certain laws against the black population, justified on the ground that a lesser standard of morality prevails and that it is therefore unwise to apply the general legal standards to them. On this rationale arrests of blacks are often not made for such offences as bigamy, open and notorious co-habitation, and, most strikingly, felonious assault where both the aggressor and the victim are black and the latter declines to complain. This, of course, constitutes a form of discrimination no less significant than the commonly charged overzealous arrest of blacks, in view of its perpetuation of a lower moral standard in an underprivileged cultural subgroup and by the failure to use the criminal law for one of its central purposes as a solidifier and communalizer of moral values. A practice which gives rise to problems of a related character is the decision not to arrest a minor offender in order to use him as an informer or decoy to detect and arrest persons whom the police regard as major offenders. A dramatic example is the grant of a police "license" to narcotics users to continue their use so long as they cooperate in apprehending larger sellers. Apart from the moral issue of police participation in crime, it may be doubtful that in exhibiting nonenforcement the police contribute to deterring traffic in narcotics; and it would seem clear that in following this pattern of nonenforcement against known users, the police are depriving the victims of the opportunity for rehabilitation, presumably one of the ends of the narcotics laws.[29]

What has been said would seem to point to the inevitable selectivity of judgment required in evaluating rule and discretion at the police level. Police discretion owes its existence to a variety of causes and serves varying values and purposes, some weightier and less dispensable than others. Judgments reached out of apprehension of the potential for abuse and discrimination and the subtler kinds of evils, which fail to pass on the case for discretion in particular situations and the relative feasibility of eliminating it, can neither be rounded nor reliable. But there is a further task, which arises after deliberative judgment has decided to retain the discretionary judgment in those situations where its usefulness outweighs its dangers, or to abide with it where it appears ineradicable. This is the task of devising means whereby abusive judgments may be minimized or neutralized and conscientious judgments guided to ensure consistency with the totality of goals of a criminal law system. The traditional means of guiding the exercise of discretionary judgment, through the legislative (or administrative) formulation of criteria for nonenforcement, is probably unsuitable for this purpose in view of the need to avoid weakening the deterrent and moralizing force of the substantive criminal law.[30] Other suggestions have been to provide mechanisms or arrangements whereby the nonarrest decision is shared by the police and some other agency; or to create an "Appraisal and Review Board" in order "to increase visibility and hence reviewability of these police decisions."[31] How far these proposals would constitute improvements in the end over existing allocations of responsibility among police, prosecutors, and trial judges is hard to say.[32] Certainly the challenge of making accountable the policeman's exercise of power not to arrest is formidable. Neither the perpetuation of the myth of full enforcement nor of the myth of the benignity and inevitability of unfettered discretion will move us towards an acceptable accommodation.

II. SENTENCING DISCRETION

The individualization of penal dispositions, principally through the institutions of the indeterminate sentence, probation, and parole, is a development whose value few would contest.[33] Whether or not individualization significantly advances the goal of crime prevention is, in one sense, less important than that it constitutes a moral commitment to the worth of the individual. Such basic conceptions of the relationship between man and his social environment could hardly escape expression in society's legal and institutional structures any more than it could in its architectural structures. At the same time the new penology has resulted in vesting in judges and parole and probation agencies the greatest degree of uncontrolled power over the liberty of human beings that one can find in the legal system.[34]

Consider first the sentencing and probation decision made by courts, and the related decisions when and whether to release on parole made by parole agencies. The discretion of the judge and agency in these matters is virtually free of substantive control or guidance. Where the judge has power to select a term of imprisonment within a range the exercise of that authority is left fairly at large. The probation and parole decision is usually confined solely by legislative exclusion of certain classes of offenders and crimes[35] and by the general adjuration to grant parole or probation when satisfied of a reasonable likelihood that the offender will be law-abiding and that the public welfare will be furthered.[36] Judicial review of sentencing is the exception in this country;[37] and the denial of probation and parole is viewed altogether as a discretionary judgment reversible only for patent violations of law.[38]

There is a comparable legal relaxation in the adjudicative process. During judicial sentencing a hearing and counsel are normally available.[39] However, the use of the confidential and ex parte pre-sentence report, which is usually unavailable to the offender or his counsel,[40] tends to deprive the hearing of much of its significance. In administrative parole proceedings there is no right to a hearing beyond what is granted by the statutes, and even where statutes provide for a hearing the obligation is usually interpreted as requiring no more than an attenuated interview, permission to have counsel and to present evidence being solely at the discretion of the board and often denied.[41]

Consider second the decision to revoke probation or parole for breach of the stated conditions of a conditional release. Legal standards to control and guide decision in this area are minimal. It is often the case that the court or agency is not limited to finding a breach by the offender of one of the conditions of his release in order to justify a revocation.[42] Even where a violation of a condition must be shown,[43] the effect of the limitation is impaired by several factors. Courts and agencies have complete freedom to devise such conditions as they deem appropriate, and these conditions are often either extremely vague (*e.g.*, "straighten-up," "good behavior," "clean moral life") or exceedingly intrusive, requiring such behavior as total abstinence or regular church attendance.[44] Moreover, they have untrammeled discretion to revoke where one of these "technical" violations is found; expectedly, there is a notorious disparity in the numbers and kinds of cases in which revocations are ordered where technical violations are found.[45]

Procedural standards are similarly informal.[46] Under some statutes a supervising officer is limited in his right to arrest a conditional releasee by standards similar to, though generally less strict than, those which govern arrest of other persons.[47] In many states, however, he is free to arrest for mere suspicion and sometimes without judicial or administrative control over the exercise of his judgment.[48] In some instances the parole or probation officer finds a ready means of imposing discipline on what he takes to be a recalcitrant releasee by arresting and imprisoning him for a brief period of time. Hearings on the issue of breach of the conditions of the release are sometimes dispensed with by statute altogether[49] and generally are discretionary with the paroling authorities.[50] Commonly, where some hearing is provided, the normal hallmarks of fair procedure, such as advance notice, right to present and rebut evidence, and representation by counsel, are denied.[51] For example it was the practice of the United States Parole Board after 1910 to refuse to hear a parolee's witnesses or his counsel at the hearing.[52] Only in 1961 was this position altered, apparently in deference to legal advice in pending litigation.[53] Moreover, these same procedures govern where the charge is not a technical violation but the commission of another crime, whether or not the offender has previously been acquitted of that crime.[54]

In the correctional area, then, the discretionary judgment does not permeate *de facto* into a contrary *de jure* system, as in the police area, but is openly embraced as the governing ideal. Furthermore, although resembling in its ameliorative character police discretion not to enforce the law against putative defendants, it is further reaching in its consequence for human values, affecting the nature and duration of the authoritative disposition of all persons against whom the laws have been enforced. When one seeks reasons and justifications for the deliberate abandonment of the legal norm after conviction, the answers appear to lie in two principal conceptions: that the discretion exercised entails solely the dispensing of leniency which an offender may receive as a matter of grace, but never as a matter of right; and that the exercise of the discretion turns on a purely professional diagnostic judgment by experts, rendering substantive and procedural restraints inappropriate, destructive, and unnecessary.

A. THE GRACE CONCEPTION

The idea of individualization of punishment as the dispensation of grace has been derived from several sources. One is the imposition of the relatively modern penology of individualization upon an older penology of fixed punishment apportioned to the nature of the crime. Some of the older theory of a just entitlement of the offender to a designated punishment tended to carry over, with the consequence that dispensing less punishment than the legislature authorized was regarded as an act of merciful leniency[55] to which there could be no legal claim, and hence, in the orthodox view, was a privilege and not a right.[56] Another source of the idea is the ancient view that a convicted defendant becomes an outlaw, a person with no legal rights whose property and even identity may be forfeit.[57] So one reads in opinions that after conviction prisoners are "naked criminals, hoping for mercy but entitled only to justice,"[58] neither a "citizen, nor entitled to invoke the organic safeguards which hedge about the citizen's liberty."[59] Further contributing influences may be found in two other sources. First there was an inevitable tendency to analogize the new penology of individualization to the earlier and more traditional forms of remissions of punishment, such as executive clemency and the prerogative of mercy, which, as their names imply, were indeed acts of mercy.[60] Secondly, the grace conception provided a ready rationale for upholding indeterminate sentence laws against constitutional attack as void for uncertainty, and as prohibited delegations of the power to punish. Thus, it was said that the indeterminate sentence was legally a definite sentence to the maximum imposed by the judge, the administrative agency acting only to remit a portion of the duly imposed punishment when circumstances appeared to warrant the granting of this favor.[61]

The use of the privilege-right dichotomy as a justification for decision-making without legal obligation to procedural regularity or substantive principle is, of course, well known in other areas. Its inadequacy as a rather complete begging of the question has been often and well demonstrated by others.[62] Analysis of the correctional decision in more meaningful terms requires consensus preliminarily on two propositions of fact. First, the decisions that are administratively made in this area by judges and agencies affect fundamental human values, the authoritative disposition of individuals, and not merely such matters as entitlement to a license to operate a barber shop or to receive such governmental benefits as social security or loans. Second, the modern system of individualization of punishment rests principally not upon the sentiments of grace and charity, but upon the premise that the treatment of individuals and the prevention of crime through the use of the criminal law can better be accomplished through accommodation of the kind and duration of authoritative disposition to the relevant characteristics of the offender. Accepting so much, it is at once apparent that it is inappropriate and unhelpful to talk in terms of a right only to no more than the maximum term provided by law. Nor is it any more appropriate or helpful to talk of a right to probation or to the minimum term or to parole. The issue is the appropriateness of any penal disposition of a particular offender in view of his crime and his characteristics, measured against the criteria of relevancy derived from the governing aims and premises of the criminal law.

What kind of reasoned argument, then, may be made for freedom of the ameliorative correctional judgment from legal restraint? The legislature has chosen, it may be argued, only a partial and experimental adoption of the penology of individualization because it is unprepared to accept the cost in delay, inconvenience, and expense of its total implementation and because it distrusts its potential for subverting the goals of deterrence and incapacitation. Therefore, in order to minimize these costs and yet achieve some of the gains, a minimum of substantive and procedural restraints should be imposed. This has the effect of expediting the decisional process by precluding the time-consuming and expensive processes of the traditional forms of adjudication and of subsequent litigation in the courts, and of tending to reduce the incidence of the use of this ameliorative individualization.

The first consequence is obvious enough. The latter requires a word of explanation. The absence of legal standards would not appear necessarily to serve this end. Legislative standards might as well increase the use of the ameliorative discretion as decrease it. In point of fact, however, the absence of standards probably tends to decrease it for three reasons. First, there is an inevitable pressure upon agencies responsible for release to avoid making favorable discretionary judgments where they have to face the consequence of public chastisement in the event of further criminal acts by the person released. This pressure is heightened where they cannot avoid sole responsibility by resting it in part, at least, upon a legislative direction.[63] Secondly, the legislature has in fact been explicit in the formulation of standards where its purpose has been to direct that probation and parole should not be granted, as for example by excluding classes of crimes and offenders from probation or parole eligibility.[64] The legislature has been inexplicit principally about when probation and parole should be granted.[65] Thirdly, the lack of standards tends to preclude an offender from making an affirmative case for probation or parole before the agency itself or in the courts on appeal. As for the absence of procedural requirements in the release and revocation process, the end of reducing the incidence of early or continued release would clearly be served, to some degree, at least, by depriving the offender of the opportunity to adduce evidence and argument in its favor—certainly the incidence of release could not be increased by depriving the offender of an effective opportunity to be heard.

One may disagree with these arguments on penological grounds. But the issue here is first principles. Are these judgments unacceptably destructive of values of legality and fairness? A negative answer may be reasoned in the following way. First as to the principle of legality: crimes must be defined with precision and in advance of the act in order to avoid the insecurity of the general community and the occasion for injustice to the morally innocent who are otherwise deprived of knowledge of how they are to act to avoid the threatened sanction of the law. However, there is no such threat when the issue is the remission of punishment of those duly convicted just as there generally is not where remedial law is involved. There is no problem of affording standards to guide conduct since the issue is what the offender is, what he did, and what he may do, not what he should do. This is somewhat less so in cases of revocation for breach of a condition, but it is still largely so here as well since authority to revoke is not limited to breach of condition. Further, there is no danger of injustice to the morally innocent since the guilt of the persons involved has been established by due process of law.

Second, as to the principle of procedural fairness: since the persons affected are limited to those who have been convicted of crime, there is no threat to the general community in the absence of safeguards against erroneous determinations and the loss of a sense of justice. In psychological terms there is a sympathetic identification with the accused in a trial. His erroneous or unfair conviction is viewed as threatening all. But this is not so where the issue is whether a duly convicted offender will be relieved of part of his due punishment. Further, in social terms the danger of undermining the social order by official abuse of the power of the criminal law or through the insecurity of tolerating a relatively wide margin for erroneous convictions does not exist where the issue is relieving a convicted offender of a portion of his punishment.[66]

The plausibility of this reasoning is undermined by two considerations of fundamental importance: the argument is immoral;[67] and it underrates the danger to the general community. A first tenet of our governmental, religious, and ethical tradition is the intrinsic worth of every individual no matter how degenerate. It is a radical departure from that tradition to accept for a defined class of persons, even criminals, a regime in which their right to liberty is determined by officials wholly unaccountable in the exercise of their power and through processes which deprive them of an opportunity to be heard on the matters of fact and policy which are relevant to the decisions made. In the words of an acute observer:

> "There is no liberty whenever the laws permit that under certain conditions man ceases to be a person and becomes a thing." I never tire of repeating this sentence of Cesare Beccaria at every opportunity, because it seems to me that in these apparently simple words there lies the hope of mankind and the program of the future.[68]

Second, attitudes and values are infectious. The way official power is exercised over the criminal is bound to have repercussions on how it is exercised over the accused; and how it is exercised over the accused is bound to affect how it is exercised over the general community. Such considerations have been central to a large number of Supreme Court decisions dealing with procedural due process for the criminally accused. Brutal police practices have been outlawed whether or not they prove effective in producing real evidence of guilt, because officially condoned brutality is itself a substantially brutalizing influence in the general community.[69] And arguably minor deviations from constitutional requirements have been nonetheless proscribed on the ground that "illegitimate and unconstitutional practices get their first footing in that way, namely, by silent approaches and slight deviations from legal modes of procedure."[70] The same considerations make unduly perilous any venture in systematically departing from root principles in dealing with the class of persons duly convicted of crime.

A small but, I think, relevant digression: These conclusions are directed to the sentencing-type dispositions of convicted offenders, specifically those entailing judgments whether to imprison, how long to incarcerate, when and whether to release on condition or to revoke and imprison. The query may fairly be put, however, why the reasoning is not equally applicable to the daily running of correctional institutions to govern such decisions as the imposition of discipline, the awarding of privileges, or the assignment of duties. The point is a natural one since a common justification for plenary power over parolees is that they are no less in custody than those physically within the prison walls simply because they are probationally permitted outside.[71] The answer must be that the principle remains constant for those within as well as those without the prison, but that the implications of the principle are not necessarily identical. Certainly an arbitrarily run institution in which discipline and favors are dispensed monarchically or anarchically is no less objectionable than a regime in which sentencing-type dispositions are similarly made.[72] But this is not to say that substantive standards and procedural mechanisms need meet the same specifications. Daily housekeeping decisions in the conduct of an institution are not of the same order as sentencing-type decisions governing release and term, either in their impact upon the individual and their significance to him, in the closeness of relationship to the original processes of guilt determination, or in their potential for contaminating the mainstream of tradition with regard to notions of the rule of law. Moreover, so far as the particular case of the parolee is concerned, his presence in the general community removes him from the scope of housekeeping decisions, no matter how insistently the metaphor be asserted that he is still within the prison walls, although extended and invisible.[73]

B. THE EXPERT CONCEPTION

But even accepting a full commitment to the penology of individualization and rejecting a regime of second-class human beings, the denial of law in these areas has another and quite different rationale. This is that the judgments called for are professional and diagnostic in character, rendering legal controls both inappropriate and destructive, and unnecessary to afford safeguards against abuse. "For they are not questions about principle, but about matters of fact; and for such *cuiquam in sua arte credendum*."[74]

The natural history of this conception, of course, lies in the rapid development of the behavioral sciences in recent years. Criminal behavior, like all behavior, has its antecedents and its conditions. A rigorously scientific study of those causal antecedents in the particular offender will reveal modes of ordering his personality structure and his environment toward the end of reducing the threat of his further criminality. The duration and nature of the authoritative treatment, therefore, involve clinical and professional judgments, in which legal rules cannot operate except to impair the reliability of the ultimate judgment.

This is a rather neat picture, and it may be added in all fairness, one motivated by humane and rational considerations. But it is beset by difficulties. First of all, the rehabilitative goal is not exclusive in our society. Whatever may be postulated as the ultimate ideal, in fact our system plainly rests on a multiplicity of ends, including general and special deterrence, moral vindication, and perhaps in some instances, even retribution. Weighing and effectuating these goals in no sense involve a scientific clinical diagnosis, but command the same adherence to articulated principle and procedural regularity as any legal judgment.

But even within the area of the rehabilitative judgment itself, the claimed irrelevance of the legal norm is repudiated by several considerations. First, few would deny the conspicuous lack of the reliable scientific knowledge needed to effect the goal of rehabilitation. Confidence in scientific capabilities created by awesome successes in exploring the physical world may depreciate the claimed immunity of the human psyche from scientific understanding and control. But potentiality is not fulfillment and the formidable gap between the capabilities and the responsibilities of those charged with rehabilitative functions is one of the axioms of the profession. If ever scientific advances render this no longer true, there indeed may be a forceful analogy to the so-called pure administrative process in which scientific testing and examination dispense with the need for legal norms.[75] Until then, the imperative need is for opportunity to challenge the premises and assumptions of the professional clinician. It is precisely in guaranteeing this continuous opportunity that legal structures make their singular contribution to the dilemma of the obligation to make and act on judgments where lack of knowledge makes the reliability and validity of those judgments uncertain. Rigid insistence upon an absolute professional judgment, on the other hand, insulates the judgment from scrutiny and resolves the dilemma only by assuming it does not exist.[76]

Second, the inadequacy of institutional resources combines with the inadequacy of knowledge to enlarge the relevance of the non-strictly-rehabilitative professional factors, so that judgments become even more clearly social and legal judgments rather than strictly clinical ones. Insofar as the sentencing or parole choice is whether to retain in inadequate prisons or release under inadequate supervision with inadequate opportunity for reform, the clinical judgment is marginal—rehabilitation becomes speculative and other factors tend to predominate. What consideration, for example, should be given to the effect on prison overcrowding of prolonged detention? What part should the factor of prison discipline play in the release decision? How should the balance be struck between the public danger of a predicted likelihood of recidivism, large or small, against the supposed superior chances for reform of an early release? These are judgments no doubt ill-suited to precise legislative commands, but the nature of our value commitments makes them equally ill-suited to the arrant subjectivism of undisciplined and unguided discretion.

Third, correctional judgments turn on matters of historical fact concerning the offender, as well as scientific ones. Insofar as the issue is sentencing or release, the diagnostic determination turns on the offender's past history—past arrests, personal difficulties, employment history, marital relations, and the like. And when the issue is revocation of a release conditionally granted, issues of fact become even of more direct import, since the issue is joined whether the offender has or has not behaved in compliance with the conditions upon which the release was granted. There is no ready and reliable mechanism for revealing such historical facts comparable, for example, to the blood test for determining intoxication. Especially in view of the human values at stake, therefore, the position that in these inquiries the subject may be deprived of the elementary concomitants of a hearing, wherein he may be advised of the factual issues of relevance with an opportunity to contest their accuracy and their implications, is at war with fundamental conceptions of procedural justice. Indeed, the cultivation of a sense of fairdealing in the offender would appear itself to be helpful, if not essential, in attaining the avowed goal of rehabilitation.[77] There is, moreover, the more general point made by Professors Hart and Sacks in another connection:

> Among the major instruments of control of the exercise of official powers are the arrangements which prescribe the procedure to be followed in exercising the power: the information which must be secured; the people whose views must be listened to; the findings and justification of the decision which must be made; and the formal requisites of action which must be observed. . . . A procedure which is soundly adapted to the type of power to be exercised is conducive to well-informed and wise decisions. An unsound procedure invites ill-informed and unwise ones.[78]

Finally, social workers and clinicians are men subject to human fallibility no less than policemen and politicians. Indeed the occasion for error and abuse is heightened by the endemic overburdening and understaffing of sentencing and correctional agencies, making quick judgments and shortcuts the inevitable human solution. There is no less need here than in other areas where power is exercised over the individual for the protective mechanisms of legal norms and procedural regularity. The point is made, perhaps overmade, by C. S. Lewis:

> Of all tyrannies, a tyranny sincerely exercised for the good of its victims may be the most oppressive. It may be better to live under robber barons than under omnipotent moral busybodies. The robber baron's cruelty may sometime sleep, his cupidity may at some point be satiated; but those who torment us for our own good will torment us without end for they do so with the approval of their own conscience.[79]

CONCLUDING OBSERVATIONS

A primary issue to be faced in resolving the dilemma of making discretionary judgments in the administration of criminal justice compatible with values of the rule of law is to determine specifically the areas of choice in which primary reliance may acceptably (or must) be vested in the discretionary judgments of public officials, and in which it need (and must) not. In the police area the existence of discretion may be eliminated in particular situations, or at least substantially reduced, as for example by legislative revision, but in other situations there is no alternative to accepting its existence, given the uses we want to make of the criminal law. As for sentencing discretion, it is plain that the alternative to the existence of discretion is an unacceptable reversion to the strict classical view of a fixed statutory penalty for designated offenders. Few would doubt that this is a price too great to pay for the full extension of the rule of law.[80]

The second issue to be faced is the development of structures and arrangements which tend to maximize in particular areas of choice the guidance and control of law without self-defeating rigidity and, at the same time, the wisdom and flexibility of individualized judgment without oppression or folly. Development of such pragmatic accommodations between rule and discretion is not a problem unique to the criminal law. It is, of course, only an aspect of the larger challenge to a democratic community of making accountable those who exercise power in the name of the state.[81] Indeed, this is the heart of the matter: that this perennial dilemma inheres as well in the administration of justice as in other areas of government, though often masked, as in the case of the police by the myth of full enforcement and absence of discretion, and, in the case of correctional agencies, by the myths of the dispensation of grace and the immunity of the professional diagnostic judgment from the legal norm.

The lines of accommodation await a wider consensus on the nature of the dilemma. Certainly the existence of room for choice in the public official poses differential consequences for the values associated with ordered legality. The policeman's choice not to arrest, if unwisely and needlessly expanded by inadequately conceived legislative formulations, has serious though not overwhelming potential for impairment of important values. Likely modes of control and accommodation, however, are subtle and elusive. All one can safely assert in general terms is that their development is not likely to precede a candid acceptance of the areas of choice and a revised view of the role of the policeman. The correctional choice, on the other hand, poses maximum potential dangers to values of the most fundamental character, involving root conceptions regarding the norms and procedures whereby official power is brought to bear upon the life and liberty of individuals. But here the lines of accommodation between professional expertise and legality are less uncertain. The wide experience with administrative law over the past several decades furnishes a uniquely appropriate and useful body of knowledge. The central task of administrative law—accommodating within the legal order the need for regulation through the individualized expertise of officials where the traditional processes of regulation through legislation and judicial litigation are unwieldy and unsuitable—is precisely the task created by the development of the penology of individualization. In a word, where in the business and economic sphere it was the emergence of the philosophy of public control over an increasingly complex society which produced the challenge, in the peno-correctional sphere it was the emergence and acceptance of the philosophy of the penology of individualization which produced it. But the challenge is not essentially different. Indeed the common demand twenty-five years ago for freedom of the administrator to get on with his job free of the harassment of legal imperatives is the same demand made today by those who administer the new penology. A beginning in the correctional area awaits a general recognition that the correctional agency is not sui generis, but another administrative agency which requires its own administrative law if it is to make its maximum contributions harmoniously with the values of the general social order in which it functions.[82]

POSTSCRIPT

The wide discretion of the judge and correctional official to affect the sentence of a defendant, the subject of the second part of the foregoing essay, has been reduced in the intervening years. First, individualized penal dispositions are no longer so widely accepted, and the institutions associated with this approach—indeterminate sentence and parole—have yielded in a number of jurisdictions to the determinate sentence and the abolition of parole. See ALLEN, THE DECLINE OF THE REHABILITATIVE IDEAL (1981).

Second, the Supreme Court has dealt extensively with due process requirements in sentencing and correctional decisionmaking, and has held some due process restrictions to be applicable. See *Mempa v. Rhay*, 389 U.S. 128 (1967) (defendant has right to assistance of counsel at sentencing stage); *Morrissey v. Brewer*, 408 U.S. 471 (1972) (due process at parole revocation requires notice and opportunity to be heard, to present evidence and to confront and cross-examine hostile witnesses); *Greenholtz v. Inmates of Nebraska Penal and Correctional Complex*, 442 U.S. 1 (1979) (*Morrissey v. Brewer* not applicable to parole release decisions); *Gagnon v. Scarpelli*, 411 U.S. 778 (1973) (indigent not entitled to appointment of counsel at probation or parole revocation except where particular circumstances make self-representation unfair); *Gardner v. Florida*, 430 U.S. 349 (1977) (failure to disclose facts in presentence report relied on by judge in sentencing defendant to death held to violate due process).

NOTES

NOTES TO ESSAY 1

1. Wechsler, *The Challenge of a Model Penal Code*, 65 HARV. L. REV. 1097, 1097–98 (1952).
2. Zimring, *Punishing Homicide*, 43 U. OF CHI. L. REV. 227 (1976).
3. O. W. HOLMES, THE COMMON LAW 45 (1881).
4. *Id.* at 48.

NOTES TO ESSAY 2

1. CALIF. EDUCATION CODE §9255.
2. *Idem* at §11955.
3. CALIF. ELECTIONS CODE §29003.
4. CALIF. GOVERNMENT CODE § 6650.
5. CALIF. WATER CODE §307.
6. See the telling account of Moynihan, *The War Against the Automobile,* The Public Interest, No. 3 (Spring 1966), especially at 21 *et seq.*
7. See Essay 4, The Use of Criminal Sanctions in Enforcing Economic Regulations, *intra.*
8. J. F. STEPHENS, LIBERTY, FRATERNITY AND EQUALITY (1873).
9. DEVLIN, THE ENFORCEMENT OF MORALS 23 (1959).
10. J. S. MILL, ON LIBERTY (1859).
11. H. L. A. HART, LAW, LIBERTY AND MORALITY (1963).
12. GREAT BRITAIN COMMITTEE ON HOMOSEXUAL OFFENSES AND PROSTITUTION, REPORT, COMMAND No. 247 (1957) (Wolfenden Report), Paras. 61 and 62.
13. KINSEY, POMEROY, and MARTIN, SEXUAL BEHAVIOR IN THE HUMAN MALE 392 (1948).
14. See SKOLNICK, JUSTICE WITHOUT TRIAL (1966), chap. iii.
15. THURMAN ARNOLD, SYMBOLS OF GOVERNMENT 160 (1936).
16. MODEL PENAL CODE §207.11, comments at 111 (Tent. Draft No. 9, 1959).
17. KINSEY, MARTIN, AND GEBHARD, SEXUAL BEHAVIOR IN THE HUMAN FEMALE 392 (1953).
18. Chief Judge Craven in Perkins v. North Carolina, 234 F. Supp. 333, 339 (W.D.N.C. 1964).
19. As recently as August 1966 a nationwide extortion ring was uncovered which used blackmail of homosexuals to extort millions of dollars from thousands of victims, many of whom were prominent personalities in entertainment, business, education, and government. Time, August 26, 1966, p. 14.
20. See Project, *The Consenting Adult Homosexual and the Law: An Empirical Study of Enforcement in Los Angeles County,* 13 U.C.L.A. LAW REV. 643 (1966).
21. See Bielicki v. Superior Court, 57 Cal.2d 600, 371 P.2d 288 (1962); Britt v. Superior Court, 58 Cal.2d 469, 374 P.2d 817 (1962); Smayda v. United States, 352 F.2d 251 (9th Cir. 1965).
22. See Project, *supra,* note 20, at 690–691: "The decoy method is utilized by undercover officers who 'operate' by intentionally providing homosexuals with the opportunity to

make a proscribed solicitation. . . .The decoy's modus operandi at a public restroom may be to loiter inside engaging a suspect in friendly conversation, using handwashing or urinal facilities, or even occupying a commode for long periods of time. If the suspect makes a lewd solicitation or touching, the decoy will usually suggest going elsewhere to consummate the act and the arrest will be made outside of the restroom. When a street area is a known rendezvous location for homosexuals and male prostitutes, the decoy will operate by loitering on the street or by using a car to approach the suspect. In bars frequented by homosexuals, the decoy will order a drink and engage in friendly conversation with a suspect. Enforcement in bathhouses may necessitate operation by nude and semi-nude decoys."

23. *Supra,* note 12 at 247.

24. Kinsey, *supra,* note 13 at 597.

25. LaFave, Arrest: the Decision to Take a Suspect into Custody 450 (1965).

26. Skolnick, *supra,* note 14 at 100.

27. See the sobering testimony of the Assistant Chief of the Division of Preventive Medical Services of the State Department of Public Health before the California Assembly Interim Committee on Criminal Procedure, July 20, 1964, quoted in U.S. President's Commission on Law Enforcement and Administration of Justice, Task Force Report: The Courts 5 (1967).

28. See the sources in Model Penal Code, §207.11, Comments at 147 (Tent. Draft No. 9, 1959).

29. Packer, *The Crime Tariff,* 33 American Scholar 551 (1964).

30. For a detailed description, see U.S. President's Commission on Law Enforcement and Administration of Justice, Task Force Report: Organized Crime (1967).

31. Sorrels v. U.S., 287 U.S. 435 (1932).

32. Sherman v. U.S., 356 U.S. 370 (1958).

33. E.g., Johnson v. U.S. 333 U.S. 10 (1948) (narcotics); Draper v. U.S. 358 U.S. 307 (1959) (narcotics); Beck v. Ohio, 379 U.S. 89 (1964) (gambling).

34. E.g., Carrol v. U.S., 267 U.S. 132 (1925) (prohibition); Agnello v. U.S., 269 U.S. 20 (1925) (narcotics); Marron v. U.S., 275 U.S. 192 (1927) (prohibition); Go-Bart Co. v. U.S., 282 U.S. 344 (1931) (narcotics); Lefkowitz v. U.S., 285 U.S. 452 (1932) (prohibition); Johnson v. U.S., 333 U.S. 10 (1948) (narcotics); Rochin v. California, 342 U.S. 165 (1952) (narcotics); Jones v. U.S., 362 U.S. 267 (1960) (narcotics); Wong Sun v. U.S., 371 U.S. 471 (1963) (narcotics); Ker v. California, 374 U.S. 23 (1963) (narcotics).

35. E.g., Olmstead v. U.S., 277 U.S. 438 (1928) (prohibition); Nardone v. U.S., 302 U.S. 379 (1938), 308 U.S. 338 (1939) (smuggled alcohol); On Lee v U.S., 343 U.S. 747 (1952) (narcotics); Irvine v. California, 347 U.S. 128 (1954) (gambling); Benanti v. U.S. 355 U.S. 96 (1957) (illicit alcohol); Silverman v U.S. 365 U.S. 505 (1961) (gambling).

36. The Model Anti-Gambling Act deliberately overgeneralizes the prohibition in this way even though recognizing "that it is unrealistic to promulgate a law literally aimed at making a criminal offense of the friendly election bet, the private, social card game among friends etc.," on the ground that "it is imperative to confront the professional gambler with a statutory facade that is wholly devoid of loopholes." 2 ABA Comm'n on Organized Crime, Organized Crime and Law Enforcement 74–78 (1953).

37. See the review of the evidence in the papers of Messrs. Blum and Rosenthal in U.S. President's Commission on Law Enforcement and Administration of Justice, Task Force Report: Narcotics and Drug Abuse (1967), especially at pp. 24–26, 126–131.

38. American Bar Foundation, Pilot Project Report on the Administration of Criminal Justice in the United States, Vol. III, 570 (1959); LaFave, *supra,* note 25 at 118; Frank Miller and Frank Remington, *Procedures Before Trial,* 335 The Annals, 111, 114 (1962).

39. *Ibid.*

40. People v. Tylkoff, 212 N.Y. 187, 201, 105 N.E.2d 835, 836 (1914).

41. Model Penal Code, §250.1, Comments at 2 *et seq.* (Tent. Draft No. 13, 1961).

42. See Adlerberg and Chetow, *Disorderly Conduct in New York Penal Law Section 722*, 25 BROOKLYN L. REV. 46 (1958).

43. U.S. FBI, UNIFORM CRIME REPORTS 108 (1965).

44. Note, *Use of Vagrancy-Type Laws for Arrest and Detention of Suspicious Persons*, 59 Yale L. J. 1351 (1950); Foote, *Vagrancy-Type Law and Its Administration*, 104 U. PA L. REV. 603 (1956); Justice Douglas, *Vagrancy and Arrest on Suspicion*, 70 YALE L. J. 1 (1960); LaFave, *supra*, note 25 at 87–88, 151–152, 343–363. See N.Y. Law Revision Commission Report 591 (1935); "The underlying purpose [of vagrancy laws] is to relieve the police of the necessity of proving that criminals have committed or are planning to commit specific crimes."

45. MODEL PENAL CODE, *supra*, note 41 at 2.

46. TASK FORCE REPORT: COURTS, *supra*, note 27 at 103–104.

47. BENTHAM, PRINCIPLES OF MORALS AND LEGISLATION 281–288 (Harrison ed., 1948).

48. See *supra*, note 27.

49. DEVLIN, THE ENFORCEMENT OF MORALS 17 (1959). It is noteworthy that, as a practical matter, Lord Devlin became convinced of the undesirability of continuing to consider consenting homosexuality a crime. See Dworkin, *Lord Devlin and the Enforcement of Morals*, 75 YALE L. J. 986, 987 n.4 (1966).

50. E.g., H. L. A. HART, THE MORALITY OF THE CRIMINAL LAW, chap. ii (1964).

51. See the quotation from the statement of a representative of the FBI before the National Crime Commission, *supra*, note 27 at 107.

52. H. S. BECKER, OUTSIDERS: STUDIES IN THE SOCIOLOGY OF DEVIANCE (1963); Kai Erikson, *Sociology of Deviance*, in SOCIAL PROBLEMS 457 (J. Simpson ed., 1965).

53. GUSFIELD, SYMBOLIC CRUSADE: STATUS POLITICS AND THE AMERICAN TEMPERANCE MOVEMENT (1963); Joseph Gusfield, The Symbolic Process in Deviance Designation (Ms. 1967).

54. Westley, *Violence and the Police*, 59 AMER. J. SOCIOLOGY 34 (1953); Skolnick, *supra*, note 14.

NOTES TO ESSAY 3

1. *See* Essay 2, *The Crisis of Overcriminalization*, supra.

2. Id.

3. *See, e.g.,* Zimring, *Is Gun Control Likely to Reduce Violent Killings?*, 35 U. CHI. L. REV. 771 (1968).

4. Johnson, Book Review, 7 TRANS-ACTION 57, 59 (1969).

NOTES TO ESSAY 4

1. See, *e.g.*, Tigner v. Texas, 310 U.S. 141, 148 (1940) (Frankfurter, J.); BENTHAM, THEORY OF LEGISLATION 358 (2d ed. 1871); FREUND, LEGISLATIVE REGULATION 339 (1932); LANDIS, THE ADMINISTRATIVE PROCESS 89–91 (1938); ARENS & LASSWELL, IN DEFENSE OF PUBLIC ORDER 3 (1961).

2. *E.g.,* BENTHAM, INTRODUCTION TO THE PRINCIPLES OF MORALS AND LEGISLATION (1st ed. 1789).

3. BARNES & TEETERS, NEW HORIZONS IN CRIMINOLOGY 43 (3d ed. 1959); CLINARD, THE BLACK MARKET 243 (1952); SHAW, THE CRIME OF IMPRISONMENT 34 (1946); SUTHERLAND & CRESSEY, PRINCIPLES OF CRIMINOLOGY 40–47 (5th ed. 1955). Feelings sometimes run high. See, *e.g.*, SUTHERLAND, WHITE COLLAR CRIME 85 (1949): "This change

in the economic system from free competition to private collectivism has been produced largely by the efforts of businessmen. Although they have not acted en masse with a definite intention of undermining the traditional American institutions, their behavior has actually produced this result."

4. See the statements submitted by the American Bar Association and the Association of the Bar of the City of New York in *Hearings on S.* 996, 2252–2255 *before the Subcommittee on Anti-trust and Monopoly of the Senate Committee on the Judiciary,* 87th Cong., 1st Sess. 97, 100 (1962). See also the observations of Senator Hruska during the hearings in disapproval of the proposals to tighten criminal penalties. *Id. passim.* Counsel for the defendants in the Electrical Equipment cases made the interesting observation: "What is to be served by prison sentences? . . . If the Government regards prison sentences as a means of deterring future violations of this type, then it has adopted a penological theory that was discarded 100 years ago." Wall Street Journal, Feb. 7, 1961, p. 15, col. 3 (Midwest ed.).

5. *E.g.,* HALL, THEFT, LAW AND SOCIETY (2d ed. 1952).

6. *Compare* People v. Ashley, 42 Cal. 2d 246, 267 P.2d 271 (1954), *with* Chaplin v. United States, 157 F.2d 697 (D.C. Cir. 1946). See MODEL PENAL CODE app. A at 103 (Tent. Draft No. 1, 1953).

7. *Cf.* HURST, LAW AND THE CCONDITIONS OF FREEDOM 21 (1956): "Characteristically, nineteenth century criminal and tort law involved not only limitations in the interest of free private decision, but also positive regulations looking to that end. Criminal law extended its reach in the eighteenth and nineteenth centuries nowhere more conspicuously than in the law of theft. Growth of the law concerning embezzlement, theft by bailees, and the receipt of stolen goods went along with the expansion of the market economy; increased dealings at a distance, in reliance on others, and in volume created an impersonality of dealing which called for more intervention by law to secure the working minimum of reliable conduct."

8. See *id.* ch. III *passim.*

9. *But see* SUTHERLAND, *supra,* note 3, at 45.

10. See CLINARD, *supra,* note 3, at 238; Newman, *White Collar Crime,* 23 LAW & CONTEMP. PROB. 735, 739 (1958). See the data in SUTHERLAND, *supra,* note 3, at 22, on the relative use of criminal and civil sanctions in his sample of seventy corporations. For an account of the relative use of the criminal prosecution under the antitrust laws, see Whiting, *Antitrust and the Corporate Executive,* 47 VA. L. REV. 929, 948 (1961) (appendix).

11. See, *e.g.,* the provisions of the OPA Manual reproduced in DESSION, CRIMINAL LAW ADMINISTRATION AND PUBLIC ORDER 198 (1948), entitled, "General Policies and Standards in the Selection of the Criminal Sanction." See also the statement of the Assistant Attorney General in charge of the Antitrust Division in ATT'Y GEN. NAT'L COMM. ANTITRUST REP. 350 (1955).

12. See, *e.g.,* Federal Food, Drug and Cosmetic Act § 306, 52 Stat. 1045 (1938), 21 U.S.C. § 336 (1961): "Nothing in this chapter shall be construed as requiring the Secretary to report for prosecution . . . minor violations of this chapter whenever he believes that the public interest will be adequately served by a suitable written notice or warning."

13. 26 Stat. 209 (1890), 15 U.S.C. §§ 1, 2 (1958).

14. Quoted in Cahill, *Must We Brand American Business by Indictment as Criminal?,* 1952 A.B.A. SECTION ON ANTITRUST LAW, 26, 30 n.5.

15. Jackson & Dumbaud, *Monopolies and the Courts,* 86 U. PA. L. REV. 231, 237 (1938): "[I]t must be confessed that there is no consistent or intelligible policy embodied in our law by which public officials and businessmen may distinguish bona fide pursuit of industrial efficiency from an illicit program of industrial empire building." See *id.* at 232, quoting Senator Wagner: "Half of the laws enacted by Congress represent one school of thought, the other half another. No one can state authoritatively what our national policy is."

16. MANNHEIM, CRIMINAL JUSTICE AND SOCIAL RECONSTRUCTION 159 (1946).

17. Boyce Motor Lines v. United States, 342 U.S. 337 (1952).

18. United States V. Ragen, 314 U.S. 513 (1942).

19. See Screws v. United States, 325 U.S. 91, 103–04 (1945).

20. United States v. Ragen, 314 U.S. 513, 524 (1942).

21. *Cf.* Boyce Motor Lines v. United States, 342 U.S. 337, 345 (1952) (Jackson, J., dissenting).

22. Of course, a legislature might decide as well to require knowledge or reason to know of the law or regulation. The reason would not involve the vagueness of the definition, but rather the failure of the nature of the conduct forbidden to give notice. See text accompanying note 94 *infra*.

23. Statement of Assistant Attorney General in charge of the Antitrust Division in ATT'Y GEN. NAT'L COMM. ANTITRUST REP. 350 (1955).

24. 1 DAVIS, ADMINISTRATIVE LAW TREATISE § 5.03 (1958). See *id.* at 358: "A legislative rule is the product of an exercise of legislative power by an agency, pursuant to a grant (whether explicit or not) of legislative power by the legislative body; a court will no more substitute judgment on the content of a valid legislative rule than it will substitute judgment on the content of a valid statute. A legislative rule is valid if it is (a) within the granted power, (b) issued pursuant to proper procedure, and (c) reasonable."

25. Since United States v. Grimaud, 220 U.S. 506 (1911), there has been no doubt of the constitutionality of such provisions.

26. See United States v. Petrillo, 332 U.S. 1, 18 (1947) (Reed, J., dissenting).

27. See 1 DAVIS, *supra*, note 24, § 2.03.

28. 60 Stat. 239 (1946), 5 U.S.C. § 1004 (1958).

29. See GELLHORN & BYSE, ADMINISTRATIVE LAW 700 (1960).

30. *Cf.* WILLIAMS, CRIMINAL LAW 579 (2d ed. 1961).

31. *But see* MODEL PENAL CODE § 2.07(5), comment at 155 (Tent. Draft No. 4, 1955), for a discussion of difficulties encountered in some jurisdictions.

32. See Whiting, *supra*, note 10, at 931; Note, 71 YALE L.J. 280, 291 (1961).

33. For discussion of the principles of complicity, see Essay 8, Complicity, Cause and Blame, *infra*. See also MODEL PENAL CODE § 2.04, comment (Tent. Draft No. 1, 1953).

34. WILLIAMS, *supra*, note 30, at 360.

35. Judge Ganey observed during sentencing: "[O]ne would be most naive indeed to believe that these violations of the law, so long persisted in, affecting so large a segment of the industry and finally, involving so many millions upon millions of dollars, were facts unknown to those responsible for the conduct of the corporation...." N.Y. Times, Feb. 7, 1961. p. 26, col. 3. See Watkins, *Electrical Equipment Antitrust Cases—Their Implications for Government and for Business,* 29 U. CHI. L. REV. 97, 106 (1961).

36. See the discussion of the record of convictions in Whiting, *supra*, note 10, at 942; Note, 71 YALE L.J. 280, 291 (1961).

37. Clayton Act § 14, 38 Stat. 736 (1914), 15 U.S.C. § 24 (1958).

38. S. 2254, 87th Cong., 1st Sess. (1961).

39. The difficulty is aggravated where, as in the Sherman Act, knowledge of the law is not necessary. See United States v. Griffith, 334 U.S. 100, 105 (1948).

40. See SUTHERLAND, *supra*, note 3, at 54: "The customary plea of the executives of the corporation is that they were ignorant of and not responsible for the action of the special department. This plea is akin to the alibi of the ordinary criminal and need not be taken seriously."

41. Watkins, *Federal Incorporation,* 17 MICH. L. REV. 64, 145, 238 (1918–19); Watkins, *supra*, note 35, at 108–09.

42. Watkins, *supra,* note 35, at 107–08.

43. Sherman Antitrust Act §§ 1, 2, 8, 26 Stat. 209–10 (1890), 15 U.S.C. §§ 1, 2, 7 (1958); Federal Trade Commission Act § 14, added by 52 Stat. 115 (1938), as amended, 15 U.S.C. § 54 (1958); Filled Milk Act § 3, 42 Stat. 1487 (1923), 21 U.S.C. § 63 (1958); Meat Inspection Act, 34 Stat. 1264 (1907), 21 U.S.C. § 88 (1958); Federal Food, Drug and Cosmetic Act §§ 201(e), 303, 52 Stat. 1041, 1043 (1938), 21 U.S.C. §§ 321(e), 333 (1958).

44. See, *e.g.,* United States v. Union Supply Co., 215 U.S. 50, 54–55 (1909); New York Cent. & H.R.R.R. v. United States, 212 U.S. 481, 495 (1909); United States v. George F. Fish, Inc., 154 F.2d 798, 801 (2d Cir. 1946); People *ex rel.* Price v. Sheffield Farms-Slawson-Decker Co., 225 N.Y. 25, 29–30, 121 N.E. 474, 476 (1918); State v. Dried Milk Prods. Co-op, 16 Wis. 2d 357, 114 N.W.2d 412, 414–15 (1962).

45. See, *e.g.,* United States v. Illinois Cent. R.R., 303 U.S. 239, 243–44 (1938); United States v. Armour & Co., 168 F.2d 342, 343–44 (3d Cir. 1948); United States v. Thompson-Powell Drilling Co., 196 F. Supp. 571, 574 (N.D. Tex. 1961); Regan v. Kroger Grocery & Baking Co., 386 Ill. 284, 303–07, 54 N.E.2d 210, 219–20 (1944).

46. Though not necessarily, since it cannot be known whether juries would have convicted the individuals if they could not have convicted the entity. For a collection of cases in which the individual corporate agents were acquitted but the corporation convicted, see Note, 71 YALE L.J. 280, 292 n.50 (1961).

47. MODEL PENAL CODE § 2.07, comment at 148–49 (Tent. Draft No. 4, 1955).

48. BENTHAM, *supra,* note 2, at 25 (Oxford ed. 1907).

49. Experience has varied. The OPA apparently doubted the use of corporate convictions. Its Manual stated: "Criminal prosecution against a corporation is rather ineffective unless one or more of the individuals is also proceeded against." See DESSION, *supra,* note 11, at 200. Until the recent Electrical Equipment cases (which may be in a class by themselves) the Department of Justice appeared for several years to favor a policy of prosecuting corporate defendants alone. See Kramer, *Criminal Prosecutions for Violations of the Sherman Act: In Search of a Policy,* 48 GEO. L.J. 530, 539 (1960).

50. See ARENS & LASSWELL, *supra,* note 1, at 121–22; Kramer, *supra,* note 49, at 539–40.

51. See FRIEDMANN, LAW IN A CHANGING SOCIETY 196 (1959); WILLIAMS, *supra,* note 30, at 863–64.

52. Note, 71 YALE L.J. 280, 287 n.35 (1961).

53. *Id.* at 285–86.

54. *Compare* WILLIAMS, *supra,* note 30, at 864, *with* Note, 71 YALE L.J. 280, 285 n.17 (1961).

55. It has been pointed out, for example, in opposition to a move to increase the fine for antitrust violations, that the fines actually imposed tend to be substantially lower than the authorized maximum. See Statement of the Association of the Bar of the City of New York, in *Hearings, supra,* note 4, at 100.

56. Note, 71 YALE L.J. 280, 297 (1961).

57. *But see* Lane, *Why Business Men Violate the Law,* 44 J. CRIM. L., C. & P.S. 151 (1953).

58. SUTHERLAND, WHITE COLLAR CRIME 46–47 (1949).

59. Id. at 13: "Many of the white collar crimes attack the fundamental principles of American institutions. Ordinary crimes, on the other hand, produce little effect on social institutions or social organization." See also MANNHEIM, *supra,* note 16, at 150, 152, 172–73 (1946); Newman, *White Collar Crime,* 23 LAW & CONTEMP. PROB. 734, 744 (1958).

60. See note 15 *supra.* See also MANNHEIM, *supra,* note 16, at 168.

61. FREUND, LEGISLATIVE REGULATION 253 (1932).

62. See Hart, *The Aims of the Criminal Law,* 23 LAW & CONTEMP. PROB. 401, 404 (1958).

63. MANNHEIM, *supra,* note 16, at 167–68 (1946): "Emile Durkheim has pointed out that 'the only common characteristic of all crimes is that they consist . . . in acts universally disapproved of by members of each society . . . crime shocks sentiments which, for a

given social system, are found in all healthy consciences.' Although this requirement of universal disapproval may appear somewhat exaggerated, there can be no doubt that without the backing of at least the major part of the community criminal legislation, in a democracy, must fail."

64. *Id.* at 5.

65. Fuller, *Morals and the Criminal Law,* 32 J. Crim. L. & Crim. 624, 629–30 (1942): "Ultimately the problem is one of supplementing the political sanctions of the law, which operate through threat of punishment more or less externally on individuals, with spontaneous moral sanctions which operate on the habits, attitudes, and consciences of individuals." See Andrenaes, *General Prevention—Illusion or Reality,* 43 J. CRIM. L., C. & P. S. 176, 179 (1952); Sellin, *Culture Conflict and Crime,* 44 AM. J. OF SOCIOLOGY 97 (1938).

66. In his study of OPA regulation Clinard concluded that punishment was largely ineffective beyond causing businessmen to adopt shrewd manipulative evasions. He concluded that control required "the voluntary compliance with the regulations of society by the vast majority of the citizens." CLINARD, THE BLACK MARKET 261 (1952). See VOLD, THEORETICAL CRIMINOLOGY 257 (1958).

67. See note 3 *supra.*

68. The short-lived Thurman Arnold era of vigorous criminal antitrust enforcement is a case in point. See Arnold, *Antitrust Law Enforcement, Past and Future,* 7 LAW & CONTEMP. PROB. 5 (1940). "[T]he record of enforcement shows that the high water mark for criminal antitrust suits occurred during the 1938–1944 period when, of a total of 385 suits brought by the Department, 251 or over two-thirds, were criminal prosecutions." Whiting, *Antitrust and the Corporate Executive,* 47 VA. L. REV. 929, 940 n.43 (1961).

69. See Fuller, *supra,* note 65, at 624.

70. See text accompanying notes 24–29 *supra.*

71. A bill was introduced to amend the Sherman Act so to provide in certain situations. S. 2253, 87th Cong., 1st Sess. (1961).

72. *Cf.* OPA Manual, quoted by DESSION, CRIMINAL LAW ADMINISTRATION AND PUBLIC ORDER 200 (1948): "One of the most difficult problems in this field is to combat the attitude, so prevalent in this country, that the criminal laws are made for the criminal classes and do not apply to respectable people. This attitude is clearly incompatible with enforcing general compliance on the part of the consumers. Meeting it calls for the judicious and telling selection of violations by average people in the various economic and social strata of society."

73. Congressman Thomas J. Lane of Massachusetts was convicted and imprisoned for tax evasion. He was renominated and re-elected to the House the next fall. N.Y. Times, Oct. 17, 1962, p. 23, col. 5. But having regard to Mayor Curley's experiences, Massachusetts may be a rather special case.

74. See MANNHEIM, CRIMINAL JUSTICE AND SOCIAL RECONSTRUCTION 146 (1946).

75. Revenue Act of 1924, ch. 234, § 1017, 43 Stat. 343–44.

76. See Murphy, *Criminal Income Tax Evasion,* 48 NW. U.L. REV. 317 (1953), for a description of the reforms. As to the effects of the reforms, see Department of Justice News Release, Jan. 4, 1960, as reported in 6 CCH 1960 STAND. FED. TAX REP. ¶ 8784; Schmidt, *Current Department of Justice Criminal Income Tax Policies,* 38 Taxes 293, 299 (1960).

77. See Department of Justice News Release, *supra* note 76, in which it is stated that "in the first 20 years of the [Tax] Division's existence (1933 to 1952), the Division prosecuted successfully 2,900 persons. In the past seven years (1953 to 1959) the Division convicted 4,344 persons for tax fraud. . . . "[O]f the 541 cases disposed of by trial or plea, 497, or 92%, resulted in convictions. [And] . . . 36% of all persons convicted of income tax fraud in fiscal 1959 received prison sentences. The average sentence was approximately fifteen months per person. In fiscal 1958, 31% of those convicted received jail terms

which averaged approximately twelve months per person. Total fines . . . were also more substantial in fiscal 1959, amounting to about $2.2 million as against $2.0 million in fiscal 1958 and $1.5 million in fiscal 1957."

78. MANNHEIM, *supra*, note 74, at 166.

79. Assistant Attorney General Berge, quoted in ATT'Y GEN. NAT'L COMM. ANTITRUST REP. 353 (1955).

80. FREUND, *supra*, note 61, at 302. See FRIEDMANN, *supra*, note 51, at 198.

81. See MODEL PENAL CODE § 2.05, comment at 140 (Tent. Draft No. 4, 1955): "In the absence of minimum culpability, the law has neither a deterrent nor corrective nor an incapacitative function to perform." Hart, *supra*, note 62, at 422.

82. *Cf.* H. L. A. HART, *Murder and the Principles of Punishment: England and the United States*, 52 NW. U. L. REV. 433, 451 (1957): "[Bentham] claims to show that *punishment* of such persons as we excuse on such grounds [i.e., those who have committed a crime owing to their mental condition either temporary (mistake, accident, duress, etc.) or relatively enduring (insanity, infancy)] would be wrong because it would be socially useless ('inefficacious') whereas he only shows that the *threat* of punishment would be ineffective so far as such persons are concerned. Their actual punishment might well be 'useful' in Benthamite terms because, if we admit such excuses, crime may be committed in the hope (surely sometimes realized) that a false plea of mistake, accident, or mental aberration might succeed." (Emphasis in original.)

83. MODEL PENAL CODE § 1.04, comment at 8 (Proposed Official Draft, 1962).

84. See ARNOLD, SYMBOLS OF GOVERNMENT *passim* (1935).

85. Holmes believed that the objective standard of criminal liability which disregards the personal peculiarities of the actor demonstrates that the existence of moral wrong is not a condition of punishment. HOLMES, THE COMMON LAW 45 (1923). He found support for this in the proposition that, "no society has ever admitted that it could not sacrifice individual welfare to its own existence." *Id.* at 43. *Cf.* Wasserstrom, *Strict Liability in the Criminal Law*, 12 STAN. L. REV. 731, 739 (1960).

86. Hart, *supra*, note 62, at 424: "In its conventional and traditional applications, a criminal conviction carries with it an ineradicable connotation of moral condemnation and personal guilt. Society makes an essentially parasitic, and hence illegitimate, use of this instrument when it uses it as a means of deterrence (or compulsion) of conduct which is morally neutral."

87. *Ibid.*

88. "As the concept of punishment wanes in importance, the sphere of offenses not requiring the criminal intent will widen." Million, *Limitations on the Enforceability of Criminal Sanctions*, 28 GEO. L. J. 620, 627 (1940).

89. Consider, for example, the dilution of the requirement of an agreement in conspiracies under the antitrust law, in which such evidence of agreement as conscious parallelism is sometimes made substantively sufficient. See Dunn, *Conscious Parallelism Re-examined*, 35 B.U.L. REV. 225 (1955). See also *Developments in the Law, Criminal Conspiracy*, 72 HARV. L. REV. 922, 934 (1959): "[T]ending to undermine the strict rule that agreement must be proved is the existence of what are perhaps more liberal requirements in antitrust cases, which, although they may be justified in that area, are ever likely to be extended to the general law of conspiracy." A similar dilution attributable as well, at least in part, to Sherman Act cases, has occurred in connection with the requirement in conspiracy of a specific intent to violate the law. *Compare* United States v. Patten, 226 U.S. 525 (1913), *with* Hamburg-American Steam Packet Co. v. United States, 250 Fed. 747 (2d Cir. 1918), *cert. denied*, 246 U.S. 662 (1918), and State v. Kemp, 126 Conn. 60, 9 A.2d 63 (1939). See Note, 62 HARV. L. REV. 276, 281–82 (1948).

90. For example, the felony-murder rule, the rule with respect to aggressive behavior justified on grounds of the defense of another, bigamy and statutory rape. See Packer, *Mens Rea and the Supreme Court*, 1962 SUP. CT. REV. 107, 140.

91. Hart, *supra* note 62, at 404.

92. *Cf.* WILLIAMS, CRIMINAL LAW 259 (2d ed. 1961): "To make a practice of branding people as criminals who are without moral fault tends to weaken respect for the law and the social condemnation of those who break it. 'When it becomes respectable to be convicted, the vitality of the criminal law has been sapped.'"

93. See the debate between Lord Devlin and Professor H. L. A. Hart in DEVLIN, THE ENFORCEMENT OF MORALS (1959) and HART, LAW, LIBERTY AND MORALITY (1963).

94. See Hart, *supra,* note 62, at 418. Precisely such a requirement has been incorporated into a variety of German regulatory laws. See Wirtschaftsstrafgesetz (Code of Economic Crimes) of 1954 § 6. Section 6(1) reads: "A person who in non-culpable error about the existence or the applicability of a statutory provision believed his conduct was lawful may not be punished." Section 6(2) states: "Where the person's error is a culpable one, the punishment may be mitigated." Similar provisions appear in § 12 of the Ordnungswidrigkeitgesetz (Code of Regulatory Violations) of 1952.

95. *Supra,* note 62, at 418 n.42.

96. TAPPAN, CRIME, JUSTICE AND CORRECTION 15–16 (1960). For a suggestive discussion of alternative ways of achieving favorable business sentiment, see LANE, THE REGULATION OF BUSINESSMEN 118–30 (1954).

97. The danger of the use of the criminal law to destroy a repugnant philosophy is exemplified in the revealing observation of BARNES & TEETERS, NEW HORIZONS IN CRIMINOLOGY 49 (3d ed. 1959): "White collar crime flows from a competitive economy and philosophy that reveres success based almost exclusively on money. The job of the courts of justice, legislators, and a regenerated public is to wipe out this insidious philosophy before it is too late." *Cf.* HOLMES, SPEECHES 101 (1913): "As law embodies beliefs that have triumphed in the battle of ideas and then have translated themselves into action, while there is still doubt, while opposite convictions still keep a battle front against each other, the time for law has not come; the notion destined to prevail is not yet entitled to the field."

98. Allen, *Offenses Against Property,* 339 Annals 57, 76 (1962).

99. See Morissette v. United States, 342 U.S. 246, 260 (1952); Perkins, *The Civil Offense,* 100 U. PA. L. REV. 832 (1952).

100. See, *e.g.,* Crimes and Criminal Procedure, 18 U.S.C. § 1 (1958).

101. See MODEL PENAL CODE § 1.05, comment at 8 (Tent. Draft No. 2, 1954).

102. MODEL PENAL CODE § 1.04 (Proposed Official Draft, 1962).

103. MODEL PENAL CODE § 6.03(4), (5) (Proposed Official Draft, 1962).

104. MODEL PENAL CODE § 6.02(4), (5) (Proposed Official Draft, 1962).

105. MODEL PENAL CODE § 1.04(5) (Proposed Official Draft, 1962).

106. MODEL PENAL CODE § 1.04, comment at 8 (Proposed Official Draft, 1962).

107. MODEL PENAL CODE § 2.05 (Proposed Official Draft, 1962).

108. I am indebted to Kurt G. Siehr, graduate student at The University of Michigan Law School, for providing indispensable help with the German law.

109. GERMAN PENAL CODE § 1. The classifications are *Verbrechen* (Felony), *Vergehen* (High Misdemeanor), and *Übertretung* (Petty Misdemeanor).

110. Gesetz über Ordnungswidrigkeiten of 1952 (Bundesgesetzblatt 1952, Part I, p. 177).

111. *Id.* § 1(1).

112. Rotberg, Gesetz über Ordnungswidrigkeiten 26, 44 (1952).

113. Gesetz über Ordnungswidrigkeiten of 1952 (Bundesgesetzblatt 1952, Part I, p. 177) § 48.

114. *Id.* § 54.

115. Gesetz gegen Wettbewerbsbeschränkungen of 1957 (Bundesgesetzblatt 1957, Part I, p. 1081) §§ 38–41.

116. Aussenwirtschaftsgesetz of 1961 (Bundesgesetzblatt 1961, Part I, p. 481) § 33.

117. Gesetz über das Kreditwesen of 1961 (Bundesgesetzblatt 1961, Part I, p. 881) §§ 56–59.

118. Gesetz über den Ladenschluss of 1956 (Bundesgesetzblatt 1956, Part I, p. 875) § 25.
119. Personenbeforderungsgesetz of 1961 (Bundesgesetzblatt 1961, Part I, p. 241) § 61(1)(c).
120. Wirtschaftsstrafgesetz of 1954 (Bundesgesetzblatt 1954, Part I, p. 175), as amended 1958 (Bundesgesetzblatt 1958, Part I, p. 949) §§ 1, 2, 2a.
121. *Id.* § 3

NOTES TO ESSAY 5

1. See RADZINOWICZ, IDEOLOGY AND CRIME (1966), p. 56.
2. (1843) 8 Eng. Rep. 718.
3. See *State* v. *Strasburg*, 60 Wash. 106, 110 Pac. 1020 (1910), especially concurring opinion at 110 Pac. at 1029, speaking of the State of Washington's elimination of the defense of legal insanity: "No defense has been so much abused and no feature of the administration of our criminal law has so shocked the law-loving and the law-abiding citizen as that of insanity, put forward not only as a shield to the poor unfortunate bereft of mind or reason, but more frequently as a cloak to hide the guilty for whose act astute and clever counsel can find neither excuse, justification, nor mitigating circumstances, either in law or in fact. It is therefore not strange that there should be found a legislative body seeking to destroy this evil and wipe out this scandal upon the administration of justice."
4. See the Oregon statute at issue in *Leland* v. *Oregon*, 343 U.S. 790 (1952).
5. See, *e.g.*, *People* v. *Wolff*, 61 Cal. 2d 795, 394 P. 2d 959 (1964).
6. A.L.I., Model Penal Code, Proposed Official Draft (1962), § 4.01.
7. Royal Commission on Capital Punishment, 1949–1953, Report, § 333 (Cmd. 8932, 1953).
8. *Durham* v. *United States*, 214 F. 2d 862 (1954).
9. See, *e.g.*, Morris, *Psychiatry and the Dangerous Criminal*, 41 SO. CALIF. L. REV. 514 (1968); WOOTTON, CRIME AND THE CRIMINAL LAW (1963), Chaps. 2 and 3; HART, THE MORALITY OF THE CRIMINAL LAW (1965), pp. 24–25; Weintraub, "Remarks" (1964) 37 F.R.D. 369; HALLECK. PSYCHIATRY AND THE DILEMMAS OF CRIME (1967), pp. 205–229.
10. KALVEN AND ZEISEL, THE AMERICAN JURY (1966), p. 330.
11. Walker, *The Mentally Abnormal Offender in the English Penal System*, SOCIOLOGICAL REVIEW MONOGRAPH No. 9 (1965), 133.
12. *Ibid.*
13. See Morris, *supra*, note 9 at 518–519.
14. See Hart, *supra*, note 9.
15. See *State* v. *Strasburg*, 60 Wash. 106, 110 Pac. 1020 (1910). See also *State* v. *Lang*, 168 La. 958, 123 So. 639 (1929); *Sinclair* v. *State*, 161 Miss. 142, 132 So. 581 (1931).
16. Calif. Penal Code, § 1016.
17. *People* v. *Wells*, 33 Cal. 2d 330, 202 P. 2d 53 (1949); *People* v. *Gorshen*, 51 Cal. 2d 716, 333 P. 2d 492 (1959).
18. Louisell and Hazard, *Insanity as a Defense: The Bifurcated Trial*, 49 CALIF L. REV. 805, 830 (1961).
19. Morris, *supra*, note 9 at 524–525.
20. *Robinson* v. *California*, 370 U.S. 660 (1962).
21. *Lambert* v. *California*, 355 U.S. 225 (1957).
22. *Budd* v. *California*, 385 U.S. 909, 912–913 (1966) (dissenting opinion).
23. *State* v. *Strasburg*, 110 Pac. 1020, 1025 (1910).
24. See Morris, *supra*, note 9 at 520.
25. *The Criteria of Criminal Responsibility*, 22 UNIV. OF CHI. L. REV. 367, 374 (1955).
26. *Supra*, note 9, at 520.
27. Wootton, *supra*, note 9, Chaps 2 and 3; MARSHALL, INTENTION—IN LAW AND SOCIETY (1968); Campbell, *A Strict Accountability Approach to Criminal Responsibility*, 29 FED. PROB.

33 (1965). See ANCEL, SOCIAL DEFENSE (Eng. ed. 1965); GLUECK, LAW AND PSYCHIATRY (1963), Chap. 4.

28. HART, PUNISHMENT AND RESPONSIBILITY (1968), p. 182.

29. *Id.*

30. For a like-minded, but fuller, critique of the Wootton proposal, see PACKER, THE CRIMINAL SANCTION (1968).

NOTES TO ESSAY 6

1. *Cf., e.g.,* Moore, *Causation and the Excuses,* 73 CALIF. L. REV. 1091, 1095–99 (1985).

2. ARISTOTLE, NICHOMACHEAN ETHICS, 1110a–1111b (W.D. Ross trans. 1915); T. Irwin, *Reason and Responsibility in Aristotle,* in Essays on ARISTOTLE'S ETHICS 133 (A. Rorty ed. 1980).

3. The dual character of accident and mistake defenses may be seen in CAL. PENAL CODE § 26 (West 1987), enacted in 1872:

> "All persons are capable of committing crimes except those belonging to the following classes: . . .
> "Three—Persons who committed the act or made the omission charged under an ignorance or mistake of fact, which disproves any criminal intent. . . .
> "Five—Persons who committed the act or made the omission charged through misfortune or by accident, when it appears that there was no evil design, intention, or negligence."

This formulation follows Blackstone in including accident and mistake (along with duress, infancy, and insanity) as instances of excuse based on defect of will. Blackstone, *Commentaries,* Ch. II.

4. The various approaches to duress are reviewed in MODEL PENAL CODE AND COMMENTARIES, § 2.09, commentary at 368–71 (1985).

5. W. LaFAVE & A. SCOTT, CRIMINAL LAW 432–33 (2d. ed. 1986).

6. A word needs to be said about intoxication. It is not an independent excuse: it is irrelevant that what the defendant did drunk he would not have done sober. It may provide the evidentiary basis for a *mens rea* or legal insanity defense, but it is the absence of *mens rea* or the condition of insanity that are defenses, not simply that the defendant is intoxicated. There is some authority for recognizing intoxication itself as an independent excuse if it was involuntary, but the Model Penal Code and most states allow the defense only if the incapacitation is of the kind and degree that would constitute a defense of legal insanity had it been caused by a mental disease. "The actor whose personality is altered by intoxication to a lesser degree is treated like others who may have difficulty in conforming to the law and yet are held responsible for violation." MODEL PENAL CODE AND COMMENTARIES, § 2.08, commentary at 363 (1985).

7. M'Naghten's Case, 8 Eng. Rep. 718 (1843).

8. MODEL PENAL CODE § 4.01 (1985).

9. *See infra* text accompanying notes 60–77.

10. J. BENTHAM, AN INTRODUCTION TO THE PRINCIPLES OF MORALS AND LEGISLATION 160–162 (J. BURNS & H.L.A. HART EDS. (1978). See discussion in H.L.A. HART, PUNISHMENT AND RESPONSIBILITY 41–42 (1968). For a modern version of the utilitarian argument, see Spriggs, *A Utilitarian Reply to McCloskey,* in CONTEMPORARY UTILITARIANISM 261, 291–92 (M. Bayles ed. 1968).

11. *See* H.L.A. HART, *supra* note 10; G. FLETCHER, RETHINKING CRIMINAL LAW 813–17 (1978).

12. H.L.A. HART, *supra* note 10, at 40–44.

13. *Legal Responsibility and Excuses,* in H.L.A. HART, *supra* note 10, at 28.

14. *Id.* at 46–48.

15. *But see* G. Newman, Just and Painful: A Case for the Corporal Punishment of Criminals 141–42 (1983):

   "[T]he greatest consequence of this deemphasis in prisons is that fewer persons will come under the direct control of the State (which is what we mean by prisons), and that the major portion of criminal punishment (that is, corporal punishment) will be conducted with the view that it is not criminals *per se* who are being punished at all, but free citizens who have exercised their right to break the law.

   "In this way the most basic of all freedoms in a society is preserved: the freedom to break the law."

16. Punishment and the Elimination of Responsibility, in H.L.A. Hart, *supra*, note 10 at 174–77.

17. *See* H.L.A. Hart, *supra*, note 10, at 37.

18. *See* B. Wootton, Crime and the Criminal Law 51 (1963); B. Wootton, Social Science and Social Pathology, ch. 8 (1959).

19. *See* H.L.A. Hart, *supra*, note 10 at 177–85; H. Packer, The Limits of the Criminal Sanction 27 (1968); H.L.A. Hart, Book Review, 74 Yale L.J. 1325 (1965) reviewing B. Wootten, Crime and the Criminal Law (1963).

20. *See supra*, Essay 5, *The Decline of Innocence.* This, of course, is not to embrace the retributive view that responsibility for law violation itself requires punishment, only that responsibility is necessary, but not sufficient, for punishment. *See* W.D. Ross, The Right and the Good 60–61 (1930); H.L.A. Hart, *supra* note 10, at 9–10.

21. Compare Model Penal Code § 2.09(1) (1985), where duress is defined as follows:

   "It is an affirmative defense that the actor engaged in the conduct charged to constitute an offense because he was coerced to do so by the use of, or a threat to use, unlawful force against his person or the person of another, which a person of reasonable firmness in his situation *would have been unable to resist.*" (*Italics added.*)

22. Sweet v. Parsley, 1970 App. Cas. 132 (H.L. 1968).

23. United States v. Dotterweich, 320 U.S. 277 (1943).

24. There may be injustice, however, in rare cases of foreign defendants reared in an ethically alien culture. *See* Note, *The Availability of the "Cultural Defense" as an Excuse for Criminal Behavior,* 16 Ga. J. Int'l & Comp. L. 355 (1986).

25. *See e.g.,* Kellman, *Strict Liability: An Unorthodox View,* in 4 Encyclopedia of Crime and Justice 1512 (S.H. Kadish ed. 1983); Wasserstrom, *Strict Liability in the Criminal Law,* 12 Stan. L. Rev. 731, 735–39 (1960); Note, *Criminal Liability Without Fault: A Philosophical Perspective,* 75 Colum. L. Rev. 1517, 1543–42 (1975).

26. *See* Johnson, *Strict Liability: The Prevalent View,* in Encyclopedia of Crime and Justice 1518 (S. H. Kadish ed. 1983).

27. O.W. Holmes, Common Law 48 (1881); *see also* J. Selden, Table Talk of John Selden 68 (1927): ("Ignorance of the Law excuses no man, not that all Men knowe the law, but 'tis an excuse every man will plead & no man can tell how to confute him.")

28. United States v. Dotterweich, *supra* note 23.

29. Germany does not employ strict liability. See H.-H. Jescheck, Strafrecht im Dienste der Gemeinschaft 320–322 (1980). It does allow the defense of reasonable mistake of law. *See* S.H. Kadish, S.J. Schulhofer & M.G. Paulsen, Criminal Law and its Processes 314 (4th ed. 1983).

30. Regina v. City of Sault Ste. Marie, 85 D.L.R.3d 161 (Can., 1978); Proudman v. Dayman, 67 C.L.R. 536 (Austl. 1941); *see* also Kadish, Book Review, 78 Harv. L. Rev. 907, 910–13 (1965).

31. C. Howard, Strict Responsibility 36, 79 (1963).

32. Model Penal Code § 2.02(1) (1985); *Cf.* H.-H. Jescheck, *supra* note 29.

33. *See, e.g.,* H. M. Hart, *The Aims of the Criminal Law,* 23 Law & Contemp. Probs. 401, 422–23 (1958).

34. *See* J.S. Mill, *Utilitarianism,* in *Mill's Ethical Writings* 337–38, (J.B. Schneewind ed., 1965):

"[J]ustice is a name for certain moral requirements which, regarded collectively, stand higher in the scale of social utility, and are therefore of more paramount obligation, than any others, though particular cases may occur in which some other social duty is so important as to overrule any one of the general maxims of justice. Thus, to save a life, it may not only be allowable, but a duty, to steal, or take by force, the necessary food or medicine, or to kidnap and compel to officiate, or to kidnap and compel to officiate, the only qualified medical practitioner. In such cases, as we do not call anything justice which is not a virtue, we usually say, not that justice must give way to some other moral principle, but that what is just in ordinary cases is, by reason of that other principle, not just in the particular case. By this useful accommodation of language, the character of indefeasibility attributed to justice is kept up, and we are saved from the necessity of maintaining that there can be laudable injustice."

35. Feinberg, *Justice, Fairness and Rationality* (Book Review), 81 YALE L.J. 1004, 1005 (1972) (reviewing J. RAWLS, A THEORY OF JUSTICE (1971)).

36. Another analogy is the principle of the choice of the lesser evil as a defense to what otherwise would be a crime. *See* MODEL PENAL CODE § 3.02 (1985).

37. *See infra* Essay 7, *Respect for Life and Regard for Rights in the Criminal Law.*

38. *See* Fletcher, *supra* note 11, at 818–33.

39. *See* MODEL PENAL CODE AND COMMENTARIES § 2.02 commentary at 368–71 (1985).

40. Regina v. Dudley and Stephens, 14 Q.B.D. 273 (1884).

41. *E.g.,* People v. Lovercamp, 43 Cal. App. 3d 823, 118 Cal. Rptr. 110 (1974). Escape might be justified on the view that suffering the bad conditions is a greater evil than violating prison discipline. The question here is whether the prisoner would have an excuse if the court found escaping to be the greater evil. *See* Fletcher, *Should Intolerable Prison Conditions Generate a Justification of an Excuse for Escape?*, 26 UCLA L. REV. 1355 (1979).

42. MODEL PENAL CODE § 2.09 (1985).

43. This awkward term is needed to distinguish the excuse of necessity based on coercion from the justification of choice of the lesser evil, which often is also termed necessity.

44. MODEL PENAL CODE AND COMMENTARIES, § 2.02 and commentary at 377–79 (1985). *See* S.H. KADISH, S.J. SCHULHOFER, M.G. PAULSEN, *supra* note 29, at 797–98.

45. The Criminal Codes of Queensland and Western Australia provide: "[A] person is not criminally responsible for an act or omission done or made under such circumstances of sudden or extraordinary emergency that an ordinary person possessing ordinary power of self-control could not reasonably be expected to act otherwise." Queensl. Crim. Code § 25; W. Austl. Crim. Code § 25. See also the German Criminal Code quoted in G. FLETCHER, *supra* note 11 at 833; Calif. Joint Leg. Committee for Revision of the Penal Code, Penal Code Revision Project § 520 (Tent. Draft No. 1, 1967) ("[I]t is an affirmative defense that the defendant engaged in the conduct otherwise constituting the offense in order to avoid death or great bodily harm to himself or another in circumstances where a person of reasonable firmness in his situation would not have done otherwise."). Three states (Ind. Code § 35–41–3–8 (West 1986); N.D. Cent Code Ann. § 12.1–05–10 (1985); Tex. Code Crim Proc. Ann. Art § 8.05 (Vernon 1977)) have adopted a version of this proposal suggested by the Brown Commission. 1 *Working Papers of the National Commission on Reform of Federal Criminal Laws* 276–77 (1970).

46. *See, e.g.,* MODEL PENAL CODE AND COMMENTARIES § 2.09 commentary at 373 (1985); Regina v. Hudson, [1971] 2 Q.B. 202, 207 (Crim. Appl. 1971) (duress consisted of "threats sufficient to destroy [the defendant's] will").

47. This was Aristotle's view. Speaking of actions under threats he says:

"Now the man acts voluntarily; for the principle that moves the instrumental parts of the body in such actions is in him, and the things of which the moving principle is in a man himself are in his power to do or not to do. Such actions, therefore, are voluntary, but in the abstract perhaps involuntary; for no one would choose any such act in itself."

Aristotle, *supra* note 2, at 1110a.

48. MODEL PENAL CODE AND COMMENTARIES, § 2.09 commentary at 374–75 (1985).

49. *Cf.* Macaulay and Other Indian Law Comm'rs, A Penal Code 82–84 (London 1838).

50. For a strong statement of the case for individualization, see Fletcher, *The Individualization of Excusing Conditions*, 47 S. CAL. L. REV. 1269 (1974).

51. Professor Williams has doubted the desirability of confining the duress defense to cases where the defendant acted reasonably. See G. Williams, Textbook of Criminal Law 633 (2d ed. 1983). For a contrary view see MODEL PENAL CODE AND COMMENTARIES § 2.09 commentary at 373-74 (1985).

52. State v. Williams, 4 Wash. App. 908, 484 P.2d 1167 (1971).

53. *See* O.W. HOLMES, *supra* note 27, at 48–57, 108–110.

54. *See* MODEL PENAL CODE AND COMMENTARIES § 2.02 commentary at 242 (1985).

55. There is, of course, the great issue of whether we are responsible for our characters, whether our characters are made for us rather than by us. But I don't think I am obliged to take a position on the issue, since my subject is a comparison of moral and legal blame. All I need point out is that to the extent we are not so responsible the ground beneath the whole concept of blame, moral as well as legal, is eroded.

56. H.L.A. HART *supra* note 10, at 152–57.

57. *Id.* at 154. The German law of criminal negligence seems close to what Professor Hart argues ours should be. *See* The Case of the Gable Wall (Giebelmauer) 56 RGSt 343, 349 (1922); H.-H. JESCHECK, LEHRBUCH DES STRAFRECHTS 379 (1969); Fletcher, *The Theory of Criminal Negligence: A Comparative Analysis*, 119 U. PA. L. REV. 401, 406 (1971).

58. Cf. People v. Goetz, 68 N.Y.2d 96, 111, 497 N.E.2d 41, 50, 506 N.Y.S.2d 18, 27 (1986):

> "To completely exonerate such an individual, no matter how aberrational or bizarre his thought patterns, would allow citizens to set their own standards for the permissible use of force. It would also allow a legally competent defendant suffering from delusions to kill or perform acts of violence with impunity, contrary to fundamental principles of justice and criminal law."

59. MODEL1 PENAL CODE AND COMMENTARIES § 2.02 commentary at 242 (1985).

60. I am, of course, assuming a concept of legal insanity that extends to volitional as well as cognitive incapacities. The original M'Naghten rule and rules recently developed to tighten the defense eliminate the volitional feature of the defense. See United States v. Lyons, 731 F.2d 243, 248 (5th Cir.). *cert. denied*, 469 U.S. 930 (1984); Bonnie, *The Moral Basis of the Insanity Defense*, 69 A.B.A. J. 194 (1983). I will return shortly to the case for eliminating volitional incapacity as a feature of the insanity defense.

61. *See generally* Slovenko, The Insanity Defense in the Wake of the Hinckley Trials, 14 *Rut. L. Rev.* 373 (1983); Arenella, *Reflections on Current Proposals to Abolish or Reform the Insanity Defense*, 8 AM. J. L. & MED. 271 (1982).

62. *See* Moore, *supra* note 1.

63. 61 Cal.2d 795, 394 P.3d 959, 40 Cal. Rptr. 271 (1964).

64. The California Supreme Court reversed a first degree murder conviction on the ground that "the true test [of premeditation and deliberation] must include consideration of the somewhat limited extent to which this defendant could *maturely and meaningfully reflect* upon the gravity of his contemplated act." In view of the psychiatric evidence of the defendant's diminished capacity, the court concluded that the defendant could not be found to have met this test. Id. at 821, 394 P.2d at 975, 40 Cal.Rptr. at 287. It declined to reverse a second degree murder conviction, however, because of the absence of a volitional disability feature in the California definition of legal insanity, which it felt it had no authority to revise without legislative authorization. Id. at 803, 394 P.2d at 963, 40 Cal.Rptr. at 275.

65. M. MOORE, LAW AND PSYCHIATRY 244–45 (1984). Although Professor Moore most fully develops the argument, others also have identified the defense of legal insanity with incapacity for rational conduct; *e.g.*, H. FINGARETTE, THE MEANING OF CRIMINAL

INSANITY 175–215 (1972); Morse, *Excusing the Crazy: The Insanity Defense Reconsidered,* 58 S. CAL. L. REV. 777, 782 (1985).

66. *See* N. MORRIS, MADNESS AND THE CRIMINAL LAW 53–87 (1982).

67. Professor Hart's concession that it might be desirable to eliminate the defense can only be understood on this ground, given his otherwise consistent defense of the blame principle. *Changing Conceptions of Responsibility,* in H.L.A. HART, *supra,* note 10, at 204–05.

68. *See* supra, Essay 5, *The Decline of Innocence;* Greenawalt, *"Uncontrollable" Actions and the Eighth Amendment: Implications of Powell v. Texas,* 69 COLUM. L. REV. 927, 944 (1969).

69. *See* American Psychiatric Association, Statement on the Insanity Defense 11 (1982); United States v. Lyons, 731 F.2d 243, 248 (5th cir.) *cert. denied,* 469 U.S. 930 (1984); Morse, *Failed Explanations and Criminal Responsibility: Experts and the Unconscious,* 68 VA. L. REV. 971 (1982).

70. Bonnie, *supra,* note 60, at 196–97.

71. *Id.* at 196–97.

72. *See supra* text accompanying notes 55 *et seq.*

73. *Cf.* State v. Sikora, 44 N.J. 453, 475–79, 210 A.2d 193, 205–07 (1965) (Weintraub, C.J., concurring).

74. *See Lyons,* 739 F.2d at 994 (Rubin, J., dissenting):

"Our concept of responsibility . . . is not limited to observable behavior: it embraces *meaningful* choice, and necessarily requires inferences and assumptions regarding the defendant's unobservable mental state. . . . The difference between the concepts of excusing circumstances such as coercion and the insanity defense is that the former is based on objective assumptions about human behavior and is tested against hypothetical-objective standards such as the reasonable person. 'The insanity defense [on the other hand] marks the transition from the adequate man the law demands to the inadequate man he may be.'" *Id.* at 947–98 (Rubin, J.) (emphasis in original) (quoting A. GOLDSTEIN, THE INSANITY DEFENSE 18 (1967).

75. *See* M. MOORE, *supra* note 65 at 244–45.

76. *See supra* note 63 and accompanying text. The court thought otherwise, however. People v. Wolff, 61 Cal.2d at 807, 394 P.2d at 966, 40 Cal. Rptr. at 278 (1964).

77. *Cf.* H. FINGARETTE, *supra* note 65 at 240:

"[T]he reference in the original M'Naghten rule to the defect as one involving knowledge (cognition) is not of the essence so far as the central meaning of criminal insanity is concerned. The defect of reason may show up primarily as a cognitive, a volitional, an emotional, or a behavior-control defect, or for that matter as any other specific mental sort of defect or any combination of defects."

78. *See* Delgado, *"Rotten Social Background": Should the Criminal Law Recognize a Defense of Severe Environmental Deprivation?* 3 LAW AND INEQUAL.: J. THEORY & PRAC. 9 (1985); United States v. Alexander, 471 F.2d 923, 960–61 (D.C. Cir.) (Bazelon J.), cert. denied, 409 U.S. 1044 (1972); Bazelon, *The Morality of the Criminal Law,* 49 S. CAL. L. REV. 385 (1976).

79. *See e.g.,* United States v. Brawner, 471 F.2d 969 (1972).

80. *See* Moore, *supra* note 1, at 1092–1093.

81. *See* Morse, *The Twilight of Welfare Criminology: A Reply to Judge Bazelon,* 49 S. CAL. L. REV. 1247, 1267–68 (1976).

82. United States v. Moore, 486 F.2d 1139 (D.C. Cir.) *cert. denied,* 414 U.S. 980 (1973); People v. Davis, 33 N.Y.2d 221, 306 N.E.2d 787, 351 N.Y.S.2d 663 (1973), *cert. denied,* 416 U.S. 973 (1974).

83. Commonwealth v. Sheehan, 376 Mass. 765, 383 N.E.2d 1115 (1978).

84. Powell v. Texas, 392 U.S. 514 (1968).

85. United States v. Torniero, 735 F.2d 725 (2d Cir. 1984), *cert. denied,* 469 U.S. 1110 (1985); United States v. Gould, 741 F.2d 45 (4th Cir. 1984); United States v. Llewellyn, 723 F.2d 615 (8th Cir. 1984).

86. *See* Easter v. District of Columbia, 361 F.2d 50 (D.C. Cir. 1966); Driver v. Hinnant, 356 F.2d 761 (4th Cir. 1966); State v. Lafferty, 192 Conn. 571, 472 A.2d 1275 (1984); *See* also Annotation, *Drug Addiction or Related Mental State As a Defense to a Criminal Charge*, 73 A.L.R.3d 16 (1976).

87. *See e.g.*, United States v. Moore, 486 F.2d 1139, 1147–48 (D.C. Cir.) (Wilkey, J.) (plurality opinion): "[T]he particular nature of the problem of heroin traffic makes certain policies necessary that should not be weakened by the creation of this defense."), *cert. denied*, 414 U.S. 980 (1973).

88. *See e.g.*, Powell v. Texas, 392 U.S. 514, 559–61 (1968) (Fortas, J., dissenting); *Moore*, 486 F.2d at 1235–50, 1258–60 (Wright, J., dissenting).

89. *See e.g. Moore*, 486 F.2d at 1178–80 (Leventhal, J. concurring) (stating and rejecting argument); United States v. Torniero, 735 F.2d at 730–32 (same).

90. M. MOORE *supra* note 65, at 124–126.

91. MODEL PENAL CODE § 2.01 (1985).

92. Fain v. Commonwealth, 78 Ky 183 (1879); MODEL PENAL CODE AND COMMENTARIES, § 2.01, commentary at 220–21.

93. *See supra,* note 45.

94. MODEL PENAL CODE AND COMMENTARIES, § 2.09 commentary at 374–76.

95. *Id.* at 379–80.

96. H. FINGARETTE & A. HASSE, MENTAL DISABILITIES AND CRIMINAL RESPONSIBILITY 155–72 (1979); J. KAPLAN, THE HARDEST DRUG—HEROIN AND PUBLIC POLICY 15–51 (1983); Fingarette, Addiction and Criminal Responsibility, 84 YALE L.J. 413, 427 (1975).

97. J. KAPLAN *supra* note 96, at 21–22, 35.

98. *Id.* at 35; *see also* Fingarette *supra* note 96, at 436–37 (treatment facilities are increasingly available).

99. J. KAPLAN *supra* note 96, at 33.

100. Id. at 37.

101. *Id.* 43–51; Fingarette *supra* note 96 at 431–33. The phenomenon of alcohol addiction presents a pattern different in many ways than narcotics addiction, but affords even less ground for the claim of compulsion. *See* H. FINGARETTE & A. HASSE, *supra* note 96, at 173–90; Fingarette, *The Perils of Powell: In Search of a Factual Foundation for the "Disease Concept of Alcoholism,"* 83 HARV. L. REV. 793 (1970).

102. *See supra* text accompanying notes 50–59.

NOTES FOR ESSAY 7

1. H. L. A. HART, THE CONCEPT OF LAW 188 (1961).

2. *Id.* at 189 (emphasis deleted).

3. *See* Austin, *A Plea for Excuses*, 57 PROCEEDINGS OF THE ARISTOTELIAN SOCIETY 1–2 (1956–57). As an example, *compare* section 53.1 of the recently superseded German Penal Code of 1871, which provided that "No act constitutes an offense if it was necessary in self-defense or in defense of another," *with* section 53.3, which provided that, "Excessive self-defense or defense of another is not punishable if the perpetrator has exceeded the limits of defense by reason of consternation, fear or fright," 4 THE AMERICAN SERIES OF FOREIGN PENAL CODES, THE GERMAN PENAL CODE OF 1871, at 41–42 (1961).

4. I have chosen not to burden these notes with complete citations to authority for the well-known legal doctrines discussed. *See generally* W. LAFAVE & A. SCOTT, CRIMINAL LAW 381–407 (1972); MODEL PENAL CODE §§ 3.01–.12, Comments (Tent. Draft No. 8, 1958); Note, *Justification: The Impact of the Model Penal Code on Statutory Reform*, 75 COLUM. L. REV. 914 (1975); Note, *Justification for the Use of Force in the Criminal Law*, 13 STAN. L. REV. 566 (1961).

5. *See* the opinions of Justices Brennan and Marshall In Furman v. Georgia, 408 U.S. 238 (1972).

6. It is noteworthy that popular sentiment in some states compelled reinstatement of capital punishment after courts invalidated it for a variety of reasons. In California, voters reinstated the death penalty by a 2-to-1 vote in a popular referendum held after the California Supreme Court held it unconstitutional. *Note on, the Constitutional Status of Capital Punishment*, in S. KADISH & M. PAULSEN, CRIMINAL LAW AND ITS PROCESSES 209 (3rd ed. 1975). It is also noteworthy that capital punishment is sanctioned in the European Convention on Human Rights. Article 2(1) provides: "Everyone's right to life shall be protected by law. No one shall be deprived of his life intentionally save in the execution of a sentence of a court following his conviction of a crime for which this penalty is provided by law." COUNCIL OF EUROPE, EUR. CONV. ON HUMAN RIGHTS, COLLECTED TEXTS (8th ed. 1972).

7. *See* MODEL PENAL CODE §§ 3.07(2)(b), (3) (Proposed Official Draft 1962); Note, *Justification: The Impact of the Model Penal Code on Statutory Reform*, 75 COLUM. L. REV. 914 (1975). The older tradition of the common law, found also in some European countries, allowing a broader privilege to kill for law enforcement purposes, is reflected in the European Convention on Human Rights, Art. 2(2): "Deprivation of life shall not be regarded as inflicted in contravention of this Article [see note 6 *supra*] when it results from the use of force which is no more than absolutely necessary: (a) in defence of any person from unlawful violence; (b) in order to effect a lawful arrest or to prevent the escape of a person lawfully detained; (c) in action lawfully taken for the purpose of quelling a riot or insurrection." COUNCIL OF EUROPE, EUR. CONV. ON HUMAN RIGHTS, COLLECTED TEXTS (8th ed. 1972).

8. MODEL PENAL CODE § 3.02, Comments at 6–7 (Tent. Draft No. 8, 1958).

9. The commentary to section 3.02 of the Model Penal Code states:

> "[R]ecognizing that the sanctity of life has a supreme place in the hierarchy of values, it is nonetheless true that conduct which results in taking life may promote the very value sought to be protected by the law of homicide. Suppose, for example, that the actor has made a breach in the dike, knowing that this will inundate a farm, but taking the only course available to save a whole town. If he is charged with homicide of the inhabitants of the farm house, he can rightly point out that the object of the law of homicide is to save life, and that by his conduct he has effected a net saving of innocent lives. The life of every individual must be assumed in such a case to be of equal value and the numerical preponderance in the lives saved compared to those sacrificed surely establishes an ethical and legal justification for the act. . . . So too a mountaineer, roped to a companion who has fallen over a precipice, who holds on as long as possible but eventually cuts the rope, must certainly be granted the defense that he accelerated one death slightly but avoided the only alternative, the certain death of both."

MODEL PENAL CODE § 3.02, Comments at 8 (Tent. Draft No. 8, 1958).

A number of states have recently adopted formulations of the lesser-evil principle as parts of their criminal codes. *See* Note, *Justification: The Impact of the Model Penal Code on Statutory Reform*, 75 COLUM. L. REV. 914 (1975). Wisconsin, however, excludes homicidal actions. *See* WIS. STAT. ANN. § 939.47 (1958). And *compare* Fletcher, *The Individualization of Excusing Conditions*, 47 S. CAL. L. REV. 1269, 1278 (1974): "German scholars, influenced by the Kantian tradition, have rejected the possibility of justification where the act is one of killing an innocent person."

10. Insofar as duress may excuse homicidal conduct. It often may not. *E.g.*, CAL. PENAL CODE § 26 (West 1970). *See also* W. LaFAVE & A. SCOTT, CRIMINAL LAW 376 (1972).

11. As Professor Fletcher has observed, the issue has not squarely been faced in the Anglo-American law. Fletcher, *Proportionality and the Psychotic Aggressor: A Vignette in Comparative Criminal Theory*, 8 ISRAEL L. REV. 367, 370 (1973). The Model Penal Code does allow the use of necessary defensive force in these cases. MODEL PENAL CODE § 3.11(1) (Proposed Official Draft 1962) (definition of "unlawful force" against which defensive measures are privileged). The commentary to this section of the Model Penal Code states:

"The reason for legitimizing protective force extends to cases where the force it is employed against is neither criminal no actionable—so long as it is not affirmatively privileged. It must, for example, be permissible to defend against attacks by lunatics or children and defenses to liability such as duress, family relationship or diplomatic status are plainly immaterial. We think that it is also immaterial that other elements of culpability, *e.g.* intent or negligence, are absent. Whatever may be thought in tort, it cannot be regarded as a crime to safeguard an innocent person, whether the actor or another, against threatened death or injury which is unprivileged, even though the source of the threat is free from fault."

Id. § 3.04, Comment 5, at 29 (Tent. Draft No. 8, 1958). Other commentators also support the right to take all necessary defensive measures. *See* J. SMITH & B. HOGAN, CRIMINAL LAW 262 (3rd ed. 1973); Radbruch, *Jurisprudence in the Criminal Law*, 18 J. COMP. LEG. & INT'L L. 212, 218 (3rd ser., 1936). Professor Noonan has suggested that St. Thomas found justifiable the killing of an innocent person in self-defense. Noonan, *An Almost Absolute Value in History*, in THE MORALITY OF ABORTION 24–25 (J. Noonan ed. 1970).

12. *See* Wechsler & Michael, *A Rationale of the Law of Homicide: I*, 37 COLUM. L. REV. 701, 744 (1937) [hereinafter cited as Wechsler & Michael], identifying the relevant factors as: "(1) the probability that death or serious injury will result; (2) the probability that the act will also have desirable results and the degree of their desirability, in the determination of which the actor's purposes are relevant; (3) if the act serves desirable ends, its efficacy as a means, as opposed to the efficacy of other and less dangerous means."

13. *See* Hughes, *Criminal Omissions*, 67 YALE L.J. 590 (1958).

14. *See* Feldbrugge, *Good and Bad Samaritans, A Comparative Survey of Criminal Law Provisions Concerning Failure to Rescue*, 14 AM. J. COMP. L. 630 (1966).

15. WORKING PARTY, BOARD FOR SOCIAL RESPONSIBILITY, CHURCH OF ENGLAND, ON DYING WELL—AN ANGLICAN CONTRIBUTION TO THE DEBATE ON EUTHANASIA 24 (1975) (published by the Church Information Office).

16. *See* Finnis, *The Rights and Wrongs of Abortion: A Reply to Judith Thompson*, 2 PHIL. & PUB. AFFAIRS 117, 138–39 (1973); Foot, *The Problem of Abortion and the Doctrine of Double Effect*, 5 OXFORD REV. 5 (1967) [hereinafter cited as Foot]. *See also* G. GRISEZ, ABORTION: THE MYTHS, THE REALITIES AND THE ARGUMENTS 267–346 (1970).

17. Consider Professor Hart's trenchant critique of the double-effect principle. H.L.A. HART, PUNISHENT AND RESPONSIBILITY 124–25 (1968).

18. The work of the once popular philosopher Joseph Popper-Lynkeus developed this theme. An entry on him by Paul Edwards is in 6 THE ENCYCLOPEDIA OF PHILOSOPHY (P. Edwards ed. 1967). Edwards paraphrases a passage of Popper as follows:

"Let us suppose that the angel of death were to allow Shakespeare and Newton, in the most creative periods of their lives, to go on living only on condition that we surrender to him 'two stupid day-laborers or even two incorrigible thieves.' As moral beings we must not so much as consider an exchange of this kind. It would be far better if Shakespeare and Newton were do die. One may call attention, as much as one wishes, to the pleasure produced in countless future ages by Shakespeare's plays; one may point to the immense progress of science which would be the consequence of the prolongation of Newton's life—by comparison with the sacrifice of a human being, these are mere 'luxury values.'"

Id. at 403.

19. Compare the following observations of Paul Edwards on Popper-Lynkeus' views: "In one place Popper goes so far as to assert that it would be better if all the aggressors in the world, even if they numbered millions, were to be destroyed than if a single human being succumbed to them without resistance." *Id.*

20. Wechsler & Michael, *supra*, note 12, at 739.

21. As Wechsler and Michael point out:

> "The most obvious case of homicidal behavior that serves the end of pre-serving life is that of the victim of a wrongful attack who finds it necessary to kill his assailant to save his own life. We need not pause to reconsider the universal judgment that there is no social interest in preserving the lives of aggressors at the cost of those of their victims. Given the choice that must be made, the only defensible policy is one that will operate as a sanction against unlawful aggression."

Id. at 736.

22. One finds, for example, in Locke and Blackstone the two conflicting assertions that one may not alienate his right to life (J. LOCKE, *The Second Treatise of Government,* in TWO TREATISES OF GOVERNMENT § 6, at 288–89, § 135, at 375–76 (P. Laslett ed. 1960); 4 W. BLACKSTONE, COMMENTARIES *189), but that one may forfeit that right by his actions (J. LOCKE, *supra* § 23, at 302, § 172, at 400–01; 1 W. BLACKSTONE, *supra* at *133). See the discussion in Bedau, *The Right to Life,* 52 MONIST 550, 567 (1968).

23. Professor R. Nozick finds the basis of all moral side-constraints on actions, as well as of the particular side-constraint that prohibits aggression against another, in "the fact of our separate existences" and the "root idea . . . that there are different individuals with separate lives and so no one may be sacrificed for others. . . ." R. NOZICK, ANARCHY, STATE, AND UTOPIA 33 (1974).

24. *Cf. id.* at 34; I. KANT, THE METAPHYSICAL ELEMENTS OF JUSTICE 35–36 (J. Ladd transl. 1965).

25. For an illuminating treatment of these contending principles, see Fletcher, *Proportion-ality and the Psychotic Aggressor: A Vignette in Comparative Criminal Theory,* 8 ISRAEL L. REV. 367, 376–90 (1973).

26. So much appears to be reflected by the laws of Germany and the Soviet Union which, in resisting formal recognition of any such general limitation on the use of necessary deadly force, manifest the force of the autonomy principle. *Id.* at 368, 381.

27. MODEL PENAL CODE §§ 3.04(2)(b), 3.06(3)(d), 307(2)(b) (Proposed Official Draft, 1962).

28. *See, e.g.,* People v. Jones, 191 Cal. App. 2d 478, 12 Cal. Rptr. 777 (2d Dist. 1961), in which the court held it no defense to a wife charged with manslaughter of her husband that killing him was her only means to stop his slapping assault on her.

29. I am putting aside capital punishment and the killing of fleeing felons. Both involve either a weighing of utilities—the good of law enforcement versus the good of pre-serving lives—or the issue of the retributive right of the state to punish. A discussion of these issues would largely illustrate further the dominant themes already indicated in the areas of law covered in this article.

30. *See generally* Murphy, *The Killing of the Innocent,* 57 MONIST 527 (1973).

31. It is true that the non-threatening bystander—like the families toward whose homes the floods are deflected—may possibly have a legal right to resist persons attempting the deflection. It is somewhat strange, but not illogical, to extend a right to the victim to resist, while at the same time freeing the attacker from criminal liability. Even if the law extended this right to the victim, however, the law would still be *partly* violating his right against aggression, which includes the right against the state that the aggressive conduct be criminally prohibited.

32. It is worth observing that some instances of the net-saving-of-lives principle do not produce this conflict. One such instance was suggested by Mrs. Foot; a physician denies his limited quantity of medicine to one person who needs all of it to survive in order to use it for five persons, each of whom requires one-fifth the supply to be saved. Foot, *supra* note 16, at 9. For reasons we shall see when we reach omissions (involving the distinction between letting someone die and killing him), none of the ill persons has a right over any of the others to receive the medicine. A similar instance is presented by the often-discussed hostage cases, in which a band threatens to kill two persons in their power in order to obtain the death of one person in the custody of another group. Consistent with a rights approach, the group may desist from protecting the wanted person and permit the band to enter and kill him, for in doing so they will effect a

net saving of lives and violate no one's rights. Contrariwise, it would be inconsistent with the rights approach were they themselves to kill the one person in their custody.

An instance of a quite different kind is suggested in the commentary to the Model Penal Code itself: "A mountaineer, roped to a companion who has fallen over a precipice, who holds on as long as possible but eventually cuts the rope, must certainly be granted the defense," of the net-savings-of-lives principle "because the only alternative was the certain death of both." MODEL PENAL CODE § 3.02, Comment 3, at 8 (Tent. Draft No. 8, 1958). Here, however, the dangling mountaineer is no bystander. He constitutes a threat, although an innocent one, so that the right to resist aggression suffices to justify cutting the rope.

33. There is disagreement over the justification for imposing criminal liability on the basis of negligence. *Compare* Hall, *Negligent Behavior Should be Excluded from Penal Liability*, 63 COLUM. L. RREV. 632 (1963), with H.L.A. HART, PUNISHENT AND RESPONSIBILITY 152 (1968).

34. Wechsler & Michael, *supra* note 12, at 742.

35. For an insightful examination of this aspect of the prevailing response to life-threatening conduct, see Calabresi, *Reflections on Medical Experimentation in Humans*, 98 DAEDALUS 387 (1969).

36. *See* MACAULAY, A PENAL CODE PREPARED BY THE INDIAN LAW COMMISSIONERS, Note M, 53–56 (1837).

37. Wechsler & Michael, *supra* note 12, at 751 n.175.

38. *See id.:*

"Whereas the issue [in liability for negligent acts] is . . . whether or not the act is a sufficiently necessary means to sufficiently desirable ends to compensate for the risk of death or injury which it creates, the issue [in liability for omissions] is whether or not freedom to remain inactive serves ends that are sufficiently desirable to compensate for the evil that inaction permits to befall. The extent of the burden imposed by the act is obviously a relevant factor in making such an evaluation. If the burden is negligible or very light, the case for liability is strong, and the difficulty of formulating a general rule no more insuperable an obstacle than in the case of acts."

39. *See id.*

40. *See* Skolnick, *Coercion to Virtue*, 41 S. CAL. L. REV. 588 (1968).

41. *See* Murphy, *The Killing of the Innocent*, 57 MONIST 527, 546 (1973): "When a man has a right, he has a claim against interference. Simply to refuse to be beneficent to him is not an invasion of his rights because it is not to interfere with him at all."

42. *See* Foot, *supra* note 16, at 11:

"Most of us allow people to die of starvation in India and Africa, and there is surely something wrong with us that we do; it would be nonsense, however, to pretend that it is only in law that we make a distinction between allowing people in the underdeveloped countries to die of starvation and sending them poisoned food. There is worked into our moral system a distinction between what we owe people in the form of aid and what we owe them in the way of non-interference."

It is worth noting in passing that this theory is not applicable to governments which, unlike the persons subject to them, are precisely instruments to be used by such persons. For example, the Universal Declaration of Human Rights, in Articles 22, 24, 25, 26, asserts a person's rights against his government to be provided with a variety of social services. G.A. Res. 217, U.N. Doc. A/810 at 71, 75, 76 (1948). The theory is quite applicable, however, to the relation between governments and persons belonging to other governments. On this view, the issue of the wealthier countries of the world feeding the starving ones is an issue of beneficence, not rights.

43. In suggesting that one may have a right to decline to do an act that we should criticize him for not doing, there is no inconsistency. As Professor R. Dworkin suggests, when we say a person has a right to do something (or not to do it), we imply that it would be wrong to require him to do it. But it is consistent to say that that which he has a

right to do (or not to do) in this sense is still not the right thing for him to do. Dworkin, *Taking Rights Seriously*, in Is LAW DEAD? 168, 174 (E. Rostow ed. 1975).

44. *See* S. KADISH & M. PAULSEN, CRIMINAL LAW AND ITS PROCESSES 85 (3d ed. 1975).

45. *Compare* J. HOSPERS, HUMAN CONDUCT 399–400 (1963):

"Some philosophers, such as Kant, have said that an individual human life is a thing not only of great value but of *infinite* value—that to preserve one human life it would be worthwhile not indeed to risk the collapse of civilization (for that would involve the loss of many lives), but to sacrifice for all mankind some convenience or source of happiness that would *not* involve the loss of life."

46. *See* Calabresi, *supra* note 35, at 388:

"Accident law indicates that our commitment to human life is not, in fact, so great as we say it is; that our commitment to life-destroying material progress and comfort is greater. But this fact merely accentuates our need to make a bow in the direction of our commitment to the sanctity of human life (whenever we can do so at a reasonable total cost). It also accentuates our need to reject any societal decisions that too blatantly contradict this commitment. Like 'free will,' it may be less important that this commitment be total than that we believe it to be there."

47. *See* Calabresi, *supra* note 35, at 391.

48. *E.g.*, Brody, *Abortion and the Sanctity of Life*, 10 AMER. PHIL. Q. 133 (1973); Finnis, *The Rights and Wrongs of Abortion: A Reply to Judith Thompson*, 2 PHIL. & PUB. AFFAIRS 117 (1973); 117 Foot, *supra* note 16; Thomson, *A Defense of Abortion*, 1 PHIL. & PUB. AFFAIRS 47 (1971).

49. In saying that the problem is revealed by scientific discoveries, I do not want it taken as agreeing with those who seem to suggest that the problem is answerable by such discoveries. *See, e.g.*, P. STEIN & J. SHAND, LEGAL VALUES IN WESTERN SOCIETY *171 n.36 (1974). Roe v. Wade, 410 U.S. 113, 220 (1973) (Douglas, J., concurring). Who is to be regarded as no longer a person for purposes of legal and moral judgment is hardly a scientific question. See generally* Wertheimer, *Understanding the Abortion Argument*, I PHIL. & PUB. AFFAIRS 67 (1971).

50. *See* WORKING PARTY, BOARD FOR SOCIAL RESPONSIBILITY, CHURCH OF ENGLAND, ON DYING WELL—AN ANGLICAN CONTRIBUTION TO THE DEBATE ON EUTHANASIA 58 (1975) (published by the Church Information Office). There the example is given of shooting a man trapped in a burning gun-turret. The Report comments: "Life is thereby shortened by only a matter of moments, and great agony of short duration is avoided or terminated. Can it be successfully argued that the evil asserted (great agony) is greater than the evil inflicted (death)?"

51. *See generally* Scarf, *The Anatomy of Fear*, N.Y. Times, June 16, 1974, at 10 (Magazine).

NOTES TO ESSAY 8

1. For a discussion of a current revival of scholarly interest in taking doctrine seriously, see Barnett, *Contract Scholarship and the Reemergence of Legal Philosophy* (Book Review), 97 HARV. L. REV. 1223 (1984) (reviewing E.A. FARNSWORTH, CONTRACTS (1982)).

2. O. W. HOLMES, *The Path of the Law*, in COLLECTED LEGAL PAPERS 167 (1920) (reprinting Holmes, *The Path of the Law*, 10 HARV. L. REV. 457 (1897)).

3. *Id.* at 170.

4. This also may not be enough, but it is always necessary, except in the instance of multiple independent and sufficient conditions. *See* 1 NATIONAL COMM'N ON REFORM OF FEDERAL CRIMINAL LAW, WORKING PAPERS 144–46 (1970); McLaughlin, *Proximate Cause*, 39 HARV. L. REV. 149, 153–54 (1925).

5. H.L.A. HART & A. HONORÉ, CAUSATION IN THE LAW (1959).

6. *Id.* at 296.

7. *Id.* at 296–303.

8. One of the significant contributions of Hart and Honoré's *Causation in the Law* is their identification and development of this distinction between causation of physical events and occurrences and causation of human actions ("interpersonal transactions" where "we have to deal with the concept of *reasons* for action rather than *causes* of events"). *Id.* at 48 (emphasis in original).

9. Professor Mackie took a different view that stresses the similarities in these two kinds of causal statements. J. MACKIE, THE CEMENT OF THE UNIVERSE 117 (1980). Whether or not Mackie is right, the premise that these modes of causation are significantly different is implicit in the structure of complicity and causation doctrine in the law, as much of this essay is designed to show.

10. *See* G. WILLIAMS, TEXTBOOK ON CRIMINAL LAW 390–93 (2d ed. 1983); *see also* Lewis v. Commonwealth, 19 Ky. 1139, 42 S.W. 1127 (1897); People v. Elder, 100 Mich. 515, 59 N.W. 237 (1894).

11. In *Causation in the Law*, Hart and Honoré express these basic ideas in the following language: A volitional action, they say, "has a special place in causal inquiries . . . because, when the question is how far back a cause shall be traced through a number of intervening causes, such a voluntary action very often is regarded both as a limit and also as still the cause even though other later abnormal occurrences are recognized as causes." H.L.A. HART & A. HONORÉ, *supra* note 5, at 39. Further, "A deliberate human act is therefore most often a barrier and a goal in tracing back causes in such inquiries: it is something *through* which we do not trace the cause of a later event and something *to* which we do trace the cause through intervening causes of other kinds." *Id.* at 41 (emphasis in original). And, "[t]he voluntary intervention of a second human agent . . . is a paradigm among those factors which preclude the assimilation in causal judgments of the first agent's connexion with the eventual harm to the case of simple direct manipulation." *Id.* at 69.

Hart and Honoré's conclusion that intervening volitional actions uniquely affect commonsense attributions of causal responsibility has been challenged. *See* J. FEINBERG, *Causing Voluntary Actions*, in DOING AND DESERVING 152 (1970). Feinberg argues that it is the highly unusual character of an intervening occurrence, whether a volitional action or a natural event, that is responsible for the conception of a superseding cause, and he offers some forceful counterexamples to the Hart and Honoré position. *Id.* at 166–67. But, as the argument in this essay attempts to show, the Hart and Honoré position serves as a powerful tool for understanding and accounting for the law of complicity and its relation to causation. Part of the difference between Feinberg and Hart and Honoré may be that Feinberg has chiefly in mind explanatory causal statements, while Hart and Honoré are solely concerned with statements that attribute causal responsibility. *Id.* at 181–84.

12. H.L.A. HART & A. HONORÉ, *supra* note 5, at 69.

13. I am putting to one side the exceptional cases of vicarious liability in which one is made to share in the liability of another without regard to the doctrine of complicity. These cases represent judgments of the social desirability of holding persons liable in particular situations notwithstanding the doctrinal principles that otherwise would govern. *See generally* Sayre, *Criminal Responsibility for the Acts of Another*, 43 HARV. L. REV. 689 (1930).

14. G. FLETCHER, RETHINKING CRIMINAL LAW 634–49 (1978).

15. United States v. Ruffin, 613 F.2d 408, 412 (2d Cir. 1979); *accord* Shuttlesworth v. Birmingham, 373 U.S. 262, 265 (1963) ("It is generally recognized that there can be no conviction for aiding and abetting someone to do an innocent act."); *see* cases cited in *Ruffin*, 613 F. 2d at 412; United States v. Jones, 425 F.2d 1048, 1056 (9th Cir.) ("[T]here must be a guilty principal before there can be an aider or abettor."), *cert. denied*, 400 U.S. 823 (1970); Surujpaul v. The Queen, [1958] 1 W.L.R. 1050; Morris v. Tolman, [1923] 1 K.B. 166; Cain v. Doyle, 72 C.L.R. 409 (Austl. 1946); 1 J. TURNER, RUSSELL ON CRIME 128 (12th ed. 1964) [hereinafter cited as RUSSELL ON CRIME]:

> "[W]hen the law relating to principals and accessories as such is under consideration there is only one crime, although there may be more than one person criminally liable in respect of it . . . There is one crime, and that it has been committed must be established before there can be any question of criminal guilt of participation in it."

See also Lanham, *Accomplices, Principals and Causation*, 12 MELB. U.L. REV. 490, 490 n.3 (1980).

16. Thornton v. Mitchell, [1940] 1 All E.R. 339, 341. I will consider later whether the conductor could be convicted as a principal under some other doctrinal alternative. See *infra* note 143 and accompanying text.

17. See W. LAFAVE & A. SCOTT, HANDBOOK ON CRIMINAL LAW 520–21 (1972); 1 C. TORCIA, WHARTON'S CRIMINAL LAW 186 (14th ed. 1978) [hereinafter cited as WHARTON'S CRIMINAL LAW].

18. It is otherwise, of course, when bigamy is statutorily extended to include an unmarried person who knowingly marries a person already married. *See, e.g.,* CAL. PENAL CODE § 284 (West 1984).

19. *See* Boggus v. State, 34 Ga. 275 (1866); *see also* State v. Warady, 78 N.J.L. 687, 76 A. 977 (1910).

20. *In re* Kantrowitz, 24 Cal. App. 203, 140 P. 1078 (1914); Cody v. State, 361 P.2d 307 (Okla. Crim. App. 1961). So also may a woman be guilty of rape as an accomplice to the rape of another woman by aiding a man to commit the crime, even in a jurisdiction where only a man can commit rape. People v. Reilly, 85 Misc. 2d 702, 709, 381 N.Y.S.2d 732, 739 (1976); WHARTON'S CRIMINAL LAW, *supra* note 17, at 188 & n.87.

21. *See* State v. Hayes, 105 Mo. 76, 16 S.W. 514 (1891), *overruled on other grounds by* State v. Barton, 142 Mo. 450, 44 S.W. 239 (1898); Topolewski v. State, 130 Wis. 244, 109 N.W. 1037 (1906); Regina v. Johnson & Jones, Car. & M. 218, 174 Eng. Rep. 479 (1841); Rex v. Eggington (1801), *reported in* 2 E. EAST, PLEAS OF THE CROWN 666 (1806); *see also Parties, Complicity and Liability for the Acts of Another*, in THE LAW COMM'N, WORKING PAPER NO. 43, at 11–13 (England 1972) (Proposition 3). Of course the helper could be held liable as a principal if any of his own actions constitutes the crime of burglary. Moreover, even in the situation supposed in the text, where this is not the case, there is the possibility of liability for attempt to be an accomplice. See *infra* text accompanying notes 82–84.

22. *See, e.g.,* United States v. Paszek, 432 F.2d 780 (9th Cir. 1970), *cert. denied*, 402 U.S. 911 (1971); G. WILLIAMS, CRIMINAL LAW, THE GENERAL PART 390 (2d ed. 1961) (discussing differing degrees of liability for primary and secondary parties).

23. People v. Blackwood, 35 Cal. App. 2d 728, 733, 96 P.2d 982, 985 (1939); Thomas v. State, 73 Fla. 115, 122, 74 So. 1, 3, (1917); Speer v. State, 52 Ga. App. 209, 209, 182 S.E. 824, 824 (1935); State v. Lord, 42 N.M. 638, 657–58, 84 P.2d 80, 96 (1938).

24. *See, e.g.,* Regina v. Richards, [1974] 1 Q.B. 776 (discussed *infra* at text accompanying notes 199–205); *see also* 4 W. BLACKSTONE, COMMENTARIES *36.

25. See *infra* text accompanying notes 186–205.

26. 4 W. BLACKSTONE, *supra* note 24, at *40.

27. *See* Standefer v. United States, 447 U.S. 10 (1980); Regina v. Humphreys & Turner, [1965] 3 All E.R. 689; G. WILLIAMS, *supra* note 22, at 407.

28. *See* MODEL PENAL CODE § 2.04(6) comment at 38 (Tent. Draft No. 1, 1953).

29. *Cf.* Farnsworth v. Zerbst, 98 F.2d 541 (5th Cir. 1938) (defendant may be liable despite acquittal of coconspirators on ground of diplomatic immunity).

30. *See* United States v. Azadian, 436 F.2d 81, 82–83 (9th Cir. 1971).

31. *Id.* at 83 (quoting Carbajal-Portillo v. United States, 396 F.2d 944, 948 (9th Cir. 1968)).

32. See *infra* text accompanying notes 125 et seq.

33. See *infra* text accompanying notes 187–98.

34. See *infra* text accompanying notes 170–76.

35. H.L.A. HART & A. HONORE, *supra* note 5, at 338.

36. *See e.g.*, State v. Weis, 92 Ariz. 254, 375 P.2d 735 (1962) (both defendants guilty as principals where one defendant wrote bad check and other defendant, with knowledge of its falsity, used the check to buy merchandise at a shop), *cert. denied*, 389 U.S. 899 (1967); Regina v. Kelly & M'Carthy, 2 Car. & K. 379, 175 Eng. Rep. 157 (1847) (where one defendant took victim's property and hid it on the other defendant's tram, and where the other defendant then took away that property, both defendants were principals in larceny); Cornwall's Case, 2 Strange 881, 93 Eng. Rep. 914 (1730) (servant who let thief into his master's house found guilty of burglary); *cf.* the restatement of the English law proposed by the Criminal Code Commissions, which makes everyone a party to and guilty of an indictable offense who "[a]ctually commits the offence, or does . . . any act the doing . . . of which forms part of the offence." 2 J. STEPHEN, A HISTORY OF THE CRIMINAL LAW OF ENGLAND 236 (1883).

This concept of coprincipal liability is not harmonious with the distinction between direct and derivative liability. Where a person commits only some of the actus reus himself, his liability for the crime must rest in part on the conduct of another. His liability, therefore, cannot be fully direct but must be, at least in part, derivative. As a matter of doctrinal consistency holding him as a principal just because he commits some of the actus reus would not appear sufficient. It may perhaps be regarded as an exceptional case. One can readily see the need for the exception in the case where neither actor commits the crime but together they do, as in the hypothetical of one holding the gun and the other stealing the victim's wallet. It is the same need that leads to dispensing with proof of a but-for relationship for causation in the cases of multiple sufficient conditions.

37. The help may take the form of a failure to intervene where the circumstances are such that the failure to act constitutes a kind of assistance. The principal circumstance of this kind is that in which the secondary party has legal authority to control the actions of the principal. *See, e.g.*, Moreland v. State, 164 Ga. 467, 139 S.E. 77 (1927) (defendant held liable as accomplice for manslaughter when his driver, while driving in defendant's own car, killed someone by driving recklessly); Tuck v. Robson, [1970] 1 W.L.R. 741 (licensee who knew that alcoholic drink was being consumed on his premises after hours in violation of law and made no effort to eject the offending customers or revoke their license to remain on his premises held guilty of aiding and abetting the customer's offense); Du Cros v. Lambourne [1907] 1 K.B. 40 (same as *Moreland*); Lanham, *Drivers, Control and Accomplices*, 1982 CRIM. L. REV. 419. As these cases show, allowing a driver to drive recklessly becomes equivalent to giving him the car to drive in this way. *See, e.g.*, Story v. United States, 16 F.2d 342, 344 (D.C. Cir. 1926) (owner of a car who knowingly permitted a drunken person to take the wheel held liable for aiding and abetting his criminal negligence; the owner permitted him "without protest so recklessly and negligently to operate the car as to cause the death of another"). The failure to stop the driver could equally well be seen as an implied approval and encouragement. MODEL PENAL CODE § 2.04(3) comment at 33 n.39 (Tent. Draft No. 1, 1953) ("But silence may in special situations be an expression of approval and encouragement."); *see also* G. WILLIAMS, *supra* note 10, at 348. Failure to act may also ground liability as an accomplice when a person with a duty to intervene fails to do so in order to permit the crime to succeed. Burkhardt v. United States, 13 F.2d 841, 842 (6th Cir. 1926) (sheriff who failed to prevent illegal liquor traffic found innocent of complicity only because he lacked intent to aid); Mobley v. State, 227 Ind. 335, 85 N.E.2d 489 (1949) (mother failed to intervene to stop her lover from beating her three-year-old baby to death); State v. Walden, 306 N.C. 466, 293 S.E.2d 780 (1982) (mother failed to prevent son's assault on baby brother).

38. At common law a person assisting in the execution was a principal in the second degree, while a person assisting in the preparation was an accessory before the fact. The common law expressed these ideas by defining a principal in the second degree as one who gives assistance to the principal in the first degree at the time and place of the crime (actually or constructively), and by defining as an accessory one who otherwise gives assistance.

39. *See* State *ex rel.* Attorney Gen. v. Tally, 102 Ala. 25, 15 So. 722 (1894); Commonwealth v. Kern, 1 Brewst. 350, 351 (Penn. 1867); THE LAW COMM'N, *supra* note 21, at 35

(Proposition 6(3)(a)); Attorney-General's Reference (No. 1 of 1975), [1975] 3 W.L.R. 11.

40. *See, e.g.,* Hicks v. United States, 150 U.S. 442, 449 (1893).

41. *Cf.* People v. Tewksbury, 15 Cal. 3d 953, 960, 544 P.2d 1335, 1340–41, 127 Cal. Rptr. 135, 140–41 (holding that a woman whose actions aided defendant to commit a robbery was not his accomplice unless she acted with intent to aid him), *appeal dismissed, cert. denied,* 429 U.S. 805 (1976). The court stated:

> "Although it is undisputed that [the witness] aided [the defendant] by calling the restaurant, by supplying [the defendant's girlfriend] with pencil and paper [on which to draw a diagram of the restaurant that was robbed], and by driving some of the principals to a point of rendezvous in the vicinity of the crimes, such actions do not confer upon her accomplice status unless she also acted with the requisite guilty intent."

Id. at 960, 544 P.2d at 1341, 127 Cal. Rptr. at 141; *see also* State v. Corcoran, 7 Idaho 220, 244 61 P. 1034, 1042 (1900); State v. Ankrom, 86 W. Va. 570, 574, 103 S.E. 925, 927 (1920).

42. G. WILLIAMS, *supra* note 22, at 365; *cf.* H.L.A. HART & A. HONORE, *supra* note 5, at 339–44.

43. *See, e.g.,* People v. Beeman, 35 Cal. 3d 547, 674 P.2d 1318, 199 Cal. Rptr. 60 (1984). A widely accepted formulation of the intent requirement is that of Judge Learned Hand in United States v. Peoni, 100 F.2d 401, 402 (2d Cir., 1938):

> "[D]efinitions [of aiding and abetting] have nothing whatever to do with the probability that the forbidden result would follow upon the accessory's conduct; . . . they all demand that he in some sort associate himself with the venture, that he participate in it as in something that he wishes to bring about, that he seek by his action to make it succeed."

A rival formulation of the intent requirement would make knowing aid or inducement sufficient, with no requirement of purposive action. *See* Backun v. United States, 112 F.2d 635, 637 (4th Cir. 1940); *see also* MODEL PENAL CODE § 2.04(3) comment at 27–32 (Tent. Draft No. 1, 1953).

44. *See infra* Part III, Section C.

45. *See* Wade v. State, 174 Tenn. 248, 250–51, 124 S.W.2d 710, 711 (1939):

> "Involuntary manslaughter necessarily negatives, of course, any intent on the part of the accused to kill another, but does not negative an intent to do the unlawful act, or the act not strictly unlawful in itself, but done in an unlawful manner and without due caution. Hence, one may be an aider and abettor in involuntary manslaughter because of a common purpose to participate in the unlawful act the natural and probable result of which was to kill another."

See also State v. DiLorenzo, 138 Conn. 281, 286, 83 A.2d 479, 481 (1951); State v. McVay, 47 R.I. 292, 298, 132 A. 436, 438–39 (1926); Eager v. State, 205 Tenn. 156, 168–69, 325 S.W.2d 815, 821 (1959).

46. State v. McVay, 47 R.I. 292, 298, 132 A. 436, 438–39 (1926).

47. The Model Penal Code expresses this conclusion in an explicit provision:

> "When causing a particular result is an element of an offense, an accomplice in the conduct causing such a result is an accomplice in the commission of that offense, if he acts with the kind of culpability, if any, with respect to that result that is sufficient for the commission of the offense."

MODEL PENAL CODE § 2.06(4) (Proposed Official Draft 1962).

48. It would follow from this treatment of accomplices to involuntary manslaughter that a person could also be an accomplice to a crime of strict liability. When he intentionally influences or assists the principal to do the very act that makes the principal liable, his action is indistinguishable from that of an accomplice to involuntary manslaughter. Logically, it is irrelevant whether the principal's liability is based on recklessness, negligence or strict liability. By intentionally participating in the principal's act, with the same culpability (or lack of it) as the principal, he has subjected himself to liability

for whatever crime the principal commits by that act *Cf.* Regina v. Creamer, [1965] 3 W.L.R. 583. Nonetheless, probably as a consequence of hostility to the policy of strict liability, some courts have held otherwise. *See, e.g.,* Gardner v. Akeroyd, [1952] 2 Q.B. 743; Ferguson v. Weaving, [1951] 1 K.B. 814; Johnson v. Youden, [1950] 1 K.B. 544; *see also* W. LaFave & A. Scott, *supra* note 17, at 512; G. Williams, *supra* note 22, at 394–96.

49. *Cf.* Attorney-General's Reference (No. 1 of 1975), [1975] 3 W.L.R. 11.

50. This was the situation in People v. Marshall, 362 Mich. 170, 106 N.W.2d 842 (1961). The court reversed the car owner's conviction of manslaughter, stating:

> "In the case before us death resulted from the misconduct of [the] driver. The accountability of the owner must rest as a matter of general principle, upon his complicity in such misconduct. . . . Upon these facts he cannot be held . . . with respect to the fatal accident: the killing of [the deceased] was not counseled by him, accomplished by another acting jointly with him, nor did it occur in the attempted achievement of some common enterprise."

Id. at 173, 106 N.W.2d at 844. The court rejected the theory of the prosecution because it would make the liability of the owner for manslaughter "depend upon whatever unlawful act the driver commits while in the car" *Id.* at 174, 106 N.W.2d at 844.

Courts have imposed liability where the owner was riding in the car when the inebriated driver committed the reckless acts that caused death. *See, e.g.,* Story v. United States, 16 F.2d 342 (D.C. Cir. 1926), *cert. denied,* 274 U.S. 739 (1927); Freeman v. State, 211 Tenn. 27, 362 S.W.2d 251 (1962); Annot., 95 A.L.R.2d 175, 191–96 (1964). But in these cases, the owner's failure to intervene could perhaps be construed as an encouragement of the driver's reckless actions, as the court in *People v. Marshall* appeared to suggest. Noting the court's observation in *Story* that the owner sat by the driver's side and permitted him "without protest so recklessly and negligently to operate the car as to cause the death of another," *Story,* 16 F.2d at 344, the court in *Marshall* stated: "If defendant Marshall had been by [the driver's] side an entirely different case would be presented, but on the facts before us Marshall . . . was at home in bed." 362 Mich. at 172, 106 N.W.2d at 843. Query where the owner was neither beside the driver nor at home, but following in another car. Stacy v. State, 228 Ark. 260, 263–64, 306 S.W.2d 852, 854 (1957) (owner could be liable for manslaughter). (The other issue raised by these cases—that failure to act may be encouragement— is considered *supra* in note 37.)

Cases raising comparable issues are those in which a road race participant is charged with manslaughter arising out of the reckless driving of his competitor. These are usually seen as raising a causation question, and are discussed *infra* at text accompanying notes 231–60. However, to the extent that the reckless act of the competing driver which caused the death was simply his excessive speed, complicity liability is plausible on the view that his speeding was precisely the act the defendant encouraged. *See* Stallard v. State, 209 Tenn. 13, 348 S.W.2d 489 (1961) (starter of race and first racer held guilty as accomplices where second racer collided with deceased); Regina v. Swindall & Osborne, 2 Car. & K. 230, 175 Eng. Rep. 95 (1846).

51. Technically, the accomplice can never satisfy the mens rea of the crime, which requires that the one doing the prohibited acts do so with a certain mens rea. More precisely, therefore, one should perhaps formulate the requirement as being that the accomplice should act with an "equivalent" mens rea.

52. This is subject, of course, to the inevitable looseness in characterizing the precise scope of the intended acts. *See infra* text accompanying notes 56–59.

53. *Cf.* G. Williams, *supra* note 10, at 359–60 (discussing Regina v. Salmon, 6 Q.B.D. 79 (1880)).

54. People v. McKeighan, 205 Mich. 367, 171 N.W. 500 (1919); Rex v. Hawkins, 3 Car. & P. 392, 172 Eng. Rep. 470 (1828); *see also* 1 Wharton's Criminal Law, *supra* note 17, at 181.

55. *See* 1 Russell on Crime, *supra* note 15, at 161. He could, of course, be held for soliciting the crime he intended the primary actor to commit.

56. *See* Regina v. Anderson & Morris, [1966] 2 Q.B. 110, where the court held in this situation that the secondary party could not be convicted of manslaughter. *See also* Davies v. Director of Pub. Prosecutions, 1954 A.C. 378, 401.

57. *See, e.g.*, Regina v. Bainbridge, [1959] 3 W.L.R. 656, 659; Regina v. Bullock, [1955] 1 W.L.R. 1, 5.

58. Director of Pub. Prosecutions v. Maxwell, [1978] 1 W.L.R. 1350.

59. *But see* Buxton, *Complicity and the Law Commission,* 1973 CRIM. L. REV. 223, 228.

60. *See* Williams v. United States, 308 F.2d 664 (9th Cir. 1962); Benchwick v. United States, 297 F.2d 330 (9th Cir. 1961); McGhee v. Commonwealth, 221 Va. 422, 270 S.E.2d 729 (1980); G. WILLIAMS, *supra* note 10, at 356; Sayre, *supra* note 13, at 702–03, 703 n.55; *see also* 1 RUSSELL ON CRIME, *supra* note 15, at 161; *cf.* M. FOSTER, CROWN LAW 369 (3d ed. London 1792) (1st. ed. Oxford 1762).

61. *See* MODEL PENAL CODE § 2.04(3) comment at 24 (Tent. Draft No. 1, 1953).

62. *See, e.g.*, State v. Kennedy, 85 S.C. 146, 149, 67 S.E. 152, 154 (1910); *cf.* G. WILLIAMS, *supra* note 10, at 357–58. But the result is otherwise, as we shall see, if the principal intentionally chooses a different victim. *See infra* notes 116–19 and accompanying text.

63. *See* W. LaFAVE & A. SCOTT, *supra* note 17, at 252–55. *See generally* Ashworth, *Transferred Malice and Punishment for Unforeseen Consequences,* in RESHAPING THE CRIMINAL LAW 77 (P. Glazebrook ed. 1978).

64. G. WILLIAMS, *supra* note 22, at 402; Sayre, *supra* note 13, at 699–706.

65. J. STEPHEN, A DIGEST OF THE CRIMINAL LAW art. 20 (9th ed. 1950). This apparently formed the model for § 22(2) of the Canadian Criminal Code:

> Every one who counsels or procures another person to be a party to an offence is a party to every offence that the other commits in consequence of the counseling or procuring that the person who counselled or procured knew or ought to have known was likely to be committed in consequence of the counseling or procuring.

CAN. REV. STAT. ch. C-34, § 22(2) (1970).

66. This is the ground on which it has attracted its chief criticism. *See* MODEL PENAL CODE § 2.04(3) comment at 26 (Tent. Draft No. 1, 1953); W. LaFAVE & A SCOTT, *supra* note 17, at 515–17; G. WILLIAMS, *supra* note 22, at 402–03.

67. *Cf.* People v. Michalow, 229 N.Y. 325, 128 N.E. 228 (1920).

68. A natural and probable consequence rule is also applied in distinguishable situations. In the examples we have been considering, the issue is the secondary party's liability for the primary party's unintended acts and their consequences, where those acts were the natural and probable consequence of the criminal actions the secondary party intended the principal to commit. For example, in Regina v. Radalyski, 24 Vict. L.R. 687 (Austl. 1899), the issue was the liability of the accomplice to an abortion for the death of the woman caused by the action of the principal in covering the woman's mouth to stifle her screams. This differs from situations in which the issue is the liability of a person for unintended acts (and their consequences) committed by a second person, not in any sense a party to the first person's intended crime, which were the natural and probable consequences of the first person's criminal actions. An example is the case of the policeman who accidentally kills a bystander in seeking to prevent armed robbery by the defendant. These situations, properly conceived, raise problems for causation, not complicity liability. *See infra* text accompanying notes 207–31.

69. *See* KAN. STAT. ANN. § 21–3205(2) (1981); ME. REV. STAT. ANN. tit. 17-A, § 57(3)(A) (1983) ("A person is an accomplice . . . to any crime the commission of which was a reasonably foreseeable consequence of his conduct."); MINN. STAT. ANN. § 609.05(2) (West 1964); WIS. STAT. ANN. § 939.05(2)(c) (West 1982).

70. *See infra* Part III, Section C.

71. *See supra* note 43.

72. *See* G. WILLIAMS, *supra* note 22, at 368–69.

73. MODEL PENAL CODE § 2.04 comment at 27–32 (Tent. Draft No. 1, 1953).

74. *See infra* Part III, Section C.1.

75. *See* W. SEAVEY, STUDIES IN AGENCY 70 (1949).

76. *See* RESTATEMENT (SECOND) OF AGENCY §§ 7–8 (1958).

77. *See generally* W. SEAVEY, *supra* note 75, at 32–34.

78. *See infra* Part III, Section C.

79. Whether this is more suitably accomplished by a causation analysis is considered *infra* in Part III, Section C.

80. This does not mean that the principal must himself succeed in achieving his criminal objective. He must, of course, violate the criminal law, since that is the basis of the criminal liability of the accomplice. But the principal's crime may be an attempt to commit a crime, since attempt is itself a crime, though an inchoate one. *See, e.g.,* United States v. Johnson, 319 U.S. 503, 515 (1943) (conviction for aiding and abetting attempt to evade income tax); United States v. Phillips, 664 F.2d 971, 1036–37 (5th Cir. 1981) (conviction for aiding and abetting attempt to import marijuana), *cert. denied,* 457 U.S. 1136 (1982); People v. Berger, 131 Cal. App. 2d 127, 280 P.2d 136 (1955) defendant convicted of attempting to attempt an abortion). Some recent codes explicitly so provide. *See, e.g.,* FLA. STAT. ANN. § 777.011 (West 1976); TENN. CODE ANN. § 39-1-303 (1982). *See generally* Smith, *Secondary Participation and Inchoate Offences,* in CRIME, PROOF AND PUNISHMENT: ESSAYS IN MEMORY OF SIR RUPERT CROSS 21, 26–27 (C. Tapper ed. 1981).

81. As J. Stephen summarized the law in *A Digest of the Criminal Law*: "Article 18. . . . An accessory before the fact is one who directly or indirectly counsels, procures, or commands any person to commit any felony . . . *which is committed in consequence of* such counseling, procuring or commandment." J. STEPHEN, *supra* note 65, at 18 (footnotes omitted) (emphasis added).

82. Compare the suggestion of "a general offence of aiding or encouraging crime, . . . whether or not [the] principal crime is in fact committed." Buxton, *supra* note 59, at 227; *see also* Buxton, *Complicity in the Criminal Code,* 85 LAW Q. REV. 252, 268 (1969).

83. MODEL PENAL CODE § 2.06(3)(a) (Proposed Official Draft 1962). Some statutes following the Model Penal Code in this respect include: HAWAII REV. STAT. § 705–501(1) (1976); KY. REV. STAT. ANN. § 502.020 (Michie 1985); N.J. STAT. ANN. § 2c:2-6c (West 1982); OR. REV. STAT. § 161.155 (1983); PA. CONS. STAT. ANN tit. 18, § 306(c) (Purdon 1983); TEX. PENAL CODE ANN. § 7.02 (Vernon 1974). The law is apparently otherwise in England, *see* Smith, *supra* note 80, at 32–34, 38, and most American jurisdictions.

84. Of course, the effort to induce another to commit a crime, successful or not, itself constitutes the separate inchoate crime of incitement.

85. G. FLETCHER, *supra* note 14, at 677.

86. 102 Ala. 25, 15 So. 722 (1894).

87. *Id.* at 69, 15 So. at 738–39.

88. [1951] 1 All E.R. 464.

89. *Id.* at 466.

90. *See also* United States v. Garguilo, 310 F.2d 249, 253 (2d Cir. 1962). On a proper instruction as to purpose, the court was prepared to grant that a person whose only role was to carry the photographic negatives for the principal counterfeiter could be found to be an accessory, stating that "evidence of an act of relatively slight moment may warrant a jury's finding participation in a crime." *Cf.* Commonwealth v. Soares, 377 Mass. 461, 471–72, 387 N.E.2d 499, 507 (1978), *cert. denied,* 444 U.S. 881 (1979) (defendant who gave no assistance to the principal but who stood ready to do so with the knowledge of the principal may be found guilty as an accomplice, if his readiness to give aid may have encouraged the actor); Commonwealth v. Pierce, 437 Pa. 266, 268, 263 A.2d 350, 351 (1970) ("[G]uilt or innocence of the abettor . . . is not deter-

mined by the quantum of his advice or encouragement.") (quoting Perkins, *Parties to Crime*, 89 U. PA. L. REV. 581, 598 (1941)'; Judgment of May 10, 1883, 8 RGSt 267 (W. Ger.) (discussed in G. FLETCHER, *supra* note 14, at 677–78) (defendant who lent friend a smock so as not to dirty his clothes while administering a beating held as an accomplice in the beating); *see also* Weston v. Commonwealth, 111 Pa. 251, 2 A. 191 (1885). It is sometimes held that the actions of the secondary party must be proven to have encouraged the principal. *See* State v. Birchfield, 235 N.C. 410, 414, 70 S.E.2d 5, 7–8 (1952); McGhee v. Commonwealth, 221 Va. 422, 270 S.E.2d 729 (1980). But what is meant, quite plainly, is not that the prosecution must prove the encouragement to have been a but-for condition of the principal's action, but only that the secondary party's actions were encouraging, so that they might have had this effect.

91. *Cf.* G. WILLIAMS, *supra* note 22, at 382.

92. *See* State v. Hoffman, 199 N.C. 328, 333, 154 S.E. 314, 316 (1930) ("Mere presence, even with the intention of assisting in the commission of a crime, cannot be said to have incited, encouraged, or aided the perpetrator thereof, unless the intention to assist was in some way communicated to [the principal]. . . ."); *see also* Hicks v. United States, 150 U.S. 442, 449–50 (1893); State v. Birchfield, 235 N.C. 410, 414, 70 S.E.2d 5, 7–8 (1952).

93. *See* MODEL PENAL CODE § 5.02(2) (Proposed Official Draft 1962): "It is immaterial . . . that the actor fails to communicate with the person he solicits to commit a crime if his conduct was designed to effect such communication."

94. *See* State v. Tazwell, 30 La. Ann. 884 (1878) (though the burglar did not use the tools given by another, the other would be liable as an accomplice in virtue of the encouragement and support provided by the proffer of aid); *see also* cases cited *supra* in note 92; *cf.* Judgment of April 20, 1882, 6 RGSt. 169 (W. Ger.) (discussed in G. FLETCHER, *supra* note 14, at 677–78). In the Judgment of April 20, 1882, the secondary actor gave the principal a key with which to enter a cellar to steal. Though the key did not work and the principal had to break in by other means, the secondary actor was held to be an accessory to the theft because the aid could have strengthened the principal's resolve.

95. *See* Commonwealth v. Haines, 147 Pa. Super. 165, 169–70, 24 A.2d 85, 87 (1942); West v. Commonwealth, 156 Va. 975, 979, 157 S.E. 538, 539–40 (1931).

96. Unless one were to argue that a proper description of the result is "the death of the victim, Tally having instructed the operator not to send the telegram," just as the proper description in the burglary hypothetical in the preceding paragraph is "the principal's entry, using the jimmy supplied by the secondary party." However, while the latter description is apt, the former lacks conviction, since the use of the jimmy and the entry are connected in a way that the message and the death are not.

97. *See* G. WILLIAMS, *supra* note 22, at 359: "[I]t is enough that the accused has facilitated the crime, even though it would probably have been committed without his assistance." *See* State v. Tally, 102 Ala. 25, 15 So. 722 (1894); Wilcox v. Jeffery, [1951] 1 All E.R. 464; *see also supra* note 90.

98. *See* Commonwealth v. Soares, 377 Mass. 461, 471–72, 387 N.E.2d 499, 507 (1978), *cert. denied*, 444 U.S. 881 (1979); State v. Jarrell, 141 N.C. 722, 725, 53 S.E. 127, 128 (1906).

99. *See* Judgment of May 10, 1883, 8 RGSt 267 (W. Ger.), discussed *supra* in note 90.

100. *See* Note, *Developments in the Law of Criminal Conspiracy*, 72 HARV. L. REV. 920, 999 (1959).

101. *See* Interstate Circuit, Inc. v. United States, 306 U.S. 208 (1939); United States v. Bruno, 105 F.2d 921 (2d Cir.), *rev'd on other grounds*, 308 U.S. 287 (1939); Anderson v. Superior Court, 78 Cal. App. 2d 22, 177 P.2d 315 (1947); Johnson, *The Unnecessary Crime of Conspiracy*, 61 CALIF. L. REV. 1137, 1146–50 (1973); Note, *supra* note 100, at 933–35.

102. 328 U.S. 640 (1946).

103. *Id.* at 647.

104. *See* text Part II. Section *A.; cf.* G. WILLIAMS, *supra* note 10, at 294 ("As a matter of common sense, a person who gives very minor assistance ought not to be held as an

accessory.") "Substantial" assistance or encouragement is required in tort law to make one person civilly liable for the tortious wrong of another, RESTATEMENT (SECOND) OF TORTS § 876(b) (1979). A similar requirement has been developed by courts for the imposition of civil liability on a person for assisting another to commit a fraud under § 10b of the Securities Exchange Act. *See* Note, *Liability for Aiding and Abetting Violations of Rule 10b-5: The Recklessness Standard in Civil Damage Awards*, 62 TEX. L. REV. 1087, 1092 (1984). The Model Penal Code also proposed requiring substantial aid where the secondary party knew of the primary party's intention to commit a crime, but had no purpose to further it. *See* MODEL PENAL CODE § 2.04(3)(b) (Tent. Draft No. 1, 1953). The proposal was subsequently withdrawn when the decision was made to require purposive aid in all cases. *Cf.* MODEL PENAL CODE § 2.06(3)(a) (Proposed Official Draft 1962).

Perhaps the one case in which a substantiality requirement would be problematic is that in which the contribution consists of the massing of small actions of many persons, where each person alone could not be regarded as making a substantial difference. So, for example, in Wilcox v. Jeffery, [1951] 1 All E.R. 464, discussed *supra* in text accompanying note 88, the encouragement derived from the presence and expressed approval of an audience of many. These cases resemble those involving multiple sets of sufficient conditions in causation.

105. *Cf.* German and Soviet law, discussed in G. FLETCHER, *supra* note 14, at 636. Compare the lesser crime of criminal facilitation in the New York Penal Law for cases where the secondary party renders aid believing it is probable, but not intending, that the principal will commit a crime. N.Y. PENAL LAW §§ 115.00, 115.01, 115.05, 115.08 (McKinney Supp. 1984).

106. State v. Tally, 102 Ala. 25, 15 So. 722 (1894); *see supra* text accompanying note 86.

107. 3 J. STEPHEN, *supra* note 36, at 8.

108. *See* H.L.A. HART & A. HONORÉ, *supra* note 5, at 339–40.

109. Consider the hypothetical put by Professor Greenawalt in another connection: "A knows that his neighbor B is an important figure in organized crime, but A conceals his knowledge of this fact from B. Wishing that C, one of B's employees, might be killed, A lets the fact that C is a police informer 'slip out' in a conversation with B." Greenwalt, *Speech and Crime*, 1980 AM. B. FOUND. RESEARCH J. 645, 662.

110. The Model Penal Code originally proposed to deal with the Othello case by including among the ways of influencing another (commanding, requesting, encouraging) the provoking of another to commit a crime. MODEL PENAL CODE § 2.04(3)(a)(1) (Tent. Draft No. 1, 1953); *id.* § 2.06(3)(a)(1) (Tent. Draft No. 4, 1955). A suggestion was made from the floor of an annual meeting that "induce" would do the job better than "provoke." *See* AMERICAN LAW INSTITUTE, 1953 ANNUAL MEETING, TRANSCRIPT 164 (1953) (mimeograph). On subsequent reconsideration neither term was used in the final draft, apparently on the view that the term "encourage" sufficed. The revised commentaries support this reading:

> "Encouragement also covers forms of communication designed to lead the recipient to act criminally, even if the message is not as direct as a command or request. Whether one can "encourage" without communicating a desire that a crime be committed may be more arguable, but the term is probably broad enough to cover such cases as well if a criminal purpose exists."

2 MODEL PENAL CODE AND COMMENTARIES pt. I, § 5.02 comment at 372 (1985). It appears from this, as well as the hypothetical used to illustrate these observations, that liability is contemplated even where the defendant speaks only the truth, so long as his criminal purpose is proven. *Id.*

111. *See infra* Part III, Section B.

112. *Cf.* MODEL PENAL CODE § 2.03(2)(b), (3)(b) (Proposed Official Draft 1962) (excluding a result if it is "too remote or accidental in its occurrence to have a [just] bearing on the actor's liability or on the gravity of his offense").

113. *But see* Sayre, *supra* note 13, where they are analyzed in terms of proximate cause.

114. *See supra* notes 54–55 and accompanying text.

115. [1966] 2 Q.B. 110.

116. *Id.* at 120.

117. *See supra* notes 61–63 and accompanying text.

118. *See* State v. Lucas, 55 Iowa 321, 323, 7 N.W. 583, 584 (1880) (defendant who undertook to aid theft from a company's safe was held not to be liable for the intentional robbing of its watchman by his confederates); *see also* State v. Craft, 338 Mo. 831, 839–42, 92 S.W.2d 626, 630–31 (1936); WHARTON'S CRIMINAL LAW 143 (7th ed. 1874):

> "[I]f the access[o]ry order[s] or advise[s] . . . the principal . . . to commit a crime against A., [and] instead of so doing he commit[s] the same crime against B., the access[o]ry will not be answerable; . . . but if the principal commit[s] the same offen[s]e against B. by mistake, instead of A., it seems it would be otherwise."

119. The old and much discussed English case of The Queen v. Saunders & Archer, 75 Eng. Rep. 706 (1575), can be construed as another instance of the volitional act of the principal departing from the plan serving to preclude liability in the second party. Saunders, at the urging of Archer, gave a poisoned apple to Saunders' wife with intent to kill her. When she unexpectedly gave the apple to her child in Saunders' presence, he took no action to stop the child from eating it, and the child died. The court's holding that Archer was not guilty as an accessory can be explained as a product of the court's view that Saunders' deliberate inaction in permitting the plan to miscarry in this way was equivalent to a deliberate action to kill the child, a volitional act to change the crime intended that precluded holding Archer as an accomplice. *See* H.L.A. HART & A. HONORÉ, *supra* note 5, at 343 ("The act of the principal in not revealing the fact that the apple was poisoned when he became aware of the changed situation amounted to a new independent decision relieving the instigator of liability."); G. WILLIAMS, *supra* note 10, at 358.

120. In cases where *A* incites *B* to incite *C* to commit a crime, courts typically impose liability on *A* (as well as, of course, on *B*). *E.g.*, State v. Davis, 319 Mo. 1222, 6 S.W.2d 609 (1928). The situation is quite distinguishable from the hypothetical, however, because the contribution takes precisely the form that *A* intended and is not marked by the occurrence of anything accidental or abnormal. In one unusual case of this kind, the court nevertheless denied liability of the first inciter on the ground of remoteness. *See* Regina v. Bodin & Bodin, 1979 Crim. L. Rev. 176. The concept was correct, though it was not properly applicable in this case.

121. *See supra* text accompanying notes 31–34.

122. *See supra* text accompanying notes 24–25.

123. *See supra* text accompanying notes 54 et seq.

124. *See supra* Part II, Section A.

125. H.L.A. HART & A. HONORÉ, *supra* note 5, at 134–50, 296–313 & *passim*.

126. However, cases of intended justified responses are theoretically possible. *See* S. KADISH, S. SCHULHOFER & M. PAULSEN, CRIMINAL LAW AND ITS PROCESSES 499 (4th ed. 1983):

> "Suppose two felons are holed up in a house and engaged in a gun battle with police officers surrounding the house. Felon *A* tells felon *B* to run out the back door where, he says, the coast is clear. He says this because he wants felon *B* dead and he knows the police have the back door well covered. As felon *B* dashes out, gun in hand, he is shot dead by police."

Consider also the case of a key witness who gives perjured testimony in a successful effort to secure the conviction and execution of an innocent person. *See* H.L.A. HART & A. HONORÉ, *supra* note 5, at 325; G. WILLIAMS, *supra* note 22, at 350.

127. 1 E. EAST, A TREATISE OF THE PLEAS OF THE CROWN 228 (Philadelphia 1806).

128. 1 RUSSELL ON CRIME, *supra* note 15, at 129.

129. The Queen v. Manley, 1 Cox Crim. Cas. 104 (1844) (dictum).

130. M. FOSTER, *supra* note 60, at 349; J. KELYNG, PLEAS OF THE CROWN 52–53 (2d ed. London 1739) (1st ed. London 1708); J. SMITH & B. HOGAN, CRIMINAL LAW 119–20 (5th ed. 1983).

131. United States v. Kenofsky, 243 U.S. 440 (1917); Glenn v. United States, 303 F. 2d 536, 541 (5th Cir. 1962).

132. A person may intentionally cause the action of another even where the action is not innocent, so long as it is less than fully volitional, as when the "accused makes use of threats, lies, or authority to induce the second actor to act in a particular way." H.L.A. HART & A. HONORÉ, *supra* note 5, at 327. This proposition is exhibited in decisions interpreting a variety of statutory offenses prohibiting a person from "causing" something to be done by another. They are reviewed in *id.* at 326–33; and in J.L.J. EDWARDS, MENS REA AND STATUTORY OFFENSES (1955).

133. *See supra* text accompanying notes 11–12. It is not clear how faithful courts would be to the metaphor of a person as manipulated instrumentality. Fidelity to that image would require the prosecution to establish the defendant's action as a but-for cause of the other person's conduct. In many cases this may not be possible. Consider, for example, a defendant who urges a mentally incompetent person to continue his assault on another. If he does so, could it be established that but for the urging he would not have continued to beat his victim? It would not seem so any more where the assaulter is incompetent than when he is competent. If the assaulter were competent, allowing complicity doctrine to operate, the difficulty is overcome, as we saw, by requiring only that the urger's action could have made a difference. But if the direct causation mode of liability is employed, on the footing that the assaulter is an instrumentally of the urger, there can be no liability without establishing that the urging was a but-for condition of the assaulter continuing his assault.

134. *See supra* note 21 and accompanying text.

135. G. WILLIAMS, *supra* note 10, at 372–73; *see also* THE LAW COMM'N, *supra* note 21, at 17: "[I]t would seem unreal to saddle the defendant with the acts of the innocent agent when the agent acts solely for the sake of frustrating him."

136. *See* the cases collected in the MODEL PENAL CODE comment at 15 n.5 (Tent. Draft No. 1, 1953).

137. This is true as well for attempts to commit result crimes, since if one can cause the result by using a person as an instrumentality, it follows that one can attempt to cause the result by that means.

138. 1 M. HALE, PLEAS OF THE CROWN 555–56 (1778 ed.).

139. Regina v. Flatman, 14 Cox Crim. Cas. 396 (1880).

140. Regina v. Butcher, 169 Eng. Rep. 1145 (1858).

141. Regina v. Clifford, 2 Car. & K. 202, 175 Eng. Rep. 84 (1845). For other cases, see G. WILLIAMS, *supra* note 22, at 351 n.5.

142. *See* J. SMITH & B. HOGAN, *supra* note 130, at 113; G. WILLIAMS, *supra* note 22, at 351.

143. Other examples could be put. *See* Regina v. Cogan & Leak, 1975 CRIM. L. REV. 584, 586 (commentary):

> "A, a constable on duty, induces B, the holder of a justice's license to sell him liquor by falsely representing that he is not on duty. B. is not guilty if he reasonably believes A is off duty. A is incapable of being the principal offender, not only because he is not the holder of a justice's license, but also because he cannot sell to himself. Again, suppose that A "refreshes B's memory" falsely, intending that B shall give false evidence on oath and B does so. B cannot be convicted of perjury because he lacks the mens rea and it is difficult to envisage A as a principal perjurer since he never went near the court, let alone took the oath."

Sometimes it is unclear whether an action is proxyable or not. Consider the action of driving a vehicle. In Thornton v. Mitchell, [1940] 1 All E.R. 339, a conductor negligently signaled an innocent bus driver that it was safe to back up his bus, resulting in injury to disembarking passengers. Professor Williams has argued that the conductor could not be held to have driven the bus negligently, in contravention of the Road Traffic Act. One of his reasons is that the conductor could not be said to have driven the bus, since the verb "drive," must be taken to have such a strong bodily connotation that only the actual driver can be the perpetrator of a driving offense."

G. WILLIAMS, *supra* note 10, at 370. As Williams argues, his conclusion is strengthened by the use of the same term, "drive," in the laws governing driving licenses, where it is plain that the license requirement applies onnly to the actual driver. Apart from the particular context of this legislation, however, it is not clear that the act of driving is necessarily incapable of being done by proxy. It does not seem implausible to hold that a ground control commander "pilots" a plane when he "talks down" a nonpilot in an emergency, or that a conductor "drives" a bus when he encourages a six-year-old child to steer the bus down a hill. *See* A. HOOPER, HARRIS'S CRIMINAL LAW (21st ed. 1968). After all, driving is an action which is characteristically done through instrumentalities, mechanical or animal, and it is therefore not unnatural to speak of driving through the instrumentality of another person.

144. A working paper for the English Law Commission captures the two limitations to the innocent-agent doctrine in a proposal that would exclude from the scope of that doctrine cases where "the law provides or implies that an offense can be committed only by one who complies with a particular description which does not apply to that person, or specifies the offense in terms implying personal conduct on the part of the offender." *Parties, Complicity and Liability for the Acts of Another*, in THE LAW COMM'N, *supra* note 21, at 11 (Proposition 3(2)(a)).

145. 220 Va. 770, 263 S.E.2d 392 (1980).

146. Cody v. State, 361 P.2d 307, 318 (Okla. Crim. 1961).

147. *Cf.* People v. Damen, 28 Ill. 2d 464, 193 N.E.2d 25 (1963); Rozell v. State, 502 S.W.2d 16 (Tex. Crim. 1973); State v. Kennedy, 616 P.2d 594, 596, 597 (Utah 1980) (defendant guilty of "forcible sexual abuse" when he induced another to take "indecent liberties"). For earlier cases, see Annot., 84 A.L.R.2d 1017, 1022 (1962).

148. State v. Dowell, 106 N.C. 722, 725, 11 S.E. 525, 525 (1890). The dissent, however, concluded that the conviction of the husband could not stand where the guilt of the other man could not be established.

149. State v. Blackwell, 241 Or. 528, 407 P.2d 617 (1965).

150. People v. Hernandez, 18 Cal. App. 3d 651, 96 Cal. Rptr. 71 (1971).

151. *Id.* at 657, 96 Cal. Rptr. at 74:

> "We do not, as urged by [the defendant], find her conviction of rape to be 'unique in the annals of American criminal law.'. . . Women have been convicted as 'aiders and abettors' and therefore principals . . . to the crime of rape . . . It would be unreasonable to hold a woman immune from prosecution for rape committed by a man who under her 'threats or menaces sufficient to show that [he] had reasonable cause to and did believe [that his life] would be endangered if [he] refused.'"

152. *Id.*

153. State v. Dowell, 106 N.C. 722, 724, 11 S.E. 525, 525 (1890) cited with approval in Cody v. State, 361 P.2d 307, 318 (Okla. Crim. 1961)). *But see* Meyers v. State, 19 Okla. Crim. 129, 135, 197 P. 884, 896 (1921): "[O]ur statutory definition of rape takes out of its operation the offense committed by the husband alone acting against his wife, although done through the instrumentality of an innocent third person."

154. People v. Hernandez, 18 Cal. App. 3d 651, 96 Cal. Rptr. 71 (1971).

155. 36 Crim. App. 125 (1952).

156. *Id.* at 128.

157. [1976] 1 Q.B. 217 (1975).

158. Director of Pub. Prosecutions v. Morgan, 1976 A.C. 182.

159. *Cogan & Leak*, [1976] 1 Q.B. at 222.

160. *Id.* at 223. "Leak was using him as a means to procure a criminal purpose." *Id.*

161. "The reason a man cannot by his own physical act rape his wife during cohabitation is because the law presumes consent from the marriage ceremony. . . . There is no such presumption when a man procures a drunken friend to do the physical act for him." *Id.*

162. G. WILLIAMS, *supra* note 10, at 371.

163. People v. Hernandez, 18 Cal. App. 3d 651, 96 Cal. Rptr. 71 (1971).

164. *See* G. WILLIAMS, *supra* note 10, at 371.

165. *Id.* at 372. *But see* Curley, *Excusing Rape,* 5 PHIL. & PUB. AFF. 325, 342 (1976).

166. *See supra* text accompanying note 160.

167. *See* J. SMITH & B. HOGAN, *supra* note 130, at 142.

168. 1975 CRIM. L. REV. 584, 587 (case commentary); *see also* State v. Dowell, 106 N.C. 722, 725, 11 S.E. 525, 525 (1890) ("The law . . . couples the act of the instrument with the felonious intent of the instigator. . . .").

169. *See supra* text accompanying note 21.

170. G. FLETCHER, *supra* note 14, at 664.

171. Taylor, *Complicity and Excuses,* 1983 Crim L. Rev. 656; Williams, The Theory of Excuses, 1982 CRIM. L. REV. 732, 735–38.

172. *See supra* Part II, Section *A.*

173. *See* Taylor, *supra* note 171.

174. *Cf.* Thornton v. Mitchell, [1940] 1 All E.R. 339.

175. *See* Taylor, *supra* note 171, at 658.

176. *Cf.* R. BRANDT, A THEORY OF THE GOOD AND THE RIGHT 357 (1979).

177. But *see* Lanham, *supra* note 15.

178. See the cases reviewed in United States v. Ruffin, 613 F.2d 408, 415–16 (2d Cir. 1979).

179. *See* S. REP. NO. 1020, 82d Cong., 1st Sess. 7, *reprinted in* 1951 U.S. CODE CONG. & AD. NEWS 2578, 2583.

180. Act of Oct. 13, 1951, Pub. L. No. 82–248, 65 Stat. 710, 717 (codified as amended at 18 U.S.C. § 2(b) (1982)). This follows § 2(a), which provides: "Whoever commits an offense against the United States or aids, abets, counsels, commands, induces or procures its commission, is punishable as a principal." 18 U.S.C. § 2(a) (1982).

181. For a review of the legislative history, see the majority and dissenting opinions in United States v. Ruffin, 613 F.2d 408, 413–15, 421–25 (2d Cir. 1979) (Mansfield, J.) (Wyatt, J., dissenting).

182. *See* MODEL PENAL CODE § 2.04(2)(a) comment at 16–17 (Tent. Draft No. 1, 1953). Referring to several similar provisions in state codes, the comment states: "None of these statutory formulations is quite satisfactory. It is paradoxical to speak of counseling or encouraging irresponsible persons to commit a crime, since their behavior by hypothesis is not criminal; and this is even clearer in the case of innocent, responsible agents." *Id.* at 16. Turning to the federal provision, the comment continues:

> "The federal formulation seeks to meet this difficulty by speaking of an act that would be criminal "if directly performed" by the defendant "or another" but the solution is inadequate on many grounds. It is not limited to acts of an innocent or irresponsible person, though this is the situation with which the Reviser's Note suggests it is designed to deal. Even if limited to that case by construction, it does not make clear whether or when the state of mind of the main actor is to be imputed to the defendant, even though he did not share it; whether the conduct would be criminal had he performed it may depend on that. Even more obscure is the test whether the act would be criminal if performed by "another," which the statute makes sufficient to establish liability."

Id. at 17.

183. *See* United States v. Tobon-Builes, 706 F.2d 1092, 1099 (11th Cir. 1983) ("[B]ecause of the operation of § 2(b), [defendant's] legal incapacity to commit the crime of concealment himself, owing to his lack of any duty to report currency transactions exceeding $10,000, does not detract from his liability . . . for willfully causing the innocent but duty-bound financial institutions not to disclose such transactions."); United States v. Ruffin, 613 F.2d 408, 413 (2d Cir. 1979) (defendant, though legally incapable of personally committing offense of fraudulently obtaining certain federal

funds, held nevertheless liable where he caused innocent agent meeting capacity requirement to engage in proscribed conduct); United States v. Smith, 584 F.2d 731, 734 (5th Cir. 1978); United States v. Wiseman, 445 F.2d 792, 794–95 (2d Cir.), *cert. denied*, 404 U.S. 967 (1971); United States v. Lester, 363 F.2d 68 (6th Cir. 1966), *cert. denied*, 385 U.S. 1002 (1967). For discussions of § 2(b), see Lanham, *supra* note 15, at 502–06; Note, *The Scope of Accomplice Liability Under 18 U.S.C. § 2(b)*, 31 CASE W. RES. L. REV. 386 (1981).

184. *See* statutes cited in 1 WHARTON'S CRIMINAL LAW, *supra* note 17, at 160 n. 15.

185. MODEL PENAL CODE § 206(2)(a) (Proposed Official Draft 1962).

186. The Model Penal Code's formulation introduces still another change in the traditional innocent-agency doctrine by dispensing with the requirement of intent. It has generally been required that the defendant intentionally use the actions of the innocent agent for his purpose. *See infra* note 209 and accompanying text. However, it is enough under the Model Penal Code that the defendant act with the mens rea required for the offense. Thus, a defendant may be held liable for causing the acts of an innocent agent even if he does so recklessly or negligently, so long as no greater mens rea is required for the crime with which he is charged. I will return to this feature of the Model Penal Code's provision in the next Section when dealing with the problem of the liability of a defendant for unintended actions of another person. *See infra* text accompanying notes 225-31.

187. 2 W. HAWKINS, A TREATISE OF THE PLEAS OF THE CROWN ch. 29, § 15, at 442 (8th ed. London 1824) (1st ed. London 1716); *see also* 4 W. BLACKSTONE, *supra* note 24, at *36 (footnote omitted): "It is a maxim, that *accessorius sequitur naturam sui principalis:* and therefore an accessory cannot be guilty of a higher crime than his principal; being only punished, as a partaker of his guilt."

188. 1 E. EAST, *supra* note 127, at 350; 2 W. HAWKINS, *supra* note 187, ch. 29, § 7, at 438-39. This passage of East has been cited to support the proposition that at common law the instigator could be held liable for a greater crime than the principal. *See* G. WILLIAMS, *supra* note 10, at 373 & n. 2. However, East's comment concerned an "abettor" present at the scene of the crime and instigating the primary party to commit the crime. He was stating the conventional poisition for second-degree principals rather than announcing a novel position for accessories.

189. Commonwealth v. Knapp, 26 Mass. (9 Pick.) 495, 513 (1830) (emphasis in original):

> "By the most ancient common law, as it was generally understood, those persons only were considered as principals in murder, who actually killed the man, and those who were present, aiding and abetting, were considered as accessories. So that if he who gave the mortal blow were not convicted, he who was *present* and aiding, being only an accessory, could not be put upon his trial. But the law was otherwise settled in the reign of Henry IV. It was then adjudged, that he who was *present, aiding* and *abetting* him who actually killed, was to be considered as actually killing, as much as if he had given the deadly blow. The law has been so understood from that time to the present. . . ."

This was manifest in the rules permitting a principal in the second degree, unlike an accessory, to be prosecuted even though the principal in the first degree had not been convicted. *See* Standefer v. United States, 447 U.S. 10, 15 (1980); *Knapp*, 26 Mass (9 Pick.) at 513-14; *see also* 1 E. EAST, *supra* note 127, at 351 (one present aiding and abetting may be convicted notwithstanding acquittal of perpetrator); M. FOSTER, *supra* note 60, at 427:

> "[At one time] the law was taken to be, that persons present aiding and abetting were to be considered in the rank of accessaries, not liable to answer till the principal was convicted or outlawed: but the mischiefs of this rule were very great and many. The persons who were then esteemed the only principals might die before conviction: their accomplices might dispatch them, in order to produce their own immunity. . . . "

But see 2 W. HAWKINS, *supra* note 187, at 449-51 (accessory may not be convicted if principal has been acquitted or, through death, absence, or some other circumstances, is unavailable for prosecution).

190. Regina v. Richards, [1974] 1 Q.B. 776, 780.

191. *See, e.g.,* J. SMITH & B. HOGAN, *supra* note 130, at 139-40; G. WILLIAMS, *supra* note 10, at 373-74; 1974 CRIM. L. REV. 96 (case commentary).

192. *See, e.g.,* Bridges v. State, 48 Ala. App. 249, 251-52, 263 So. 2d 705, 707-08 (1972); State v. Gray, 55 Kan. 135, 144-45, 39 P. 1050, 1053 (1895); State v. McAllister, 366 So. 2d 1340, 1342-43 (La. 1978); State v. Dault, 25 Wash. App. 568, 572-74, 608 P.2d 270, 273-74 (1980); *see also* Moore v. Lowe, 116 W. Va. 165, 168-71, 180 S.E. 1, 2-4, *cert. denied,* 296 U.S. 574 (1935), *overruled on other grounds by* State v. Petry, 273 S.E.2d 346 (W. Va. 1980); G. WILLIAMS, *supra* note 22, at 390-91. Cases to the contrary seem to go off on the now generally discarded view that the prior conviction of the principal determines the crime of which the accomplice may be convicted, regardless of what can be proven in the subsequent trial of the accomplice. *See, e.g.,* Schmidt v. State, 261 Ind. 81, 81-83, 300 N.E.2d 86, 87-88 (1973); State v. Ward, 284 Md. 189, 201-07, 396 A.2d 1041, 1049-52 (1978), *overruled on other grounds by* Lewis v. State, 285 Md. 705, 404 A.2d 1073 (1979).

193. G. WILLIAMS, *supra* note 10, at 374.

194. G. WILLIAMS, *supra* note 22, at 391.

195. H.L.A. HART & A. HONORÉ, *supra* note 5, at 323-24.

196. *See infra* "*1. Nonviolent Actions*", text accompanying note 207 et seq.

197. H.L.A. HART & A. HONORÉ, *supra* note 5, at 296–304.

198. This explanation would not work if the case had been that Iago was speaking the truth. But, as we saw earlier, there is a real question whether in that event as a matter of penal policy any liability at all, based either on complicity or causation, is appropriate. *See supra* text accompanying notes 109–10.

199. [1974] 1 Q.B. 776.

200. *See* J. SMITH & B. HOGAN, *supra* note 130, at 140; G. WILLIAMS, *supra* note 10, at 373–74.

201. *See supra* text accompanying note 191.

202. J. SMITH & B. HOGAN, *supra* note 130, at 140; *see also* Note, *Proof of Principal Offences and Liability of Secondary Party,* 90 LAW Q. REV. 314, 318 (1974).

203. The same argument applies to Professor Williams' criticism of the *Richards* case. *See* G. WILLIAMS, *supra* note 10, at 373–74.

204. *See, e.g., id.* at 372–73.

205. *See supra* note 21 and accompanying text.

206. *See supra* text accompanying notes 170–77.

207. MODEL PENAL CODE §204(2)(a) comment at 17 (Tent. Draft No. 1, 1953).

208. *Id.*

209. *See* H.L.A. HART & A. HONORÉ, *supra* note 5, at 323–25.

210. *See supra* text accompanying notes 4–7.

211. *See, e.g.,* Commonwealth v. Almeida, 362 Pa. 596, 68 A.2d 595 (1949), *cert denied,* 339 U.S. 924 (1950), *overruled by* Commonwealth *ex rel.* Smith v. Myers, 438 Pa. 218, 261 A.2d 550 (1970); Commonwealth v. Moyer, 357 Pa. 181, 53 A.2d 736 (1947).

212. *See* State v. Canola, 73 N.J. 206, 213, 374 A.2d 20, 23 (1977).

213. People v. Washington, 62 Cal. 2d 777, 783, 402 P.2d 130, 134, 44 Cal. Rptr. 442, 446 (1965); *see also* State v. Canola, 73 N.J. 206, 374 A.2d 20 (1977); Commonwealth v. Allen, 475 Pa. 165, 379 A.2d 1335 (1977).

214. *See* State v. Canola, 73 N.J. 206, 225, 374 A.2d 20, 30 (1977). Recent statutory formulations of the felony-murder doctrine have taken various positions. These statutes commonly exclude the death of one of the felons as a basis for felony murder, regardless of who does the killing. *See, e.g.,* CONN. GEN. STAT. ANN. § 53a–54c (West Supp. 1984); N.Y. PENAL LAW § 125.25 (McKinney Supp. 1984). For some doubts on the defensibility of this position, see S. KADISH, S. SCHULHOFER & M. PAULSEN, *supra* note 126, at 498–500. Many statutes appear to confine felony murder to killings committed personally by the felon or his accomplice (the agency theory), although

the statutory language sometimes leaves room for doubt. *See, e.g.,* COLO. REV. STAT. § 18-3-102 (1978); N.J. STAT. ANN. § 2C : 11-3 (West 1982).

215. However, this is the conclusion reached in California under a peculiar interpretation of its homicide statutes. Pizano v. Superior Court, 21 Cal. 3d 128, 577 P.2d 659, 145 Cal. Rptr. 524 (1978); Taylor v. Superior Court, 3 Cal. 3d 578, 477 P.2d 131, 91 Cal. Rptr. 275 (1970).

216. *Cf.* Taylor v. State, 41 Tex. Crim. 564, 572, 55 S.W. 961, 964 (1900).

217. *See, e.g.,* People v. Washington, 62 Cal. 2d 777, 781, 402 P.2d 130, 133, 44 Cal. Rptr. 442, 445 (1965) ("When a killing is not committed by a robber or by his accomplice but by his victim, malice aforethought is not attributable to the robber, for the killing is not committed by him. . . .").

218. 63 Cal. 2d 690, 408 P.2d 365, 47 Cal. Rptr. 909 (1965), *vacated on other grounds,* 388 U.S. 263 (1967).

219. *Id.* at 704, 408 P.2d at 373, 47 Cal. Rptr. at 917 (emphasis added). The formula the court uses is the formula in California for elevating an egregiously reckless killing to murder.

220. *See* Taylor v. Superior Court, 3 Cal. 3d 578, 477 P.2d 131, 91 Cal. Rptr. 275 (1970); People v. Washington, 62 Cal. 2d 777, 402 P.2d 130, 44 Cal. Rptr. 442 (1965).

221. It should be said that third-party felony-murder cases in other jurisdictions are also consistent with this interpretation. The cases that adopt the so-called proximate cause theory of the felon's liability most clearly rest on just such a causation analysis. The felony-murder artificialities enter the picture only after causation has been established. The cases and statutes adopting the agency approach reject the causation approach only for the purposes of the stringencies of the felony-murder rule. They do not consider the liability of the felon for manslaughter (or even murder) apart from the felony-murder doctrine.

222. *In re* Pagett, 76 Crim. App. 279 (1983).

223. *Id.* at 288–90.

224. *See* MODEL PENAL CODE § 2.04(2)(a) comment at 17-18 (Tent. Draft No. 1, 1953).

225. *Id.* § 2.06(2)(a) (Proposed Official Draft 1962).

226. H.L.A. HART & A. HONORÉ, *supra* note 5, at 327-28. See the proposal of the English Law Commission purporting to restate existing law: "A person acts through an innocent agent when he intentionally causes the external elements of the offence to be committed by . . . a person who is himself innocent of the offence charged by reason of a lack of a required fault element, or lack of capacity." THE LAW COMM'N, *supra* note 21, at 11 (Proposition 3); *cf.* United States v. Chiarella, 184 F.2d 903, 909–10 (2d Cir. 1950), *cert. denied,* 341 U.S. 956 (1951) (L. Hand, J.).

227. It is possible to read the Model Penal Code provision as not embracing liability for *unintentionally* causing nonvoluntary conduct. Literally, it only stipulates accountability when two conditions are met: when the defendant causes the innocent person to engage in the conduct, and when he acts with the mens rea required for the offense. The reading I have given the language, however, is apparently the one intended. *See* MODEL PENAL CODE § 2.04(2)(a) comment at 17–18 (Tent. Draft No. 1, 1953):

> "When the crimes call for no more than recklessness or negligence for their commission, it should suffice . . . that one with such recklessness or negligence causes the required overt conduct by an innocent or irresponsible person; there is no reason for demanding that such conduct be caused purposively. . . . In short, the draft proposes to determine liability by the culpability and state of mind of the defendant, coupled with the overt behavior he has caused another to perform."

228. *Id.* at 17.

229. G. WILLIAMS, *supra* note 22, at 352.

230. The Model Penal Code eliminates strict liability (except for nonimprisonable infractions, MODEL PENAL CODE § 2.05 (Proposed Official Draft 1962)), but the analysis in the text would apply in any jurisdiction retaining strict liability if it adopted the Model Penal Code complicity provisions.

231. It is worth noting that in other situations raising the issue of liability of one person for what another does, the Model Penal Code has adhered strictly to the requirement of intention, manifesting a sensitivity to widening the net of liability. To be guilty as an accomplice, for example, a person must purposively solicit or knowingly aid another to commit a crime. MODEL PENAL CODE § 2.04(3) (Tent. Draft No. 1, 1953). The comment to this section states: "Whatever may be law upon the point, it is submitted that the liability of an accomplice ought not to extend beyond the criminal purposes that he shares or knows." *Id.* § 2.04(3) comment at 26. It is not immediately apparent why the Model Penal Code chose to cast the net wider when a person causes an innocent person to commit a criminal action than when he influences or helps a guilty person to do so. It is also worth noting that to be guilty of criminal homicide by causing another to commit suicide under the Model Penal Code, a person must *purposely* cause the suicide by force, duress or deception. *Id.* § 210.5(1) (Proposed Official Draft 1962).

232. People v. Marshall, 362 Mich. 1970, 106 N.W.2d 842 (1961) (defendant, who lent automobile keys to drunk who was then involved in fatal crash, found not guilty of involuntary manslaughter, but could be held for negligence).

233. Commonwealth v. Root, 403 Pa. 571, 170 A.2d 310 (1961) (conduct of defendant in accepting challenge to engage in automobile race could not justify conviction for involuntary manslaughter for death of the challenger).

234. Jacobs v. State, 184 So. 2d 711 (Fla. Dist. Ct. App. 1966) (defendant who recklessly drove in automobile race where driver of oncoming vehicle was killed held guilty of manslaughter).

235. Commonwealth v. Atencio, 345 Mass. 627, 189 N.E.2d 223 (1963) (defendants, who participated in Russian roulette, liable for involuntary manslaughter).

236. *See supra* text accompanying notes 44–48.

237. *See* State v. McVay, 47 R.I. 292, 132 A. 436 (1926).

238. *See supra* notes 64–70 and accompanying text.

239. *See supra* text accompanying note 185.

240. 403 Pa. 571, 170 A.2d 310(1961).

241. In commenting on the decision of the intermediate appellate court, which had affirmed the conviction, Professor Williams advances a different reason for reversal than that later invoked by the Supreme Court: since the deceased committed no crime in causing his own death by his reckless action, there was no homicidal crime for which the competitor could be held as a secondary party. G. WILLIAMS, *supra* note 22, at 393–394. This, however, is to treat the defendant's liability in terms of complicity, rather than causation. Complicity in any event does not fit here, since the deceased died as a result of a dangerous action his competitor did not intend. Professor Williams adds in a footnote that neither can the doctrine of causation make a person a party to a nonexistent crime. *Id.* at 394 n. 13. But the issue is the survivor's liability for recklessly causing the death of the competitor, which *is* a crime.

There may be good reasons for not extending liability to one who helps another to expose himself deliberately to a great risk. Professor Williams instances two mountain climbers who undertake a foolhardy climbing attempt under particularly dangerous circumstances in the course of which one of them falls to his death. *Id.* at 393. There is force in the policy argument that a person should not suffer criminal liability for helping another to subject himself to risks he is free to assume. But that policy is consistent with the standard causation doctrine, as the decision of the Pennsylvania Supreme Court reveals, since it precludes regarding the helper as causing the other party's wholly volitional action. In any event, the issue does not affect our main concern, for as far as the logic of the court's decision was concerned the decision might just as well have involved the death of a nonparticipant. *Root,* 403 Pa. at 589, 170 A.2d at 318 (Eagen, J., dissenting).

242. *Root,* 403 Pa. at 574, 170 A.2d at 311.

243. *Id.* at 576, 170 A.2d at 312.

244. *Id.* at 575–78, 170 A.2d at 311–13.

245. Actually, there was a simpler basis for distinguishing the tort cases, which involved in one case a 16-year old, and in the other, a drunken person, since the actions of these persons might be regarded as sufficiently unfree to permit the causal chain to be traced through them.

246. *Root*, 403 Pa. at 583, 170 A.2d at 315 (Eagen, J., dissenting). Very much the same exchange of arguments occurred in another road race case where a bystander was killed. This time the majority affirmed the conviction. Jacobs v. State, 184 So. 2d 711 (Fla. Dist. Ct. App. 1966); *see also* People v. Kemp, 150 Cal. App. 23 654, 310 P.2d 680 (1957).

247. *See supra* notes 48–50 and accompanying text.

248. *But see* State v. Hopkins, 147 Wash. 198, 265 P. 481, *cert. denied*, 278 U.S. 617 (1928).

249. W. LaFave & A. Scott, *supra* note 17, at 511–12.

250. Commonwealth v. Atencio, 345 Mass. 627, 189 N.E.2d 223 (1963).

251. *Id.* at 629, 189 N.E.2d at 224 (citation omitted). *But see supra* note 241 (discussing Professor Williams' view).

252. *Cf.* Commonwealth v. Malone, 354 Pa. 180, 47 A.2d 445 (1946).

253. The court sought to distinguish *Root* on the ground that in the road race case much is left to the driver's skill (or lack of it), while in the Russian roulette case it is a matter of luck whether the revolver discharges. Commonwealth v. Atencio, 345 Mass. 627, 631, 189 N.E.2d 223, 225 (1963). But it is questionable that this is a relevant distinction. Perhaps it was thought more likely that harm would occur from the playing of Russian roulette than from engaging in the road race, since in the latter the deceased competitor may not take outrageous risks while driving, or might safely extricate himself if he did. But the decision in *Root* explicitly conceded that defendant's actions were reckless enough to constitute manslaughter if he could be said to have caused the death. *Root*, 403 Pa. at 573–74, 170 A.2d at 311.

254. *See supra* text accompanying notes 64–73.

255. *See supra* text accompanying notes 85–96.

256. The Second Restatement of Torts asserts: "If the likelihood that a third person may act in a particular manner is the hazard or one of the hazards which makes the actor negligent, such an act whether innocent, negligent, intentionally tortious, or criminal does not prevent the actor from being liable for harm caused thereby." Restatement of Torts (Second) § 449 (1965); *see id.* §§302A, 302B; W. Keeton, D. Dobbs, R. Keeton & D. Owen, Prosser and Keeton on the Law of Torts § 33, at 201–03, § 44, at 302 (5th ed. 1984).

257. An argument for extending the concept of causation to cover cases where a defendant recklessly or negligently facilitates another person's criminal conduct, even when it is wholly volitional, is made in Note, *Causation in the Model Penal Code*, 78 Colum. L. Rev. 1249, 1277-84 (1978). The author also argues that the causation provisions of Model Penal Code § 2.03 provide for such liability.

258. Cal. Joint Legislative Comm. for Revision of the Penal Code, Penal Code Revision Project § 408(1)(b)(i) (Tent. Draft No. 2, 1968). I should disclose my role as the Reporter responsible for this draft. It seemed to me at the time to represent desirable legislative policy. I still think so, but with less certainty.

259. Consider the following cases in which tort liability has been imposed: Kendall v. Gore Properties, Inc., 236 F.2d 673 (D.C. Cir. 1956) (landlord held negligent in killing of tenant by employee whose background he did not sufficiently investigate); Liberty Nat'l Life Ins. Co. v. Weldon, 267 Ala. 171, 100 So. 2d 696 (1957) (insurer that issued policy on life of child to one without insurable interest in child held negligent when child was murdered by beneficiary); Weirum v. RKO Gen. Inc., 15 Cal. 3d 40, 539 P.2d 36, 123 Cal. Rptr. 468 (1975) (radio station held liable for careless driving by fans trying to win award for being the first person to locate roving disc jockey). For further cases, see Restatement (Second) of Torts §449 app. (1966 & Supp. 1983).

260. Consider the case of a police guard who negligently leaves his gun in the open ward of a mental hospital. If an incompetent person uses the gun to kill, the criminal law

permits the guard to be held for manslaughter on a causation theory. There is no greater peril to ordinary behavior if the guard is also made liable when a competent visitor uses the gun to kill.

261. *Cf.* H.L.A. HART & A. HONORÉ, *supra* note 5, at 357:

> "[W]hatever else may be vague or disputable about common sense in regard to causation and responsibility, it is surely clear that the *primary* case where it is reluctant to treat a person as having caused harm which would not have occurred without his act is that where another voluntary human action has intervened."

NOTES FOR ESSAY 9

1. For a review of the importance of several earlier criminal law writers, see Ashworth, *The Making of English Criminal Law, (4) Blackstone, Foster and East,* 1978 CRIM. L.R. 389.

2. 10 WORKS OF JEREMY BENTHAM 469 (Bowring ed. 1843) [hereinafter cited as BENTHAM WORKS].

3. J. BENTHAM, *Papers Relative to Codification and Public Instruction,* in 4 BENTHAM WORKS, *supra* note 2, at 453, 507.

4. *Id.* at 468.

5. *Id.* at 476.

6. *Id.* at 514.

7. J. BENTHAM, *Specimen of a Penal Code,* in 1 BENTHAM WORKS, *supra* note 2, at 164. *See also* Jolowicz, *Was Bentham a Lawyer?,* in JEREMY BENTHAM AND THE LAW 1, 11–12 (G. W. Keeton & G. Schwarzenberger eds. 1948).

8. Lord Bryce attributed the legal and governmental reforms in the last two-thirds of the nineteenth century to several factors, the first being "the general enlightenment of mind due to the play of speculative thought upon practical questions which marked the end of the last and beginning of this [the 19th] century, and of which the most conspicuous apostles were Adam Smith in the sphere of economics and Jeremy Bentham in the sphere of legal reform." 2 J. BRYCE, STUDIES IN HISTORY AND JURISPRUDENCE 768 (1901). *See generally* C. PHILLIPSON, THREE CRIMINAL LAW REFORMERS ch. IV (1923); 1 L. RADZINOWICZ, A HISTORY OF ENGLISH CRIMINAL LAW 355–96 (1948); Alfange, *Jeremy Bentham and the Codification of Law,* 55 CORNELL L. REV. 58 (1969); Holdsworth, *Bentham's Place in English Legal History,* 28 CALIF. L. REV. 568 (1940).

9. For a discussion of his background, see Moore, *The Livingston Code,* 19 J. AM. INST. CRIM. L. & CRIMINOLOGY 344, 346–47 (1928). Moore's bibliography of writings by and about Livingston is the most exhaustive one to come to my attention. *Id.* at 363.

10. See the comment on Bentham in Sir John Romilly's letter to Dumont in 1791: "Bentham leads the same kind of life as usual at Hendon,—seeing nobody, reading nothing, and writing books which nobody reads." J. DILLON, THE LAWS AND JURISPRUDENCE OF ENGLAND AND AMERICA 327 n.1 (1895). *See also id.* at 330 n.1.

11. 1 COMPLETE WORKS OF EDWARD LIVINGSTON ON CRIMINAL JURISPRUDENCE 1 (1873) [hereinafter cited as LIVINGSTON WORKS]; W.B. HATCHER, EDWARD LIVINGSTON 237 (1940).

12. *See* W. B. HATCHER, *supra* note 11; C.H. HUNT, LIFE OF EDWARD LIVINGSTON (1864).

13. *See* Everett, *Bentham in the United States of America,* in JEREMY BENTHAM AND THE LAW, *supra* note 7, at 185, 193.

14. *See* Letter from Plumer to Bentham (Sept. 15, 1826), *reprinted in* 10 BENTHAM WORKS, *supra* note 2, at 556–57: "[Livingston] has often spoke of you to me in terms of the highest veneration and respect, and informed me, more than once, that his attempts at Codification grew out of what he learnt of your views in the works published by Dumont. He considers you as his master in the service: and you could hardly deserve a more zealous or more enlightened disciple." *See also* Letter from Livingston to Bentham (Aug. 10, 1829), *reprinted in* 11 BENTHAM WORKS, *supra* note 2, at 23.

15. C. H. HUNT, *supra* note 12, at 83.

16. W. B. HATCHER, *supra* note 11, at 245–62.

17. Bentham appears to have realized this. He helped Livingston by arranging for needed material to be sent him, and he engineered the publication of Livingston's completed Code in England and a favorable review in an English journal. *See* 11 BENTHAM WORKS, *supra* note 2, at 35, 37, 51.

18. *See* Letter from Livingston to Bentham (July 1, 1830), *reprinted in* 11 BENTHAM WORKS, *supra* note 2, at 51: "I . . . take pleasure in acknowledging, that although strongly impressed with defects of our actual system of penal law, yet the perusal of your works first gave method to my ideas, and taught me to consider legislation as a science governed by certain principles applicable to all its different branches, instead of an occasional exercise of powers called forth only on particular occasions, without relation to, or connexion with, each other."

19. *See Introductory Report to the System of Penal Law, reprinted in* 1 LIVINGSTON WORKS, *supra* note 11, at 87–95, 148, 163.

20. *See* 1 LIVINGSTON WORKS, *supra* note 11, at 86–87: "I have taken truth for the foundation of all my statements, utility for the sole object of my provisions, and reason alone as the means of supporting my conclusions. . . ."

21. 11 BENTHAM WORKS, *supra* note 2, at 23.

22. C. H. HUNT, *supra* note 12, at 257–58; 1 LIVINGSTON WORKS, *supra* note 11, at 81.

23. For Bentham's arguments for giving reasons, see 1 BENTHAM WORKS, *supra* note 2, at 159.

24. CODE OF CRIMES AND PUNISHMENTS art. 499, *reprinted in* 2 LIVINGSTON WORKS, *supra* note 11, at 130.

25. *Id.* art 689, *reprinted in* 2 LIVINGSTON WORKS, *supra* note 11, at 180–81.

26. 1 LIVINGSTON WORKS, *supra* note 11, at 237.

27. *Preamble to Draft Code and Book 1, reprinted in* 2 LIVINGSTON WORKS, *supra* note 11, at 3, 14.

28. This is why he thought it indelicate to include the crime of homosexuality. But another reason was as modern as that reason was quaint: that it is susceptible of use (because of the difficulties of proof) as an engine of extortion. 1 LIVINGSTON WORKS, *supra* note 11, at 27. He also thought it couldn't happen in Louisiana, but we may charitably pass that. None of the Penal Codes eliminated homosexual offenses until the Model Penal Code. Livingston did include the crime of adultery for married women. 2 *id.* at 286–87; CODE OF CRIMES AND PUNISHMENTS art. 344, *reprinted in* 2 LIVINGSTON WORKS, *supra* note 11, at 97. Bentham would have eliminated both. Bentham, *Offences Against Taste,* in THE THEORY OF LEGISLATION 476 (Ogden ed. 1931).

29. 1 BENTHAM WORKS, *supra* note 2, at 450.

30. 1 LIVINGSTON WORKS, *supra* note 11, at 185–224.

31. *See* Franklin, *Concerning the Historic Importance of Edward Livingston*, 11 TUL. L. REV. 163, 182 (1937): "Livingston's thought represents the most concerted attack on judicial supremacy in the history of American law. . . ."

32. CODE OF CRIMES AND PUNISHMENTS art. 7, *reprinted in* 2 LIVINGSTON WORKS, *supra* note 11, at 15.

33. "An ambiguous penal law, is no law; and judicial decisions cannot explain it without usurping authority which does not belong to them." 1 LIVINGSTON WORKS, *supra* note 11, at 170.

34. CODE OF CRIMES AND PUNISHMENTS arts. 7, 8, *reprinted in* 2 LIVINGSTON WORKS, *supra* note 11, at 15.

35. CODE OF PROCEDURE art. 431, *reprinted in* 2 LIVINGSTON WORKS, *supra* note 11, at 294–95.

36. CODE OF CRIMES AND PUNISHMENTS arts. 205–208, *reprinted in* 2 LIVINGSTON WORKS, *supra* note 11, at 59–60.

37. *Id.* art. 213, *reprinted in* 2 LIVINGSTON WORKS, *supra* note 11, at 70–71.

38. *Id.* arts. 138–143, *reprinted in* 2 LIVINGSTON WORKS, *supra* note 11, at 44–45.

39. *Id.* art. 146, *reprinted in* 2 LIVINGSTON WORKS, *supra* note 11, at 46.

40. *Id.* art. 20, *reprinted in* 2 LIVINGSTON WORKS, *supra* note 11, at 17.

41. *Id.* art. 240, *reprinted in* 2 LIVINGSTON WORKS, *supra* note 11, at 69–70.

42. An insightful treatment of the main themes in Livingston's Code appears in Hall, *Edward Livingston and His Louisiana Penal Code*, 22 A.B.A.J. 191 (1936).

43. CODE OF CRIMES AND PUNISHMENTS art. 15, *reprinted in* 2 LIVINGSTON WORKS, *supra* note 11, at 16.

44. *Id.* art 12, *reprinted in* 2 LIVINGSTON WORKS, *supra* note 11, at 16.

45. *Id.* art 239, *reprinted in* 2 LIVINGSTON WORKS, *supra* note 11, at 69.

46. *Id.* art 356, *reprinted in* 2 LIVINGSTON WORKS, *supra* note 11, at 99.

47. 1 LIVINGSTON WORKS, *supra* note 11, at 15.

48. CODE OF CRIMES AND PUNISHMENTS arts. 19, 20, *reprinted in* 2 LIVINGSTON WORKS, *supra* note 11, at 17.

49. *Id.* art. 386, *reprinted in* 2 LIVINGSTON WORKS, *supra* note 11, at 104–05.

50. *Id.*

51. *Id.* arts. 621, 622, *reprinted in* 2 LIVINGSTON WORKS, *supra* note 11, at 166.

52. 1 LIVINGSTON WORKS, *supra* note 11, at 223. *See* Mackey, *Edward Livingston on the Punishment of Death*, 48 TUL. L. REV. 25 (1973).

53. *See* Roberts, *Edward Livingston and American Penology*, 37 LA. L. REV. 1037 (1977); Smith, *Edward Livingston, and the Louisiana Codes*, 2 COLUM. L. REV. 24 (1902).

54. *Introductory Report to the Code of Reform and Prison Discipline, reprinted in* 1 LIVINGSTON WORKS, *supra* note 11, at 507, 537–89.

55. "A man of worth and integrity may be guilty of breaking the provisions of mere positive law; but it would be confounding all sense of proportion in punishment to conduct him to the same prison with the thief or assassin." *Id.* at 544–45.

56. *Id.* at 546.

57. *Id.* at 547–48.

58. *Id.* at 555–56.

59. *Id.* at 558.

60. *Id.* at 528.

61. CODE OF REFORM AND PRISON DISCIPLINE art. 294, *reprinted in* 2 LIVINGSTON WORKS, *supra* note 11, at 598.

62. 1 LIVINGSTON WORKS, *supra* note 11, at 533.

63. *Id.* at 533–34.

64. Apparently Guatemala adopted the Code of Reform and Prison Discipline in Spanish translation. *See* C.H. HUNT, *supra* note 12, at 279.

65. *See* Beckman, *Three Penal Codes Compared*, 10 AM. J. LEGAL HIST. 148, 166–67 (1966).

66. *See* Franklin, *Concerning the Historic Importance of Edward Livingston*, 11 TUL. L. REV. 163, 209–12 (1937).

67. C. H. HUNT, *supra* note 12, at 278. For other testimonials and recognition, see Moore, *supra* note 9, at 344, 355–60.

68. "My own forensic experience, gentlemen, has been extremely small; for my only recollection of an achievement that way is that at quarter sessions I once convicted a boy of stealing a parcel of cocks and hens." 1 G.O. TREVELYAN, LIFE AND LETTERS OF LORD MACAULAY 368 n.1. (1876).

69. E. STOKES, THE ENGLISH UTILITARIANS AND INDIA 191 (1959).

70. India Charter Act, 1833, 3 & 4 Will. IV, c. 85, §53. A discussion of the historical context and contents of the Charter Act of 1833 may be found in C. ILBERT, THE GOVERNMENT OF INDIA 81–89 (3d ed. 1915).

71. *See* 1 G.O. TREVELYAN, *supra* note 68, at 343 (1876).

72. Public Dispatch of 10 December 1834, *reproduced in* C. ILBERT, THE GOVERNMENT OF INDIA 492 (1898), *quoted in* E. STOKES, *supra* note 69, at 193.

73. *See* J. CLIVE, MACAULAY: THE SHAPING OF THE HISTORIAN 435 (1973). In a letter to his barrister-friend, Ellis, at this time he wrote: "I have immense reforms in hand such as you Knight Templars would abhor, but such as would make old Bentham jump in his grave—oral pleadings—examination of parties—single seated justice—no institution fees—and so forth." E. STOKES, *supra* note 69, at 213 n.4.

74. E. STOKES, *supra* note 69, at 190–233.

75. Macaulay wrote to Hobhouse in 1835: "our criminal code, whatever credit it may do us in the opinion of Benthamites at home, will do very little good to the people of this country, until it be accompanied by a thorough reform of prison-discipline." J. CLIVE, *supra* note 73, at 448.

76. *Id.* at 440.

77. 1 G.O. TREVELYAN, *supra* note 68, at 419.

78. Stephen, *Macaulay*, in 12 DICTIONARY OF NATIONAL BIOGRAPHY 411 (1921).

79. *See* J. CLIVE, *supra* note 73, at 453: "The philosophical, Benthamite, approach to codification was to think of law as it ought to be as well as law as it was; to dissect every idea; to ask of every rule what useful purpose it served."

80. "I am firmly convinced that the style of laws is of scarcely less importance than their substance. When we are laying down the rules according to which millions are, at their peril, to shape their actions, we are surely bound to put those rules into such a form that it shall not require any painful effort of attention or any extraordinary quickness of intellect to comprehend them." Macaulay, Minute (May 11, 1835) *quoted in* E. STOKES, *supra* note 69, at 199.

81. *See* E. STOKES, *supra* note 69, at 191–92.

82. *See* Stephen, *supra* note 78, at 417:

    "The tenants of the Whig party were for him the last word of political wisdom. The essay on Bacon is a deliberate declaration of the worthlessness of all speculation not adapted to immediate utility. His attack upon the utilitarians expresses a more thorough-going empiricism than that of their own official advocates. . . . The philosophical and imaginative tendencies represented by such men as Wordsworth, Coleride, or Carlyle, struck him as mere mystical moonshine."

83. Clive, *Macaulay*, in 9 INTERNATIONAL ENCYCLOPEDIA OF THE SOCIAL SCIENCES 499 (1968).

84. J. BENTHAM, *On the Influence of Time and Place in Matters of Legislation*, in 1 BENTHAM WORKS, *supra* note 2, at 169.

85. *See* A PENAL CODE PREPARED BY THE INDIAN LAW COMMISSIONERS i–iv (1838) [hereinafter cited as INDIA PENAL CODE]. The criminal laws prevailing in India at the time are described in great detail in J. CLIVE, *supra* note 73, at 437; M. LANG, CODIFICATION IN THE BRITISH EMPIRE AND AMERICA 69–76 (1924); Banerjee, *The Substantive Criminal Law Prior to the Indian Penal Code*, in 1 INDIAN LAW INSTITUTE, ESSAYS ON THE INDIAN PENAL CODE 1 (1961).

86. INDIA PENAL CODE, *supra* note 85, at i: "the system of penal law which we propose is not a digest of any existing system, and . . . no existing system has furnished us even with a ground work."

87. *Id.* at i, iv.

88. He follows his acknowledgment of Livingston's assistance with the comment: "We are the more desirous to acknowledge our obligation to that eminent jurist because we have found ourselves under the necessity of combatting his opinions on some important questions." *Id.* at iv. *See, e.g., id* at 72, 73, 75 note (fines), 104 note (omissions), note 106–09 (homicide) (discussion of Livingston's Code). But he rejected Livingston's provisions in almost every instance.

89. *See* 3 J. STEPHEN, HISTORY OF THE CRIMINAL LAW OF ENGLAND 300 (1883); 1 W. STOKES, THE ANGLO-INDIAN CODES xxvi (1887); M. SETALVAD, THE COMMON LAW IN INDIA 126–29 (1960); Rankin, *The Indian Penal Code*, 60 LAW Q. REV. 37, 42–43 (1944).

90. 3 J. STEPHEN, *supra* note 89, at 300.

91. Vesey-FitzGerald, *Bentham and the Indian Codes,* in JEREMY BENTHAM AND THE LAW, *supra* note 7, at 222, 227. He further observes, "That the Indian Penal Code is founded on English Criminal Law is true only in the sense in which it might be contended that without a Blackstone to excite his critical faculty we might never have had a Bentham." *Id.*

92. *See* Brinton, *Macaulay,* in 10 ENCYCLOPEDIA OF THE SOCIAL SCIENCES 648 (1935).

93. *See* E. ERICKSON, GANDHI'S TRUTH 276 (1969), which includes this telling sentence from Macaulay's Minute on Indian education: "We must at present do our best to form a class who may be interpreters between us and the millions whom we govern; a class of persons, Indian in blood and colour, but English in taste, in opinions, in morals, and in intellect."

94. "A single shelf of a good European library was worth the whole native literature of India and Arabia . . . Neither as the languages of the law, nor as the languages of religion, have the Sanskrit and Arabic any peculiar claim to our engagement." T. MACAULAY, PROSE AND POETRY 729 (1852), *quoted in* E. ERIKSON, *supra* note 93, at 276.

95. *See* 1 W. STOKES, *supra* note 89, at xvi.

96. INDIA PENAL CODE, *supra* note 85, at 70 note.

97. *Id.* at 81–82 note.

98. *Id.* at 102 note. For other examples, see discussion in J. CLIVE, *supra* note 73, at 452–55; 1 W. STOKES, *supra* note 89, at xxvi; Rankin, *supra* note 89, at 45–46.

99. India Charter Act, 1833, 3 & 4 Will. iv, c.85.

100. INDIA PENAL CODE, *supra* note 85, at i.

101. E. STOKES, *supra* note 69, at 227. *See* Vesey-FitzGerald, *supra* note 91, at 231:

> "But it was Bentham's peculiar merit that he taught lawyers—at any rate lawyers of the high quality of those who framed the Indian Codes—to think always of the law as a symmetrical and logical whole and of the law not merely as it is but as it ought to be; to dissect every idea; to base themselves always on first principles and to ask of every rule, 'what useful purpose does this serve?' "

102. J. BENTHAM, *Codification Proposal,* in 4 BENTHAM WORKS, *supra* note 2, at 543–45.

103. INDIA PENAL CODE, *supra* note 85, at v.

104. J. CLIVE, *supra* note 73, at 459.

105. J. BENTHAM, *Essay on the Promulgation of Laws and the Reasons Thereof, With Specimen of a Penal Code,* in 1 BENTHAM WORKS, *supra* note 2, at 159–63. J. BENTHAM, *supra* note 102, at 543 ("Rationale, interwoven not detached."). One reason Macaulay chose to omit the reasons, apparently, was his expectation of difficulty in obtaining legislative consensus. *See* E. STOKES, *supra* note 69, at 199–200.

106. INDIA PENAL CODE, *supra* note 85, at iv.

107. 3 J. STEPHEN, *supra* note 89, at 302–03.

108. INDIA PENAL CODE, *supra* note 85, at v.

109. 1 W. STOKES, *supra* note 89, at xxiv.

110. *See, e.g.,* M. LANG, *supra* note 85, at 81; F. POLLACK, A DIGEST OF THE LAW OF PARTNERSHIP iv (4th ed. 1888); E. STOKES, *supra* note 69, at 231.

111. 1 LIVINGSTON WORKS, *supra* note 11, at 178–79.

112. *See.* R. RANTANLAL & K. DHIRAJLAL, THE LAW OF CRIMES (22d ed. 1971).

113. 1 W. STOKES, *supra* note 89, at xxvi.

114. M. C. SETALVAD, *supra* note 89, at 129–30.

115. F. POLLOCK, *supra* note 110, at iv. *See also* 3 J. STEPHEN, *supra* note 89, at 302–03.

116. HER MAJESTY'S COMMISSIONERS ON CRIMINAL LAW, FOURTH REPORT, CD. No. 168, at xvi (1839), *reprinted in* 3 BRITISH PARLIAMENTARY PAPERS (CRIMINAL LAW) 233, 248 (I.U.P. 1971) [hereinafter cited as PARL. PAP.].

117. Stephen appreciated the value of illustrations but believed they would be unacceptable to the English Parliament and to the English judges. 3 J. STEPHEN, *supra* note 89, at 304.

118. *Id.* at 322.

119. E. STOKES, *supra* note 69, at 192.

120. *See, e.g.,* 9 BENTHAM WORKS, *supra* note 2, at 213–64 (bureaucracy contemplated in his Constitutional Code). *See also* J. CLIVE, *supra* note 73, at 433–34.

121. INDIA PENAL CODE, *supra* note 85, at 85 note.

122. *Id.* at 131 note. "It would weaken a class already too weak. It will be time enough to guard the matrimonial contract by penal sanctions when that contract becomes just, reasonable, and mutually beneficial."

123. *Id.* cl. 470, at 64. Paradoxically, John Stuart Mill criticized this provision on the ground that the truth of charges relating to private life would be too difficult to adjudicate. *Review of A Penal Code prepared by the Indian Law Commissioners,* 31 LONDON & WEST-MINSTER REV. 393, 403–04 (1839) (unsigned, but generally attributed to Mill); *see, e.g.,* J. CLIVE, *supra* note 73, at 462; E. STOKES, *supra* note 69, at 239. ·

124. INDIA PENAL CODE, *supra* note 85, cls. 275–86, at 36–37.

125. *Id.* at 101 note.

126. CODE OF CRIMES AND PUNISHMENTS arts. 110–14, *reprinted in* 2 LIVINGSTON WORKS, *supra* note 11, at 38–39.

127. INDIA PENAL CODE, *supra* note 85, cl. 113, at 16. Although he did include an "explanation" stating that disapprobation of governmental measures "compatible with a disposition to render obedience to the lawful authority of the Government" is not "disaffection."

128. *Id.* cl. 75, at 10.

129. *Id.* cls. 62, 63, at 7.

130. *E.g., id.* cls. 471–78, at 64–66 (defamation), where "good faith" belief in such non-factual matters as opinion and aesthetic judgment are made defenses to defamation.

131. *Id.* cl. 63, at 7, speaks of an action "done by a person in the exercise, to the best of his judgment exercised in good faith of any power given to him by law," which would be odd if "good faith" imported an objective standard of reasonableness.

132. Later changes to Macaulay's Code as enacted included a provision expressly stating otherwise. 1 W. STOKES, *supra* note 89, at 103: "Nothing is said to be done or believed in good faith, which is done or believed without due care and attention."

133. INDIA PENAL CODE, *supra* note 85, cl. 294, at 38.

134. *Id.* at 105 note. "In general however the penal law must content itself with keeping men from doing positive harm, and must leave to public opinion, and to the teachers of morality and religion, the office of furnishing men with motives for doing positive good." The same libertarian position appears in his reasons for not making adultery a crime:

> "We cannot admit that a Penal Code is by any means to be considered as a body of ethics, that the legislature ought to punish acts merely because those acts are immoral, or that because an act is not punished at all it follows that the legislature considers that act as innocent. Many things which are not punishable are morally worse than many things which are punishable."

Id. at 130 note. Compare the quite different perspective of Livingston in defending his proposal to criminalize indecent advances to women. 1 LIVINGSTON WORKS, *supra* note 11, at 286.

135. *See, e.g.,* J. CLIVE, *supra* note 73, at 447–48; Rankin, *supra* note 89, at 47.

136. INDIA PENAL CODE, *supra* note 85, at 69–70 note.

137. *Id.* at 77 note:

> If it were possible to devise a punishment, which should give pain proportioned to the degree in which the offender was shameless, hard-hearted, and abandoned to vice, such a punishment would be the most effective means of

protecting society. On the other hand of all punishments the most absurd is that which produces pain proportioned to the degree in which the offender retains the sentiments of an honest man.

138. E. STOKES, *supra* note 69, at 217–18.

139. SUMMARY OF REPORT OF LAW COMMISSION, *quoted in* E. STOKES, *supra* note 69, at 217–18.

140. INDIA PENAL CODE, *supra* note 85, at 70 note.

141. *See id.* at xx.

142. *Cf.* 1 W. STOKES, *supra* note 89, at 26 ("The framers of the Code do not seem to have troubled themselves much about the rival theories of punishment, respecting which German jurists and philosophers have written so copiously.").

143. INDIA PENAL CODE, *supra* note 85, at vi.

144. CODE OF CRIMES AND PUNISHMENTS arts. 487, 488, *reprinted in* 2 LIVINGSTON WORKS, *supra* note 11, at 127, 128.

145. INDIA PENAL CODE, *supra* note 85, at 107 note.

146. *See id. See also* text accompanying note 35 *supra.*

147. For a summary of prison terms provided by the Indian Penal Code as later enacted, see 1 W. STOKES, *supra* note 89, at 25.

148. CODE OF CRIMES AND PUNISHMENTS art. 90, *reprinted in* 2 LIVINGSTON WORKS, *supra* note 11, at 33; INTRODUCTORY REPORT, *reprinted in* 1 LIVINGSTON WORKS, *supra* note 11, at 224–25.

149. INDIA PENAL CODE, *supra* note 85, at 72–73 note.

150. CODE OF CRIMES AND PUNISHMENTS art. 647, *reprinted in* 2 LIVINGSTON WORKS, *supra* note 11, at 170.

151. INDIA PENAL CODE, *supra* note 85, at 120–21 note.

152. CODE OF CRIMES AND PUNISHMENTS art. 535(4), *reprinted in* 2 LIVINGSTON WORKS, *supra* note 11, at 146.

153. INDIA PENAL CODE, *supra* note 85, cl. 297, at 39; *id.* at 108–09 note.

154. *Id.* at 119 note.

155. *Id.* cl. 61, at 7; *id.* at 78 note. *See also* MODEL PENAL CODE §223.1(1) (Proposed Off. Draft, 1962).

156. INDIA PENAL CODE, *supra* note 85, cl. 73, at 9. *See also* MODEL PENAL CODE §2.12 (Proposed Off. Draft 1962).

157. INDIA PENAL CODE, *supra* note 85, at 81 note.

158. *Id.* cl. 470, at 64. *See also text accompanying note 123 supra.*

159. *Id.* cl. 297, at 39. *See also* text accompanying note 153 *supra.*

160. *Id.* at 131 note. *See also* text accompanying note 122 *supra.*

161. *Id.* cls. 74–84, at 411. *See also* text accompanying note 97 *supra.*

162. "Nothing is an offence which is in the exercise of the right of private defense, or which would be an exercise of private defense if the circumstances under which it is done were such as the person who does it believes in good faith that they are." *Id.* cl. 84, at 11. I find myself compelled to read "good faith" in this way for the reasons stated in notes 130, 131 *supra,* and because it is not clear how otherwise the self-defense provisions were an enlargement, as Macaulay meant them to be. Another noteworthy feature of the self-defense provisions involves the person who, knowing his life is not imperilled, uses deadly force to protect an interest for which only lesser defensive force is justified (assault, recovering property). His offense is "voluntary culpable homicide in defense" and not murder. INDIA PENAL CODE, *supra* note 85, cl. 299, at 40.

> "The chief reason for making this separation is that the law itself invites men to the very verge of the crime which we have designated voluntary culpable homicide in defence . . . And it seems difficult to conceive that circumstances which would be a full justification of any violence short of homicide should not be a mitigation of the guilt of homicide."

Id. at 110 note.

163. *Id.* at 111 note m.

164. *Id.* at 111–12.

165. *Id.* cls. 294, 295, at 112.

166. *Id.* at iii–iv.

167. *Id.* cl. 305, at 112. Macaulay states that Livingston framed his Code on the same principles, *id.* at 112 note, but I think he was mistaken. CODE OF CRIMES AND PUNISHMENTS art. 532, *reprinted in* 2 LIVINGSTON WORKS, *supra* note 11, at 144, provides that the punishment for negligent homicide is to be increased if the act is done in committing an unlawful act—if the unlawful act is a misdemeanor not against the person, the punishment is increased by one-fourth; if the act is an offense against the person, it is to be increased by one-half; if the act is punishable with hard labor, it is to be doubled. Article 597 makes murder any death, accidental or negligent, apparently, resulting from illegal burning. The upshot is that the principle of felony-murder and misdemeanor-manslaughter is retained for negligent actions, though not for accidental ones, except in the case of burning. Moreover, article 41 states a broad "lesser-crime" principle that reaches all cases other than homicide: if one in intentionally committing an offense "shall through MISTAKE or ACCIDENT, do another act which, if voluntarily done, would be an offense, he shall incur the penalty for the act really done." Livingston was concerned, with reason, that this "is in apparent contradiction to the general other provision, that the will must concur with the act in order to constitute an offense [Art. 27]." CODE OF CRIMES AND PUNISHMENTS art. 41, *reprinted in* 1 LIVINGSTON WORKS, *supra* note 11, at 234–35.

168. Except once, as far as I can find. INDIA PENAL CODE, *supra* note 85, cl. 257, at 34: "Whoever malignantly or wantonly does any act which he knows to be likely to spread the infection of any disease dangerous to life. . . ."

169. *Id.* cl. 267, at 35.

170. *E.g., id.* cls. 265, 266, 268, at 35.

171. *Id.* cl. 260, at 34.

172. *Id.* cl. 261, at 34.

173. *Id.* cl. 294, at 38. Macaulay equates for purposes of punishment acts of intentional killings with those done with knowledge of the likelihood of causing death—both may be murder. One may quarrel with the choice but one at least knows it is being made.

174. *Id.* cl. 304, at 40.

175. *Id.* cl. 399, at 54.

176. *Id.* cl 456, at 61.

177. *E.g., id.* cls. 253, 254, at 33–34.

178. *Id.* cl. 16, at 3.

179. Act XLV of 1860, 11 INDIA A.I.R. MANUAL 947 (2d ed. 1961).

180. The most detailed account of the revisions of Macaulay's draft by subsequent Indian LAW COMMISSIONS is given in Patra, *Historical Introduction to the Indian Penal Code,* in INDIAN LAW INSTITUTE, *supra* note 85, at 33–46. *See also* Rankin, *supra* note 89, at 40–41. Stephen speculates that the long delay:

> "is probably to be accounted for by the extreme aversion which for a long time before the mutiny was felt by influential persons in India to any changes which boldly and definitely replaced native by European institutions. It appeared in every way the safer course to alter and interfere as little as possible. . . . "

3 J. STEPHEN, *supra* note 89, at 299.

181. He wrote that long delay in its enactment had the beneficial result of providing the opportunity "for a minutely careful revision by a professional lawyer [Sir Peacock Barnes], possessed of as great experience and as much technical knowledge as any man of his time. An ideal code ought to be drawn by a Bacon and settled by a Coke." 3 J. STEPHEN, *supra* note 89, at 300.

182. Stephen himself saw to reinserting this provision of Macaulay's Code, cl. 304, when he served as legal member of the Council of India. *Id.* at 311.

183. INDIA PEN. CODE §497 (1860), *reprinted in* 1 W. STOKES, *supra* note 89, at 283.

184. Stephen himself spoke of the enacted Code's homicide provisions as "the weakest part of the Code." 3 J. STEPHEN, *supra* note 89, at 313.

185. Stephen, *Codification in India and England,* 18 FORTNIGHTLY REV. 644, 654 (1872).

186. 3 J. STEPHEN, *supra* note 89, at 299. Lord Bryce travelled through India in 1888 and 1889 seeking opinions from competent persons on the Penal Code, as well as the other Indian Codes. The Penal Code received the best press: "The Penal Code was universally approved; and it deserves the praise bestowed on it, for it is one of the noblest monuments of Macaulay's genius." 1 J. BRYCE, *supra* note 8, at 108–09.

187. Sir John Holker, Attorney-General, so stated in introducing the Bill. 239 HANSARD 1938, *quoted in* M. LANG, *supra* note 85, at 56.

188. See the bibliography in L. RADZINOWICZ, SIR JAMES FITZJAMES STEPHEN (1829–1894) AND HIS CONTRIBUTIONS TO THE DEVELOPMENT OF CRIMINAL LAW 49 (Seldon Soc'y Lecture 1957). I am indebted to Sir Leon for this probing study.

189. Stephen's book was out of print from 1914 until 1967 when the second edition (1874) was republished by the Cambridge University Press.

190. L. STEPHEN, LIFE OF SIR JAMES FITZJAMES STEPHEN 248 (1895).

191. 1 J. BRYCE *supra* note 8, at 109; M. LANG, *supra* note 85, at 84–85.

192. 1 J. BRYCE, *supra* note 8, at 110.

193. Cahn, *Fact-Skepticism: An Unexpected Chapter,* 38 N.Y.U.L. REV. 1025, 1027 (1963).

194. *See* Stephen, *supra* note 18, at 644.

195. DIGEST OF THE CRIMINAL LAW iv (1877).

196. REPORT OF THE ROYAL COMMISSION APPOINTED TO CONSIDER THE LAW RELATING TO INDICTABLE OFFENSES (1879) [hereinafter cited as REPORT], *reprinted in* 6 PARL. PAP.,*supra* note 116, at 369.

197. By Stephen's own testimony "by far the greater part both of the Code and of the Report" was his composition. 3 J. STEPHEN, *supra* note 89, at 349.

198. P. MILLER, THE LIFE OF THE MIND IN AMERICA 254 (1965).

199. John Austin, for example, one of Bentham's most powerful disciples, had a more modest view of codification than Bentham did. He did not favor a *beau ideal* of all possible codes, preferring a code based on existing law; he did not think it important that the average reader be able to understand and know the code's provisions; and he thought the arguments against judge-made law exaggerated. *See* 2 AUSTIN ON JURISPRUDENCE 620-81 (Lectures 37-39), 1021-39 (Notes on Codification) (5th ed. Campbell 1885).

200. L. RADZINOWICZ, *supra* note 8, chs. 15, 16 (1948); Fry, *Bentham and English Penal Reform,* in JEREMY BENTHAM AND THE LAW, *supra* note 7, at 34.

201. "Mr. Peel is for consolidation in contradistinction to codification: I for codification in contradistinction to consolidation." 10 BENTHAM WORKS, *supra* note 2, at 595.

202. *See* text accompanying notes 69, 70 *supra.*

203. FIRST REPORT OF HIS MAJESTY'S COMMISSIONERS ON CRIMINAL LAW (1834), *reprinted in* 3 PARL. PAP., *supra* note 116, at 9.

204. These reports and drafts occupy three volumes of the Irish University Press Series of British Parliamentary Papers (volumes 3, 4, and 5—"Criminal Law") and cover over 2,000 pages.

205. FOURTH REPORT FROM HER MAJESTY'S COMMISSIONERS FOR REVISING AND CONSOLIDATING THE CRIMINAL LAW (1848), *reprinted in* 5 PARL. PA., *supra* note 116, at 414, A Fifth Report in 1849 contained a draft of a criminal procedure bill. 5 PARL. PAP., *supra* note 116, at 559.

206. *See* L. RADZINOWICZ, *supra* note 188, at 18; REPORT, *supra* note 196, at 6, *reprinted in* 6 PARL. PAP.,*supra* note 196, at 374. A fuller account of the history of these movements for reform is given in M. LANG, *supra* note 85, at 42–58.

207. The close affinity between his moral thinking and that of Justice Holmes is explored in Mark D. Howe's biography of Holmes. *See* M.D. HOWE, JUSTICE OLIVER WENDELL HOLMES—THE SHAPING YEARS 213, 227–28 (1957), and its sequel, M.D. HOWE, THE PROVING YEARS 171–73 (1963).

208. Stephen acknowledged that in certain areas he was a utilitarian.

> "That is to say, I think that from the nature of the case, some external standard must always be supplied by which moral rules may be tested; and happiness is the most significant and least misleading word that can be employed for that purpose. . . . I know not on what other footing than that of expediency, generally in a wider or narrower sense, it would be possible to discuss the value of a moral rule or the provisions of a law."

J. STEPHEN, LIBERTY, EQUALITY, FRATERNITY 227 (White ed. 1967).

209. *Stephen*, 18 DICT. NAT. BIOG. 1051, 1053 (1921).

210. L. STEPHEN, *supra* note 190, at 107.

211. J. STEPHEN, *supra* note 208, at 211.

212. *Id.* at 118.

213. *Id.* at 219.

214. *Id.* at 212.

215. *Id.* at 220.

216. *Id.* at 238.

217. J. STEPHEN, ESSAYS BY A BARRISTER 78 (1862) ("Doing Good").

218. J. STEPHEN, *supra* note 208, at 229.

219. *Id.* at 228.

220. *Id.* at 150.

221. *Id.* at 144.

222. *Id.* at 152.

223. 2 J. STEPHEN, *supra* note 89, at 81–82.

224. INDIA PENAL CODE, *supra* note 85 at xx.

225. J. STEPHEN, DIGEST OF THE CRIMINAL LAW xxiii (1877).

226. REPORT, *supra* note 196, at 5, *reprinted in* 6 PARL. PAP., *supra* note 116, at 373.

227. 3 J. STEPHEN, *supra* note 89, at 361. Bentham's views on this kind of codification, which he pejoratively called consolidation, are exemplified in the following earthy passage from his tract addressed to his "Fellow-Citizens of France on Houses of Peers and Senates," 4 BENTHAM WORKS, *supra* note 2, at 419, 425 n. a:

> "Have you a receptacle, the odour of which is troublesome? Employ a set of men—*nightmen* is with us the official name of them—not to empty it, but to look into it, and report, more particularly, how it smells. So doing, you will follow the precedent set by our law-reformers. . . . "

228. 4 BENTHAM WORKS, *supra* note 2, at 350.

229. REPORT, *supra* note 196, at 12–13, *reprinted in* 6 PARL. PAP., *supra* note 116, at 380–81.

230. "On this very delicate subject we do not undertake to suggest any alteration of the law." 6 PARL. PAP., *supra* note 116, at 388.

231. See, for example, the separate provisions on mischief depending on the object damaged—ships, wrecks, piles and sluices, fish ponds, cattle, hopbinds, telegraphs, etc. Draft code §§ 390–407, *reprinted in* 6 PARL. PAP., *supra* note 116, at 516–520.

232. 3 J. STEPHEN, *supra* note 89, at 357.

233. Draft Code § 164, *reprinted in* 6 Parl. PAP., *supra* note 116, at 466.

234. REPORT, *supra* note 196, at 7–8, *reprinted in* 6 PARL. PAP., *supra* note 116, at 375–376.

235. *Id.* at 9, *reprinted in* 6 PAR. PAP., *supra* note 116, at 377.

236. *Id.*

237. Draft Code § 141, *reprinted in* 6 PARL. PAP., *supra* note 116, at 462.

238. REPORT, *supra* note 196, at 21, *reprinted in* 6 PARL. PAP., *supra* note 116, at 389.

239. Draft Code § 147, *reprinted in* 6 PARL. PAP., *supra* note 116, at 463; REPORT, *supra* note 229, at 22, *reprinted in* 6 PARL. PAP., *supra* note 116, at 390.

240. Draft Code § 5, *reprinted in* 6 PARL. PAP., *supra* note 116, at 431; REPORT, *supra* note 196, at 9–10, *reprinted in* 6 PARL. PAP., *supra* note 116, at 377–378.

241. Draft Code § 19, *reprinted in* 6 PARL. PAP., *supra* note 116, at 435.

242. REPORT, *supra* note 196, at 10, *reprinted in* 6 PARL. PAP., *supra* note 116, at 378.

243. 3 J. STEPHEN, *supra* note 89, at 361. At another point Stephen revealed a different reason for leaving such defenses as necessity or choice of evils unstated: "There is no fear that people will be too ready to obey the ordinary law. There is great fear that they would be too ready to avail themselves of exceptions which they might suppose to apply to their circumstances." *Id.* at 110. The issue is even today a live one in England. *See* Williams, *Defences of General Application, Necessity,* 1978 CRIM. L. REV. 128.

244. L. RADZINOWICZ, *supra* note 188, at 35.

245. Draft Code § 178 (murder), *reprinted in* 6 PARL. PAP., *supra* note 116, at 469; *id* § 75 (treason), *reprinted in* 6 PARL. PAP., *supra* note 116, at 445; *id.* § 106 (piracy with violence), *reprinted in* 6 PARL. PAP., *supra* note 116, at 454; *id* § 81 (burning ship of war or government arsenals), *reprinted in* 6 PARL. PAP., *supra* note 116, at 447.

246. 1 J. STEPHEN, *supra* note 89, at 479.

247. Draft Code § 10, *reprinted in* 6 PARL. PAP., *supra* note 116, at 433.

248. 2 J. STEPHEN, *supra* note 89, at 92.

249. 3 *id. at* 367. Stephen had come far from Bentham who regarded the pronouncement of moral guilt as beyond the competence of and therefore inappropriate to the criminal law. *See* Fry, *supra* note 200, at 20, 26–27. The contrast with Macaulay is also great. *See* note 134 *supra.*

250. Draft Code § 13, *reprinted in* 6 PARL. PAP., *supra* note 116, at 433.

251. REPORT, *supra* note 196, at 14, *reprinted in* 6 PARL. PAP., *supra* note 116, at 382.

252. Draft Code § 12, *reprinted in* 6 PARL. PAP., *supra* note 116, at 433.

253. *Id.* § 119, *reprinted in* 6 PARL. PAP., *supra* note 116, at 457.

254. *Id.* pt. 15, *reprinted in* 6 PARL. PAP., *supra* note 116, at 463.

255. *Id.* §§174, 175, *reprinted in* 6 PARL. PAP., *supra* note 116, at 468.

256. *Id.* §§ 174(d), 175(a), *reprinted in* 6 PARL. PAP., *supra* note 116, at 468.

257. *Id.* § 176, *reprinted in* 6 PARL. PAP., *supra* note 116, at 468.

258. *Id.*

259. Id. § 74, *reprinted in* 6 PARL. PAP., *supra* note 116, at 445.

260. *Id.* § 201, *reprinted in* 6 PARL. PAP., *supra* note 116, 474.

261. *Id.* § 56, *reprinted in* 6 PARL. PAP., *supra* note 116, at 441.

262. *Id.* § 71, *reprinted in* 6 PARL. PAP., *supra* note 116, at 444.

263. *Id.* § 62, *reprinted in* 6 PARL. PAP., *supra* note 116, at 442.

264. *Id.* § 61, *reprinted in* 6 PARL. PAP., *supra* note 116, at 442. He makes the same move in defining bigamy. *Id.* § 216, *reprinted in* 6 PARL. PAP., *supra* note 116, at 477.

265. Sir Leon Radzinowicz's kinder judgment may be fairer: "By extracting principles out of the 'endless myriad of precedents' and 'wilderness of single instances', he raised the status of criminal law as a legal discipline in a most remarkable way." L. RADZINOWICZ, *supra* note 188, at 22.

266. *See* note 231 *supra.*

267. Draft Code § 254, *reprinted in* 6 PARL. PAP., *supra* note 116, at 485.

268. *Id.* § 255, *reprinted in* 6 PARL. PAP., *supra* note 116, at 485.

269. *Id.* § 256, *reprinted in* 6 PARL. PAP., *supra* note 116, at 486.

270. *Id.* § 260, *reprinted in* 6 PARL. PAP., *supra* note 116, at 486.

271. *See* note 243 *supra.* He might have yielded here to the wisdom of his colleagues since he did draft a necessity provision in his *Digest of the Criminal Law* (art. 32).

272. Draft Code §§ 159–164, 170–173, *reprinted in* 6 PARL. PAP., *supra* note 116, at 465–66, 467–68.

273. Stephen "remains the greatest draftsman and codifier of criminal law this country has ever produced, a worthy peer of the most prominent amongst Continental lawyers who have left their mark in this field." L. RADZINOWICZ, *supra* note 188, at 22.

274. *See* M. LANG, *supra* note 85, at 56–58.

275. The Criminal Code Act, 1893, is a very close copy. 57 Vict., c. 56 (N.Z.).

276. Sir Samuel Griffiths produced a code for Queensland, heavily based on the Stephen Code, which, in turn, was borrowed in the other jurisdictions. *See* P. BRETT & P. WALLER, CRIMINAL LAW 4 (4the ed. 1978).

277. *See* J. CRANKSHAW, CRANKSHAW'S CRIMINAL CODE OF CANADA xv (6th ed. 1935).

278. Hicks, *David Dudley Field,* in 6 DICT. OF AMER. BIOG. 360, 362 (1943).

279. FIRST REPORT OF THE COMMISSIONERS OF THE CODE (1858), *cited in* Reppy, *The Field Codification Concept,* in DAVID DUDLEY FIELD CENTENARY ESSAYS 17, 40 (A. Reppy ed. 1949) [hereinafter cited as FIELD ESSAYS]. *See also* Moore, *Wm. Curtis Noyes,* in 13 DICT. OF AMER. BIOG. 592 (1943).

280. Reppy. *supra* note 279, at 40.

281. H. FIELD, THE LIFE OF DAVID DUDLEY FIELD 78, 81 (1898).

282. *See* Field, Address to the Law Reform Society (1883), *reprinted in* 2 DAVID DUDLEY FIELD, SPEECHES, ARGUMENTS AND MISCELLANEOUS PAPERS 476, 480 (Sprague ed. 1884) [hereinafter cited as FIELD SPEECHES]: "Night after night the commissioner met at each other's houses and re-examined carefully every section, every line, and every word [of the Penal Code Draft]."

283. His only political office was Congressman from New York to which he was appointed to fill the remaining two months of the term of the resigned incumbent. RECORD OF THE LIFE OF DAVID DUDLEY FIELD 45 (E. Field ed. 1931).

284. Roscoe Pound was of the view that Field's codification efforts might have changed the whole course of American law if they had come a quarter century earlier when the law was still in its formative stage. Pound, *David Dudley Field: An Appraisal,* in FIELD ESSAYS, *supra* note 279, at 5, 16 (1949).

285. As we saw earlier, *see* text accompanying notes 46–63 *supra,* Livingston, a friend and counsellor of Jackson, who served in his administration, early represented the legal side of Jacksonian sentiment. Bentham himself was lionized by the Jacksonian Democrats. He was toasted at a Democratic Fourth of July celebration in 1835 as "the modern apostle of liberty and reform. . . . [M]ay every democrat and workingman remember that he has most happily combined the essence of their principles in one short line—'The greatest good of the greatest number.' " A. SCHLESINGER, JR., THE AGE OF JACKSON 330–31 (1945).

286. *See* A. SCHLESINGER, JR., *supra* note 285, ch. 24.

287. See his arguments, in 3 FIELD SPEECHES, *supra* note 282, at 239, 411.

288. F. VON SAVIGNY, ON THE VOCATION OF OUR AGE FOR LEGISLATION AND JURISPRUDENCE (1831 ed. A. Hayward trans). *See* E. PATTERSON, JURISPRUDENCE: MEN AND IDEAS OF THE LAW 421–424 (1953).

289. J. CARTER, THE PROPOSED CODIFICATION OF OUR COMMON LAW (1884). Carter's objections, however, did not extend to codifying the criminal law. *Id.* at 14–18, 76.

290. R. POUND, *supra* note 284, at 7. Professor George Fletcher is one of the few contemporary scholars who leans in this direction. *See, e.g.,* Fletcher *The Right Deed for the Wrong Reason: A Reply to Mr. Robinson,* 23 U.C.L.A. L. REV. 293, 294 (1975), where he praises Robinson, *A Theory of Justification: Societal Harm as a Prerequisite for Criminal Liability,* 23 U.C.L.A. L. REV. 266 (1975), in terms that evoke the historical school:
    "Robinson does not claim that his position efficiently furthers any or all aims of the criminal law. Rather he starts from a construction of the criminal law as a received set of principles that ought to be binding on our deliberations

when conduct should be punished. The authority for these principles is not their instrumental value, but their grounding in a theory of just punishment implicit in the patterns of liability that have accrued in the common law."

See also Fletcher, *The Metamorhosis of Larceny,* 89 HARV. L. REV. 469 (1976).

291. P. MILLER, *supra* note 198, at 244, 255.

292. N.Y. CONST. of 1846, art. VI, §§ 2, 4, 8, 12 (F. Hough ed. 1867) (annotated). *See* C. WARREN, A HISTORY OF THE AMERICAN BAR 532 (1911).

293. M. LANG, *supra* note 85, at 118; Pound, *supra* note 284, at 9.

294. N.Y. CONST. OF 1846, art. VI § 24 (F. Hough ed. 1867).

295. *Id.* art. I, § 17.

296. *See* Reppy, *supra* note 279, at 30–36.

297. *See* Clark, *Code Pleading and Practice Today,* in FIELD ESSAYS, *supra* note 279, at 55, 56.

298. H. FIELD, *supra* note 281, at 74; M. LANG, *supra* note 85, at 132–36.

299. *See* Reppy, *supra* note 279, at 36–42.

300. COMMISSIONERS OF THE CODE, DRAFT OF A PENAL CODE FOR NEW YORK (1864); COMMISSIONERS OF THE CODE, THE PENAL CODE OF THE SATE OF NEW YORK (1865) (reported complete).

301. I will be considering primarily the 1864 draft. The 1865 version differs little from the earlier draft.

302. A. SCHLESINGER, *supra* note 285, at 33.

303. P. MILLER, *supra* note 198, at 260.

304. A curious shade on his legal career arose over his representation, and alleged participation in some of the questionable deals of Jay Gould, Jim Fisk, and "Boss" Tweed in connection with Erie Railroad activities. *See* C. ADAMS & H. ADAMS, CHAPTERS OF ERIE 36, 134, 183 (1956); Hicks, *David Dudley Field,* in 6 DICT. AMER. BIOG. 360–362 (1931). The evidence of serious improprieties is great, although lawyer's ethics at the time were in flux and judging by the standards of another day may be unfair. *See* Schudson, *Public, Private, and Professional Lives: The Correspondence of David Dudley Field and Samuel Bowles,* 21 AM. J. LEGAL HIST. 191 (1977). In any event, though a combination of public spirit and private improbity is always unexpected, it is hardly unknown. *See, e.g.,* F. OWEN, TEMPESTUOUS JOURNEY: LLOYD GEORGE, HIS LIFE AND TIMES 225–40, 628, 686–93 (1955); 2 C. FUESS, DANIEL WEBSTER 389–94 (1930).

305. *See* P. MILLER, *supra* note 198, at 259.

306. *Id.*

307. Field, *Judicial Delays: Second Report to the American Bar Association,* in 3 FIELD SPEECHES, *supra* note 282, at 199, 225. See also Field's 1889 address where, though late in his career, he observed: "[O]ur profession is one of the great conservative forces of society;. . . . it forms a group around the judges, serving the double purpose of oversight and defense. . . . In the incessant conflict between law and lawlessness, an immense majority of lawyers have always stood on the side of law." *The True Lawyer,* in 3 FIELD SPEECHES, *supra* note 282, at 399, 402.

308. *See* H. FIELD, *supra* note 281, at 73–74. (His ambition "was not to be a breaker of the precious traditions of the past. He had no purpose or desire to destroy the Common Law but to preserve it and exalt it by cutting off its excrescences, and by translating it into the language of the people. . . .").

309. Address by D. Field at the New York University Law School (April 7, 1884), *reprinted in* 2 FIELD SPEECHES, *supra* note 282, at 503, 509.

310. COMMISSIONERS OF THE CODE, DRAFT OF A PENAL CODE FOR NEW YORK § 241(2) (1864).

311. *Id.* § 241(3).

312. *Id.* § 224(5).

313. *Id.* § 260(2).

314. *Id.* preliminary note, at iii.

315. Ch. 26, 1857 N.Y. Laws.

316. H. FIELD, *supra* note 281, at 74.

317. COMMISSIONERS OF THE CODE, DRAFT OF A PENAL CODE FOR NEW YORK § 404 (1864).

318. *Id.* § 406.

319. *Id.* § 408.

320. *Id.* §§ 410–414.

321. *Id.* § 417.

322. *Id.* § 449.

323. *Id.* § 459.

324. *Id.* § 467.

325. *Id.* §§ 503–510.

326. *Id.* § 713.

327. REPORT, *supra* note 196, at 12, *reprinted in* 6 PARL. PAP., *supra* note 116, at 380.

328. COMMISSIONERS OF THE CODE, DRAFT OF A PENAL CODE FOR NEW YORK iv (1864), (preliminary notes).

329. *Id.* at vi.

330. *Id.* at iv.

331. *Id.* § 150 note.

332. *See, e.g., id.,* §§ 319 (tightening the law of rape), 131 (spelling out the five ways of improperly influencing a juror).

333. *Id.* § 241 note.

334. *See* Draft Code § 176, *reprinted in* 6 PARL. PAP., *supra* note 116, at 468.

335. COMMISSIONERS OF THE CODE, DRAFT OF A PENAL CODE FOR NEW YORK §§ 248, 252 (1864).

336. *Id.* § 260(2).

337. *Id.* § 2.

338. *Id.* at iv.

339. *Id.* § 248 note.

340. *Id.* § 584.

341. *Id.* note.

342. *Id.* § 540 note.

343. J. DILLON, *supra* note 10, at 316.

344. *See* Beckman, *supra* note 65, at 148, 172.

345. Ch. 676, 1881 N.Y. Laws, I, 913.

346. *See* M. LANG, *supra* note 85, at 146.

347. *Id.* at 152–59.

348. *Preface* to N. DAK. REV. CODE iv (1895).

349. CAL. PENAL CODE (1872). 3 *Appendix* to JOURNALS OF THE SENATE AND ASSEMBLY, 19th Sess. 316, 349 (1872).

350. *See* PROPOSED CAL. REVISED LAWS, PENAL CODE §§ 187, 188 (1870).

351. Some credit for Field's success in California apparently belongs to his brother, Stephen J. Field, who stated in his *Reminiscences* that as a California state assemblyman in 1851 he adapted to California circumstances and helped secure the passage of the civil and criminal practice codes his brother had proposed for New York. C. SWISHER, STEPHEN J. FIELD, CRAFTSMAN OF THE LAW 54–55 (1930). Later, while a Justice of the United States Supreme Court in 1873, he served, remarkably, on a committee of code examiners, appointed by the Governor of California, to re-examine the political, civil, penal and civil procedure codes enacted earlier and to propose amendments. *See* THE CODE EXAMINER'S NOTES FROM DRAFT OF AN ACT TO AMEND THE CIVIL CODE 3, 11 (M. Dodge ed. 1916).

352. *See Preface* to ARIZ. PENAL CODE, ARIZ. REV. STAT. (1913).

353. IDAHO REV. STAT. pt. 4 (Penal) (1887). IDAHO CODE § 18 (Crimes and Punishment) comp. leg. notes (1940).

354. MONTANA PENAL CODE (1895); *see* H. FIELD, *supra* note 281, at 91.

355. 3 OREGON COMPILED LAWS ANNOT. CODE, comp. leg. notes (1940).

356. UTAH CODE ANN. § 76 (Penal Code), historical notes (1953).

357. 1890 WYO. SESS. LAWS, ch. 73.

358. The contest between legislatures and courts over which should govern reappeared, of course, in the bitter controversy over judicial review.

359. Wechsler, *A Thoughtful Code of Substantive Law*, 45 J. CRIM. L.C. & P.S. 524, 526 (1955).

360. Id. at 525.

361. Wechsler, *The Model Penal Code and the Codification of American Criminal Law, in* CRIME, CRIMINOLOGY AND PUBLIC POLICY 419, 424–25 (R. Hood ed. 1976).

362. Wechsler, *supra* note 359, at 525.

363. Wechsler, *supra* note 361, at 420–21.

364. *Id.* at 421.

365. J. MICHAEL & H. WECHSLER, CRIMINAL LAW AND ITS ADMINISTRATION (1940); Wechsler & Michael, *A Rationale of the Law of Homicide* (pts. 1 & 2), 37 COLUM. L. REV. 701, 1261 (1937).

366. Wechsler, *The Challenge of a Model Penal Code*, 65 HARV. L. REV. 1097, 1098 (1952).

367. Wechsler & Michael, *supra* note 365.

368. Wechsler, *supra* note 366, at 1098.

369. Wechsler, *supra* note 361, at 424.

370. MODEL PENAL CODE § 211.2 (Proposed Off. Draft, 1962).

371. *Id.* § 2.04.

372. *Id.* § 5.01.

373. *Id.* § 2.06.

374. Wechsler, *supra* note 361, at 442; Wechsler, *supra* note 359, at 529–30.

375. Wechsler, *The American Law Institute: Some Observations on its Model Penal Code*, 42 A.B.A.J. 321, 322 (1956).

376. MODEL PENAL CODE § 2.03, Comment 132 (Tent. Draft No. 4, 1955).

377. MODEL PENAL CODE § 2.03 (Proposed Off. Draft, 1962).

378. MODEL PENAL CODE § 3.02 (Proposed Off. Draft, 1962); MODEL PENAL CODE § 3.02 Comment 5 (Tent. Draft No. 8, 1958).

379. MODEL PENAL CODE § 2.02(2)(d) (Proposed Off. Draft, 1962); Wechsler, *supra* note 361, at 435–38.

380. Wechsler, *supra* note 361, at 432.

381. The Code's point of departure is that the criminal law should not

> "vary legal norms with the individual's capacity to meet the standards they prescribe, absent a disability that is both gross and verifiable, such as the mental disease or defect that may establish irresponsibility. The most that it is feasible to do with lesser disabilities is to accord them proper weight in sentencing."

MODEL PENAL CODE § 2.09, Comment 6 (Tent. Draft No. 10, 1960). The Code makes some concession to the individual's circumstances by requiring that the reasonableness of the defendant's action, whenever that is in issue, be judged from the viewpoint of a person "in the actor's situation." *E.g., id.* §§ 210.3(1)(b) (provocation), 2.02(2)(d) (negligence) (Proposed Off. Draft, 1962). While this deliberately introduces an area of flexibility, it is plain that no wholly individualized standard was contemplated. *Id.* § 2.02, Comment 126 (Tent. Draft No. 4, 1955); *id.* § 2.09, Comment 6 (Tent. Draft No. 10, 1960). In the interest of furthering the preventive purposes of the law the Code does not accept the position that severe emotional distress should suffice for provocation, *id.* § 210.3, Comment 47–48 (Tent. Draft No. 9, 1959). *See also* Williams, *Provocation and the Reasonable Man* 1954 CRIM. L. REV. 740, 741–42; that duress may rest solely on the actors inability to act otherwise because of his terror at the threat,

MODEL PENAL CODE § 2.09, Comment 6–7 (Tent. Draft No. 10, 1960). *See also* G. WILLIAMS, CRIMINAL LAW: THE GENERAL PART 756 (2d ed. 1961); that the right of self-defense exists so long as the actor actually believed his life was endangered, MODEL PENAL CODE § 3.09(2) (Proposed Off. Draft, 1962); or that negligence should require a showing that the actor was capable of taking reasonable precautions, *id.* § 2.02(2)(d). *See also* H. L. A. HART, PUNISHMENT AND RSPONSIBILITY 154 (1968); G. WILLIAMS, *supra*, at 122–124.

382. MODEL PENAL CODE § 2.05 (Proposed Off. Draft, 1962).

383. Wechsler, *supra* note 361, at 438.

384. *Id.* at 447–49.

385. MODEL PENAL CODE art. 3 (Proposed Off. Draft, 1962).

386. *Id.* § 2.02.

387. Note Wechsler's acceptance of Professor Packer's characterization of the dominant tone of the Code "as one of principled pragmatism." Wechsler, *supra* note 361, at 465.

388. MODEL PENAL CODE § 210.6 (Proposed Off. Draft, 1962).

389. *Id.* § 210.2(1)(b).

390. *Id.* § 2.08(2).

391. Wechsler, *supra* note 361, at 441.

392. S. KADISH & M. PAULSEN, CRIMINAL LAW AND ITS PROCESSES 570–71 (3d ed. 1975).

393. Wechsler, *supra* note 361, at 445.

394. *Id.* at 419–24.

395. ALI ANNUAL REPORT 19 (1978).

NOTES TO ESSAY 10

1. It is illuminating to observe that from the single point of view of the number of persons directly affected, the preaccusation and postconviction processes have a greater significance than the processes of trial. Of all persons touched by the criminal process only the relatively small percentage who are brought to trial and acquitted or convicted are directly affected by the safeguards of trial. On the other hand, none of these persons escape the impact of enforcement decisions of the police and the prosecutor. And of those who are convicted, only the 10–15% whose convictions follow not-guilty pleas are affected by the safeguards of trial, while virtually all are directly affected by the exercise of correctional discretion.

2. There are, of course, other stages in the criminal process in which wide scope for the discretionary judgment raises the problem of compatibility with the rule of law. At the pretrial stage, for example, the problem is raised by the exercise of the accusatorial judgment by such institutions as the prosecutor and the grand jury: when to charge, with what crimes to charge, whether to reduce a charge to a lesser offense. At the trial stage the judge himself has considerable discretion; for example, in the decision to accept guilty pleas to lesser offenses and in formulating a charge to the jury. At the postconviction stage, the problem is raised by the administration of penal institutions, including the imposition of discipline upon convicts. See Breitel, *Controls in Criminal Law Enforcement,* 27 U. CHI. L. REV. 427, 428 (1960). It is acutely raised as well in connection with modes of dealing with specialized classes of offenders, such as sexual psychopaths, mental delinquents, juvenile delinquents, and persons acquitted on grounds of insanity.

3. Consideration will not be given to deliberative judgments by police to enforce the criminal law by actions which either clearly violate legal proscriptions or skirt the boundaries of rules amorphously defined; for example, the unlawful search, the harassment raid, the arrest with no purpose of prosecution.

4. See Remington & Rosenblum, *The Criminal Law and the Legislative Process,* 1960 U. ILL. L.F. 481, 491–92.

5. See generally ARNOLD, THE SYMBOLS OF GOVERNMENT 149–71 (1935). His observation concerning prosecutorial discretion is equally applicable to police discretion:

> "The idea that a prosecuting attorney should be permitted to use his discretion concerning the laws which he will enforce and those which he will disregard appears to the ordinary citizen to border on anarchy. The fact that prosecuting attorneys are compelled to do this very thing is generally ignored, or, when attention is called to it, regarded as evidence of some kind of social degeneration which must be preached away in public speech and judicial utterance."

Id. at 151.

6. For a compilation of such statutes see Goldstein, *Police Discretion Not To Invoke the Criminal Process: Low-Visibility Decisions in the Administration of Justice*, 69 YALE L.J. 543, 557 n.26 (1960).

7. See, *e.g.*, People v. Woodward, 220 Mich. 511, 515, 190 N.W. 721, 723 (1922). The view is that "the lodgment in an officer of the power to enforce a law necessarily implies the duty of enforcement." Gowan v. Smith, 157 Mich. 443, 459, 122 N.W. 286, 291 (1909). See also the cases dealing with mandamus to compel a magistrate to issue an arrest warrant where a proper complaint has been filed. Such proceedings are often upheld on the ground that police enforcement is a compulsory ministerial act. *E.g.*, Marshall v. Herndon, 161 Ky. 232, 170 S.W. 623 (1914). Where relief has been denied it is often for the reason that relator lacked a necessary special and personal interest in the arrest sought. See State *ex rel.* Skilton v. Miller, 164 Ohio St. 163, 128 N.E.2d 47 (1955); Annot., 49 A.L.R.2d 1285 (1956).

8. Bargain City U.S.A. Inc. v. Dilworth, The Philadelphia Legal Intelligencer, June 22, 1960, p. 1, col. 1 (Phila. Ct. C.P. 1960).

9. *Id.* at p. 6, col. 2.

10. *But see* Comment, *The Right to Nondiscriminatory Enforcement of State Penal Laws*, 61 COLUM. L. REV. 1103, 1118 (1961), where it is concluded that United States Supreme Court decisions support the conclusion that "administrative agencies charged with enforcing penal laws possess the power to make reasonable classifications of a legislative nature."

11. See the compilation in Goldstein, *supra* note 6, at 558 n.27.

12. Thoughtful commentators have recently been turning their attention to these problems. For positions generally favorable to a rule-of-law approach, see Goldstein, *supra* note 6; Hall, *Police and Law in a Democratic Society*, 28 IND. L.J. 133 (1953). For positions generally favorable to freedom for the discretionary judgment, see Breitel, *supra* note 2; Remington & Rosenblum, *supra* note 4, at 491.

13. Most of the illustrations which follow are based upon or suggested by two of the American Bar Foundation studies in connection with the continuing program of research into the administration of criminal justice in the United States: II PILOT PROJECT REPORT—THE ADMINISTRATION OF CRIMINAL JUSTICE IN THE UNITED STATES (1959), and LaFAVE, ARREST IN MICHIGAN (1960). The present confidential status of these preliminary studies precludes further acknowledgment of my indebtedness to them through specific references. None of these arrest situations will be new to those who have read Professor Goldstein's acute analysis based on the data revealed by these studies, *supra* note 6.

14. See Walton, *"Selective Distribution" of Police Patrol Force*, 49 J. CRIM. L., C. & P.S. 165, 379 (1958).

15. But however intelligently this power is used, the fundamental question remains, should the police have the recognized right to dispense with the criminal law at will?

> Dicey believed that the rule of law meant that the citizen should be free from arbitrary power. A discretion to withhold a punishment may result in just as much arbitrary power as discretion to use extralegal punishment.

Hargrove, *Police Discretion*, 25 SOL. 337 (1958).

16. Goldstein, *supra* note 6, at 562.

17. See Comment on § 3 of the Model Anti-Gambling Act in 2 AMERICAN BAR ASSOCIATION COMMISSION ON ORGANIZED CRIME, ORGANIZED CRIME AND LAW ENFORCEMENT 75 (1953):

> "[A]bout half [of the states] impose penalties for all gambling, apparently leaving the problem of the social gambler to the discretion of enforcement authorities and the courts . . . .
>
> "The Commission has. . . had great difficulty with. . . finding a formula which would exclude the social or casual gambler from prosecution and punishment, yet which would not result in opening a large breach in the statute for the benefit of professional gamblers and their patrons. The Commission recognizes that it is unrealistic to promulgate a law literally aimed at making a criminal offense of the friendly election bet, the private, social card game among friends, etc. Nevertheless, it is imperative to confront the professional gambler with a statutory facade that is wholly devoid of loopholes."

18. *Cf.* James & Son Ltd. v. Smee, [1955] 1 Q.B. 78, 93: "Where legislation, as here [strict liability statute], throws a wide net it is important that only those should be charged who either deserve punishment or in whose case it can be said that punishment would tend to induce them to keep themselves and their organization up to the mark."

19. Hart, *The Aims of the Criminal Law*, 23 LAW & CONTEMP. PROB. 401, 424 (1958). See People v. Bunis, 9 N.Y.2d 1, 4, 172 N.E.2d 273, 274, 210 N.Y.S.2d 505, 507 (1961), in which the court of appeals invalidated § 436 d of the N.Y. Penal Law proscribing the sale of coverless magazines, stating: "What is wrong is not the sale of coverless magazines, but rather their sale by a vendor who takes part in a scheme to defraud a magazine publisher. Admittedly by denominating as criminal all sales, section 436-d necessarily tends to prevent corrupt sales. But . . . it is unreasonable and beyond the legitimate exercise of the police power for the Legislature to interdict all sales, permissible and illicit alike, in order to prevent those which are illicit."

20. For attempts to draft more narrowly defined gambling statutes, see MONT. REV. CODE ANN. § 94-2403 (1947); MODEL ANTI-GAMBLING ACT § 3[(2)], note 17 *supra*.

21. See Remington & Rosenblum, *supra* note 4, at 491, 493.

22. KINSEY, POMEROY & MARTIN, SEXUAL BEHAVIOUR IN THE HUMAN MALE 392 (1948): "The persons involved in these activities [illicit sexual activities punishable as crimes] taken as a whole, constitute more than 95 per cent of the total population."

23. SYMBOLS OF GOVERNMENT 160 (1935).

24. See Remington & Rosenblum, *supra* note 4, at 493.

25. See *id.* at 494.

26. *Cf.* KINSEY, MARTIN & GEBHARD, SEXUAL BEHAVIOUR IN THE HUMAN FEMALE 18 (1953):

> "The prodding of reform group, a newspaper-generated hysteria over some local sex crime, a vice drive which is put on by the local authorities to distract attention from defects in their administration of the city government, or the addition to the law-enforcement group of a sadistic officer who is disturbed over his own sexual problems, may result in a doubling . . . in the number of arrests on sex charges, even though there may have been no change in the actual behaviour of the community, and even though the illicit sex acts that are apprehended and prosecuted may still represent no more than a fantastically minute part of the illicit activity which takes place every day in the community."

27. See Allen, *The Borderland of the Criminal Law: Problems of 'Socializing' Criminal Justice*, 32 SOCIAL SERVICE REV. 107, 109 (1958).

28. See note 13 *supra*.

29. The problem is carefully examined in Goldstein, *supra* note 6, at 562–73.

30. However, on occasion this has been done. Article 88 of the *Uniform Code of Military Justice* makes it an offense for an officer to use contemptuous words against certain officials of the United States Government. 10 U.S.C. § 888 (1958). The comment upon this provision in the *Manual for Courts-Martial*, however, states that "expressions of

opinion made in a purely private conversation should not ordinarily be made the basis for a court martial charge." MANUAL FOR COURTS-MARTIAL, UNITED STATES 318 (1851). Another well known example was the detailed OPA guide to price-control enforcement policy during World War II. These are summarized in Schwartz, *Federal Criminal Jurisdiction and Prosecutors' Discretion*, 13 LAW & CONTEMP. PROB. 64, 84 (1948).

31. Goldstein, *supra* note 6, at 586.

32. While nonenforcement judgments by prosecutors and trial judges may often influence police not to arrest (except where the police motive is other than prosecution, *e.g.*, harassment), they do not reach independent judgments of police not to arrest in the first place. Beyond this, there appears to be little systematic formulation and communication of standards from prosecutors to police. Furthermore, it cannot be assumed that prosecutorial discretionary judgments and policies are not generative of cognate dangers themselves.

33. *But see* Lewis, *The Humanitarian Theory of Punishment*, 6 RES JUDICATAE 224 (1953).

34. There are now two classic studies of this problem: the five volumes comprising *The Attorney General's Survey of Release Procedures* in 1939, and the *Model Penal Code* more recently. See MODEL PENAL CODE arts. 6, 7, 301–06. (Prop. Final Draft No. 1, 1961) and supporting comments in earlier drafts.

35. The exclusions usually embrace defendants with prior records of convictions and those convicted of more serious offenses posing a threat of personal injury. See the table summarizing the probation laws of the various states in MODEL PENAL CODE § 6.02, comment at 14–21 (Tent. Draft No. 2, 1954). For a summary of statutory parole eligibility exclusions, see MODEL PENAL CODE § 305.10, comment at 85–89 (Tent. Draft No. 5, 1956).

36. See, *e.g.*, ARIZ. REV. STAT. ANN. § 13-1657 (1956) (Court may place on probation, "if it appears that there are circumstances in mitigation of the punishment, or that the ends of justice will be subserved thereby."); FLA. STAT. § 948.01(3) (1959) (Probation may be granted "if it appears . . . that the defendant is not likely again to engage in a criminal course of conduct and that the ends of justice and the welfare of society do not require that the defendant shall presently suffer the penalty imposed by law."); ARIZ. REV. STAT. ANN. § 31-412 (1956) (The board may release on parole when it appears "that there is reasonable probability that the applicant will live and remain at liberty without violating the law."); FLA. STAT. § 947.18 (1959) (The Parole Commission shall not grant parole unless there is a reasonable probability that on parole the defendant "will live and conduct himself as a respectable and law abiding person, and that his release will be compatible with his own welfare and the welfare of society."). See also MODEL PENAL CODE § 305.13, comment at 98 (Tent. Draft No. 5, 1956) ("[P]arole decisions rest on the intuition of the paroling authority, largely unguided by the laws that establish this broad grant of power or even by specific board standards. The paroling authority may release those who appear clearly to be 'good risks' and simply deny the remainder.").

37. See United States v. Rosenberg, 195 F.2d 583, 604–05 (2d Cir. 1952); Hall, *Reduction of Criminal Sentences on Appeal*, 37 COLUM. L. REV. 521, 522 (1937); Note, *Appellate Review of Primary Sentencing Decisions: A Connecticut Case Study*, 69 YALE L.J. 1453 (1960).

38. See, *e.g.*, Hines v. State Bd. of Parole, 293 N.Y. 254, 56 N.E.2d 572 (1944).

39. On the right to counsel at sentencing see Kadish, *The Advocate and the Expert—Counsel in the Peno-Correctional Process*, 45 MINN. L. REV. 803, 806 (1961). It is doubtful that there is any constitutional compulsion upon the sentencing judge to hold any hearing at all on the issue of punishment. See Williams v. New York, 337 U.S. 241, 251–52 (1949); Thomas v. Teets, 220 F.2d 232, 239 (9th Cir. 1955). Where statutes impose trial-type procedures on sentencing hearings, the premise appears to be that they apply only if the judge chooses to hold a hearing in the first place. *E.g.*, IDAHO CODE ANN. § 19-2515 (1947); ORE. REV. STAT. § 137.080 (1959).

40. Note, 58 COLUM. L. REV. 702, 705–06 (1958); see Williams v. New York, 337 U.S. 241 (1949).

41. See Kadish, *supra* note 39, at 812. In Losieau v. Hunter, 193 F.2d 41 (D.C. Cir. 1951), a two minute "hearing" was held to satisfy due process requirements.

42. Probation is thus conferred as a privilege and cannot be demanded as a right. It is a matter of favor, not of contract. There is no requirement that it must be granted on a specified showing. . . . There is no suggestion in the statute that the scope of the discretion conferred for the purpose of making the grant is narrowed in providing for its modification or revocation.

Burns v. United States, 287 U.S. 216, 220–21 (1932); *accord*, Kaplan v. United States, 234 F.2d, 345, 348 (8th Cir. 1956).

Parole is a "mere privilege—which the State Board of Pardons and Paroles had the unquestioned right to take from him at its uncontrolled discretion—for reasons satisfactory to it, or for no reasons at all." State *ex rel.* McQueen v. Horton, 31 Ala. App. 71, 76, 14 So. 2d 557, 560, *aff'd*, 244 Ala. 594, 14 So. 2d 561 (1943). See generally MODEL PENAL CODE § 305.21, comment at 115–18 (Tent. Draft. No. 5, 1956).

43. *E.g.*, United States v. You, 159 F.2d 688 (2d Cir. 1947); United States v. Van Riper, 99 F.2d 816 (2d Cir. 1938); State v. Bonza, 106 Utah 553, 150 P.2d 970 (1944).

44. See Note, *Legal Aspects of Probation Revocation*, 59 COLUM. L. REV. 311, 315 (1959). For a discussion of probation conditions, see MODEL PENAL CODE § 301.1, comment at 141–46 (Tent. Draft No. 2, 1954); for a discussion of parole conditions, see MODEL PENAL CODE § 305.17, comment at 103 06 (Tent. Draft No. 5, 1956). For a typical set of parole conditions, see Bates, *On the Uses of Parole Restrictions*, 33 J. CRIM. L., C. & P.S. 435, 441–42 (1943).

45. See MODEL PENAL CODE § 305.21, comment at 117–24 (Tent. Draft No. 5, 1956).

46. See generally Note, *Legal Aspects of Probation Revocation*, 59 COLUM. L. REV. 311 (1959); Note, *Parole Revocation Procedures*, 65 HARV. L. REV. 309 (1951); Comment, *Revocation of Conditional Liberty—California and the Federal System*, 28 SO. CAL. L. REV. 158 (1955).

47. *E.g.*, *18 U.S.C. § 3653 (1958) ("for cause")*; ALA. CODE tit. 42, § 10 (1958) ("reasonable cause to believe"); COLO. REV. STAT. ANN. §. 39-16-9 (1953) ("reason to believe").

48. *E.g.*, ARIZ. REV. STAT. ANN. § 13-1657(B) (1956); CAL. PEN. CODE § 1203.2; MASS. GEN. LAWS ANN. ch. 279, § 3 (1956); *cf.* Story v. Rives, 97 F.2d 182, 188 (D.C. Cir. 1938) (fourth amendment restrictions on arrest and search not applicable to persons on conditional release).

49. *E.g.*, DEL. CODE ANN. tit 11, § 4321 (1953); IOWA CODE § 247.26 (1958); MINN. STAT. § 610.39 (1957); MO. REV. STAT. § 549.090 (1959).

50. ATTORNEY GENERAL, SURVEY OF RELEASE PROCEDURES 245–48 (1939).

51. See 2 ATTORNEY GENERAL, SURVEY OF RELEASE PROCEDURES 329 (1939); Annot., 29 A.L.R.2d 1074 (1953).

52. See Washington v. Hagan, 287 F.2d 332 (3rd Cir. 1960) (upholding practice); Fleming v. Tate, 156 F.2d 848 (D.C. Cir. 1946) (practice found inconsistent with statutory grant of an "opportunity to appear").

53. See Kadish, *supra* note 39, at 822, for an account of the reversal of the Board's policy.

54. *E.g.*, Jianole v. United States, 58 F.2d 115 (8th Cir. 1932) (not acquitted); Galyon v. State, 189 Tenn. 226 S.W.2d 270 (1949) (acquitted).

55. See H.R. REP. NO. 1377, 68th Cong., 2d Sess. 2-3 (1925) (in support of proposed federal probation legislation), quoted in United States v. Murray, 275 U.S. 347, 355 (1928). The notion of probation and parole as merited leniency also appears to lie behind the common exemptions of certain classes of offenders from eligibility therefor. See note 35 *supra*.

56. See Burns v. United States, 287 U.S. 216, 220–21 (1932); Hiatt v. Compagna, 178 F.2d 42, 45 (5th Cir. 1949), *aff'd by an equally divided Court*, 340 U.S. 880 (1950).

57. See Tappan, *The Legal Rights of Prisoners*, Annals, May 1954, p. 99.

58. People v. Riley, 376 Ill. 364, 368, 33 N.E.2d 872, 875 (1941).

59. Fuller v. State, 122 Ala. 32, 40, 26 So. 146, 148 (1899).

60. See Solesbee v. Balkcom, 399 U.S. 9, 15–16 (1950) (dissenting opinion).

61. *E.g., In re* Lee, 177 Cal. 690, 171 Pac. 958 (1918); State v. Meyer, 228 Minn. 286, 37 N.W.2d 3 (1949).

62. *E.g.,* 1 DAVIS, ADMINISTRATIVE LAW TREATISE § 7.20, at 507–10 (1958); Davis, *The Requirement of Opportunity To Be Heard in the Administrative Process,* 51 YALE L.J. 1093, 1122–25 (1942); Schwartz, *Procedural Due Process in Federal Administrative Law,* 25 N.Y.U.L. REV. 552, 569–71 (1950). The doctrine has sometimes been authoritatively rejected for certain purposes. See Slochower v. Board of Educ., 350 U.S. 551 (1956) (lack of a right to public employment does not negative constitutional protection against unfair discharge); *cf.* Schware v. Board of Bar Examiners, 353 U.S. 232 (1957).

63. See Wechsler, *Sentencing, Correction, and the Model Penal Code,* 109 U. PA. L. REV. 465, 488 (1961).

64. See note 35 *supra.*

65. See note 36 *supra.*

66. This would appear to be the rationale of the usual argument that a person conditionally at liberty need not be furnished procedural protections because he was given these protections at the time of trial. See, *e.g.,* Fuller v. State, 122 Ala. 32, 26 So. 146 (1899); *In re* Patterson, 94 Kan. 439, 146 Pac. 1009 (1915).

67. *Cf.* Hall, *Nulla Poena Sine Lege,* 47 YALE L.J. 165, 192 (1937).

68. CALMANDREI, PROCEDURE AND DEMOCRACY 103 (1956).

69. Rochin V. California, 342 U.S. 165, 173–74 (1952); see Kadish, *Methodology and Criteria in Due Process Adjudication—A Survey and Criticism,* 66 YALE L.J. 319, 347 (1957).

70. Boyd v. United States, 116 U.S. 616, 635 (1886); see Reid v. Covert, 354 U.S. 1, 39 (1957): "Slight encroachments create new boundaries from which legions of power can seek new territory to capture."

71. See, *e.g.,* United States *ex rel.* Nicholson v. Dillard, 102 F.2d 94, 96 (4th Cir. 1939); *Ex parte* Anderson, 191 Ore. 409, 424–28, 229 P.2d 633, 640–41 (1951); McCoy v. Harris, 108 Utah 407, 160 P.2d 721 (1945).

72. See People *ex rel.* Brown v. Johnston, 9 N.Y.2d 482, 174 N.E.2d 725, 215 N.Y.S.2d 44 (1961), in which the court of appeals rejected the lower court's view that place of detention is an administrative matter and held that it is the duty of the courts to protect inmates against arbitrary and unlawful treatment. "An individual, once validly convicted and placed under the jurisdiction of the Department of Correction . . . is not to be divested of all rights and unalterably abandoned and forgotten by the remainder of society. If these situations were placed *without* the ambit of the writ's protection we would thereby encourage the unrestricted, arbitrary and unlawful treatment of prisoners, and eventually discourage prisoners from cooperating in their rehabilitation." *Id.* at 485, 174 N.E.2d at 726, 215 N.Y.S.2d at 45–46. The *Model Penal Code* proposes a hearing on the disposition of good-time allowances, MODEL PENAL CODE § 305.8 (Tent. Draft No. 5, 1956), and a structured adjudicatory proceeding for the imposition of prison discipline, MODEL PENAL CODE § 305.7 (Tent. Draft No. 12, 1960). See also AMERICAN CORRECTIONAL ASSOCIATION, MANUAL OF CORRECTIONAL STANDARDS 241–42 (1959).

73. See Note, *Parole, Revocation Procedures,* 65 HARV. L. REV. 309, 311 (1951), suggesting the "inherent difference between the custody involved in imprisonment in a cell and 'custody' as applied to a person who is at liberty in the world." A suggestive analogy is the difference in the application of constitutional standards to the exclusion as opposed to the expulsion of aliens. Once members of the community, constitutional proscriptions govern their expulsion, Japanese Immigrant Case, 189 U.S. 86 (1903), which do not apply to the exclusion of those who never joined the community, United States *ex rel.* Knauff v. Shaughnessy, 338 U.S. 537 (1950). See Bridges v. Wixon, 326 U.S. 135, 154 (1945).

74. Lewis, *supra* note 33, at 226; see Allen, *Criminal Justice, Legal Values and the Rehabilitative Ideal,* 50 J. CRIM. L., C. & P.S. 226, 230 (1959).

75. *Cf.* 1 DAVIS, ADMINISTRATIVE LAW TREATISE § 7.09 (1958); GELLHORN & BYSE, ADMINISTRATIVE LAW: CASES AND COMMENTS 657–65 (4th ed. 1960).

76. *Cf.* Allen, *The Borderland of Criminal Justice: Problems of "Socializing" Criminal Justice,* 32 SOCIAL SERVICE REV. 107, 119 (1958): "Our great problem today and for the future is to domesticate scientific knack and technique so that they may operate compatibly with the values and assumptions of a legal order and, at the same time, make their important contributions to our needs."

77. Fleming v. Tate, 156 F.2d 848, 850 (D.C. Cir. 1946).

78. HART & SACKS, THE LEGAL PROCESS: BASIC PROBLEMS IN THE MAKING AND APPLICATION OF LAW 173 (tent. ed. 1958); *cf.* Solesbee v. Balkcom, 339 U.S. 9, 25 (1950) (dissenting opinion of Frankfurter, J.): "The fact that a conclusion is reached in good conscience is no proof of its reliability. The validity of a conclusion depends largely on the mode by which it was reached."

79. Lewis, *supra* note 33, at 228.

80. To accomplish the purpose of the [probation] statute, an exceptional degree of flexibility in administration is essential. It is necessary to individualize each case, to give that careful humane and comprehensive consideration to the particular situation of each offender which would be possible only in the exercise of a broad discretion.

   Burns v. United States, 287 U.S. 216, 220 (1932) (Hughes, C.J.).

81. See HART & SACKS, *supra,* note 78, at 155–79.

82. The proposals and supporting studies of the *Model Penal Code* constitute a major breakthrough in this area. See generally Wechsler, *Sentencing, Correction, and the Model Penal Code,* 109 U. PA. L. REV. 465 (1961). See also Allen, *Law and the Future: Criminal Law and Administration,* 51 Nw. U.L. REV. 207, 213–14 (1956); Tappan, *The Legal Rights of Prisoners,* Annals, May 1954, pp. 99–100.

INDEX

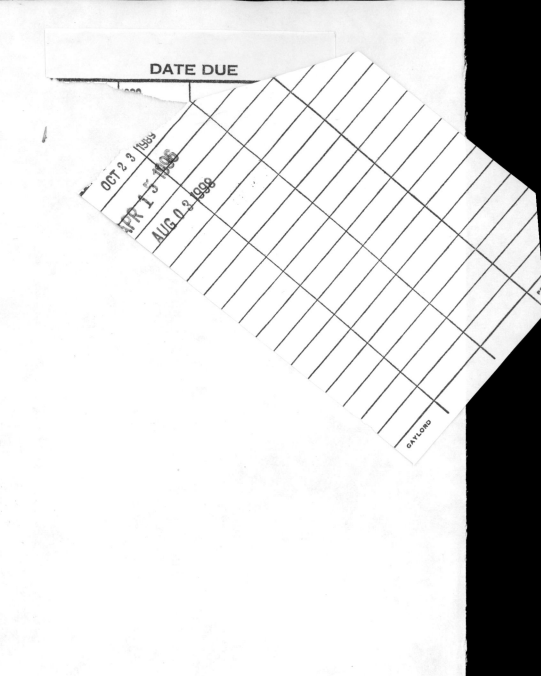